Designing Complex Web Information Systems:
Integrating Evolutionary Process Engineering

Roberto Paiano
University of Salento, Italy

Anna Lisa Guido
University of Salento, Italy

Andrea Pandurino
University of Salento, Italy

Information Science REFERENCE

INFORMATION SCIENCE REFERENCE

Hershey · New York

Director of Editorial Content: Kristin Klinger
Senior Managing Editor: Jamie Snavely
Managing Editor: Jeff Ash
Assistant Managing Editor: Carole Coulson
Typesetter: Jeff Ash
Cover Design: Lisa Tosheff
Printed at: Yurchak Printing Inc.

Published in the United States of America by
        Information Science Reference (an imprint of IGI Global)
        701 E. Chocolate Avenue, Suite 200
        Hershey PA 17033
        Tel: 717-533-8845
        Fax: 717-533-8661
        E-mail: cust@igi-global.com
        Web site: http://www.igi-global.com/reference

and in the United Kingdom by
        Information Science Reference (an imprint of IGI Global)
        3 Henrietta Street
        Covent Garden
        London WC2E 8LU
        Tel: 44 20 7240 0856
        Fax: 44 20 7379 0609
        Web site: http://www.eurospanbookstore.com

Copyright © 2009 by IGI Global. All rights reserved. No part of this publication may be reproduced, stored or distributed in any form or by any means, electronic or mechanical, including photocopying, without written permission from the publisher.
    Product or company names used in this set are for identification purposes only. Inclusion of the names of the products or companies does not indicate a claim of ownership by IGI Global of the trademark or registered trademark.

Library of Congress Cataloging-in-Publication Data

Paiano, Roberto, 1953-Designing complex web information systems : integrating evolutionary process engineering / by Roberto Paiano, Anna Lisa Guido, and Andrea Pandurino.
       p. cm.
Includes bibliographical references and index.

Summary: "This book gives the reader a complete view of the architectures, problems and solutions linked to the design and development of modern web information systems"--Provided by publisher.

ISBN 978-1-60566-300-5 (hardcover) -- ISBN 978-1-60566-301-2 (ebook) 1. Web sites--Design. 2. Information storage and retrieval systems. I. Guido, Anna Lisa, 1973- II. Pandurino, Andrea, 1958- III. Title.
  TK5105.888.P33 2009
  006.7--dc22

                          2008043765

British Cataloguing in Publication Data

A Cataloguing in Publication record for this book is available from the British Library.

All work contributed to this book is new, previously-unpublished material. The views expressed in this book are those of the authors, but not necessarily of the publisher.

Dedication

To my beloved wife Terry that is my life
To my parents Angelo e Giuseppina for their love and support
To the memory of my father-in-law Antonio that guided me from the heaven

Roberto

To my husband for his love for me
To my father and my mother: their love for me is special
To my brother because he believes to me

Anna Lisa

To my beloved wife Maria Lucia. Her love lights up my life.
To my family for inspiring me to be the best person that I can.
To Roberto and Anna Lisa for the unwavering support. I couldn't have done it without them.

Andrea

Table of Contents

Section I
Background

Section II
The Methodologies

Section III
Automatic Code Generation and the Tools

Foreword

Information systems are a traditional field of computer science: they put ICT to work in order to solve real-life problems ranging from accounting, managing organization, ticketing, airline reservations, and so forth.

Web technology is something (relatively) new: it started from niche-applications (outside of the traditional areas) and it has become pervasive, covering all kinds of realms, information systems included. With respect to traditional ways of using information systems, Web technology has brought a number of novelties:

- A new concern for interactive-visual interfaces
- A new approach to information structuring, hyper textual rather than hierarchical
- A new approach to information "consumption" emphasizing browsing and navigation (over links) in addition to the more traditional hierarchical exploration or querying

These novelties added further complexity to information systems design, that have always involved several concerns, and therefore several different methodologies and skills. In order to develop a complex information system (whether implemented traditionally or via Web technology), at least the following is needed:

- Understanding the "domain" (or the domains) relevant for the application, that is, the knowledge concerning the specific context. It could be banking, it could be customer relationships management, it could be shoe manufacturing, it could be airline reservations, and so forth.
- Understanding "who" the people are involved: who does produce information (how, when, why, through which actions, etc.), who "consumes" information (when, why, through which actions, etc.), who monitors or supervises information (why, how, when, etc.)

- Understanding the "business," that is, the socio-economic context into which the application is embedded. Who are the "external players": What do they do? How do they operate? What is the overall business flow? How are the "goods" or "services" exchanged? How is the information exchanged? and so forth.
- Understanding the internal "business processes," that is, the flow of actions that are needed within the application itself. Some business processes can be very well-defined and organized, with precise rules to follow. Other business processes, instead, could be "ill-defined" with loose definitions are not precise rules to follow. A user trying to choose a hotel is a typical example of an ill-defined task: we know the goal, we know the information likely to be needed, and we know the operations needed for booking; we cannot predict, however, the precise sequence of actions, nor all of the steps that will be necessary.

Above are just the main concerns that need to be taken into consideration while designing a complex information system; others also could be mentioned and have their own relevance.

Given this situation, we can ask ourselves basic questions about "designing information systems": is it one discipline, or several disciplines combined? Can we find a unified methodology, a unified notation, a unified approach, or do we need to combine several different pieces together, in an "ill-defined" puzzle, where the individual pieces do not always fit well together in the global picture?

The book takes a "realistic" point of view: there have been specific answers to specific needs; different approaches, different methodologies and different notations have been developed, for the different areas involved in information systems design.

Instead of trying to develop yet another universal approach, by solving all of the problems in a unified framework, it is wiser to expose all of the different approaches that have been proposed for each part of the design problem. A synthetic picture explaining and comparing different approaches for the same part of the design is a needed contribution, lacking in published literature. Each research group, in fact, puts all of its efforts into explaining the advantages and the details of its approach; references to other works are not well-developed, and focus on showing that they have limitations.

An independent assessment of different approaches is therefore welcome and needed.

In terms of what is being covered, the list of issues covered is impressive:

- Business process: most relevant approaches are introduced and compared
- Web design: again all relevant approaches are synthesized and compared
- Ontologies (necessary for domain modeling): they are introduced and explained
- Specific methodologies are proposed, in order to put all of the pieces of the puzzle together in a meaningful picture

Not everything possible is covered, but a lot is being covered in a synthesis that could become a valid working tool for teachers, students and professionals.

Prof. Paolo Paolini
Politecnico di Milano (Italy)

Preface

Today, dealing with information systems appears to be very complex because the term, by now, is used in order to indicate any application capable of solving any problem in a specific business area.

Over the years, we have used this term in a very general way, often with divergent meanings between them.

Moreover, several and different design methodologies have been used, from the functional decomposition to those relative to the big framework, as those realized by SAP® (that put together different specific applications with the goal—above all marketing goals—to supply integrated information systems simply choosing some configuration parameters) and, besides these, several and different philosophies of design like ERP, MRP, CRM, and so forth.

Moreover, the advent and the extraordinary spread of the Internet and, therefore, the expansion of information systems on the Web, have generated a remarkable increment of methodologies and technologies for the design and the development of applications for the Web, forcing to review well-known methodologies, such as the object-oriented, with the result to make the effective use of UML® (Rumbaugh, Jacobson, & Booch, 2004) for the design of information systems extremely complex.

In general terms, we can assert that any methodology, to be truly effective, must allow the designer to concentrate him/herself on the problem of solving rather than trying to understand the use of the same methodology in order to express the specific problem.

It appears, therefore, necessary to try to make order in this chaotic universe of acronyms, philosophies, and methodologies that often approach similar problems and offer similar solutions, even if they address innovation and oneness, supplying a clear point of reference to which we will relate within this book.

INFORMATION SYSTEMS

The term information systems means "the set of the procedures and the infrastructures that support and describe the flowing of the information inside an organizational structure" (Pighin, 2005).

In other words, an information system allows describes, in detail, as any company (public or private) carries out the job to which it is deputy and to which the material and immaterial resources are available.

Such definition does not take account, and it must not take account, of the use of an eventual automation related to the use of computer-based systems.

For an information system to become "automated," partially or completely, means to design and to develop a computer-based system that supports and implements how much described previously; in other words, the application must adapt itself completely to the way the company works, and not vice versa.

Very often, today, many software houses try to impose on the companies the way of working already implemented within their applications, prescinding from the peculiarities of the companies, their history and the resources available.

Of course, to develop an ad hoc application requires remarkable economic investments and it is not always affordable for the average and small productive realties and, therefore, often it is indispensable to balance these two divergent requirements.

The goal of the book and of the methodology that is described inside is to realize a compromise between the economic effort and the necessity, for the companies, to differ from other concurrent economic realities.

Information Systems: From Business Process Design to the Business Process Reengineering

In the 1990, Hammer (1990) published his theory on the necessity of reengineering the business processes starting from the observation of the reality and from the experience that many computer experts had experimented in their professional life.

He asserted that the introduction of innovative technology on old business processes had the highest probabilities of failure.

Such affirmation, however obvious, had the merit to raise the problem of the understanding of how the company carried out its own job and with which resources before proposing innovation.

This is, in our opinion, the guideline that would have to always drive the proposal of innovation to a company, but as pointed out previously, it is not how many things happens in the majority of the cases.

The theory of the BPR—business process reengineering—(Hammer & Stanton, 1995), in brief, is made up of three main phases:

1. *AS-IS*: the definition of present BPs (business processes). This is supposed to be the fundamental phase of the analysis because it allows identification of the primary processes (or macro-processes) that they describe as the company works currently.
2. *Comparison and diagnosis*: it is provided for a quantitative and qualitative evaluation of what is found, using well-known techniques of benchmarking, and eventually a comparison with companies of the same typology.
3. *TO-BE*: re-definition of BPs according to the requirements of a company.

There are least four variables to be considered in each phase, in particular:

- **The flow of BPs:** the decomposition of the processes in activity flows
- **The organizational structure**: the contribution and the responsibility of the productive units to BP
- **The human resources:** the characteristics, skills and the availabilities to the change
- **Systems of values (motivation and boosting):** a system that aims both to reduce the opportunistic individual factor and to measure the productivity

Globally considering these variables, there are three strategies of reengineering that have substantially been asserted:

1. **Buy-side strategy:** related to the part of the information system regarding suppliers of raw materials and/or services (B2B, e-procurement, etc.)
2. **In-side strategy:** related to the part of the information system inside the company (ERP)
3. **Sell-side strategy:** related to the part of the information system that involves the final users (B2C, etc.)

Any design of reengineering always begins with the necessity of a change and the definition of a new business vision.

Therefore, in the first phase (AS-IS), it is indispensable to understand how the company currently operates, by which organizational structure and the specific level of responsibility within the activities, with which kind of human resources (skills, availability to the change, etc.), and which system of values defining both the individual and structure goals and the system of incentive in order to reduce most possible what in literature it is called "opportunistic individual behavior" (Williamson, 1975).

This phase is, in our opinion, the most difficult and most expensive from the economic and employed resource point of view, but if well executed, it concurs to carry out BPR with success.

In fact, starting from the detailed analysis of the present situation and using opportune tools of simulation, it is possible to carry out a first rationalization of the organizational structure and the flows of business processes.

Such affirmation, justified from the experience of a quarter of a century in the field of the high-level information systems of one of the authors, is based on the fact that often the operating procedures and the information exchange inside the companies is the result of a series of adjustments that they have contributed to create, in the course of time, a superstructure not justified and often unknown to the company's people.

AS-IS analysis would have to identify a few primary processes for being able to effectively manage a reengineering of the same ones and, in particular, we think that for a big company, approximately 15 processes would have to be characterized.

Both the primary processes and the support process (or secondary processes) are represented using the value chain of Porter (Millar & Porter, 1985) identifying the processes that create value for the company according to their mission.

The first activity, therefore, concerns the decomposition of these processes in a harmonic and reasoned flow of tasks.

For many years, from the introduction of the concept of business process, it has been a complete anarchy in the use of an effective notation for the graphical representation of the flow of the activities regarding the first variable into play. Some big software houses have developed their own method (for instance, FILENET™, now an IBM® subsidiary) while others have used standard methods like IDEF0 (IEEE, 1998).

The fundamental characteristic of these models of representation of the processes is that they are not user-oriented, that is, they are particularly complex to use and too cryptic so that the final user could understand them.

Finally, in 2004, the more important companies in this sector have gathered in a consortium to aim to develop a common and effective notation to be used to model the BPs in an understandable way for the final customer.

Such notation, BPMN™—business process management notation—which is the base of this book and will be shortly illustrated later on, (OMG, 2006) is now maintained from the OMG™.

The representation of the processes through BPMN uses, for its formal representation, specific machine-readable languages, such as the initial BPEL and the actual XPDL, that the companies of the sector use in order to develop all of the support tools that are not free of charge.

For many years, our research group has used OWL (Web ontology language) (W3C, 2004) as the main language for the modeling and the definition of metamodel because it is considered more suitable to represent the concepts and the base rules understanding a methodology. The choice to use the ontologies in the field of software engineering has been confirmed by a recent paper published by IEEE (Cardoso, 2007).

The use of ontologies, that will be discussed, allow us homogeneity of modeling being a platform/company-independent.

The second phase, defined as comparison and diagnosis, provides a first activity of appraisal using the techniques of benchmarking, certainly complex and articulated, but basically determinist.

Instead, the comparison with other similar companies is different. In literature, often it refers to such a comparison with the term of "best practice" that means some success cases of companies that operate in the same segment of market with equal dimensions: in other words, concurrent companies.

It is obvious that the companies cannot have approached, legally, sensitive data of concurrent companies in order not to incur in the crime of industrial espionage.

It is equally obvious that the big consultant companies, thanks to the elevated number of customers, could have such information, but they would not have to use them for the same reason expressed previously.

The term "best practice" comes instead from wide use in the business field but with obvious scope to propose to the customer something pre-assembled.

According to our opinion, the true comparison would have to instead be carried out between how much is found using benchmarking and the goals of the company according to the vision that has generated the change necessity.

Finally, the third phase, called TO-BE, consist of redesigning the way by which the company must work in order to aim its goals.

The change, of course, will include all of the involved variables described previously and the result will be absolutely integrated.

It is interesting to notice that, until now, we have spoken exclusively about information systems and not about applications by agreement with the separation between the two systems, information systems and computer-based systems, described previously.

During the last few years, the business process management (BPM), that "is a field of knowledge at the intersection between management and information technology has been asserted, encompassing methods, techniques and tools to design, enact, control, and analyze operational BPs involving humans, organizations, applications, documents and other sources of information" (Van der Aalst, 2003).

This mixture between information systems and computer-based systems was already present de facto on the market for many years.

In fact, when the big consultant companies with their associated software companies propose the notorious "best practices," they certainly sell effective software applications, but these applications are pre-manufactured and customizable through an opportune set of parameters, so it is possible that these applications are not the best possible solution for that specific company.

In short, the consultant proposes to the company a solution to the problems that have driven the change, but this solution does not take into account some of their own peculiarities.

Some of the more important companies of the sector pursue this type of approach, which could be useful for some companies of small and average dimensions, but the economic effort required is often times unsuitable for these kinds of companies.

The market is currently global and too competitive, so there are various reasons that induce change. Moreover, the change necessities take part very frequently (in some cases, also many times in the same year), so the information system must be flexible for being able to adapt itself easily to the new reality without the necessity of dramatic reengineering.

In the same way, the support computer-based system must be equally flexible for effectively being able to adapt itself to the new requirements.

The philosophy of the BPM proposes exceeding the logic of the BPR, just for the ability to implement flexible systems in order to follow the continuous evolution of BP; it considers as the main software instrument the workflow engines that have the job of automating the repetitive activities above all (the operating job) usually oriented inside the company, putting into effect the transformation of the processes according to the inside strategy that generated the ERP.

In this book, we will not deal with ERP, because however many software companies currently continue to advertise their products like ERP, practically having unique DBMS and allowing the sharing of the information between all the business software systems is a norm for good design.

Therefore, the BPM is more modern, more flexible and a softer approach of the BPR. However, is it true?

No, it is not in our opinion. In fact, very often before would it be opportune to carry out, where necessary, a radical transformation using the BPR and successively to follow the continuous evolutions through the techniques of the BPM.

In fact, using directly BPM in order to model BPs in the point of view of their automation, it is the high risk to fall back in the error described by Hammer: to graft computer-based innovation on an inadequate organizational structure represents a high probability of failure.

The failure risk increases considering which professional figure should model the BPs.

From the point of view of automating the execution of this flow of activities, it seems natural to design such a flow using the necessary sagacity to the implementation and, therefore, the key figure would have to be an expert of design of applications.

Such a choice does not seem adequate to us. In the methodology proposed in the book, the first hypothesis regards just the knowledge that a cultural gap exists between the specialists of business and organization and the specialists of software applications.

Web Application: The Concept of User Experience

Today, Web applications (WA) are widely dealt with, but everyone interprets this definition in their own way.

We think, therefore, it is opportune to clarify for the reader what we mean by Web application.

First, it is necessary to clarify what we certainly do not mean by such a term, and that unfortunately, many specialists of the field adopt instead.

The WA is not a traditional application that uses the browser as interface.

The WA is, instead, a tightened marriage between the necessity to carry out operations, being an active part of a business process, with the typical usability and the navigation of a static Web site.

The greater causes of failure in the area of Web applications are determined from the inability of the visitor to find the information that he/she needs and to surf between these.

For this reason, some methodologies of Web application design have been developed in the last years that will be further illustrated in this book.

At the dawn of the Web, also with the knowledge of the concept of hypertext, that is, a semantic relation between information, many have undertaken the development of such applications without using a design methodology; they discovered absolutely unusable WA in which the visitor "got lost" and that the user desperately abandoned the application never to return.

When it became apparent that it is necessary to use this type of application for design methodology also, many turned to the only noted and widely used UML®.

Many practitioners continue to think about this methodology without taking into some account the fact that it has been created in order to model system-oriented applications, and they continue to ignore the requirements of usability of the user. UML® has evolved in order to try to model anything, without losing its own originaal sin represented by the base rules of the Object-Orientation, thus becoming potentially a methodology able to model anything (also BPs) but, de facto, so complicated to be unusable even for the same specialists of applications.

The user of a WA needs, instead, "to feel at ease" in a world to which it belongs, and that it agrees before still to find the information which it needs.

Modeling the user experience means modeling the interaction of the user with the application by agreement with its requirements and not modeling the application according to the requirements of the system.

The approach used in this book aims to model the interaction of the user with the WA using the paradigm of the "dialogue," considering both the peculiarities of the user (multi-user) and those of the device that it is using (multi-device).

Moreover, the user of a WA uses information not closely tied to the data, but that instead is related to the marketing and to the creation of a world able to attract a new user.

The approach used for modeling the WAs is based on three levels: conceptual level, logical level and page level. The details of every level will be illustrated more ahead; in this moment, we only notice that the more advanced point of the modeling, mainly close the implementation (page level), loses a few semantic to advantage details to the necessary developer.

The attention of the specialists, therefore, is moving more and more towards the application domain rather than towards the classic design of applications (OO).

This area of research, confirmed from the result of the workshop on the DSM (domain-specific modeling) in the conferences OOPSLA 2006 and 2007, does not consider the effective use of standard methodologies in order to model anything in any application domain.

The main reason is the limitations that these methodologies of course introduce and the key concepts of an application domain "make up" that they force to express that make it lose clarity and acquaintance (Paiano, 2006; 2007).

During a conference in 2006, IBM® tried to illustrate the use of UML® from the point of view of the DSM, and the result was a sort of old-style functional decomposition, brought up-to-date with some of the typical terms of the OO.

In any case, one of the key concepts of this area of research is represented by the automatic generation of the final application starting from the model.

We almost perfectly agree with this tendency.

The domain we consider is the Web, and we model the WAs using a methodology that is absolutely suitable for the Web in order to model applications in different application domains with the awareness that, if will be further clarity and representativeness requirements, it is possible to modify the below meta-model thanks to the use of ontology that allow us to express very complex concepts with the needed semantic and clarity.

Finally, starting from the model of the application, we automatically generate the final WA using two different open source frameworks.

Complex Web Information Systems: The Challenge

At this point, a question cannot be deferred anymore: What is a complex Web information system?

A complex Web information system is an information system, usable via the Web, which includes the way a company performs its activities inside, the BPs. This system must be usable and must be arranged to easily follow the changes of the activities of the company according to the vision of a company as an "open system" (Galbraith, 1973), adopting, therefore, a contingent perspective about its position in the business world. This vision, after 35 years, is not only actual but unavoidable in the global market of the third millennium.

As the reader can see, the answer appears to be quite simple, however, to aim the goal of designing a "contingent" information system capable to effectively adapt itself to the continuous changes forced by the solicitations coming from the outside of the company, a complex work of analysis and integration of several methodologies is needed.

Therefore, the **challenges** of this book are:

- To design information systems approaching two main problems: on one hand those relative to the development of Web applications and on the other hand to the design and integration, inside of the information system, of the business processes that, although their importance and unquestioned usefulness, they found it hard to enter in a pervasive way in the design and the development of the Web information systems.
- To implement the information systems through the automatic code generation tools that, starting from the design model in a machine readable format, help the IT expert to obtain the Web information system very close to the design and without the little personal choices that are very often dangerous.

The methodology that is the foundations of this book has the goal of proposing a solution to several problems related to the development of information systems usable via the Web.

Regarding the BPs, as argued previously, it is thought to be fundamental to start from a deepened analysis of the actual situation without considering eventual automations.

Moreover, being that this activity is much more complex and embraces every aspect of the business life, the experience and the skill of the analysts who, apart from some cases ascribable to small business reality, are experts of organizations and models of business and are not expert of development of applications, are decisive.

This clear separation of the jobs represents our first hypothesis.

In fact, currently we can identify two situations.

The first represents how much happens using the techniques of the BPM. The consultant companies aim to design BPs from the point of view of the developer of applications, allowing, therefore, the ability to use the workflow engines or similar techniques.

In this case, they completely lose sight of the company in its wholeness, so this technique represents just a way to design applications with look and feel more attractive but are substantially similar to the functional decomposition of approximately 20 years ago.

Of course, in some cases, this technique can be equally effective, but it is impossible to generalize its use.

The second situation represents, instead, exactly the opposite. A big consultant company designs the new BPs correctly considering the company in its wholeness and acting on all of the variable ones into play.

Successively, when they will develop the computer-based system, which must support the new way to work of the company, the developers will use well-known techniques of applications design considering BPs just as requirements.

Therefore, it needs to bridge the gap between the design of BPs and the design of the Web applications.

Our research work, that is the base of this book, has the goal of bridging this gap through a methodology that takes into account the requirements and the peculiarities that are apparent.

The research activity, therefore, starts from the foundation that the activity of the business experts (those who have the task of redesigning a company in its wholeness) stop at a detail level unsuitable to those who, instead, must implement the applications.

Therefore, the first methodological step carried out from the designers of applications is that of refining the flow of the processes in order to render them apt to being a true input (and not just as a requirement) for the developers.

Moreover, two possible scenarios are proposed. The first regards the part of Web information systems turned to the internal users by agreement with the strategy of reengineering of the BPs defined "in-side" to which often it is associated, erroneously to our opinion, the acronym ERP.

This type of user often has the necessity of applications data or process-driven, and therefore, the philosophy of designing the user experience could be not be suitable, in the sense that in the majority of the cases, it coincides with the semantic structure of an ER model with the timing based on the flow of the operations.

For the internal users, the use of a workflow engine could be suitable also, but we have thought it opportune to give a greater freedom to such users in order to build a "virtual desktop" according to their needs.

For this reason, and by agreement with the philosophy of the DSM, we have preferred to generate automatically the Java™ Portlet or the Webparts in Microsoft® environment.

In this way, the user could personalize his/her virtual desktop, adding to the business activities also others Portlet about individual productivity or social communication.

The second scenario concerns instead the external users of the company and therefore essentially, but not only, by agreement with the strategy of reengineering of BPs defined "sell-side."

The external users essentially use a WA in order to navigate between the information and to activate BPs having integrated part of the same ones.

This scenario allows making a design of the user experience independent from the processes and by agreement with how much is described in the previous paragraph to which successively will be integrated the BPs.

According to these considerations, this book aims to introduce two new methodologies: the first one is a result of the extension and a reasoned integration of existing methodologies at conceptual and logical levels which introduces a new publishing model; the second one, is oriented to the internal users, as an enhancement of the generation of applications through workflow engines.

This book deals with new methodologies and is clearly oriented to the scholars demanding their contribution to improve our approach; however, since the book also deals with tools and automatic code generation starting from the models of the Web information systems, it could be an essential guide for practitioners that have to design, manage and maintain information systems. The development process model is not completely classified into the well-known models such as, waterfall, agile, and so forth.

According to the philosophy of domain-specific modeling, the programmers have to develop the tools for the automatic generation of the code to build the final applications. They are completely free in using whatever they like in terms of development process.

Furthermore, to build the final complex Web information system, our methodology does not constrain a specific process; in fact, it is possible to generate a prototype starting from the only conceptual model to verify with the customer the good quality of the modeling analysis. This iteration could be always done. In the last analysis, it is possible to affirm that the development process is quite similar to the agile unified process (AUP) (Ambler, 2002), but not completely equal.

ORGANIZATION OF THE BOOK

The research work, that is the base of this book, realizes an integrated and flexible methodology in order to model complex Web information systems, which safeguard both the peculiarities of the Web and adopting a right methodology for the design of the information system, performed by experts of the field, that becomes integrating part of the final model being reused and adapted to the requirements of the development.

All the models are in OWL format and through a code generator an application is obtained very closer to the final.

The book is divided into three sections with an overview for each section that summarizes the content and the goals of the section providing the reader with a helpful orientation.

The first section provides a background about the existing methodologies with a critical discussion about their strengths and their weakness; in Chapter I, the main notations for modeling the BPs will be described in detail; in Chapter II, the main methodologies for the modeling of WAs will be described; in Chapter III, the IDM (interactive dialogue model) methodology for designing WAs will be presented; in Chapter IV, after a short review of the fundamental concepts of the ontology, the use of OWL language for the realization of meta-model and models will be described.

The second section is of this book concerns the presentation of the two new methodologies using case studies to better understand them. Chapter V describes, in detail, the overall design vision of the architectures that are the base of the methodologies; in Chapter VI, the complete methodology of design for Web information systems for external users will be described using a simple case study to improve the readability; in Chapter VII, such methodology is applied to a more complex real case study; in Chapter VIII, the methodological approach for the internal users will be presented through a simple case study; furthermore, in Chapter IX, the methodology for internal users is applied to a real and complete case study.

The third section concerns the description of the support tools, used essentially as editors, and the tools that allow for generating the final application in an automatic way. In detail, in Chapter X, we will deal with the problems related to the automatic generation of code; in Chapter XI, the technological choices will be described; in Chapter XII, a configurable editor as an indispensable tool in order to model BPs and WAs will be described; in Chapter XIII, the code generators will be described and in the Chapter XIV, the application of these tools to real case studies will be presented.

Finally, in Chapter XV, we will draw a conclusion and a panoramic view of the future work.

REFERENCES

Ambler, S. (2002). *Agile modeling: Effective practices for extreme programming and the unified process.* John Wiley & Son, Ltd.

Cardoso, J. (2007). The semantic Web Vision: Where are We?. *IEEE Intelligent Systems*, 22-26.

Galbraith, J.R. (1973). *Designing complex organizations.* Reading, MA: Addison-Wesley Publishing Company, Inc.

Hammer, M. (1990). *Reengineering work: Don't automate, obliterate.* Boston, MA: Harvard Business Review.

Hammer, M., & Stanton, S. (1995). *The reengineering revolution.* New York, NY: Harper Business.

IEEE Std 1320.1-1998. (1998). IEEE Standard for Functional Modeling Language—Syntax and Semantics for IDEF0. New York: IEEE.

OMG. (2006). *Business process modeling notation specification.*

Paiano, R., Pandurino, A., & Guido A. (2006). Conceptual design of Web application families: The BWW approach. *Proceedings from the 6th ACM OOPSLA Workshop on Domain-Specific Modeling,* (pp. 23-32). Portland, OR.

Paiano, R., Sánchez-Ruíz, A., Motoshi S., & Langlois, N. (2007). Domain-specific software development terminology: Do we all speak the same language. *Proceedings from the 7th OOPSLA Workshop on Domain-Specific Modeling (DSM'07).* Montreal, Canada.

Pighin, M., & Marzona, A. (2005). *Sistemi informativi aziendali.* Pearson Education.

Porter, M.E., & Millar V.E. (1985). *How information gives you competitive advantage. Harvard Business Review, 63*(4), 149-161.

Rumbaugh, J., Jacobson I., & Booch, G. (2004). *Unified modeling language reference manual.* Addison-Wesley.

Van der Aalst W.M.P., der Hofstede, A.H.M., & Weske, M. (2003). Business process management: A survey. *Proceedings from the First International Conference in Business Process Management,* (pp. 1-12) Eindhoven, PAYS-BAS.

W3C. (2004). *OWL Web ontology language reference.*

Williamson, O.E. (1975). *Markets and hierarchies: Analysis and antitrust implications.* New York, NY: Free Press.

Acknowledgment

The authors would like to acknowledge the publishing team at IGI Global, and especially Rebecca Beistline, whose suggestions throughout the overall development of this book were very effective.

I wish to thank IBM because it was fundamental in my technical and professional education. Furthermore, IBM gave me the opportunity to be introduced to high-level research.

Special thanks go to Salento University that is giving me the opportunity to research in a stimulating and very satisfying environment. I would like to thank the students of computer engineering that first experimented on the use of the methodologies described in this book, validating them in exam projects and especially in graduation and doctoral theses.

Above all, I wish to express my gratitude to Professor Paolo Paolini that not only has introduced me to academic research, but also because he is my mentor and an extraordinary man.

Roberto Paiano
Salento University, Lecce, Italy

Section I
Background

The purpose of this section is to provide the readers with a detailed view of the most known methodologies in the area of BPM and Web application design. Of course, these methodologies are well known in general terms, however here they are presented according to the final goal of this book: to design Complex Web Information Systems. For this reason the coverage of each methodology concerns both its peculiar characteristics and its usefulness to accomplish the task to design a modern and complete Information System. Furthermore, a useful comparison among these methodologies is provided; in particular, in the second chapter a comparison among the most known methodologies to design Was is presented. In the third chapter, the methodology IDM is presented in detail; IDM is the last evolution of a family of methodologies oriented to the design of modern and usable Web Applications. Finally, in the Chapter IV, this book deals with ontology. The ontology is spreading everywhere, however we were among the first to use the expressiveness of the ontology to realize meta-models. All the methodologies we adopt in this book are described through the OWL (Web Ontology Language) that allows us to better express the concepts of our methodologies without constrains.

Chapter I
Evolution of Business Process Notation

WHY PROCESS NOTATION IS IMPORTANT

The analysis of the business processes, realized through visits and interviews to the employees, must necessarily aim to provide for visibility to a large range of operation of the whole process knowledge; this misses very often to the company: each operator sees only the part of the process that tightly competes with it and only an analysis realized by an external team (or that succeeds in abstracting from the specific problems of every actor of the business process) can gather the process in its entirety.

The analysis, of course, has to be documented in a precise and punctual way, and surely it is necessary to find a tool of representation of the business processes that allows providing a clear vision, precise and not technical at the same time. Such representation has to initially be a tool of discussion between an analyst and the company and, then, a tool of connection among business analysts, involved eventually also in the phase of reengineering, and IT analysts.

To achieve this goal, it is essential to carefully analyze the various techniques of representation of the business processes existing in the international panorama

Copyright © 2009, IGI Global, distributing in print or electronic forms without written permission of IGI Global is prohibited.

and among these to select the technique that whose results are more suitable to our purposes.

This chapter describes the actual methods of representation of the business processes identifying that appears more proper for the design of complex Web information systems and defining it in detail. Specifically, three notations will be analyzed: IDEF0, UML® and BPMN™.

IDEF0:1993

IDEF0 (Draft Federal Information, 1993) is the acronym for integration definition for function modeling; it is a standard born in 1993 with the goal of providing for a manner to model in a consistent and complete way the activities, functions, processes, operations as well as the relationships intervening between them. IDEF0 has the followings characteristics:

- *Generic,* or rather it suits it for the analysis of systems with various goals and complexity
- *Rigorous and precise* with the purpose of providing a correct model and easily usable
- *Concise to facilitate the communication,* the approval and the validation of the model
- *Conceptual* for the representation of the functional requisites
- *Flexible* to support different phases of the cycle of life of a project

The use of IDEF0 is recommended for the projects that:

- Require proper techniques of modeling for the analysis, development, and reengineering of an information system
- Require a description of how the company works through an analysis of its processes

The IDEF standard, in which is included the IDEF0 standard, is constituted by three other levels:

- **IDEF0**, used for producing a "functional model." A "functional model" is a structure that represents the functions, the activities and the processes inside the system or in the area of interest.
- **IDEF1** is used for producing a "information model" that represents the structure and the semantics of the information in the area of interest.

Copyright © 2009, IGI Global, distributing in print or electronic forms without written permission of IGI Global is prohibited.

- **IDEF2** is used for producing "dynamic model." A dynamic model represents the varying behavior in the time of the system.

Among these three levels, the first one (IDEF0) is mostly used, and it is probably the reason for which often the terminology IDEF or IDEF0 it is used for pointing out the same thing.

IDEF0 is not limited to providing only for the primitive types of modeling, but also possible methodologies with which to be able to conduct the activities of modeling.

The IDEF0 diagrams are organized into a hierarchical structure, or rather, the sketches are refined for following levels.

In the first level, level A0, the high-level functions are contained, and they are modeled through inputs, controls, output and mechanism and are purposely represented through arrows outgoing or incoming.

- **Inputs:** represent the information that will be transformed, through special functions, in information of output.
- **Outputs** express the output of an IDEF0 diagram, or rather, the data object produced by the functions.
- **Mechanism:** they express the mean by which to realize one determined action.
- **Control:** they express the conditions required to produce the correct output.

The following figure provides for a graphic representation of the level A0.

One of the main characteristics of an IDEF0 diagram is the hierarchical structure with which the various diagrams are organized (of which, above, just the first level is shown). This structure is obtained by associating some graphic elements, named parents, and another diagram child that explores how much is represented in the graphic parent. In this way, it is possible to gradually go down to a deeper level of detail guaranteeing a good readability.

Every function is modeled as a box whose children are detailed in the following level. All the children have to be inside the scope of the high-level diagram.

Diagrams Child

The single function represented in the high-level diagram could be decomposed in its main sub-functions creating the diagram child. In their turns, every sub-function could be decomposed creating the respective diagram's children, and so forth. In every diagram, it is possible to decompose one, all, or only some functions. Every

Copyright © 2009, IGI Global, distributing in print or electronic forms without written permission of IGI Global is prohibited.

Figure 1. Graphic representation of level A0

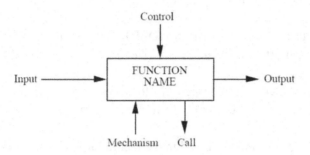

child diagram contains the relative boxes and arrows that provide for a level of detail on the diagram father.

Diagrams Parents

A parent diagram can be both a diagram father and a diagram child that details its parent. The fact that a child box is detailed, and therefore is a diagram parent, is suitable from the presence of a detail reference expression (DRE) or rather a brief code written in the low right of the box father, that points to the child box.

The DRE can be:

- A "C-number" that it identifies univocally a particular version of the diagram child
- A number of pages that points out where, in the document, the diagram child will appear
- The number of the node of the relative diagram child
- A numbered note whose text specifies the condition for the selection of a diagram child

The specifications of IDEF0 also include a methodology that details some procedures to develop or to criticize models realized in a work team. The same methodology also provides for details on how to realize, always in a team, the revision of a project. These methodologies, provided together with the specifications, can also be used however with other types of notations.

Furthermore, the creation of a model is a dynamic process that requires more effort from a person. Through the project, the authors create an initial diagram that is distributed to the members of the project for possible revisions and comments. The discipline requires that every person that wants to make comments does so in

Copyright © 2009, IGI Global, distributing in print or electronic forms without written permission of IGI Global is prohibited.

writing to who has realized the diagram. The author always answers in writing. This procedure continues until the diagram is now officially accepted.

During this cycle, the diagrams can be modified for answering to decisions and comments. The final model represents an acceptance of the representation of the system, and it is the input to organize the job with the purpose of answering to the change.

Because IDEF0 diagram is mostly focused on representing the interactions among the activities, the flows of information and documents and the used resources, it does not take into account the "times." In the representation of the processes temporal constrains, possible precedence and succession constrains are not considered, for which a further diagram is used, IDEF3, in combination with the first one.

In conclusion, the standard IDEF is particularly useful to represent in a top-down way the business processes, but, it really does not allow either to provide information on the actors of the system, neither does it contribute to give semantics to the very frequent decisional choices inside a design of process. Demanding the possibility to represent the information and the dynamics of interaction among the various functions to the models IDEF1 and IDEF2, it provides for a fragmented vision of the process which is difficult to understand.

UML: 2004

UML® (Rumbaugh, Jacobson, & Booch, 2004) is an acronym for Unified Modeling Language™, or rather language of unified modeling; it is a language based on the object-oriented paradigm. Currently, since 2004, it is available the version 2 that, since 2005, is officially an OMG™ standard.

Already since the 1.5 version (the precedent to the actual 2.0 version), UML® has been used and easily understood by everybody, technical or not, in the definition of the specifications of a project. UML® is characterized by its capability of synthesis and for its simplicity.

UML® is often used within the software engineering where the modeling is an important step, and it is directed to assure that the business functionalities are correct and complete, that the needs of the customers have been satisfied and that the system has the requirements of sturdiness, reliability, safety and extendibility; before that, the phase of real implementation begins. UML® helps to really create the models of the software independently from the hardware, from the operating system, from the programming language or from the net: in few words, UML® is independent from the technology of reference and, therefore, it is particularly useful in a phase that comes even before the choice of such a technology. Of course, a good design realized using UML® makes the following phase of coding easier,

Copyright © 2009, IGI Global, distributing in print or electronic forms without written permission of IGI Global is prohibited.

and it facilitates the communication among the different actors involved in this process of development.

UML® is constituted by a series of graphic elements and by a series of syntactic and semantics rules that regulate its use. UML® makes around ten types of diagrams, each of which offers a different "view," but correlated among them of the system that is wanted to realize. Of course, the possibility to use all of these views depends on the complexity of the system to realize, but generally the designers tend to use all of the diagrams because these views are oriented to enhance the communication among experts of different areas.

Following, we shortly list the various views provided by UML:

- *Static View - diagram of the classes*: it shows the structure of the classes that compose the system or the sub-systems in terms of attributes, methods and associations. This diagram inherits all the characteristics of the object-oriented programming: polymorphism, inheritance and encapsulation.
- *Use cases views - diagram of the use cases*: it represents a scenario of use of the system, the functional requirement or specifications of a test. A diagram of the use cases can specify: the actions completed by the system (use cases), people that interact with the system (actors) and relationships between them.
- *Implementation view - diagram of the components and diagram of deployment*: the first one describes the components that constitute the software system—source file, executable, documents, libraries, data—the second the hardware elements—devices and interconnections, disposition of the software components on the hardware devices—that is the logical, and physics architecture of the system.
- *State view - diagram of the states*: it is produced during the logical modeling of the system and through following refinements; it is based on the diagram of the activities. It describes the behavior of the classes focusing itself on a single entity (class) for turn: it is possible to represent nested, competing and synchronous states.
- *Activities view - diagram of the activities*: it is the UML® view that it mostly draws close to the modeling of processes: every atomic operation of the process is represented as activity; the decisional points find correspondence in the branches and the changeover from a task to the other automatic transitions to the completion of the preceding activity is how they are realized. The activity diagram could be considered as an extension of the state diagram: this lastly represents the various states crossed by an object during its elaboration while the first one focuses on the activities.
- *Interaction view - sequence diagram and collaboration diagram*: these two diagrams express as the collaboration happens among the objects of the

Copyright © 2009, IGI Global, distributing in print or electronic forms without written permission of IGI Global is prohibited.

system to realize the use cases. The first one focuses on the temporal aspect of the exchanged messages; the second focuses on the relationships among the objects. They are equivalent and the one can be turned into the other: in the transformation from the sequence diagram to the collaboration, diagram information is lost on the relationships while information is lost on the temporal constrains in the transformation from the collaboration diagram to the sequence diagram.

A main characteristic of UML® is the possibility to realize some mechanisms of controlled extension (stereotypes, new properties, constrains), thanks to which the semantics of the elements of the original meta-model can be modified according to the specific requirements of the designer.

The mechanisms of extension allow creation of new "profiles of UML®," that are a collection of stereotypes, properties and rules that enrich the standard UML®, and they make it more proper to model systems and entities in specific domains. Some profiles have already been standardized by OMG™; others are in progress of standardization. The profiles currently adopted by OMG™ are:

- **Profile for the business modeling:** used to allow modeling of the business processes, the organizational roles involved in such processes, and the information elements of the domain.
- **Profile for the process of software development**.

The version 2.0 of UML® concerns improving the extendibility of the notation and providing for some details omitted in the 1.5 version.

Business Modeling by UML

One of the most important aspects of UML®, already present in the version 1.5 and improved in the version 2.0, is the extendibility of the notation known as the possibility to add new graphic elements with the goal to answer to particular needs of modeling. One of the extensions of UML® was proposed by Hans-Erik Eriksson and Magnus Penker in 2000 (Erickson & Penker, 2000; Sparks, 2000) with the purpose of modeling the business processes.

The proposed extension starts from the assumption that the modeling of the business processes:

- can influence one or more organizational units
- has a horizontal organizational impact
- creates value for different types of customers.

Copyright © 2009, IGI Global, distributing in print or electronic forms without written permission of IGI Global is prohibited.

Table 1. Graphic elements of the UML extension for the business processes

ELEMENTS		USE
Business Process		It is a collection of activities that produce an output for a particular customer or market. The notation implicates a flow of activities from left to the right.
Inputs	Information	The business processes "use" the information coming from customers, from external resources or from the inside of the organization to complete the activities. They are related to the symbol of the process by relationships of <<supply>>
	Resources	The business processes "consume" the resources: they are related to the symbol of the process by relationships of <<input>>
Events		It can be the receipt of an object, the arrival of a date or any cause that provokes the starting of the process.
Outputs		It can be a physical object, the completion of the order of a customer or any object that has a logical value for the organization.
Goals		It is the business motivation for the execution of an activity.

The customers can be both external and inside. The extension proposes the elements described in Table 1.

An example of modeling of a process realized with this extension is shown in Figure 2.

The link types <<implement>> are used for guaranteeing the traceability among the model of process and other elements of the notation such as use cases, packages and artifacts. In this way it is possible to individualize what function is already implemented inside the process (Figure 3).

The Support to the Business Process in the UML Version 2.0

The UML® Version 2.0 has brought substantial improvements, especially in the area of the modeling of the business processes. The modeling of the business

Copyright © 2009, IGI Global, distributing in print or electronic forms without written permission of IGI Global is prohibited.

Figure 2. Representation of a business process by UML extension

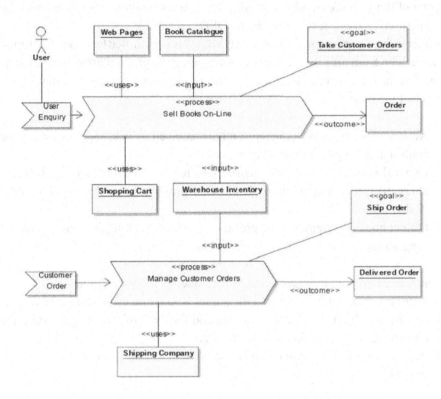

Figure 3. Traceability of a business process in an implementation diagram

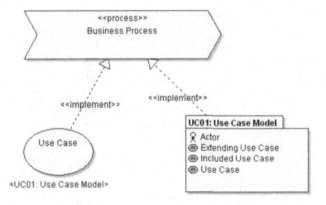

Copyright © 2009, IGI Global, distributing in print or electronic forms without written permission of IGI Global is prohibited.

processes in the version 2.0 has been realized thanks to a complete revision of the diagram of the activities, and it also allows the representation of analysis made by the structured analysis techniques as the DFD.

The activity diagram contemplated in UML® 2 is constituted by nodes connected between them from arcs for the goal to form a complete graph. Particularly UML® 2 provides for the existence of three typologies of nodes that allow regulations of the flow of the processes:

- **Action nodes** that check the data and the received values, and they supply the control and the data to the other actions
- **Control nodes** that include constructions to allow a choice among different alternatives (decision point) or to allow the prosecution of the flow in parallel (forks)
- **Object nodes** that temporarily preserve some data waiting for their movement through the graph

The related graphic representation of the nodes is shown in Table 2.

We observe that, contrary to what the names would make you think, the control nodes coordinate both the flow of the data and the flow of the process while the object nodes can manage both objects and data.

The activity nodes can be connected between them through direct arcs; there are two types of arcs:

Table 2. Graphic representation of nodes

NODES	GRAPHIC REPRESENTATION	
Action nodes		
Control nodes	Decision and merge	
	Fork and join	
	Initial node	
	Final nodes	
Object node		Label
		Label

Copyright © 2009, IGI Global, distributing in print or electronic forms without written permission of IGI Global is prohibited.

- **Control flow:** they connect the actions to point out that the following action cannot begin until the end of the preceding one; just one token can pass through the control flow.
- **Object flow:** they connect nodes for the purpose of providing for input to the actions. Only objects and token can pass among the flows objects.

The activity models coordinate actions, some of which could invoke behaviors defined by the user, including other activities. All of the actions are pre-defined: for instance, UML® 2 defines actions to create objects, to set attributes, to connect objects between them and to invoke behaviors defined by the user. The actions can have input and output, called "pins," that are connected through flow to appear as the values pass through the various objects.

The activities are behaviors defined from the user and, as the other behaviors in UML® 2.0, they can be activated by the invocation of an action, and they support parameters with the purpose to receive and to provide for data from who invokes the action. To access the values of the parameters, the actions are modeled as a special type of node.

Finally, UML® 2.0 provides the possibility of defining some roles that, de facto, are translated in the formal representation of the actors of the process.

BPMN: 2006

The BPMN™ (OMG, 2006) or Business Process Management Notation™, derived from the Business Process Management Initiative (BPMI™) consortium that boasts important names, among which include Adobe Systems, Inc., Axway Software, Bea happy Systems, Inc., Bluespring Software, Inc., British American Tobacco, BroadVision, Casewise Systems, Inc., FileNET Corporation, IBM Corporation, SAP AG, Select Business Solutions and many other important names. In June 2005, BPMI™ joined OMG™ (Object Management Group) with the goal to formalize some useful standards for the companies.

The primary goal of the notation is to be easily understandable by all of the business users: the business analysts that realize the first draft of the design of the process, the developers responsible of the implementation of the process in the reference technology, and finally the business users that manipulate and monitor the modeled processes. By doing this, the notation has tried to create a standard that succeeds in uniting different notations and different points of view.

The members of the Working Group have treasured their experience coming from the use of a lot of notations trying to consolidate the best ideas of every notation in BPMN™.

Copyright © 2009, IGI Global, distributing in print or electronic forms without written permission of IGI Global is prohibited.

The specifications provided by the consortium define the notation and the semantics of the so-called business process diagram (BPD). BPMN™ is constituted by two fundamental parts:

- **Visual part:** a key element of BPMN™ is the choice of the icons used for the graphic elements defined in the specifications. The goal is to create a visual language that all of the designers of processes can recognize and to understand independently from the subject of the diagram itself. There is an elevated level of flexibility in the colors, in the dimension, in the style and in the position of the text inside every icon. It is possible to extend the notation, but also, always respecting some base rules:
  - ° It is possible to add new elements or new symbols associated with existing elements. The extension can also be realized for an object or to change the styles with which the lines are drawn. The extensions must not be, however, in any way, in conflict with how much is defined in the specifications.
  - ° The extensions cannot change the forms present in the specifications (it is not possible to change a rectangle into a triangle).
  - ° It is possible to add other elements, but without entering into a conflict with those already existing.
- **Semantics part:** the notation specifies also, as the various elements interact between them and the rules of interconnection, that it is necessary to respect both during the definition of a new diagram and during the developing of a tool to support the notation.

Business Process Diagram

BPMN™ defines the concept of business process diagram (BPD).

A BPD allows provision of a general vision of one or more processes and to visualize the involved subjects showing their interrelations and their assignments.

A BPD, if opportunely structured, provides for a lot of information on the work of the company, but it does not provide, for a precise choice of the inventors of the notation, information about:

- the organization, the structure and the resources of the company
- the functional subdivision of the company
- information related to data and information models of the company
- business strategies
- business rules

Copyright © 2009, IGI Global, distributing in print or electronic forms without written permission of IGI Global is prohibited.

Of course, this does not mean that these aspects are not important during the analysis of an information system, but they are deferred to other methodologies.

IT Expert - Business Expert

A well precise goal that the notation aims to reach is fulfilling the existing gap among business expert, professional figures that are in charge of understanding the processes, and eventually undertaking corrective actions to improve the carrying out, and IT expert, professional figures that, on the field, take care to operate a process, or rather they realize the application that is the best adaptation to the problems that emerged during the modeling. Very often, the IT experts do not find, in the drawing of the process realized by the business expert, all of the information they need, therefore they make a "translation" from the language used in the design of the process to a language more close to the requirements of development distorting, very often, the reality.

The BPMN™, introducing de facto two levels of detail, a more visual and a more detailed (based on the properties of every element), contributes to fill this gap allowing the two professional figures to opportunely discuss always on the same base diagram properly specialized according to the particular needs.

Business Process

BPMN™ treats three different typologies of processes that allow to offer different visions of a same process to the different typologies of actors involved. Of course, according to the particular needs of analysis, the more proper type of business process will be selected. With BPMN™, it is possible to represent three types of business processes:

- **Private business processes:** take place all inside a single organizational unit (they coincide with the workflow)
- **Abstract processes:** processes that show the interactions among a private business process and another organizational unit
- **Collaboration processes:** represent the interaction among two or more organizational units

Of course, by combining the various types of diagrams, it is possible to get different BPD such as the high-level representation of the processes; the AS-IS and TO-BE of business processes; detailed diagrams (workflow): it is important that the designer focuses it on a particular aspect of the analysis of the processes avoiding to realize diagrams that are too complicated and therefore difficult to understand.

Copyright © 2009, IGI Global, distributing in print or electronic forms without written permission of IGI Global is prohibited.

For every typology of process, it is possible to define the relative participants or the subjects (human or software modules) that are assigned to the accomplishment of the tasks.

BPMN™ provides for four different categories of primitives of modeling with which it is possible to represent the processes: flow object, connecting object, swimlane and artifact.

Every primitive of modeling belonging to each of the four typologies allows provisions of a further level of detail, this time not graphic but just textual: the addition of this level of detail (or rather of the level of property) is particularly useful to give the necessary information to the IT expert that, only from the graphic primitives, would not be able to understand all the necessary details for modeling.

Figure 4 shows the four different graphic primitives of BPMN™.

You can observe that every element, which is explained below, can have different icons that, when properly used, are suitable to represent the whole business process.

The main graphic elements of the notation are the flow objects that allow defining of the behavior of the business process. Three different types of flow objects exist: events, activities and gateway. The various flows objects are connected through the connecting objects that, in the specific one, are sequence flow, message flow and association. There are, instead, two ways to group the modeling elements rendering explicit the actors assigned to execute the tasks (specified by the flows objects): pools and lanes. There are finally the artifacts used to provide additional information on the process and that are used only for modeling purposes: there are three categories of artifacts or rather the data objects, the groups and finally the annotations.

Now we can see in detail the graphic representation in each of the categories of elements that are pointed out.

Figure 4. BPMN overview

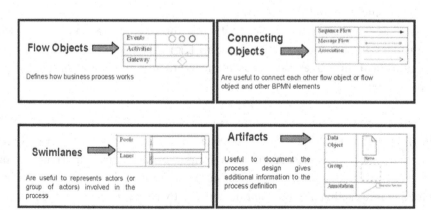

Copyright © 2009, IGI Global, distributing in print or electronic forms without written permission of IGI Global is prohibited.

Flow Object

- **Event:** all that "happens" inside a process. They affect the flow of the process (often they are really delegated to create an instance of it), and they have a cause (trigger) and an effect (result). Three typologies of event exist (Figure 5): start event, intermediate event, and end event according to if they respectively own an incoming flow, both incoming and outgoing, or just outgoing.
- **Activity:** A generic term to denominate an activity made by a participant of the process. Activity (Figure 6) can be atomic (task) or not atomic (sub-process).
- **Gateway:** It is used for checking the divergence (forking) or the convergence (joining) of the flow. It owns some conditions that allow performing conditional choices and some internal markers indicate a specific behaviour (Figure 7).

Figure 5. Typology of events

Figure 6. Typology of activities

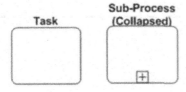

Figure 7. Gateway example

Copyright © 2009, IGI Global, distributing in print or electronic forms without written permission of IGI Global is prohibited.

Swimlane

The swimlanes represent "who does what" in the diagram. They are rectangles that define the processes and the relative participants.

The two typologies of the existing swimlane are:

- **Pool:** it represents a participant inside a process (Figure 8)
- **Lane:** It subdivides the pools into more logical entities (e.g., the branches of a company) (Figure 9).

Artifact

The artifacts are elements that do not influence the change of the flow of execution, but they stay in a background of the execution of the process, or they have a pure goal of documentation.
It is possible to define new artifacts, but three canonical versions already exist in the specification of the BPMN™:

- **Data object:** It provides information on what an activity requires as input, and what it produces as output (Figure 10)
- **Group:** It allows, for purposes exclusively related to the documentation, group activities to belong to a different pool (Figure 11)
- **Annotation:** It adds additional information to the diagram or to parts of it (Figure 12).

Figure 8. Pool example

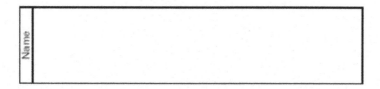

Figure 9. Lane example

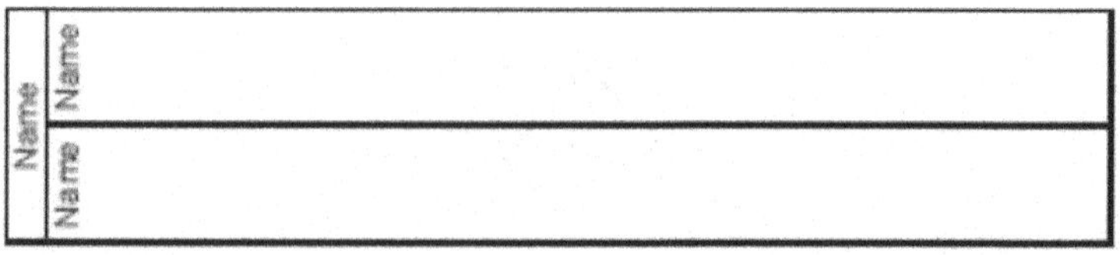

Copyright © 2009, IGI Global, distributing in print or electronic forms without written permission of IGI Global is prohibited.

Figure 10. Data object example

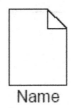

Name

Figure 11. Group example

Figure 12. Annotation example

Descriptive Text Here

Connecting Object

A connection object connects (also in an oriented way) the elements of the notation. They can be one of three types:

- **Sequence flow:** It indicates the order in which activities are executed inside the process (Figure 13)
- **Message flow:** It indicates the flow of the messages that intervenes among two participants (Figure 14)
- **Association:** It is used for associating information (textual or graphical) to flow objects (Figure 15).

Every basic element can change the stereotype of visualization inside the diagram. Different types of start, intermediate, and end events that, for instance, model the start of a process according to the receipt of a message or the expiration of a determined time range, exist. It is possible to make the same discourse for the

Copyright © 2009, IGI Global, distributing in print or electronic forms without written permission of IGI Global is prohibited.

Figure 13. Sequence flow example

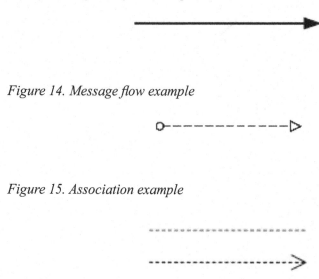

Figure 14. Message flow example

Figure 15. Association example

gateways that are used for sorting the flow among different possible alternatives: the inside markers will serve to give an intuitive and immediate vision of the possible practicable alternatives.

When a sub-process is defined, it is necessary to indicate an activity in whose inside, there is a symbol of "+," the so-called sub-processes, containers of other processes. The sub-process cannot, every case, overcome the boundary of the activity.

Inside the process, it is possible to define some loops. BPMN™ makes two mechanisms of loop available:

- **Activity loop:** suitable with a small circle with an arrow inside the icon that represents the activity. An attribute of the process will point out if it can be repeated or performed once.
- **Sequence flow looping:** The loop can be realized as shown in Figure 16:

It is possible to define some transactions that are represented inside a double frame.

Finally, from the semantic point of view, the specifications also establish the possible interconnections among the objects previously introduced. It is possible to have rules of interconnection for both the categories of connecting objects: sequence flow and message flow. The symbols inside Table 3 point out that the element of the line can be connected with the present element in the column. It is not possible to connect elements of sub-processes with the process that contains them.

Copyright © 2009, IGI Global, distributing in print or electronic forms without written permission of IGI Global is prohibited.

Figure 16. Example of loop using a gateway

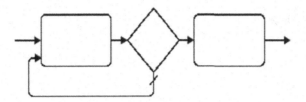

Table 4 points out, instead, that the various objects of the notation can be connected through message flow. A message flow cannot connect objects that are inside the same lane.

Comparison between LRC Table and BPMN Diagram

The flow of the process, even though important, is not the only key element in the study of the process suitable to a continuous improvement. Furthermore, the organization structure is extremely important. From the intersection among these two organizational variables (flow of process and organization structure), several conclusions can be drawn. It is possible to observe, for instance, that organizations with a parallel structure are proper for repetitive and simple assignments and to tall volumes, while flat organizations with very limited duties are proper for complex jobs and limited volumes.

An accurate study of the business processes cannot very often be completed without taking the business organization chart into account: the organization charts can be deepened for following levels of detail going from the head of the company down to the lower level employees that have the burden to perform manual assign-

Table 3. Sequence flow: Interconnection rules

Source\Target	◯	▭	▭⊞	◇	◎	◉
◯		✓	✓	✓	✓	✓
▭		✓	✓	✓	✓	✓
▭⊞		✓	✓	✓	✓	✓
◇		✓	✓	✓	✓	✓
◎		✓	✓	✓	✓	✓
◉						

Copyright © 2009, IGI Global, distributing in print or electronic forms without written permission of IGI Global is prohibited.

Table 4. Message flow: Interconnection rules

Source\Target	◯	▢	▢	Pool	◯	◯
◯						
▢	✓	✓	✓	✓	✓	
▢	✓	✓	✓	✓	✓	
Pool	✓	✓	✓	✓	✓	
◯						
◯	✓	✓	✓	✓	✓	

ments or better the activities that allow for the daily carrying out of the normal flow of business.

Up to a few year ago, the LRC charts were used (Linear Responsibility Charting) (Cleland, 1983) to define "who does what" inside the company. The techniques of process design used in those years did not underline any roles inside the company, but they focused only on the flow of the activities showing, at same time in a separate documentation, at what level of responsibility the various activities was taken in charge by the several actors interested in the process. The LRC diagram was used precisely as a useful tool of linking the flow of a process and the organization chart. A LRC diagram exist in a chart in which are positioned on the columns the various actors of the diagram and on the lines the main activities performed inside the process. At the intersection between lines and columns, the assignment of the actor is pointed out for a well precise activity. The assignments can be:

D = it decides, it authorizes, it confirms
E = it performs activity
A = it participates in part-time, it provides for assistance and support
I = it is systematically informed

An example of an LRC chart is described in the Table 5.

With the introduction of the BPMN™ for the design of the business processes, the use of a chart of this type to point out "who does what" is almost useless because all the suitable information in the chart is already visually evident in the BPMN™ diagram.

All of the actors of the system are pointed out with the pools or with some lanes inside of the pools and, to have an idea of the information transit among the vari-

Copyright © 2009, IGI Global, distributing in print or electronic forms without written permission of IGI Global is prohibited.

Table 5. LRC chart: example

	Actor 1	Actor 2	Actor 3
Activity 1	E	D	I
Activity 2	I		E
Activity 3	A	D	E
Activity 4	D	D	I

ous actors of the process, it is possible to directly represent the actors not involved in a specific process but that are constantly informed, as a black box connected to the other actors with some messages flow to specify that an actor is Informed about a specific activity or about a specific group of activities. Of course, the actor that performs an activity will have the relative task inside the lane or pool that represents it.

The activity of decision and sharing inside a specific process is referred to as the semantics attributed to the name of the various tasks.

We can affirm, therefore, that the LRC chart is included in the design of the BPMN™ diagram according to the rules of mapping described in Table 6.

The centrality of the actors that perform the various tasks inside the process is fundamental today, with a horizontal vision of the company, was also useful in the past years in which, despite the existing notations, did not allow to focus on the actors, it placed side by side to the design of the process the useful LRC chart to understand in that terms the various actors had involved in the carrying out of the various activities.

The same information is present today in the BPMN™ diagrams where, in optics to provide a wide vision of company, and that it also crosses the boundary of the business area also involving in the process external actors, they cannot only find users that directly belong to the business organization chart but also external actors that belong to the process in different ways (e.g., instance, customers, suppliers, other corporate bodies, other companies).

CONCLUSIVE NOTES ON THE GRAPHIC REPRESENTATION OF THE BUSINESS PROCESSES

The notations presented here are just examples of the possible existing notations for the representation of a business process. If, for instance, the various suites of BPM (Business Process Management) that currently exist on the market and that allow realization of the whole process of development of business processes-based

Copyright © 2009, IGI Global, distributing in print or electronic forms without written permission of IGI Global is prohibited.

Table 6. Mapping rules between the BPMN and the LRC chart

LRC	BPMN™
System Actors	Pool/Lane
Execute	The task is represented in the relative pool/lane
Decide	The task semantics assigned to an actor that takes a specific decision.
Part-time partecipation, providing for assistance and support	The task semantics assigned to an actor that participates part-time and provides for assistance and support.
Always Informed	The information arrives to the actor systematically informed through message flows coming from other actors of the process.

applications from the definition of the process and up to the realization of the final application with relative maintenance are considered, it is possible to observe a great difference among the notations used by each. Typically, the big companies of this sector, such as Filenet, ILog and so forth, that are involved in the realization of such tools, are oriented to use their own notations to preserve the know-how of the company.

The tendency to use a proprietary notation for the design of the business processes could derive from the difficulty to use a standard notation, such as IDEF0, for the definition of the process. Such notation, in fact, misses many details, for instance, a clear distinction among the different actors of the system, and it requires, therefore, being able to be inserted into an executive project, of extensive "adjustments" that make its use complicated.

The use of UML® and the relative extensions, de facto, not only implicates a considerable effort for the person who has to use the notation that is forced to study a series of constructions and rules not always proper of the business modeling (we remember that the fundamental characteristic of UML® is not to represent business processes but to represent in general a system), but also for those that, also not being technical, have to read the design and validate it.

A good alternative, in terms of simplicity, completeness and clarity, could be the BPMN™ that as reference notation has been selected in the design of a complex Web information system.

Copyright © 2009, IGI Global, distributing in print or electronic forms without written permission of IGI Global is prohibited.

REFERENCES

Cleland, D.I., & King W.E. (1983). *Systems analysis and project management.* McGraw-Hill.

Draft Federal Information Processing Standards Publication 183 (1993) *Integration definition for function modeling (IDEF0).*

Eriksson, H. E., & Penker M. (2000). *Business modeling with UML: Patterns at work.* John Wiley & Sons.

OMG. (2006). *Business Process Modeling Notation Specification.*

Rumbaugh, J., Jacobson I., & Booch, G. (2004). *Unified modeling language reference manual.* Addison-Wesley.

Sparks, G. (2000). An introduction to UML: The business process model. Retrieved January 2007, from http://www.uml.co.il/WhitePapers/The_Business_Process_Model.pdf

Copyright © 2009, IGI Global, distributing in print or electronic forms without written permission of IGI Global is prohibited.

Chapter II
Web Information System Design Methodolgies Overview

INTRODUCTION

In the previous chapter, an in-depth analysis of several methodologies used to model the business processes was provided. In detail, the analysis was direct to choose a specific methodology able to satisfy the requirement of simplicity and clarity needed for the design of the business processes.

In this chapter, the main methodologies of Web application design established into the international scientific panorama are presented. Each of these methodologies is characterized for its capability to suitably structure the informative contents and to define a navigational structure. These features allow the user an easy and intuitive navigation through the Web site contents, avoiding cognitive errors.

In a nutshell, these methodologies drive the designer in the project of the Web application. Many of these methodologies are born after the evolution of the simple sites into more complex applications that are in need of a specific design phase made before the technical development phase.

Between these methodologies in this chapter, we have analyzed WebML (Ceri, Fraternali, & Bongio, 2000), OOHDM (Schwabe & Rossi, 1998) and UWE (www.

Copyright © 2009, IGI Global, distributing in print or electronic forms without written permission of IGI Global is prohibited.

Webml.org) (Koch & Kraus, 2002; 2003). The IDM (Perrone, Bolchini, & Paolini, 2005; Bolchini & Paolini, 2006; Paolini, Mainetti, & Bolchini, 2006) methodology, which was established into the international scientific panorama and born as a natural evolution of W2000 (Baresi, Garzotto, Mainetti, & Paolini, 2002), is analyzed in more detail. IDM is a good starting point for the design task in the realization of a complex Web information system.

IMPORTANCE OF THE DESIGN METHODOLOGIES FOR MODERN WEB-ORIENTED INFORMATION SYSTEMS

The design is surely the core phase into the software development life cycle, and it allows for describing a complete vision of application requirements without focusing on development and technological detail. At the same time, the design is rigorous and formal.

The importance of the design into the analysis of the Web application is highlighted more than other kinds of application: in the development of a Web application, it is central to join the technical aspects and the user experience aspects.

The first generation of design methodologies considered the Web application as a display of static content, structured into a database, where navigational paradigm could be based on the relationship between the entities.

In a short time, the designers were aware that this content organization did not appeal to the user that became harder to please; thus, the introduction of a different kind of management of information content was essential. This new management was based not on the information structure, but on the user perception.

During these years, the designers discovered that, in order to make a good Web application project, different aspects must be considered; between these aspect, the information is surely the most important, but also the navigational and the trans-actional aspects must be properly considered during the design.

Thus, the "user experience" vision became widely accepted in the international scientific community. This concept allows focusing the attention on the dialogue between the user and the Web application.

In order to apply the user experience concept, it is essential to focus on the user; thus, the real application player is not the data but instead the way the users use these data.

The design methodologies of Web application are inclining to split the design into different "thematic" area and to focus the analysis every time on a different design aspect: the informative, navigational, and the transactional.

Indeed, very often, different analysis levels focusing on a specific aspect are present in these methodologies. This feature is common between the examined

Copyright © 2009, IGI Global, distributing in print or electronic forms without written permission of IGI Global is prohibited.

methodologies: the separation between the aspects enables the designer to focus in a different moment on a different Web application aspect.

As the other design methodologies, the Web application methodologies also allow the designer to think carefully on the application design before starting with the development phase.

A valid design, in fact, increases the quality of the final application and, in particular, allows quick correction of project errors that could compromise the entire project.

It is clear that during the Web application design where different important aspects are jointed into unique context, these concepts are empathized. On one hand, the Web application design methodologies allow focusing on several aspects in different momens; on the other hand, they allow, in some cases, having a global and clear view of how these aspects must be connected in order to model the final application.

The situation becomes more complex when, over the complexity of the design of a standard Web application, the complexity derived from introduction of the business processes must be added. The design of business processes must be a part of the entire design of Web application and adds a very high complex level.

In this chapter, the main design methodologies of Web application are presented by focusing on the specific one selected for the design of a complex Web information system. In the following chapter, the studies will focus on the business processes analysis.

THE WEB DESIGN METHODOLOGIES

OOHDM: 1998

Initially, OOHDM was a methodology developed to model hypermedia applications and then extended to Web applications. OOHDM (object-oriented design method) is based on object-oriented paradigm.

OOHDM, as the other analyzed methodologies, distinguishes four design levels:

- Conceptual design
- Navigation design
- Abstract interface design
- Implementation

Copyright © 2009, IGI Global, distributing in print or electronic forms without written permission of IGI Global is prohibited.

In each level, a specific model is created. The model is an object model that describes a specific design area. The specific level model is obtained from the model of the previous level enhanced.

In brief, we analyze the different design levels.

Conceptual Modeling

The first modeling phase, conceptual modeling, allows for designing of the semantic of the application domain. In other words, it consists of identifying the elements that describe the system without focusing on a different kind of user and tasks.

The model of conceptual modeling is realized using the object-oriented paradigm and UML® notation. The output is a complete schema of classes and relationships. The diagram differentiates a little by UML®, for example, the use of multiple attributes and the use of relations with direction.

The conceptual classes that describe the domain are built using aggregations and generalization/specialization concepts of OO. There is no specific method to create the conceptual model, but a generic object-oriented method could be used to create a class diagram.

Navigational Design

The navigational design is realized as a view based on the conceptual model. OOHDM acknowledges that the objects used by the user to navigate are not the same objects of the conceptual model because they are objects created on only one or more conceptual objects.

The created view is valid for a specific user group that performs a specific set of tasks into the application. The navigational schema is composed of a cluster of pre-defined elements as nodes, links, anchors and access structures, which is the same semantic used in the Web application and thus the nodes are the information objects.

The nodes are derived as composition of the objects previously defined. The nodes are related using the links that represent the relations from the point of view of the final user.

After the navigational classes are defined, it is possible to define the navigational space in order to allow for a well-known user group to access the information. Therefore, the navigational objects are grouped in a defined set called "contexts."

For each context, the visual elements are defined with the entry point, the constraints from user, the classes and operation and the associated access structures. The navigational structures are defined into the context diagram that shows all of

Copyright © 2009, IGI Global, distributing in print or electronic forms without written permission of IGI Global is prohibited.

the access structures and the contexts defined for the entire application and shows all possible navigation between the contexts.

Into the context diagram, it is possible to model classes that share some properties, configurable classes, simple links and derived links (that could be changed to adapt to specific navigation) and access structures to show the information.

The context diagram does not describe all of the needed structures to describe all contexts: each context will be detailed using the CRC cards. A CRC card (Beck & Cunningham, 1989) is an index card that is used to represent the responsibilities of classes and the interaction between the classes; in this case, it is used to define the context. Each card is composed of five sections: (i) its super and sub classes (if applicable), (ii) the responsibilities of the class, (iii) the names of other classes with which the class will collaborate to fulfill its responsibilities, and (iv) authors.

The main CRC card benefits are: (i) the complexity of the design is at a minimum, (ii) they are portable, (iii) they allow the designer to focus on the essentials of the class and prevent him from getting into its details, and (iv) they are simple to manage.

After the different contexts are defined, it is possible to extend the class definition with decorator (called "InContext" class).

This class adds attributes to a defined class; these attributes are valid only for a specific context.

Therefore, the navigational output is made up of three parts:

- A navigational class schema in which the classes and relationships are already defined in the previous phase and are re-defined to represent the user's point of view
- A context schema to describe the different context in which the users operate
- The CRC cards that define the extra detail in every defined context

Abstract Interface Design

In this phase, the interface aspect is defined. This aspect is related to the ability of the users to interact with the application layout. In this design phase, by putting the user at the center of Web application design, it is possible to specify the interface as the user appreciates it.

We have to define the difference between the navigation and the interface: not all that happens on the interface is related to navigation. It is useful to model the interfaces independently from the technological aspects.

The abstract interface design provides a description of the activated navigation, which interfaces will be synchronized and which interfaces will be shown to the user.

Copyright © 2009, IGI Global, distributing in print or electronic forms without written permission of IGI Global is prohibited.

OOHDM uses ADV (abstract data view) to describe the user interfaces. ADV describes:

- The static and structural aspects using the composition technique
- How these aspects are related with the navigational object
- How these aspects operate when they are activated by external events

It is clear that a specific ADV exists for a specific page of a final Web application.

Implementation

In this phase, the appropriate developer environment is chosen. In spite of OOHDM, which is based on an object model, it does not require an environment based on OO paradigm to develop a Web application.

In Table 1, the main phases of methodology are summarized.

WEBML: 2000

WebML (Web modeling language) is a language that makes a conceptual model of a complex Web site; thus, the language does not describe the architectural and development aspects, but it models the design one having a high-level of abstraction. The conceptual modeling with WebML is composed of four perspectives:

- **Structural model:** describes the information site content as entity and relationship with a classical entity-relationship diagram; in this model a first organization of the content is made. The data are structured using the common rules of an E-R model.
- **Hypertext model:** allows making user-oriented structures of Web application. The hypertext model defines the hypertext that will be published on Web. In this model, the information structure of having a global view of the entire site is done. The global view is called site view. The hypertext model splits the design intp two macro-areas: one to model the information infrastructure as the user appreciates it and the second to model the navigation inside the information structure defined before. Thus, the hypertext model is composed of two models: the composition model that models the pages of the hypertext and the information elements of each page and the navigational model that indicates the allowed navigation between the page and how the different contents are linked to create the hypertext.

Copyright © 2009, IGI Global, distributing in print or electronic forms without written permission of IGI Global is prohibited.

Table 1. Methodology main phases

PHASE	INPUT	OUTPUT	GOAL
Conceptual Modelling	Domain analysis	OO diagram to model the domain	Provide a semantic vision of analyzed domain
Navigational Design	OO diagram to model the domain	Navigational schema Context Schema CRC cards	Define the navigational structures for each user
Abstract Interface Design	Context Schema	Graphic interface design	Give an idea of the final application.
Implementation	Navigational schema; Context Schema; CRC cards; Graphic interface design	Web Application	The final application

- **Presentation model:** this model is oriented to the graphical aspect of Web application. It allows defining the layout and the graphical properties of the pages. It is possible to define the layout and the graphical properties for single pages (page-specific layout) or for a set of pages (generic layout).
- **Personalization model:** every user class is modeled with two entities: group and user. These entities store the preferences for each user used in the composition of the information units or in the specific navigation.

The language used in the design methodology is graphical and very simple and it is very simple to be understood by technical and no-technical users.

The development of a Web application with WebML is obtained reiterating the presented model. The number of iteration depends on the application complexity.

In detail, the single steps are:

- Requirement elicitation
- Data model
- Hypertext design in-the-large
- Hypertext design in-the-small
- Presentation model

Copyright © 2009, IGI Global, distributing in print or electronic forms without written permission of IGI Global is prohibited.

- Users and groups design
- Customization design

It is important to better describe the data model and hypertext model. We have to highlight that WebML was developed to design Web applications starting from the E-R model. WebML describes the application information contents with entities (as in the database design).

Starting from this data model, the designer models one or more hypertexts (called site views) that describe how to publish and/or manage the data modeled into E-R schema. The site view is a diagram of pages that will be published on the Web.

The pages are formed from content units that are autonomous fragments of information to be published (for instance, an item to select specific objects or input form, etc.). The pages could be linked with links in order to make the complete navigational maps of a site.

In addition to the simple navigation between contents, WebML provides infrastructures to support the operations (also simple) such as the filling of a shopping bag or the update of contents (insert or update of instance of relationships).

UML-BASED WEB ENGINEERING: 2000

The UML-based Web engineering (UWE) methodology covers the entire life cycle of Web application development. It proposes an object-oriented approach based on the unified software development process (Rumbaugh, Jacobson, & Booch, 1999).

The used design notation is a "light" profile of UML®. In this case, profile is an extension of the methodology. The extension is based on extension mechanism defined into UML® and uses a standard notation easily supported by case tools.

The UWE profile includes the stereotypes and tagged values defined to model the different aspect of Web application such as navigation, presentation, users and operations. For each aspect, a model is defined following the guide lines provided with UWE.

To contain the classical elements of UML® meta-model, the UWE meta-model introduces new elements. Each one of these elements has private properties and relations and properties and relations inheritance from other UML® meta-model.

Therefore, as the well-formedness rules of UML®, UWE use OCL (object constraint language) constraints to describe the semantic of added elements. In Figure 1, a view of meta-model of elements of UWE and UML® is described.

The foundation package contains all of the base elements of the model and is divided into two packages: core and context. The first contains three levels related

Copyright © 2009, IGI Global, distributing in print or electronic forms without written permission of IGI Global is prohibited.

Figure 1. UWE meta-model

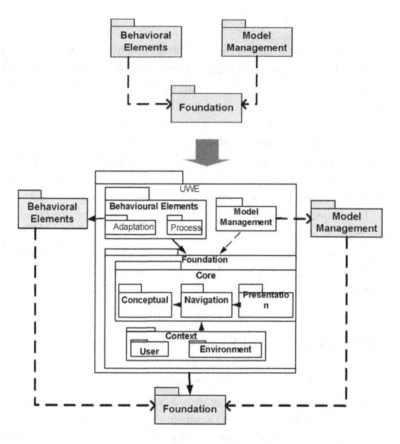

to the conceptual, navigational, and presentational aspect; the second depends on "core" and contains the two packages "user" and "environment."

The behavioral elements package (connected with the foundation package) consists of two sub-packages: the process (task), to model the workflow elements, and adaptation, to model the customization aspect of the application. The model management package describes the conceptual, navigation and presentation aspects, and it derives from a foundation model.

The conceptual model is not very different from the classical model used in the creation of classical application. In this package (Figure 2), in fact, the classes contained into the schema and the mutual relation are modeled. As in the traditional object-oriented system, the classes, the inheritance structures, and the restrictions are defined.

The model elements are divided into conceptual classes, operation, attribute and associations. The conceptual class elements are sub-classes of UML®. Classes with

Copyright © 2009, IGI Global, distributing in print or electronic forms without written permission of IGI Global is prohibited.

Figure 2. Conceptual package

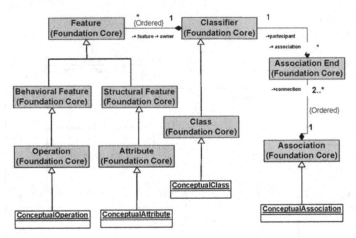

the navigation model attribute are added. This attribute specifies that the conceptual class is relevant to the navigation model. Furthermore, the attribute, operation and associations attributes use the same logic of UML® attributes.

Navigation Package

The navigation package (Figure 3) is the design of the navigational structures of Web application; thus, the base elements are the NavigationNode and links that derive, respectively, from the class and association elements of UML® core.

The meta-class NavigationNode is an abstract class, so only its specialized class could be instantiated: for each ConceptualClass (with the navigational property activated), a specific NavigationClass class is created; while, the association between the NavigationClass is derived from the corresponding ConceptualClass or derived ex novo in order to model the navigational paths.

The abstract class link is abstract and links a source NavigationNode with one or more target nodes; its attribute is automatic and allows for distinguishing between system links and user links.

A NavigationClass is composed by only NavigationAttributes that are derived from the ConceptualAttribute of conceptual model. Constraints on the meta-model forces the ConceptualAttributes (from which NavigationAttributes of Navigation-Class are derived) to be ConceptualAttributes of only one ConceptualClass associated with NavigationClass.

This constraint is expressed using the OCL restriction. In Figure 4, it is possible to view a piece of the complete design in order to clarify the mutual relationships.

Copyright © 2009, IGI Global, distributing in print or electronic forms without written permission of IGI Global is prohibited.

Figure 3. Navigation package

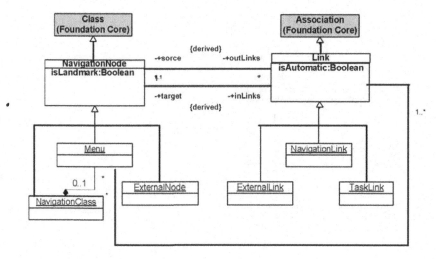

Figure 4. Relationships between conceptual and navigation package

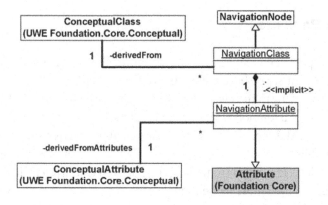

The specialization of link class could be of a different type:

- **NavigationLink:** used to model the navigation (static) with the classic semantic used into the hypermedia application; it could contain a set of AccessPrimitives (index, query and guided tour) associated with one or more NavigationAttributes.
- **TaskLink:** it connects a source node with TaskGraph (an element that describes the dynamic behaviour of a node defined in the UWE Task Model).
- **ExternalLink:** it allows describing the connection with resources external to the application.

Copyright © 2009, IGI Global, distributing in print or electronic forms without written permission of IGI Global is prohibited.

Presentation Package

This package contains the presentation primitives of Web application (Figure 5). The core element is the abstract class location that, through its specialization Location-Group, allows modeling a list of subclass locations; while alternative presentations between different locations are modeled using the LocationAlternative class.

All the UI elements are specializations of abstract class UIElements that could be associated to more NavigationAttributes. The user interface elements are group-like or primitives such as image, text o text input. The collections are used to individuate homogeneous series of NavigationNodes; while the subtype, AnchoredCollection, is related to the index elements that describe the corresponding list of elements. The UI elements contained in the element group collection are used to model specific features of a set of NavigationNodes. At last, the anchor is related to an element of link type.

User Package, Adaptation Package

The base element of the user meta-model is the meta-class user, a specialization of the UML® actor element. Every user is defined by a unique user ID and could be associated to a different UserRole. Every UserRole has a UserProfile that could be assigned to a single user or to a group of users. The UserProfile is the element that, by differentiating the users though its properties, allows modeling of different Web application behaviors.

Figure 5. Presentation package

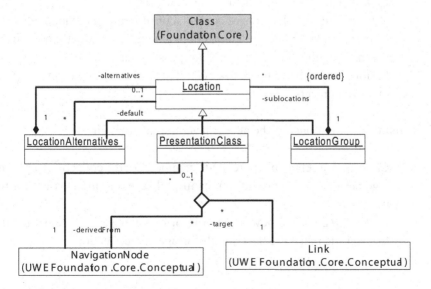

Copyright © 2009, IGI Global, distributing in print or electronic forms without written permission of IGI Global is prohibited.

The main elements in the adaptation model are the rules (AdaptationRule) and its events (RuleTrigger) that activate themselves. The AdaptationRule derives from the transition elements of the UML® state machine and the RuleTrigger one from the event. The AdaptationRules are classes related to user properties and to core elements of conceptual, navigation and presentation packages. The rules are activated by other rules or by other events (called RuleTrigger in the meta-model) through the user behavior (navigation) or context behavior (mobility, network changes, etc.).

W2000: 2000

W2000 methodology is organized in the following parts:

- **Information Design:** the purpose is the identification of the relevant information to be handled by the application, and the provision of an overall organization of the information structures, independently from any specific intended usage.

The main concept introduced is the distinction between the hyperbase and the access layer. The hyperbase is the place where most of the content is defined, and it is the most stable part of the application. The main design notions for the hyperbase are the following:

- ○ *Entity*: a virtual object of interest for the user, organized into components
- ○ *Components*: the constituents of an entity
- ○ *Slots*: the atomic elements of content, constituents of components
- ○ *Semantic associations*: the connections among the parts of the hyperbase, that provide the "infrastructure" for possible navigation
- ○ Entities may exist as instances of entity types or as single entities (one-of-a-kind objects)

The main design notions for the access layer are the following:

- ○ *Collection*: a set of objects (called "members" of the collection), grouped together in order to provide a meaningful access to information for the user.
- ○ *Collection center*: a new piece of information (e.g., an index) allowing the user the make the best possible usage of a collection.

Copyright © 2009, IGI Global, distributing in print or electronic forms without written permission of IGI Global is prohibited.

- ○ *Collection topology*: the inner organization of a collection, for allowing an optimal "reading" of it.
- ○ *Collection filter*: providing the possibility of searching, within a collection, members with specific properties.
- ○ Collections may exist as instances of collection types or as single collections (one-of-a-kind groupings).

- **Navigation Design:** the purpose is the organization of the information into pieces (nodes) oriented toward "user consumption;" furthermore, navigation paths are provided in order to allow user navigation, which is one of the most distinctive features of hypermedia applications.

Navigation design is organized upon a limited set of design notions. The main concepts are the following:

- ○ *Node*: a set of slots, specifically chosen in order to provide a "unit of consumption" for the users. Nodes may appear as instances of node types or as single nodes (one-of-a-kind units). Nodes, for the greatest parts, derive from entities, or semantic associations or collection centers.
- ○ *Cluster*: a set of nodes, which can be navigated across. Clusters of nodes are generated from entities (structural clusters), from semantic associations (association clusters) or collection (collection clusters).
- ○ *Accessibility relationship*: a connection among nodes that support navigation. Accessibility relationships "tie" together the nodes of the same cluster, supporting navigation within it.
- ○ *Navigation pattern*: it describes the actual way navigation across nodes (within a cluster) is allowed. The description of all possible navigation patterns is outside the scope of UWA, but designers are allowed to define (informally or formally) any navigation pattern they wish to use.

- **Publishing Design:** the purpose is the organization of the information into "pages," which are the units of "physical consumption" for the user.

The main notions being used are page, section, publishing units and interaction spot.

- ○ *Page*: it is the "physical unit delivered to the user. A page can be an instance of a page type, or a single page. A page is organized into sections. The sections within the same page are semantic units, independent one from the others.

Copyright © 2009, IGI Global, distributing in print or electronic forms without written permission of IGI Global is prohibited.

- ○   *Section*: a section is the semantic constituent of a page. It contains a single piece of information (roughly corresponding to a node) or a set of correlated pieces of information (roughly corresponding to a cluster). A section consists of one or several publishing units.
- ○   *Publishing unit:* it is the atomic part of a section. It may derive from the navigation design ("content" publishing unit), or it provides new content added for publishing purpose ("decorator" publishing unit) or provides interaction elements ("interaction" publishing units).
- ○   *Interaction spot*: it provides a way to "operate" with the application. An interaction spot may provide a link to a different page (instance), a link within the same page (instance), an interaction with the content (e.g., zoom, play, start, stop, etc.), the activation of an operation (see below) or the control over a transaction execution (see corresponding document).

- •   **Operations Design:** the purpose is to provide the user with operations (other than standard hypermedia operations, such as navigation) that allow the user to invoke application dependent "functions" (such as "register," "submit," etc.).

It provides the ingredients to add operational functionalities to hypermedia applications. The main design notions are the following:

- ○   *Pre-conditions*: the conditions that must be satisfied before the user can invoke the operation. Pre-conditions may involve the "hypermedia state" (i.e., the state of the objects defined by the hypermedia design), or the "application state" (i.e., the state of additional information handled by the application) or other system and environment states.
- ○   *Post-conditions*: the conditions that will be satisfied after the completion of the operation. Post-conditions may involve all the elements of preconditions and also "output", that is, actions sending "messages" outside of the strict environment of the application.

In detail, the model is composed by:

- •   **Application Schema.** An application schema is the description of an application; the description involves what the application offers to the user, in terms of information, available operations and page structures. It does not involve how the application is implemented and the graphical layout, although it pro-

Copyright © 2009, IGI Global, distributing in print or electronic forms without written permission of IGI Global is prohibited.

vides requirements for both. An application schema consists of a hypermedia schema, a customization schema and an operation-transaction schema.

- **Hypermedia Schema.** A hypermedia schema describes the information structures, the navigation patterns and the browsing capabilities. It captures the hypertext part of a Web application. A hypermedia schema consists of a hyperbase schema and an access schema. A hyperbase schema describes the "kernel" of an application, the content, its organization and the basic navigation patterns.
- **Access Schema.** An access schema describes the information structures and the navigation patterns that allow the user to organize its way to locate and access the objects of the hyperbase.
- **Customization Schema.** A customization schema describes how the design of an application can be "customized" in order to accommodate different needs, originating from different contexts. A specific important aspect of changing context is represented by the need of using different devices (with different capabilities) and ubiquitousness.
- **Operation-Transaction Schema.** An operation-transaction schema describes which services are offered by the application, divided in simple services (operations) and more complex services (transactions). Operations are described later in this document, while transactions are described elsewhere.

The different parts of design are conceived as different aspects of an overall design process, but different possibilities are taken in consideration:

- *Pure waterfall*: the different parts of design are performed one after the other in the order. It makes sense for training purposes or simple cases, but it is unrealistic otherwise.
- *Mixed waterfall*: the basis is a waterfall process, but different parts of design can be anticipated (e.g., doing a little of publishing design before completing navigation design) or postponed.
- *Incomplete design*: within each part, only a portion of design is performed (e.g., skipping details, or focusing upon critical portions of the application).
- *Partial waterfall*: some parts of the design are skipped (e.g., starting with navigation design, or going from information to publishing design, skipping navigation design).
- *Reverse waterfall*: starting with a part and "moving backward" (e.g., starting with publishing, a common practice, and then moving to navigation and information).

The W2000 methodology does not allow describing the page layout in detail.

Copyright © 2009, IGI Global, distributing in print or electronic forms without written permission of IGI Global is prohibited.

IDM – INTERACTIVE DIALOGUE MODEL: 2006

Interactive dialogue model (IDM) is a design technique to model the dialogue structure of information-intensive applications. This kind of application rests on the assumption that the main important aspect is the presentation of information to the user. The IDM methodology is especially effective because it is founded on the linguistic concepts of human dialog applied to the interaction between user and application.

IDM is really simple to learn: the graphical elements describe the main application features in terms of dialogue contents and of how the dialogue is unfolding between the users.

Using the experience of the others methodologies analyzed before, the IDM methodology is based on the design separation: it has a specific design to model the dialogue between user and application that defines the information content and the semantic relationships to be presented to the final user.

This part of design is called IDM. At the same time, at the definition of the information contents, the designers can model the page structures that compose the final application. This design is called P-IDM (publishing IDM).

In the first step of the design in which the information contents are defined, there are two levels of design: the first one called conceptual IDM and the second one logical IDM. The conceptual IDM is very useful to agree with the customers about the requirements, and it does not detail the technical aspects of information structures but it models in-the-large the dialogue objects and the relationships between them. The logical IDM is more detailed: it breaks down the dialogue objects into their component and describes the allowed transitions from an information object to one other.

IDM

The two levels of IDM methodology use three simple elements: topic, relevant relation and group of topics. These elements describe all interaction mechanisms of Web application.

The user could be interested in viewing the specific information about a specific topic and afterwards he/she could be navigated to other topics related to the first.

The user could start his/her navigation from a group of topics that groups more topics of the same type and navigate inside the specific group.

Furthermore, during the definition of the logical level from the conceptual one, in the IDM methodology the designer can define the access structures to the information using the IDM element called introductory act. The introductory act allows defining the information used by the user to navigate through the topic.

Copyright © 2009, IGI Global, distributing in print or electronic forms without written permission of IGI Global is prohibited.

It is clear that all of the design could be made following the piece of advice of the buyer that, using marketing strategies, defines the ways in which the user could reach the information.

Further, into the logical level, the designer could describe in detail the topics in order to better define their information structure and content. Thus, the dialogue act concept is used into the model.

Each topic could be composed by one ore more dialogue acts. In order to emphasize that IDM methodology models the user modalities to dialogue with the application, the IDM output is the conceptual schema called "dialogue map."

The choice to model the dialogue experience instead of the information structure makes the used notation really close to user needs and makes it very simple to learn without extra knowledge. The concise and intuitive schema is the starting point to make suggestions, alternative proposals, brainstorming and preliminary discussions about strategic decisions.

P-IDM

P-IDM is the second level of IDM methodology in which using the information structures defined in IDM model the designer models the application pages. Thus, P-IDM is the intermediate changeover from the content and navigation definition to their presentation to the final user.

The P-IDM goals are:

- **Acceptability:** its modular structures makes itself very simple to use and makes itself adapt to the real company needs. Its standard notation (UML® derived) offers a great compatibility with well-known development and design environments.
- **Interactivity**: it analyzes and designs the allowed navigation patterns.
- **Quality:** the IDM methodology is especially suitable to describe the user dialogue, and it is very carefully to consider in detail the specific needs of specific channel, device, and interaction profile in order to model good and usable applications.
- **Object orientation:** the methodology uses some typical aspect of object-oriented languages and, thus, it is compliant with a rapid prototyping tool that produces object-oriented code.

P-IDM uses as starting point the UML® notation and the WAE (Web application extension) proposed by Conallen (2002). The methodology develops the design using several views. Each view is focused on a specific dialogue aspect in order to better model the interactions between user and application.

Copyright © 2009, IGI Global, distributing in print or electronic forms without written permission of IGI Global is prohibited.

- **The structural navigation view:** it defines the pages that present the information related to the same conceptual entity. The view includes the template design, the navigational links between pages and the content separation.
- **The association view:** it defines the navigation between pages of different entities that are linked by semantic associations. The user, starting from the source entity, can choose the target entity using a specific attribute set of the second entity. If the attribute set is not a part of a target entity, the designer could add an intermediate page that links the two entities.
- **Navigational path view:** navigational path starts from specific access structures and guides and helps the user during the navigation to choose objects of interest among those present in the general object list.
- **Navigational maps:** it provides a global view of all navigational possibilities offered to the users. The maps can be of the entire application or of a single package if planned.

The main methodology element is surely the "screen" that describes the page or a part of the page of the final Web application. The screen uses a specific template that the designer has defined with the buyers.

The P-IDM design uses as starting point the IDM design created before. Thus, the precise map rules exist that allows maximizing the effect of modeling the information contents.

More notation details are provided in Chapter III.

CONCLUSIVE NOTES ON DESIGN METHODOLOGY OF WEB APPLICATION

The analyzed Web application design methodologies are characterized by common guidelines: the importance of the final user in the definitions of the content. In order to achieve this goal, the several presented methodologies are inclined to split the design into different thematic areas; thus, the designer is forced to focus on a specific design aspect at time.

In general, it is possible to affirm that the WA design allows the designer at first to focus on the structure of information content in order to describe what the user has to perceive and then how these contents must be perceived by the user. The "how" is made by defining the navigational strategies. After these models, it is possible to describe with more details the conceptual model and then the implementation architectures: in this case, the page structures are defined without specific implementation detail that must be defined behind.

Copyright © 2009, IGI Global, distributing in print or electronic forms without written permission of IGI Global is prohibited.

Then, these features are the successful point in methodologies, and they are so important, that they are replicated in all of the presented design methodologies. The methodologies study done allows choosing IDM methodology as the main methodology to develop this work.

In fact, IDM allows having, on one hand, the easiness of the information content design that is the main element of user experience and, on the other hand, it is possible to ignore the technique formalism such as the design through the ER model (as in WebML methodology) or the difficult model of OOHDM and UWE inspired to the object-oriented paradigm.

Furthermore, IDM is a methodology really simple to learn also for non-technical user. IDM terminology is really closer to the dialogue between the user and the application.

IDM is the natural evolution of W2000 methodology, but it is preferred to W2000 because it allows describing using a single diagram (used in different design phase) the information aspect and the navigation aspect.

The page definition and so the P-IDM is particularly interesting: created as an extension of UML® for Web application, it uses a different notation; indeed, the UML® notation is really valid to model traditional application but is less effective to model Web application in which the classical design paradigm are substituted by the user interaction.

For the sake of simplicity, in table 2 there is a comparison between the methodologies presented above. In particular we focus on six different aspects of the design methodologies:

- **User center focus:** the evaluation of the focus that the methodology provides for the user
- **Standard compliance:** the evaluation of the adherence of the methodology to the standard
- Separation between the design of the information and the design of the navigation
- Separation between the design of the information and the design of the pages
- **Support for code generation:** the evaluation of the possibility to automatically obtain the Web application from the design
- **Language simplicity:** the evaluation of the understanding simplicity of the language

Copyright © 2009, IGI Global, distributing in print or electronic forms without written permission of IGI Global is prohibited.

Table 2. Comparison between Web application design methodologies

	OOHDM	WEB ML	W2000	UWE	IDM
User centre focus	* Start from navigation design	***	***	***	***
Standard compliance	*** OO-Oriented	*** OO-Oriented	*** UML® based	*** OO-Oriented	* New and simple notation introduced
Separation between the design of the information and the design of the navigation	***	***	***	***	* Information and navigation in the same diagram
Separation between the design of the information and the design of the pages	***	***	***	***	***
Support for code generation	*	*	**	*	***
Language simplicity	*** UML®-Like	*** UML®-Like	**	**	*** Based on dialogue metaphor

In Table 2 there is, where necessary, some little comment in order to better explain the symbol used really means. The symbol "***" means an excellent support to the specific item while the symbol "**" means a less excellent support to the specific item. The symbol "*" means a minor support to the specific item. The symbol "-" means that the specific item is not supported by the considered methodology.

We highlight that the table is only a comparison between methodologies and not an evaluation. For example, the symbol "*" for the item "standard compliance" in the IDM methodology does not mean that the minor support is a problem for the methodology, but in the specific case, there is a point of excellence because also a designer unskilled in the object- oriented or in the UML® language can apply the methodology.

Copyright © 2009, IGI Global, distributing in print or electronic forms without written permission of IGI Global is prohibited.

THE METHODOLOGY EXTENSIONS TO SUPPORT THE DESIGN OF PROCESS-ORIENTED WEB APPLICATION

Design Methodology for Web Application Process Oriented: Introduction

The advent of Web application more oriented to the final user where the user is an active part of the application, brings a natural evolution to the support inside the same application of the business processes reaching the goal to integrate data-centric and process-centric design primitives.

When we speak about complex Web information system, it is important to refer to business processes that are carrying elements in the information system, and require not only to be represented but also to be integrated in the same information system.

The complexity level introduced by the business processes is double: on one hand business processes combine the free navigation between pages a navigation guided by the process where the user is forced to execute well-defined steps but without losing the possibility to go out from the process in order to come back in a second time; a further complexity level is because the business processes must not be cabled in the code of the information system, but it is important to consider the process in a separate manner in order to allow a simple change of the process in order to constantly adapt the information system to the external world.

The increase of the complexity level makes it more necessary for a design phase that, now must take into account, in parallel, several problems. The Web application design methodology analyzed until now, immediately is adjusted to this new tendency providing tools useful to integrate business processes in the traditional navigation between contents.

The extension to business processes of the actual design methodologies has as a goal to integrate in the design methodologies also the design of the business processes already made in a separate design. These methodologies are interested in maintaining the separation of the design already proposed and to add the business processes as a separate view inside of the design. The final goal of the proposed extensions is to place side by side to the Web application design the process design identifying some contacts points among these two worlds forced from logics of markets and from demands of various types, to live together.

For each Web application design methodology previously examined, we will analyze the extension made up of the relative authors in order to consider also business processes. This analysis will be of the highest importance in the following parts of this work when, gathering the best of every methodology, we will propose a new design methodology that answers to well- precise requirements.

Copyright © 2009, IGI Global, distributing in print or electronic forms without written permission of IGI Global is prohibited.

Extension of OOHDM for Business Processes

The necessity to develop Web applications that support and allow executing business processes, brought OOHDM authors to think about a possible extension of the methodology to support the problems and thus to add new primitives, in the special case to add the primitives to the conceptual and navigation model (Rossi, Schmid, & Lyardet, 2003).

In the extension of OOHDM for the business processes, the conceptual model has been divided in a part oriented to the free navigation and in a part oriented to the task execution.

Of course, not all the activities that make up business processes need an interface; some of these may be an automatic task, and thus they do not need a graphical interface. The extension of the methodology is oriented only to support tasks of the business processes that need graphical interface to be executed.

To represent in the integrated design business processes tasks, OOHDM authors define the concept of *activity objects* in the conceptual design and the *activity nodes* in the navigation design.

The *activity nodes* are activities that are perceived in a well-defined way from the final user and thus are a view on the *activity object*.

The business processes are represented in the conceptual schema as aggregation relationship between activity objects that represent business processes themselves and activity objects that represent objects (activity) that support them.

In the conceptual schema is defined also the activity flow that follows each other in the business processes: this activity flow is defined through an UML® activity diagram. The uncoupling in the conceptual design of the several activities of the business processes allows a simple reuse if each activity is in other business processes.

In the navigational level, the activity nodes are navigational nodes: the definition of the navigational nodes consists of attributes, anchor and operation by which the final user interact. The abstract interface design is made up of activity nodes, buttons such as "ok," "commit," "cancel" and "submit" that control the input of the activities, and they control the flow in order to go to the next activity.

The activity nodes are in the context of the process where they belong. To each activity we can add the possibility to stop the process and to start it in a second moment. In this case OOHDM, thanks to the concept of anchor, makes a set of operations that allow assuring that the process is in a correct state.

The introduction of the activity nodes and of the activity objects solve problems of the definition and management of the process flow in the Web application design but does not solve the problems of the coexistence of the free navigation and of the navigation guided by the process:

Copyright © 2009, IGI Global, distributing in print or electronic forms without written permission of IGI Global is prohibited.

- Navigation inside a context: when the user stops the execution of a business process, the user will be unable to make operations that modify the state of the resource used in the process. A solution is to provide to the user the possibility of limiting the navigation *inside the context* of the activity node. Each business process defines a navigational context and this means that when a user stops the business process its navigation is not relative to the business process but to the navigational context of the business process. The navigational context of the process defines what restrictions or addition to apply to a node when it is used by the user in the process context. These restrictions will be defined in the class "InContext" decorator of the base class.
- It may be situation where the user needs to start more processes in the same session. The simple navigation may disorient the final user: the user must go out from the business process, start a new process and later come back in the initial business process. A solution will be the use of the landmark links that allow making simple the access to each navigational node of the Web application (the navigational node may be related to a process or not).

WebML: Extension in Order to Support Business Processes

The extension made up by authors of WebML (Brambilla, 2003) considers business process as a sequence of elementary operations with a control logic based on decision points. The extension is not able to consider complex business logic. Another choice of the WebML authors is to re-use consideration and tools already mature in the design of Web application data-centric. The proposed extension has the following features:

- The proposed approach will adapt a classical development process to the development of application process-centric and data-centric.
- The proposed approach is a mix of notation and design concepts that supports both the requirement phase and the conceptual phase.
- A set of extensions that allows considering in the classical data-centric design also a process-oriented design.

The authors of WebML consider business processes in two of the most important steps of the WebML design:

- The data model, used in order to express domain objects, was extended in order to consider information about user and about workflow.
- The hypertext model has been enriched with a set of primitives that allows to adapt the contents of each page to the workflow state.

Copyright © 2009, IGI Global, distributing in print or electronic forms without written permission of IGI Global is prohibited.

Data Model Extension

The data model that in WebMLthat is used in order to represent domain objects has been enriched with metadata concerning the business processes: in the data model, indeed, there are entities and relationships coming from the process design.

As an example, the entity "process" is related to the entity "ActivityType" in order to represent classes and activities that can be executed in the business processes (Figure 6). The entity ActivityInstance represents the activity that may assume several states such as active, not active or complete. There are the entity user and the entity group that represent actors of the process. An activity type is related to a group in order to describe that a group of actors may perform a well- defined type of activity while an instance of the activity is related to only one user because it refers only to the user that execute a process task in a well-defined point of time. In Figure 6, we can see a part of the diagram (application data model) where objects of the domain are designed as originally defined in WebML.

Finally, we observe that the workflow data model part may be linked together with the application data model depending on the special requirement of the design.

Extension of the Hypertext Model

In parallel to the extension of the data model, the authors realized also the extension of the hypertext model providing accurate indication on as to build the interfaces through which the final user will be able to read and write data in order to execute the hypertext model. The part of hypertext model that represents the area related to the business processes will be enclosed between two structures that define the

Figure 6. Extension of the data model

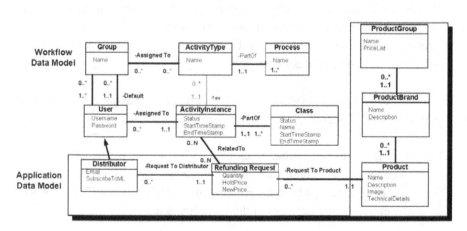

Copyright © 2009, IGI Global, distributing in print or electronic forms without written permission of IGI Global is prohibited.

start and the end of the workflow. These structures were created in order to support business processes in the WebML design and are start activity and end activity: these elements are of the highest importance because they update data related to the workflow when a part of the workflow ends. Particularly, to start a new activity (start activity) means to create an instance of the activity, to store the timestamp, to assign the activity to the correct user (the user is belonging to a group of users that can develop a well-specified activity) and to change the state of the activity to "active." It is clear that when the activity ends (EndState) it is important to set to "terminate" the state of the related activity. In order to retrieve a data object related to the instance of the activity, it is important to use content units related to the workflow that is to tag the entity that refers to an instance of the workflow. (In order to mark the entity related to the workflow, they are characterized with a "W.") It is clear that the business processes constrain the navigation in the hypertext model because the presence of the branch brings to follow a different navigational path depending on the state of the activity or on the user choice. In the hypertext model authors add the possibility to define a navigational path to follow after the evaluation of a well-defined condition.

Extension of UWE to the Business Processes

The methodology, created in order to design information-intensive Web application, has recently been extended in order to support business processes and thus process-intensive application (Koch, Kraus, Cachero, & Meliá, 2004).

The first problem faced by the authors of the methodology has been to select a simple and precise way to design business processes: the use case modeling used in the UWE to make the requirement analysis is not sufficient, so authors added another design, the process model, that enrich the analysis phase. UWE, despite that it founds on UML®, does not provide extension to UML® in order to guarantee a support to the business processes but authors think that the only usage of activity diagram is sufficient to complete the domain model. Activity diagram allows designing also sub-activity calling another activity diagram.

After the preliminary analysis, that allows understanding the problem and defining a first conceptual design of that problem, it is possible to follow two paths:

- To define a navigation model driven by a process flow when a process flow is refined in a correct way. The integration between process and free navigation expresses the relationship between the user interface and the steps defined in the process flow.

Copyright © 2009, IGI Global, distributing in print or electronic forms without written permission of IGI Global is prohibited.

- To define a navigation model enriched by concepts coming from the process flow in order to reflect a set of integration points that is a set of points where the user left the navigational view in order to access in a process view.

The approach followed in the UWE design methodology is the second approach.

A process-oriented Web application design according to UWE methodology is made up of three phases:

- Refining of the conceptual model by activity diagram that define business processes
- Integration of the business processes in the navigational design
- Refining the process model through structural view and behavioral view
- To define a presentation model based on the navigation and on the process model linked together in an opportune way

Integration of the Business Processes in the UWE Navigation Model

The UWE navigation model is made up of two steps. The first step allows specifying what object the user can visit after the navigation between contents of application: this can be applied adding to the diagram information about how the user can reach the objects to visit. The navigation model is made up of a class diagram where it is possible to see the concepts of <> and <>.

If we introduce the support to the business processes, we add two classes <<process class>> and <<process link>> where <<process class>> is used by the final user when he/she executes the business processes and <<process link>> designs the association between <> and <<process class>>. Process link needs information about the process state and this is made by OCL constraints.

In the second step, related to the definition of the navigation model, it is important to add a set of access structures of the highest importance to allow the final user to start its navigation. Access structure are defined through <<index>>, <<query>> and <<guided tour>>.

After, the navigation model is enriched by the <<menu>> class.

In the extension of the UWE methodology made up in order to support business processes, authors add only the <<process model>> and the <<process link>>. An example is in Figure 7.

Copyright © 2009, IGI Global, distributing in print or electronic forms without written permission of IGI Global is prohibited.

Figure 7. An example of navigation model extended in order to support business process

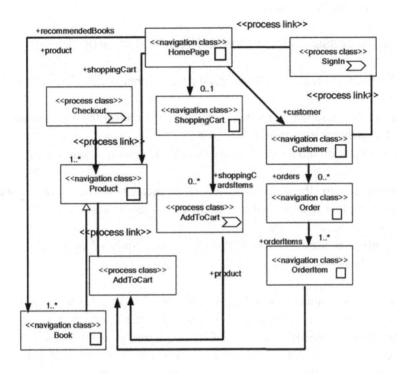

Refining of the Process Model

In order to define the process flow, the authors of UWE added two new views: the structural view and behavioral view. The structural view comes from the conceptual level, and it concerns preserving information strictly related to the process. In the structural view, it is possible to have links with cardinality 0.1 and thus implies that in some situations links do not exist.

The graphical representation is made up of by class diagrams derived from the conceptual model. It is possible, however, to have in the structural view classes that do not come from the conceptual model, but are added ex novo in order to represent information functional to the process: these classes are not represented in the conceptual model.

Each process class of the structural view refers to a well-defined UML® activity diagram (it defines the behavioral view). The process state can be defined directly adding attributes to the process class.

Copyright © 2009, IGI Global, distributing in print or electronic forms without written permission of IGI Global is prohibited.

The behavioral view is a refinement of the process model made up of UML®
activity diagram. In order to define the behavioral view, any extension to the notation UML® has not been realized.

Business Processes Support to the Presentation Model

The UWE presentation model allows specifying the presentation logic of the Web
application.

Thanks to the presentation model, it is possible to realize the representation of
the page that includes both layout and colors.

In the presentation model, it is possible to identify two different views:

- **Structural view:** the goal of this view is to indicate how to organize the space
  in the page; it is possible to define in the same view how several elements are
  grouped in the same page
- **User interface view:** the goal of this view is to define all details of the graphical interface of the page

The presentation model is based on the concept of the location that means each
element has its own well-defined position in a well-defined area of the page.

The presentation model is made up of several stereotypes: the most important
stereotype is the <<presentation class>> that represents the logic by which the
graphical interface will be presented to the user. Each <<presentation class>> is
linked to a <> in order to define how in a well-defined presentation the user can navigate.

CONCLUSIVE NOTES ON DESIGN METHODOLOGY OF WEB APPLICATION AND THEIR SUPPORT TO PROCESS DESIGN

The approach to the design of a complex Web information system, starts from the
study of Web application design methodologies that allows focusing the design on
the user and on its possible dialogue with the Web application. The study will focus
in a second moment on the integration between the Web application design and the
business processes. The problem to link together the Web application design with
the business processes design is an open problem: the presented methodologies leave
open several problems. These problems will be faced and solved in this work.

As an example, the OOHDM approach constrains to use the business processes
design made up of UML® activity diagram, and thus it is strongly lied to an object-
oriented paradigm. The OOHDM extension to the process model offers several

Copyright © 2009, IGI Global, distributing in print or electronic forms without written permission of IGI Global
is prohibited.

thinking points because it allows separating in an explicit way two different navigation that coexist when the business processes support is added to the traditional Web application design.

In the WebML, the extension consists, fundamentally, of the extension of the model of the data adding the necessary metadata to the various activities that compose the business processes (over that, of course, metadata useful for the management of the users). The proposed extension also provides a standard way to turn the diagrams of business processes into hypertext diagrams integrating the navigation related to the business process with the free navigation among the information contents of the Web application.

The same authors of WebML affirm that an important limit of the proposed methodology is that the methodology cannot be applied to business processes driven by sophisticated business logic: an activity that asks for an elevated operational complexity is modeled, indeed, as a black-box. An example of a simple business process that is well suited it for the extension proposed for WebML is one that deals with the management of contents in which the most frequent actions are the scheduling and the approval of the changes to the official documents, as orders or invoices.

Finally, UWE methodology, focus it, as OOHDM, on an object-oriented design of the Web application and, therefore, it results very tied up to UML® as a tool of representation. In UWE, it is possible to properly individualize a clear distinction among the concepts tied up to the design of the Web application that is process-intensive and those tied up to the design of the business processes. The subdivision in several steps of the methodology allows the designer to focus itself on every particular aspect of the design in different moments.

For the sake of simplicity, in Table 3 there is a comparison between OOHDM, WEBML and UWE extension for the business process previously presented.

In particular the focus is on the following items:

- Traceability of the business process in the final design: is it possible to follow the initial business process in the final design?
- Support for the stop and resume a business process
- Support for the process state: does the design consider the state of the process?
- Support for the execution of the multiple business process
- Explicit business process model: is there a business process model useful to understand the final design?
- Separation between business process and navigation process
- Support to the free navigation (not guided by the business process)

Copyright © 2009, IGI Global, distributing in print or electronic forms without written permission of IGI Global is prohibited.

Table 3. Comparison between process-oriented Web application design methodologies

	OOHDM extension	WEBML-extension	UWE-extension
Traceability of the business process in the final design	**	*	***
Support for the stop and resume a business process	* Use of a process anchor	-	***
Support to the process state	* Use of a process anchor	-	***
Support to the execution of the multiple business process	**	-	-
Explicit business process model	-	***	***
Separation between business process and navigation process	-	-	***
Support to the free navigation	***	**	***

In Table 3 there is, where necessary, some little comments in order to better explain what the symbol used really mean. The symbol "***" means an excellent support to the specific item while the symbol "**" means a less excellent support to the specific item. The symbol "*" means a minor support to the specific item. The symbol "-" means that the specific item is not supported by the considered methodology.

The study of every one of these methodologies has individualized an existing methodological gap in the design of a complex Web information system.

In the following parts of this work, we will fill this methodological gap. A new comparison table that will comprehend the methodology that covers this gap, will be presented in Chapter VI.

Copyright © 2009, IGI Global, distributing in print or electronic forms without written permission of IGI Global is prohibited.

REFERENCES

Baresi, L., Garzotto, F., Mainetti, L., & Paolini, P. (2002). Meta-modeling techniques meet Web application design tools. *Proceedings from 5th International Conference FASE 2002 (part of ETAPS 2002)* (pp. 294-307).

Beck, K., & Cunningham, W. (1989). A laboratory for teaching object-oriented thinking. *Proceedings from OOPSLA 198* (pp. 7-10).

Bolchini, D., & Paolini, P. (2006). Interactive dialogue model: A design technique for multichannel applications. *IEEE Transaction on multimedia, 8*(3), 529-541.

Brambilla, M. (2003). Extending hypertext conceptual models with process oriented primitives WebML. *Proceedings from ER 2003* (pp. 246-262). Chicago, IL.

Ceri, S., Fraternali, P., & Bongio, A. (2000). Web modeling language (WebML): A modeling language for designing Web sites. *Proceeding from the 9th World Wide Web Conference (WWW9)* (pp. 137-157). Amsterdam.

Conallen, J. (2002). *Building Web applications with UML* (2nd ed.). Addison-Wesley.

Koch, N., & Kraus, A. (2002). The expressiveness power of UML-based Web engineering. *Second Int. Workshop on Web-Oriented SoftwareTechnology (IWWOST '02). CYTED* (pp. 105-119). Malaga, Spain.

Koch, N., Kraus, A., Cachero, C. & Meliá S. (2004). Integration of business processes in Web applications models. *Journal of Web Engineering, 3,* 22-49. *Rinton Press.*

Kraus, A., & Koch, N. (2003). *A meta-model for UWE.* (Tech. Rep. 0301). Institut für Informatik, Ludwig-Maximilians-Universität München.

Paolini, P., Mainetti L., & Bolchini, D. (2006) *Progettare siti Web e applicazioni mobili.* McGraw-Hill Companies.

Perrone, V., Bolchini, D., & Paolini P. (2005). A stakeholders-centered approach for conceptual modeling of communication-intensive applications. *Proceedings of the 23rd annual international conference on design of communication: Documenting & designing for pervasive information* (pp. 25-33).

Rossi, G., Schmid, H., & Lyardet, F. (2003). Engineering business processes in Web applications: Modeling and navigation issues. *Third Int. Workshop on Web-Oriented Software Technology* (pp. 1677-1682). Oviedo.

Rumbaugh, J., Booch, G., & Jacobson, I. (1999). *The unified software development process.* Prentice Hall.

Copyright © 2009, IGI Global, distributing in print or electronic forms without written permission of IGI Global is prohibited.

Schwabe, D., & Rossi, G. (1998). Developing hypermedia applications using OOHDM. *Workshop on Hypermedia Development Processes, Methods and Models, Hypertext*, (pp. 18-34). Pittsburgh, USA.

Copyright © 2009, IGI Global, distributing in print or electronic forms without written permission of IGI Global is prohibited.

Chapter III
Details about IDM Web Application Design Methodology

INTRODUCTION

Chapter II analyzes some Web application design methodology that is well-known in the international scientific community. The idea that links together these methodologies is the centrality of the user and the ability to separate logically the information, navigation and publishing design aspects. In this way, at one time the designer focuses on a specific kind of user and takes into consideration the information, navigation and publishing aspects.

Now, we have to choose between the various analyzed methodologies able to model the complex Web information system.

The selected methodology is IDM (Perrone, Bolchini, & Paolini, 2005; Bolchini & Paolini, 2006; Paolini, Mainetti & Bolchini 2006). The dialogue metaphors proposed by IDM in particular adapt to allow the designer to focus on the communication between the user and the application instead of thinking about the graphical and transactional aspects.

IDM provides also a good organization of pages with PIDM that, producing different views, allows focusing on different design aspects. IDM inherits several aspects by W2000 (Baresi, Garzotto, Mainetti, & Paolini, 2002) such as the sepa-

Copyright © 2009, IGI Global, distributing in print or electronic forms without written permission of IGI Global is prohibited.

ration of different contents in topic (called in W2000 entity) and the separation of topic in dialogue acts (the components in W2000).

To well understand the proposed methodology, in this book, several detailed examples are presented using W2000 and IDM methodology.

The design is always in-the-large, but some guidelines in order to lead the designer to carefully design the pages are introduced in the last chapter.

IDM

The IDM methodology is structured in three levels:

- C-IDM in which an in-the-large design of information contents of application is made
- L-IDM in which a more detailed design of the contents and of the access structures is made
- P-IDM in which a detailed project of Web pages that shows the information contents is made.

A short description of the three design levels is shown below. In L-IDM, a first PageDesign in which simple guidelines are presented in order to translate in pages the conceptual ideas made in IDM is present. These guidelines are useful in order to model the PIDM that is the real application model.

C-IDM (Conceptual IDM)

The starting point for IDM methodology is the conceptual model (C-IDM). The C-IDM allows describing the application dialogue strategies before describing in detail the technological choice. In C-IDM, all of the dialogue elements (topic), the relevant relationships (relevant relation) and the argument group are defined.

In fact, an interactive application must be focused on specific arguments, but it must allow the dialogue changes choosing in a set of arguments. In the detail:

- **Topic** is the dialogue subject, in other words the interesting argument of a dialogue between user and application. Considering that the contents are the core elements of an interactive application, a lot of topics have to be designed in a single project. Thus, the entire project choice is based on contents. In some cases, the explanation of some content is the most important requirement of the application; the other contents are less important but all together

Copyright © 2009, IGI Global, distributing in print or electronic forms without written permission of IGI Global is prohibited.

are important for the good quality of the final application. The topic choice is strictly connected to the requirements analysis, because the topics are what the stakeholder wants to find in the application. A topic, a dialogue element, has to be content and information with a precise sense for the final user independently from the application and from the arguments presented inside.

- **Multiple topics (or kind of topic)** is the class that groups the possible subjects of dialogue. It is a generic argument from which it is possible to derive specific arguments for the dialogue; through this abstraction, the designer can identify the general dialogue arguments that could be modeled through a set of distinct arguments using the specific content. In other words, a topic can be an instance of a multiple topic. Defining for each multiple topic, the cardinality can help the designers and the developers to size the application content and so the needed resources.
- **Relevant semantic relation** is a theme change that could happen during the dialogue, and it allows, thus, the topic change; after the consumption of the content of interest, the user may continue the dialogue using thematics correlated with the first one. The user has to follow guided, changed arguments. A relevant semantic relation represents the possibility of moving the attention from one topic to another that are semantically related to the same argument. Furthermore, in this case, it is important to establish the cardinality that signals the minimum and maximum number of topics reachable using the relevant semantic relation.
- **Group of topics** is the group of possible dialogue arguments. During the Web application dialogue, the user is not totally free to choose the arguments to view. Accessing the site, the user chooses to start the dialogue with the application, but he/she unconsciously entrusts the stakeholders with the task of establishing the better arguments to start the dialogue. So, the stakeholders define the dialogue theme with the users and the users can only prefer specific arguments to explore between a set of possible arguments chosen by stakeholders. Of course, other standard groups of topics are available like, for instance, the index of each multiple topic.

From the IDM point of view, the dialogue starting points can be specific topics directly accessible or an explicit choice of arguments called a group of topics.

From the project point of view, the organization of access contents is more important because through it the user can access the information and can start the dialogue. In order to make an effective dialogue with a complex application, the groups of topic are the only system to view, navigate and understand the contents.

There are four standard ways to design the group of topics:

Copyright © 2009, IGI Global, distributing in print or electronic forms without written permission of IGI Global is prohibited.

- **Group of content-driven topics:** It helps the user to access the arguments of interest; indeed, the user uses it to explore categories and sub categories. In every case, it is important to model a navigation path that is not more complex in order not to disorient the user; the groups of content-driven topics have the main goal of guiding the user into a specific argument.
- **Group of task-driven topics:** Good designers have to create a model created with what the user needs, creating a final application that is satisfactory and effective for the user. This group of topic has the main goal of guiding the user into performing a specific task, organizing the dialogue arguments in order to make the search of specific themes simpler if the user has a specific goal. Depending on the application domain, the user can be interested in performing a specific task or having precise goals. The groups of task-driven topic do not only have the main goal of catching the user needs, but also of stimulating the interests for application arguments in the user.
- **Group of user-driven topics:** It is possible to organize the contents and the services offered by an application taking care of the different user profiles that could have interest in the dialogue themes of an application. To do this, the designer has to know for each kind of user some information such as his/her domain knowledge or his/her practice with the application.
- **Group of highlight topics:** Often people who navigate the Internet arrive discover during the search of other information. In this case, it is fundamental that the application creates interest in the users, suggesting new paths and attractive contents. The access strategies described before are often used in combination between themselves.
- **Multiple groups of topics:** It is a family of group of topics from which can be derived several groups of topics with the same structure features of one origin.

L-IDM (Logical IDM)

The next conceptual design phase is called logical design. In fact, it is important to detail the contents of dialogue between user and WA and to detail the navigational strategy that allows the user to interact with these contents.

Thus, starting from the conceptual choices, the designer describes and models the dialogue working with the user in a structured way using the L-IDM schema. The logic design is based on the following primitives:

- **Dialogue act:** It is a piece of dialogue with the user. Then, after the definition of the general dialogue argument hinted in the conceptual level (the topics), the designer makes the detailed model of the dialogue pieces and of the

Copyright © 2009, IGI Global, distributing in print or electronic forms without written permission of IGI Global is prohibited.

user interaction. In some cases, the dialogue act corresponds with the page presented to the user; so, it is something that could not be presented in two or more steps. In the case of Web application, the user requests a page and receives the entire page. Some elements are visualized at the same time of page visualization, while specific contents such as pop-up, video, and music will be visualized on demand. In this phase, the conceptual choices are translated into an operational choice related to the way the dialogue develops itself. There are three kinds of dialogue acts:

○ **Content dialogue act:** A piece of dialogue that represents contents for users. The goal is to communicate to the users a piece of content of a topic. The single topic and the multiple topics must be fragmented in content dialogue act; only the elementary topic could be not be fragmented. In order to well fragment a topic, the designer has to follow a set of criteria such as dimension (taking care not to show too many contents to the user), the content (splitting the different kinds of information), the user profile (defining different dialogue acts for different kinds of users), the device (distinguishing the text contents, the video, the images and the download file) and, at last, the channel for which the application is designed. This fragmentation process, on one hand, leads to a set of simpler dialogue acts, and on other hand, makes the navigation more difficult. Each topic must have at least one dialogue act.

○ **Transition act:** It is a piece of dialogue that allows the user to navigate from one topic to another. Its goal is to allow the user to change dialogue arguments, followings semantic relationships (defined in the C-IDM schema). In few words, it can be defined as a list of topics correlated between them using the semantic defined into the relationship.

○ **Introductory act:** It is a piece of dialogue that allows introducing a group of topics; its goal is to allow the user to access a group of topics. The main message of introductory act is a list of topics of the same group of topics. Sometimes, it presents additional contents.

• **The structural strategies:** The structural strategies are defined only if the topic is fragmented in different dialogue acts. The structural strategies indicate how the piece of topic into the same topic can be changed. It is the definition of the navigation that links the many content dialogue acts of the same topic in order to allow the user to access and explore the contents. A structural strategy has to define two essential elements: the default dialogue act of the topic (the default act is the first that the users see when accesses to the topic) and the navigation method to reach the other dialogue acts. The navigational strategy is defined through the navigational patterns that can be *index, all-to-*

Copyright © 2009, IGI Global, distributing in print or electronic forms without written permission of IGI Global is prohibited.

all, *guided tour*, or *index/guided tour*. The choice of the navigational pattern is made by the designer in order to accomplish the needs, the abilities, and the interests of the final users; in fact, a user with little knowledge of the contents that he/she accesses for the first time in the application prefers a simple navigational path, such as a guided tour, while domain expert users prefer an index path; in few word, they prefer the efficiency to the simplicity. The navigational strategies, defined at first in the L-IDM schema, will be better defined during the page design where the designer can better understand the usability of the chosen strategy. The designer can evaluate correctly his/her choices only when he/she tries to navigate through the pages.

- **Transition strategies:** They are defined only if the relationship between topics is of type 1:N otherwise the designer has to use the structural strategies. The modalities to move from a topic to the related one, link the source topic to the target topic of a relevant relation. A transition strategy establishes the way the user can get through the transition defined by a relevant relation using a transition act. The more used patterns are index and guided tour.
- **Introduction strategies:** They define the navigation or the interaction modality that allows accessing and navigating between the topics of a group of topics using an introductory act. An introduction strategy defines the role of the introductory act in order to access the topic of the group of topic and its exploration. Each introductory act must have its own introductory strategy without it the user could not access to the topic and so navigate into the group of topic. The typical ways are the patterns seen for the structural strategy.

In the logical design, the designer has to define the list for the introductory acts and the transition acts. If the navigational pattern is index, all-to-all or mixed, an introductory act and a transition act describe the list of topic from which it is possible to access the specific topic. In this case, the design of the list is a critical task because it is strictly connected with the application usability. Thus, it is fundamental to choose very carefully the information to present and to correlate the list elements, in order to be simpler to identify the topic. Furthermore, the order of the list elements is very important. In fact, the list should be compact and readable without the lack of clarity and expressivity in order to offer to the user a good and efficient navigation.

In order to give an idea of the possible graphical elements of the IDM notation (in the conceptual level and logical too), in the Table 1, the most common element with a little description is shown.

Copyright © 2009, IGI Global, distributing in print or electronic forms without written permission of IGI Global is prohibited.

PAGE DESIGN: Guidelines

Thus, the logical design allows defining all of the application behaviors in terms of dialogue acts (of contents, of introduction or of transition). The content corresponds to single Web pages. The transition from the logical schema to the page design is simpler and rapid even if IDM does not take care of a graphical aspect and layout. However, IDM proposes a guideline to define the pages and to establish which contents will be shown to the final user:

- Each dialogue act is mapped on a specific page. A content dialogue act of a multiple topic corresponds to a kind of page valid for each instance of the topic; for each page the designer models a single page valid for all of the relation instances; finally, the multiple introductory acts are mapped on a single page template valid for all instances of considered introductory acts.
- The single topics and the introductory acts of major interest will be translated in links on all application pages, called landmark. The landmark allows the users to access important dialogue subjects every time.
- For each page that presents a content dialogue act, the following elements must be defined:
  ○ Content of dialogue act
  ○ Structural links that allow the user to navigate to other content dialogue acts of the same topic
  ○ Transition links that allow the user to navigate to the related topics using semantic association or to navigate to others transitions presented
  ○ Landmarks
  ○ Orientation information that allows the user to understand his/her position into the dialogue and the followed path
- For each page of introductory act, the following elements must be defined:
  ○ The list of topics
  ○ Landmarks
  ○ Orientation information
- For each page of transition act, the following elements must be defined:
  ○ Introduction content (optional)
  ○ The list of topics
  ○ Landmarks
  ○ Orientation information

Copyright © 2009, IGI Global, distributing in print or electronic forms without written permission of IGI Global is prohibited.

Table 1. Elements of IDM notation

ELEMENT	DESCRIPTION	NOTATION
Kind of topic	Generic category of interest object for the user.	
Topic	An instance of kind of topic	
Group of topics	The topics are organized in a group in order to render simpler for the user to reach the interested information: a topic can be categorized into more groups.	◇
Parametric group of topics	Group of topics derived by another group through a parameter.	◇
Dialogue Act	A piece of the dialogue.	●
Transition Act	A specific dialogue act that indicates the passage from a topic to another topic..	
Introductory Act	Dialogue acts that accesses and introduces the specific group of topic.	
Group of introductory act	The introductory acts are organized in a group that allows to the user to access to more group of topic at the same time.	
Structural Strategy	It specifies how the dialogue acts will be presented to the user.	
Transition Strategy	It specifies how user can navigate between the topic of a relevant relation.	
Subject Strategy	It specifies how the topic will be accessed by the user.	⇧
Relevant Relation	It is a relation between the topics that represents the dialogue.	- - - - →

P-IDM

Starting form IDM, PIDM allows creating the design as close as possible to the final application that will be developed. Thus, PIDM, even if it remains at a high level of detail, is the first step to the development phase. PIDM fragments the design into several views, each of which focus on a specific implementation aspect:

Copyright © 2009, IGI Global, distributing in print or electronic forms without written permission of IGI Global is prohibited.

- **View of structural navigation:** It defines the pages used to present the information related to the same conceptual entity (topic). The view includes the design of templates, navigational links between pages and the division between the contents.
- **Association view:** It defines the navigation between the pages of different entities but is correlated to semantic associations. The user starts form a source entity and can choose the target entity using a set of attributes of the second entity if this set has a few elements; otherwise, an intermediate page can be introduced.
- **Navigational path view:** Navigational path starts form a specific access structure and guides the user to explore the dialogue and to choose the specific subject during his/her exploration between the sets.
- **Operation view:** It allows specifying the operation that activates the pages and the possible navigational path valid when the operation are activated.
- **Page template view:** It defines the layout of the pages specifying the links of each page and their templates.
- **Navigational Map:** It provides a global view of navigational possibility offered to the user related to the entire application.

Graphical Elements

In Table 2, the main notation elements are shown.

A specific mapping between the IDM components and PIDM components is shown in Table 3.

Table 2. P-IDM graphical elements (part 1)

ELEMENTS	DESCRIPTION	NOTATION
Layout content	Describe the sets of link or the static contents that compose a template: It allows to have a design close to the implementation one. They are used as aggregator of screen template.	<<Layout Content>>
Screen template	Represent the content common to all pages that specializes in it. They propose the general application structures and divides all the contents in functional area.	<<Screen Template>> Standard Page
Content	They are used as screen aggregator: the content class contains all the attributes and the information used into the screen.	<<Content>> Name

Copyright © 2009, IGI Global, distributing in print or electronic forms without written permission of IGI Global is prohibited.

Table 2. P-IDM graphical elements (part 2)

ELEMENTS	DESCRIPTION	NOTATION
Link	It indicates the navigational relation existing between two screens and is defined with a name that explains the meaning: if it is not oriented a bidirectional associations exists.	link
Association content	It has the goal to support the navigation offering a preview of objects or of entities.	<<Association Content>> Name
Association link	It indicates the navigation form navigation between centre and its elements: it starts from an association content and finish to a screen.	Association Link 1..n
Access content	The collection centre represents a simple access to the collection of information contents of interest for the user. A collection centre is linked to a screen using aggregation relation.	<<Access content>> Name
Collection link	It indicates the navigation form a collection centre to one of its elements. It starts from an access content and arrives at a specific screen.	Collection Link 1. n
Input form	It models the user input such as the operation of search for a specific instance or to insert an element to a specific collection. It can be used on a relation between two screens or used as an aggregate component to a screen.	

Table 3. Mapping IDM - P-IDM

IDM elements	P-IDM elements
Topic	Abstract Screen with the same name of the topic.
Dialogue act	Screen: specialize in the abstract topic of the screen and aggregate a content class with the same name of the corresponding dialogue act.
Relevant relation with transition strategy	Association content.
Transition act	Intermediated Screen with aggregated association content.
Introductory act	Screen that aggregate an access content.
Group of introductory act	Sets of screen with aggregated access content.
Subject strategy	/

Copyright © 2009, IGI Global, distributing in print or electronic forms without written permission of IGI Global is prohibited.

OPEN ISSUES ABOUT PIDM AND W2000 PUBLISHING MODEL

The W2000 methodology and its evolution IDM are good design tools to model the structure of information. In fact, they allow structuring the information to be presented to the final user (based on user-centered paradigm) and the semantic relationships between this information.

Furthermore, the structured access allows defining the starting point of the user navigation. In W2000 the information and navigation design is presented in two distinct models while in IDM the information and navigation design are presented in only one diagram to simplify the comprehension of the model for the customers.

In IDM, it is really important to highlight the metaphor in which the conceptual effort to define the several information and the navigation between them consists in designing all the possible dialogues between the user and the application.

Thus, this makes the design clearer and directly understandable, and it especially eases the communication between the designer and the customers in order to have a common point of view on the content of Web application and navigation strategy in the first phase of design.

The information structure, even if of fundamental importance, is not the only thing to define a good information system: over the design phase, it is necessary to create the page design independently from the specific implementation technology to use in a development phase.

W2000 and IDM present a design level to model the Web pages to support the information system: respectively, the publishing model and PIDM.

However, these design levels are at a high level of abstraction and do not allow the customers to understand the real page structures. It is clear that many details do not allow a generation code tool to create the application. The generation code tool could be the solution to giving the customers an idea of the final application.

In the following chapters, we will refer to the page conceptual design, thus we will consider only the PIDM level.

But, it is important to clear the possible change points to make the design level more detailed in order to plan the structure of each page balancing the usability, the features and the layout aspect. When we refer to these possible changes, we speak about *Publishing IDM*. It is clear that, as the design of each page is at deeper level of detail, as the generation code tool can produce more detailed pages closer to pages of the real Web application. On this open issue, we present possible activities useful to define a methodological level in order to render the design of the page more detailed.

Copyright © 2009, IGI Global, distributing in print or electronic forms without written permission of IGI Global is prohibited.

- *Layout information:* In all of the two methodologies, there is a lack of information to place the contents into the pages. For example, PIDM designs the screen and allows placing more screens into the same page, but it does not explain how these screens must be placed into the page.
- *Type of content:* The information of the content type of the screen is all missing. This kind of information is really important and must be explained better: text content needs a variable space in the pages while a video or an image always need the same space.
- *Interaction between application and user:* It is clear that it is necessary to better describe the interaction between the application and the user in order, for instance, to better describe, the content on which the user can directly interact, such as clickable maps or video that can be stopped or started.

Starting from these considerations, we provide here some ideas on which to define, in a following job, a further level of design useful to go down to a greater level of detail in the representation of the pages. You consider, for instance, a PIDM screen: despite that the screen virtually represents an area of the page, any indication is given relatively to its layout; it needs, therefore, to establish what the structure of the screens of the application will be. Besides, the Web applications and the multi-device applications, in general, allow the user to enjoy a series of digital contents that must be memorized using formats of coding to allow the correct production and fruition of them. If it is, therefore, crucial the format of production of the contents, generally related to the environments of editing, still even more is the possibility to easily convert such formats in formats of fruition that assure the correct vision of the data on different customer platforms and devices. It has, therefore, a certain importance to define what types of contents must be visualized in given areas of the screen, specifying somehow if the user has the possibility to interact with such a content, or if it can simply view it. It can be thought about as determining a set of publishing rules that can drive in the design of the pages of the application to be presented to the user.

Definition of a New Publishing Methodology

With the goal to propose a level of design useful to define the structuring of the pages, the best part of the two methodologies that could be taken in examination are thought about (Publishing model of W2000 and P-IDM). It puts on evidence as particularly interesting is the separation in views proposed in P-IDM and the structuring of every view in screens each of them contains some well precise information expressed in terms of content; in parallel, it is particularly suitable the structuring of every page in sections and publishing units proposed in W2000; none of the two

Copyright © 2009, IGI Global, distributing in print or electronic forms without written permission of IGI Global is prohibited.

methodologies, however, provides detailed information about the positioning of every element inside the page. Relatively to the used graphic notation, that proposed in the publishing model of W2000 is seemed more intuitive therefore it recommends the use. On the base of the detected open issues and using the best parts of both the methodologies, to define a suitable level of detail it turns out opportune:

- To define some contents that will have to be available in almost every one of the pages of the application or, rather, contents that must always be present independently from the type of navigation undertaken by the user; it is opportune to remember that both IDM and W2000 point out, respectively with the "single topic" and the "single entity" the information that can eventually be repeated in more pages of the application, but they do not point out where to place such contents.
- Definition of the model of layout that will use the pages of the application in terms of a set of frames. You remember that neither PIDM nor W2000 provide this information; at the most, W2000 points out that the page is composed of sections, but it does not provide information on their positioning.
- Definition of the navigational map that provides a general vision of the navigation among screens corresponding to different topics. You remember that this characteristic is borrowed from PIDM.
- Definition of the specializations for the screens deriving from the same topic and of the navigation among these last ones. Furthermore, this characteristic is borrowed from PIDM.
- Definition of the contents proper to every screen that composes the application and of the navigation among screens deriving from different topics.

Borrowing the view concept from PIDM, defining two fundamental views can be considered:

- *Structure view*: it defines the general structure of the application in terms of layout to be used by the pages and the contents always present in each of them
- *Contents view*: it defines in the detail the real contents of the application and the interaction that it offers the user.

To get an integrated design it tries, therefore, to introduce some methodological elements useful to provide this further level of detail. Such methodological elements relate, in terms of notation, to the publishing model of , and considering the structural shortcomings previously presented, they allow providing a more precise definition of the structuring of the pages of the Web application.

Copyright © 2009, IGI Global, distributing in print or electronic forms without written permission of IGI Global is prohibited.

Figure 1. An example of landmark group representation

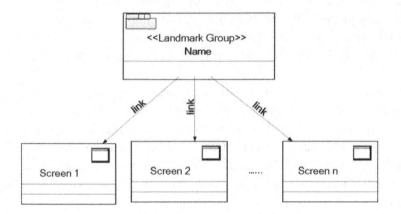

The methodological elements are the following:

• *Landmark groups*: they define a set of landmark's links organized according to a criterion chosen by the designer that, then, must be visualized together in one some area of the page. The notation proposed is in Figure 1.

As it is observed, the concept of destination screen for this kind of link remains:

• *Recurrent content type*: it is possible to identify in the design of the Web application some recurrent objects such as login, the search inside the page, the search in the Web, the setting of the language or the shopping cart. Such elements have been specified with the name of recurrent content type. Each of these elements is characterized by a well-precise symbol coming from the publishing of W2000 and presented in the Figures 2-6.

  Login RCT: it is the area related to the login and to the registration.

  Search RCT: it is the area related to the search into the site.

  Web Search RCT: it is the area related to search on the Web.

  Set Language RCT: it is the area related to set the language.

  Shopping Cart RCT: it is the area related to the shopping cart.

Copyright © 2009, IGI Global, distributing in print or electronic forms without written permission of IGI Global is prohibited.

Figure 2. Login recurrent content type

Figure 3. Search recurrent content type

Figure 4. Web search recurrent content type

Figure 5. Set language recurrent content type

Figure 6. Shopping cart recurrent content type

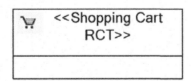

- *Page template*: resuming the analogous concept present in PIDM, the page template is characterized by the aggregation of one or more landmark groups and of one or more recurrent content types and it defines, therefore, the model of the pages according to the content that will have to appear in each of them.
- *Layout template*: it specifies the physical composition of a screen. Particularly, it is possible to divide a screen into frames, each of which will be character-

Copyright © 2009, IGI Global, distributing in print or electronic forms without written permission of IGI Global is prohibited.

Figure 7. An example of layout template

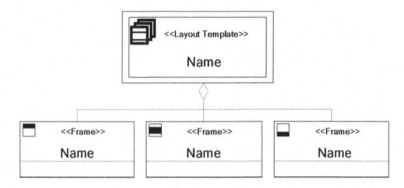

ized by a well-precise content (Figure 7). The concept of the frame is based on the concept of the section proposed in the publishing model of W2000.

- *Frame*: to represent the different frames contained in each Layout Template. A frame can be *fixed* or *dynamic*. A fixed frame is defined once, and it always has the same content; it treats, therefore, the areas of the screen that stay unchanged in all of the pages that come down from that template and that are most destined to contain navigation bars, logos, copyright information, and so forth, or rather that type of content that has to always be available to the user during the navigation. A frame type dynamic has, instead, the purpose of introducing to the user those that are the real contents of the application; it is represented through a contour outlined that it is to underline its varying character according to the subject of the dialogue in matter.

Figure 8. Fixed frame

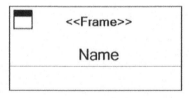

Figure 9. Dynamic frame

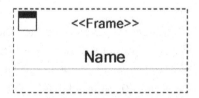

Copyright © 2009, IGI Global, distributing in print or electronic forms without written permission of IGI Global is prohibited.

The notation differs according to the place that the frame occupies inside the page; an example of notation is shown in Figures 8 and 9.

It is possible to observe once more as the notation is resumed by the publishing model of W2000.

- *Content type*: they represent the different types of content that can be introduced to the user; the aggregation of more content types build a frame. For each content type, it is possible to specify the type of content (for instance multimedia, image, link, form etc.).
- *Layout*: it is possible to think about defining some models of layout inside which to position the various contents defined by the modeling. For each model, it needs to point out in every frame the data shown in the table that follows:

The Figure 10 shows the use of the frameset inside of the page and the percentage of occupation of the frame within the screen.

Table 4. An example of frame definition

Frameset	Frameset number.
Frame	Frame number; % on the screen.

Figure 10. A layout template with its own frames

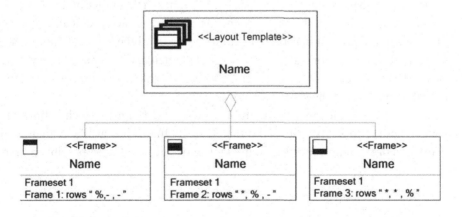

Copyright © 2009, IGI Global, distributing in print or electronic forms without written permission of IGI Global is prohibited.

From the Information Modeling to the Pages Modeling

A level of design so detailed that it also aims to define the physical positioning of each frame inside every single page, is particularly useful for two fundamental reasons:

- The design provides all of the useful details to produce, after an opportune translation in a specific language, the Web application closer to that real.
- It is possible to provide the buyer, already on paper, a precise perception as to what the application could be.

It is possible, therefore, to think about the definition of a series of methodological guidelines that allow directly passing from the information and the navigation design to the punctual design of the page skipping, if tightly considered not necessary, the design realized through the publishing model or through the PIDM methodology.

We propose then some guidelines that are useful to facilitate this direct passage from the design of the information contents to the page design.

The first thing to be done should be to identify the landmarks that the application has to have according to the single topics and to the introductory acts considered particularly interesting; such landmarks can be organized by the designer according to a particular criterion, for instance, according to the type of information toward which they want to guide the user. It is, for instance, possible to choose to separate the landmarks that aim toward pages containing the key points of the dialogue from those that want, instead, to provide technical information, related to the application or not, such as contacts, credits, disclaimer, external links, and so forth.

Then, the designer can proceed with verifying the presence or less sections related to the login and to the registration, of sections related to the summary of online orders, analyzing the opportunity to insert an inside search engine for the Web, or a forum inside the application, and so forth.

These first two phases are of the highest importance in the choice of the structure of the application; in fact, the elements listed above are at the base of any application, and they are present in different combinations in all the WAs. Therefore, according to the presence or less of such kinds of elements, the layout of every page can be selected in terms of the number of frames of which it is composed and the physical disposition of the same.

Of course, the choice is strongly influenced by the designer which defines the layout according to its experience, to the elements that it has available thanks to the analysis of the requirements and the logical design or, also, to possible preferences of the buyer.

Copyright © 2009, IGI Global, distributing in print or electronic forms without written permission of IGI Global is prohibited.

Once established, the elements (landmarks and/or others) that repeat themselves in all or in large part of the pages of the application are fundamental to understand as the navigation happens among the contents. From the IDM diagram, it is easy to understand as the user can change matter during the dialogue or rather, in terms of IDM, the possibility to pass from one topic to another semantically correlated. These relationships and the related passage to new themes of conversation by the user really correspond to the navigation among the contents provided by the application. PIDM provides the navigation view or rather, an overall vision of the application that represents the screens connected among them through association and collection links; the purpose is to provide a global view about the navigation opportunities that the application provides to the user.

At this point the information present in the various topics is positioned, for each page, inside of the frames that constitute the selected layout. It is obviously that such positioning has to respect the navigation and the contents design defined in the preceding phase.

CONCLUSION

In this chapter, we described some useful details for a deepened understanding of IDM methodology of design of Web application selected for the design of a complex Web information system. Details have been supplied both in conceptual terms and in terms of notation, and you have been provided with some guidelines that allow deriving, starting from the design of the information contents, the design of the pages.

In this chapter, we presented also a new publishing methodology called publishing IDM that considers several design aspects of the Web pages such as layout or the position of the frames inside of the page.

In the following part of the book, because at this moment the publishing IDM is not defined into the meta-model, we will consider the layout of the Web pages speaking about a layout model; it is conceptually very close to the publishing IDM but not already formalized. The layout design, as it will be clear in Chapters XIII and XIV, allows adding to the PIDM design the information useful to consider also the design of the pages. We are working to migrate the PIDM design extended by the layout design to the publishing IDM.

Copyright © 2009, IGI Global, distributing in print or electronic forms without written permission of IGI Global is prohibited.

REFERENCES

Baresi, L., Garzotto, F., Mainetti, L., & Paolini, P., (2002). Meta-modeling techniques meet Web application design tools. *Proceedings from the 5th International Conference FASE 2002 (part of ETAPS 2002),* (pp. 294-307).

Bolchini, D., & Paolini, P.(2006). Interactive dialogue model: A design technique for multichannel applications. *IEEE Transaction on multimedia, 8*(3), 529-541.

Paolini, P., Mainetti L., & Bolchini, D. (2006). *Progettare siti Web e applicazioni mobili.* McGraw-Hill Companies.

Perrone, V., Bolchini, D., & Paolini P. (2005). A stakeholders centered approach for conceptual modeling of communication-intensive applications. *Proceedings of the 23rd Annual International Conference on Design of Communication: Documenting & Designing for Pervasive Information,* (pp. 25-33).

Copyright © 2009, IGI Global, distributing in print or electronic forms without written permission of IGI Global is prohibited.

Chapter IV
A Brief Introduction to Ontology

INTRODUCTION

It is now clear that a careful initial phase of design, above all that it concerns for the complex Web information systems, it is essential to assure the quality of the final system. To reduce the necessary time development effort in order to get the final output, it is important to have tools that allow quickly obtatining tangible results; in few words, it is important to quickly obtain a consistent part of code for the final application. In this way, it is possible to provide the customer with a first draft of the information system in order to have a first validation of the design.

The key point in order to make fast the transition from the design to the development is to translate in a formal language the design choice made up by the designer. In this way, it will be possible to instruct and to configure some tools that allow, according to the MDA® (model-driven architecture®) producing the necessary code to make the design previously made tangible.

Based on these considerations, the design of complex Web Information systems is supported, in the present job, by a set of tools that will not only facilitate in the phase of validation of the result of the design, but also in the following phase of development.

Copyright © 2009, IGI Global, distributing in print or electronic forms without written permission of IGI Global is prohibited.

The input of these tools is a machine-readable representation of several design methodologies used in the design phase. It is important, therefore, to have both a machine-readable representation of the business processes and a machine-readable representation of the Web application design. As it will be possible to see in the following chapters, with the goal of obtaining a design that link together the know-how coming from the design of the business processes and the know-how coming from the design of the Web application, we will introduce some methodological guidelines that, opportunely translated in a machine readable format, will be the input for the automatic generation of the complex Web information system.

The problem to face, at this point, is to select a simple and flexible standard language, that allows representing all of its complexity the information systems.

The language that appears most appropriate for this purpose is the ontological language OWL (W3C, 2004) (a standard W3C). It is useful bacause it exploits the facilities made available by the ontologies and it provide a set of semantic constructs that allow to represent in its entirety the various aspects offered by the methodology.

Before explaining the use of this language that we intend to do within the design of complex Web information systems, it is essential to provide a brief introduction about the ontologies and their usage within the semantic Web.

The representation in the ontological format of the methodologies exposed in this job has followed a precise methodological approach; in the following part of this chapter, we expose, therefore, some of the ontology design methodologies created in the international scientific panorama and among these which will be selected as most appropriate for our purposes.

DEFINITION OF ONTOLOGY

There are many definitions of the concept of "ontology" in the philosophical field, but surely that which is more suitable to this job is the definition given by Gruber in 1993: "ontology is a formal, explicit specification of a shared conceptualization." The term "conceptualization" is the abstraction of some concept through the definition of its peculiar characteristics; the term "explicit" is connected to the fact that the constraints that contribute to the precise definition of the concept have to be expressed in a formal way, and finally the concept of "formality" points out that an ontology must be defined through a formal language.

The ontology, in conclusion, is a collection of terms and relative definitions or a map of concepts related to a well-precise domain in which it is possible to navigate.

Copyright © 2009, IGI Global, distributing in print or electronic forms without written permission of IGI Global is prohibited.

When a group of people and software systems developed for the Web have to collaborate among them, it is necessary to guarantee that they understand the applications and the information that receive. Their interaction essentially depends on the adoption of a conceptualization, a formal representation of the reality as it is perceived independently the the used dictionary.

In order to understand the reality, an ontological characterization of the information is helpful: the information may be detected, isolated, organized and integrated based on what is most important: its content.

The ontology allows formulating an exhaustive and rigorous conceptual scheme within a well- specified domain. It generally concerns a hierarchical data structure that contains all of the amazing entities, the existing relationships between them, the rules, the axioms and the specific constraints of the domain.

The terms ontology encloses:

- A *shared dictionary* is a set of terms that represent concepts and a set of relationships that define the reality under examination.
- A *language* allows expressing the conceptualization of the domain of interest. The language allows expressing the domain in terms of concepts, properties and relationships between concepts, using terms of the vocabulary.
- A set of *rules* in order to specify, in a non-ambiguous and explicit way, the meaning of the concepts and the relationships among concepts of the domain of interest and the restrictions that subsist in the domain.

The ontology is essentially made up of:

- **Concepts** (or *classes*): a set of the objects of which we want to deal. For each concept, it is important to define the properties that describe characteristics of it, the attributes and possible *restrictions* with the goal to limit the relationships of heredity pointed out by the properties themselves.
- **Relationships:** a set of the relationships that intervene among the objects. They are defined by the properties and by the attributes that characterize the classes of the domain. From a conceptual point of view, the principal relationships that can be defined among the concepts of an ontology are the following:
  - *same-as* (equivalence), it is defined between two concepts semantically equivalent, or that denote the same entity of the real world, or that have the same meaning (e.g., book same-as volume)
  - *kind-of* (subclass-of, is-a), it is defined between two concepts, c and c'; it allows organizing, in hierarchical way, concepts in taxonomies (e.g., book kind-of publication);

Copyright © 2009, IGI Global, distributing in print or electronic forms without written permission of IGI Global is prohibited.

- ◦ ***part-of***, it is defined between two concepts, *c* and *c'*,such that *c* is a component of *c'* or *c* is a part of a thing represented by *c'*. (e.g., motor part of car, slice part of cake);
- ◦ ***associates,*** is defined between two concepts in order to express a generic semantic constraint between these two concepts. (e.g., book associates author).

- **Axioms:** they are used to design an explicit way expression that is always true. Axioms may be used for several goals:
  - ◦ To define the meaning of several components of the ontology
  - ◦ To define complex relationships
  - ◦ To verify the correctness of the information or to obtain new information
- **Individuals:** they are objects of the real world and represent elements that answer to the characteristics defined in a well-defined class.

ONTOLOGY AND SEMANTIC WEB

The main use of the ontologies is what is done within the Semantic Web; a promoter of this new vision of the Web is Tim Berners Lee, inventor of the Web. The ontologies propose themselves as the tools of connection among different heterogeneous resources present on the Web.

The Web is currenlty nothing else other than a set of information through which the user tries to unravel "filtering," with a simpler mental mechanism, those more proper for his/her own purposes.

The Semantic Web proposes it to make the links among the various information more expressive than those actual, so to facilitate the user in his/her job of search.

A specific language to represent the knowledge is not sufficient in expressing the full "meaning" of the present texts in the Web. It needs to place side by side to it some rules of inference that succeed in associating the rules to logic concepts and allow the intelligent agents to extract knowledge from knowledge. And it is really the role of the ontologies to *associate concepts to logics rules.*

Tim Berners Lee imagines the Web as a virtual space in which the knowledge can be shared from everyone and to which all can enter in a simple way both to explore its contents and to create them. The possibility to enter and to exchange the information does not have to be granted alone to limited groups of people, but it has to be guaranteed to all of the people with the same naturalness with which they communicate.

Copyright © 2009, IGI Global, distributing in print or electronic forms without written permission of IGI Global is prohibited.

On the other side, Tim Berners Lee proposes that the information interchange do not happen only among people, but also between people and machines and between machines and machines. Of course, all of this will be made possible by the intelligent agents that will have the role of understanding the mechanisms of our daily life and can autonomously regulate it. This new way of seeing the Web has the goal of organizing the information in such a way to allow the processing of this information by the computers, making, in parallel, the Web most useful to the final users.

The ontology will be used for the automatic elaboration of the contents for the purpose of answering three fundamental problems:

- **Information search:** the actual systems of search are based on keywords
- **Information extraction:** until today, the final user filters the results obtained through the search going to extrapolate "manually" the part of information of interest
- **Information maintenance:** to maintain structured text updates is, above all, a strong activity when information massive structure grows. The automatic maintenance of consistence, correctness and updating of the information requires an appropriate representation of the semantics and the use of constraints that allow individualizing and correcting anomalies.

To solve these problems, it is necessary to store and to access the documents on the base of a less superficial representation of their contents so it can be generated and be managed by a computer.

DESIGN METHODOLOGY FOR ONTOLOGY

It is clear that it is very helpful to represent, through a formal language, the domain. It is important, however, to define first the ontology that will be represented through a formal language using a structured approach that drive the "knowledge engineering," that is, the engineer with the goal to make explicit the knowledge, in the definition of a well-defined domain.

There are in the international scientific panorama several design methodologies for ontology that support the designer in the hard task of the conceptualization.

Among the most important methodologies, we refer to:

- USCHOLD & KING methodology
- Gruninger & Fox methodology
- Ontology Development 101

Copyright © 2009, IGI Global, distributing in print or electronic forms without written permission of IGI Global is prohibited.

None of these methodologies has been defined as "the methodology" most effective of design ontology; usually, one of these is selected depending on the particular requirements of the designer and the peculiarities of the application domain to represent.

We provide hereafter a brief description of all of the ontologies design methodologies listed above.

USCHOLD and KING Methodology

Mike Uschold and Martin King (1995) introduced a methodology called "skeletal" for the design and the evaluation of the ontologies. This methodology it is founded on the experience of development of the *enterprise ontology*, an ontology created to design company processes, and it is made up of the following phases:

- **Feasibility study:** it consists of determining the technical and economic feasibility of the project in examination, and selecting the area on which to focus in order to determine the best solution.
- **Phase of scoping:** such a phase has the goal of clearly defining the field of application of the ontology and the goal for which it is made up to make the target of the ontology clear.
- **Construction of the ontology:** it represents the core of the process of development, and it allows getting in output the conceptualization of the domain of interest.
- **Evaluation:** it consists of valuing, according to opportune techniques, the ontology realized.
- **Maintenance:** the specifications on which the ontology if founded can often change in base to the changes of the real world. To reflect these changes, the ontologies must frequently be updated. The maintenance of the ontology is a crucial assignment from the moment that two important characteristics must always respect:
  - ∘ *adequacy* is related to how the ontology of a domain must correctly represent the reality.
  - ∘ *completeness* concerns the complete definition of all of the concepts that belong to the ontology.

It is particularly useful to subsequently detail the phase related to the construction of the ontology realized through the following sub-phases:

- **Capture of the ontology.** This is also called sub-phase of conceptualization, and it articulates in two steps:

Copyright © 2009, IGI Global, distributing in print or electronic forms without written permission of IGI Global is prohibited.

- ◦ *Identification*: identification of the key concepts and of the relationships in the domain of interest realized through brainstorming or grouping together of similar terms and potential synonymous for following considerations or other techniques that are very close to those classical of analysis of the requirements.
- ◦ *Definition*: production of precise textual definitions and not ambiguous to refer to the concepts and relationships individualized in the preceding step.

This process of capturing the ontology is independent from the particular language that is used for the coding.

- • ***Realization of the meta ontology***. The realization of the meta-ontology concerns the choice of the fundamental terms (classes and relationships) that will be used for specifying the ontology.
- • ***Construction of the taxonomy***. This phase consists of define the "is-a" relationships among the various terms of the domain, according to their definitions. One of the principal roles of the taxonomies is to give a structure to the ontology, in order to facilitate the human understanding and to allow the integration of the various ontologies.
- • ***Choice of the language of the representation of the ontology***. the taxonomy allows giving a structure to the ontology; nevertheless, since it includes only the is-a relationships existing among the various terms, to represent all of the other possible relationships (not only those is-a), it is necessary to consider other tools. There are two different currents of thought about the way to represent the knowledge: the logical trend and the anti-logic trend. The logical trend proposes using the tools of the mathematical logic to study and to develop the languages of representation of the knowledge. The logic, as a tool of representation of the knowledge, within artificial intelligence, has been criticized by different points of view. The logical representations have a poor structure; the knowledge is represented in the form of many statements independent among them. The information that concerns a well-specified object or concept or event can be scattered accordingly in different multiple formulas of the base of knowledge. From here, the demand to organize the representations in a format more consistent to the computational purposes of artificial intelligence. Besides, the developers of ontologies do not always know the discipline of the mathematical logic; accordingly, they are not able to use the logic to represent the ontologies.
- • ***Choice of the language for coding ontology***. This fifth sub-phase of the phase of construction the ontology concerns the choice of the language of

Copyright © 2009, IGI Global, distributing in print or electronic forms without written permission of IGI Global is prohibited.

coding of the ontology that allows passing from the graphic representation, "human-readable," to the writing of the code, "machine-readable." Different languages can be used for codifying the ontology that differ from each other in their syntax, terminology, expressiveness and semantics.

- *Writing of the code.* After having chosen the language that must be used for the coding of the ontology, the following phase is obviously the writing of the code, that can be performed through the help of special tools that support the language of coding chosen or through the simple notepad.

- *Integration of the existing ontologies.* During the phase of capture and writing of the ontology, there is the problem of whether or not to use the already existing ontologies. It generally deals with a very complex problem. In fact, it is simple enough to identify the synonyms and to extend them to an ontology in which concepts do not really exist. Instead, when there are similar concepts defined in the existing ontologies, it is, generally, difficult to understand when such concepts can be adapted and re-used. A way to try to integrate the existing ontologies is to make explicit all of the assumptions that are at the base of the ontology.

Gruninger and Fox Methodology

The Gröninger and Fox methodology (1995) is oriented to the design and evaluation of ontology based on the TOVE (Toronto Virtual Enterprise) project.

In few words, the methodology requires the definition of a logical knowledge model made up using several steps:

- **Capturing the motivation that makes useful the ontology definition**: The development of the ontologies is motivated from the scenarios that arise in the application. The motivating scenarios are often problems or examples that have not been considered in a suitable way by the existing ontologies. Any proposal of a new ontology or of the extension to any ontology must describe the motivation scenario in order to understand the motivation of the proposed ontology.

- **Making informal competency questions.** Based on the motivating scenario, it is of the highest importance to formulate a set of competency questions that the ontology must be able to address. These questions are not in formal language but the ontology must be able to address these questions. It is possible to define the relationships between informal competency questions and motivation scenarios; in this way, it is possible to provide an informal justification for the new or extended ontology. In few words, these questions are useful to evaluate the feasibility of the project.

Copyright © 2009, IGI Global, distributing in print or electronic forms without written permission of IGI Global is prohibited.

- **Specification in the first-order logic terminology of the ontology.** An ontology is a description of objects, properties of objects and relationships among objects. If the goal is to define a new ontology for every informal competency questions, there must be objects, attributes or relations in the proposed ontology that intuitively address the informal competency questions. It is important to identify objects in the domain of discourse: objects will be defined as constants or variables in the language. Attributes are defined as unary predicates while relationships among objects are n-ari predicates.
- **Formulating the formal competencies questions.** Once the competency questions have been defined in an informal way and the terminology has been defined, the competency questions are re-phrased in a formal way using the first-order logic and the terms specified in the preceding phase.
- **Specifying in the first-order logic axioms**. In order to obtain an ontology, it is important to explain, in a first-order logic, the semantic and constraints of the terms established.
- **Completeness theorems.** Once the competency questions have been formally stated, we must define the conditions under which the solutions to the questions are complete. It is important to provide theorems to show that it is possible to answer, through ontology, the proposed competency questions.

Methontology

METHONTOLOGY (Mariano, Gómez-Pérez, & Juristo, 1997) is a methodology developed at polytechnic of Madrid in the *Ontological Engineering Group* (Corcho, Mariano, & Gómez-Pérez, 2005).

The methodology is made up using some idea of the software engineering science. The process development of the ontology following the methontology is based on the most sophisticated techniques of the standards created to develop software. Methontology defines the life cycle of the ontology development and the activity to follow in each phase.

There are three types of activities in the ontology life cycle:

- **Management activities:** these activities include activity of scheduling, control and quality assurance.
- **Activities oriented to the development.** These activities include pre-development, development and post-development activities. During the pre-development, it is possible to study the environment where the ontology will be used and a feasibility study is made. In the development, it is possible to conceptualize, formalize and implement the ontology. In the post-development, there is the maintenance of the ontology that is the update and correction of

Copyright © 2009, IGI Global, distributing in print or electronic forms without written permission of IGI Global is prohibited.

the ontology and the integration, if it is necessary, of the ontology with other ontologies or other application.

- **Support activities.** These activities are parallel to the development, and they include knowledge acquisition activity, evaluation, integration, merging and/or alignment, documentation and configuration management.

We focus now on the ontology development phase.

The process starts with the definition of the specifications and this produces an informal output that evolves in the time increasing the level of formality.

Through the definition of the specifications, the goal of the ontology is defined, that is, it is possible to define the motivations that lead to building an ontology, what the future uses are and who the end users are.

The specifications can be informal, in natural or formal language; for instance using a set of competency questions. At the end of such activity, a document will be produced in which the requirements of the ontology (goal, level of formality, field of action, etc.) will be specified.

The work goes on with the conceptualization that allows organizing and structuring the knowledge acquired during the acquisition of the knowledge using external representations that are independent from the representation of the knowledge and from the paradigms of implementation in which the ontology will be subsequently formalized and implemented. Formally, the view of the domain is converted in a semi-formal model using intermediary representations (IRs) based on tabular notations and graphics.

At this level, we speak in terms of concepts, attributes, relationships, axioms and useful rules because these terms can be understood by the experts of the domain and from the developers of the ontology accordingly; they fill the gap between the perception of the domain of the people and the languages of implementation of the ontology.

To develop a consistent and complete conceptual model, the activity of conceptualization defines a set of tasks that must be performed in succession. These tasks increase, step by step, the complexity of the intermediary representations used for developing the conceptual model. The tasks for the conceptualization are defined below:

- **Task 1. Make a glossary of terms.** In the first place, the designer has to develop a glossary of the terms that includes all of the remarkable terms of the domain (concepts, individuals, attributes, relationships among concepts, etc.), their definition in natural language, and their synonyms and acronyms.
- **Task 2. Define the taxonomy of concepts.** When the glossary of the terms contains a rather large number of terms, the designer builds the taxonomies

Copyright © 2009, IGI Global, distributing in print or electronic forms without written permission of IGI Global is prohibited.

of the concepts to define the hierarchy of every concept, where a concept is an abstraction for one or more terms of the glossary.

- **Task 3. Define the diagram to link together concepts.** Once the taxonomy has been built and valued, the activity of conceptualization proposes to build the diagrams of binary relationship.
- **Task 4. Define the dictionary of the concepts.** In this task, for each concept, it is possible to define relationships to other concepts, the specific domain of interest of the concepts, the individual of each concept and the attributes of the concept. The attributes of the classes have the same value for all the instances of the concept while the attribute of the individual has different values for each instance of the concept.
- **Task 5. Define the details of binary relationships.** The goal of this task is to define the details of all of the binary relationships defined in the dictionary and to obtain, as output, a table of these relationships. For each relationship, the designer must define its name, the name of the source and target concept, the cardinality of the relationships, and if there exist, the inverse of the relationship.
- **Task 6. Define in detail the attributes of each individuals.** The goal of this task is to describe in the details all of the attributes of each individual already included in the dictionary.
- **Task 7. Define in detail the attributes of the classes.** The goal of this task is to describe in detail the attributes of the classes already defined when concepts has been defined.
- **Task 8. Define in detail constants.** The goal of this task is to describe in detail each constants of the glossary.
- **Task 9. Define axioms.** The designer must define formal axioms and must describe them in a precise way.
- **Task 10. Define rules.** Rules are defined to add knowledge to the ontology.
- **Task 11. Define individuals.** When the conceptual model of the ontology is ready, the designer may define the individuals that seem to be important in order to clarify the concept. For each individual, the designer may define the name, the concept to which the individual belongs and the values of the attributes.

At this point, it is important to formalize the ontology using an ontological language. It is clear that it is important to update the ontology in order to maintain this ontology compliant with the domain concepts.

Copyright © 2009, IGI Global, distributing in print or electronic forms without written permission of IGI Global is prohibited.

Ontology Development 101

Another design methodology in the international scientific panorama has been proposed by Natalya F.Noy and Deborah L. McGuinness from Stanford University (Noy & McGuinness, 2001). In reality, they propose only methodological guidelines because their idea is that *"There is no one 'correct' way or methodology for developing ontologies"* and they make their experience available in the realization of ontologies providing a set of "rules" to reference.

Such rules include:

- *There is no correct way to design a domain, but there are always several possible alternatives. The best solution depends on the future usage of the ontology and on the possible future extension of it.*
- The developing process of the ontology will be an iterative process.
- The concepts in ontology have to be close to the objects (physical or logical) and to the relationships of the domain of interest. There will probably be names and verbs in the definition of the domain that will allow individualizing, *respectively, the objects and the relationships of the ontology.*

The methodological guidelines proposed are made up of several steps listed here.

STEP 1. Define Domain and Scope of the Ontology

In a nutshell, defining tge domain and scope of the ontology means answering several basic questions. For instance:

- What knowledge will the ontology describe?
- For what will the ontology be used?
- Which type of applications will have to answer the information enclosed in the ontology?
- Who will have to use the ontology?

The answers to these questions can change during the process of ontology design, but in every instant, questions can contribute to limit the goal of the model. One of the ways to determine the goal of the ontology is to draft a list of questions which a knowledge base should be able to answer: the competency questions. These questions will be used subsequently as a test: does the ontology contain enough information to answer these types of questions? Do the answers require a particular level of

Copyright © 2009, IGI Global, distributing in print or electronic forms without written permission of IGI Global is prohibited.

detail or the representation of a particular area? These competency questions are only a draft and do not have need to be entirely exhaustive.

STEP 2. Consider the Possibility to Reuse Pre-Existing Ontologies

It is almost always correct to consider if someone has already done similar work and to see if that work can be refined. In this case, it is useful to extend the existing resources for the particular domain and assignment. To re-use existing ontologies could be a necessary requirement if the system needs to interact with other applications that already use particular ontologies or checked dictionaries.

Many ontologies are available in an electronic format, and they can easily be imported into an integrated environment of development of ontologies. The formalism with which they are expressed does not often constitute a big problem, thanks to the fact that many representation systems can import and export ontologies. Besides, the translation from one type of formalism to another usually is not particularly complex.

STEP 3. List Important Terms of the Ontology

It is useful to define a list of all terms to use in the ontology that is a list of terms of interest for a special user of the ontology. It is important to ask:

- Which terms would the user like us to talk about?
- Which properties do these terms have?
- What would we like to say about these terms?

Initially, it is important to stretch a comprehensive list of the terms without worrying about the coincidences with the concepts that they represent, with the relationships among the terms or of some ownerships that the concepts may have.

The two next phases—the development of the hierarchy of classes and the definition of the properties of each concept—are tightly related together, and it is difficult to say whether first completing the one rather than the other. Typically, few definitions of concepts are created in the hierarchy and the work goes on describing the properties of these concepts and so on, adding from time to time new concepts. These two phases are the most important.

STEP 4. Define Classes and Hierarchical Structure of the Classes

There are several approaches that are useful to develop a class hierarchy:

Copyright © 2009, IGI Global, distributing in print or electronic forms without written permission of IGI Global is prohibited.

- *Top-down.* The development process starts with the definition of the most general concepts in the domain; after this generalization, it follows a specialization of each concept.
- *Bottom-up.* The development process starts with the analysis of the most specific classes and is followed by a grouping of these classes in most general concepts (super classes).
- *A combination of the preceding approaches.* The development process is a combination of the top-down and bottom-up approaches. It is possible to first define the most important concepts, and then it is possible to generalize or to specialize these concepts. The generalization or specialization depend on the specific case under analysis.

None of these three methods is defined as the best. The approach to be chosen depends, in a very marked way, on the personal point of view of the domain. If a developer has a systematic vision with a high detail level of the system, the strategy to follow is a top-down strategy. The combined approach often turns out to be the simplest, since the concepts of intermediary level aim to be those which are more descriptive than the domain.

In general, independent from the selection of the top-down, bottom-up or combination approach, the starting point is the class definition. From the list made up in step 3, the designer selects the terms that describe objects with an independent existence rather than terms that describes these objects. These terms will become classes of the ontology. The classes are organized in a hierarchical taxonomy asking if an object will necessarily be an instance of some other classes by being an individual of a class. If class A is super-class of B, then every instance of B is also instance of A. In other words, the class B represents a concept that is a "kind of" A.

STEP 5. Define Properties of the Classes

Classes do not usually provide the necessary information to answer to the questions defined in the step 1. After defining classes, it is important to describe the internal structure of each concept.

At this step, classes has been selected from the list of terms defined in step 3.

The most parts of terms that have not been selected from that list are probably properties of the classes.

Obviously, after having individualized the main classes, many terms that remain in the same list of step 3 are good candidates to become properties of these classes. There are in general many types of properties of the objects that can become properties in the ontology:

Copyright © 2009, IGI Global, distributing in print or electronic forms without written permission of IGI Global is prohibited.

- *Intrinsic properties*: If we consider an ontology to describe wines, an intrinsic property will be the taste.
- *Extrinsic property*: For example, the name or the area of origin of the wine.
- *Parts:* If the object is a structured object, these may be both physical objects or abstract objects.
- *Relationships:* between objects in order to characterize in all its part an object.

These properties will be added to each class in order to have a complete definition of the object. A subclass inherits all of the properties of a super-class.

STEP 6. Define Restriction on the Properties

Properties may have several types of restrictions that describe the value types, the allowed values, the cardinality and other characteristics. We explain here some of these:

- *Cardinality.* The cardinality defines how many values a property may assume. The only difference between some systems is single and multiple cardinality, while others allow specifying a least value and maximum value in order to precisely describe the number of possible slots.
- *Value types.* A restriction about allowed values describes what base type can be defined for a well-specified property (for instance, string, number, boolean, etc.).
- *Domain and range*. The classes allowed for a property are the range of the property. The classes to which a property is linked are the domain of the property.

STEP 7. Create Individuals

The last step is to create all of the instances of the classes (in a few words, this is to populate classes). In order to define an instance of a class it is important to:

- Select a class
- Create the individuals
- For each individual it is important to fill all of its properties

Copyright © 2009, IGI Global, distributing in print or electronic forms without written permission of IGI Global is prohibited.

SEMANTIC WEB LANGUAGES

According to the idea of Semantic Web, W3C® is working about languages for knowledge representation. One of the main goals of the ontology is both the interoperability syntactic and semantic. Semantic interoperability means that an ontology must be "machine readable," that is, it must be interpreted by a machine in a well-defined format. Syntactic interoperability is the ability to provide a support to a reasoner that has to learn from the data. Languages created to support ontology are different: the first ontology language is RDF (resource description language) and RDF Schema (W3C, 2004).

RDF has a model close to the entity-relationship model and allows giving interoperability through applications that interact with each other in order to exchange information on the Web in a machine-readable format. RDF does not give reasoning support, but it is a useful language that will be input for reasoning tools. The three main concepts of RDF are:

- *Resource*: anything that will be defined in RDF is named "resource." Resource is named by an URI and can be a Web page or part of it; a resource can be an object in the real word not directly accessible on the Web.
- *Property*: it allows defining a characteristic of a resource through a binary relationship between two resources or between a resource and a well-defined data type.
- *Statement*: it is a sentence with a fixed structure: subject, predicate and object. Subject and predicate must be resources while an object may be a literal. The statement allows representing complex situations if an object is used as a subject on a new statement.

Successor of RDF (and RDF Schema [W3C, 2004]) are DAML (darpa agent markup language) and OIL (ontology interchange language), an ancestor of OWL, the ontology language used today.

OWL allows providing more machine readability than XML, RDF and RDF schema. In the Semantic Web, OWL is used when information must be processed by an application (and not only presented to a human). OWL allows providing a detailed description of any domain.

OWL adds new vocabulary (in comparison to RDF and DAML+OIL) to describe classes and relationships; it supports a useful mechanism to integrate different ontologies. OWL is made up of three different languages, each of them is the extension of its ancestor:

- *OWL Lite* allows giving simply a taxonomy without complex constraints.

Copyright © 2009, IGI Global, distributing in print or electronic forms without written permission of IGI Global is prohibited.

- *OWL DL* (description logic) gives high complexity, completeness and decidability.
- *OWL Full* gives expressiveness, but does not give decidability.

OWL main primitives are:

- *Classes*: they allow the abstraction of some concepts. Each class has a set of properties (each one for specific concept characteristics). A class would be composed by subclasses.
- *Properties*: There are two types of properties: DataType specific to each class and ObjectProperty used to create a link between classes. ObjectProperty has both domains: class (to which the property is connected) and range (the possible values of the property). In each class, we can indicate "restrictions" that define constraints.
- *Individuals*: individuals are objects with the characteristics defined by classes and properties. Both classes and properties may have individuals.

ONTOLOGY AND META-MODEL

Having described the concept of ontology and after the examination of some possible design methodologies for ontology definition, it is possible now to select one of them to adapt for the specific goal of this work.

In the preceding part of this work, it is clear that ontology is mainly used within the Semantic Web; in this work the use of ontology is proposed in a context quite different from the traditional ones, but in a way that ontology appears to be effective enough.

In this book, ontology has been used both to define a meta-model and the model of a specific methodology. It is important to highlight the concept of meta-model.

The meta-model idea was created about ten years ago and interest on the topic is increasing. A meta-model can be defined as a language to describe a model; therefore, to create a meta-model, it is important to work at an abstract level. A meta-model allows describing a specific methodology, so starting from the meta-model, it will be possible to define a model. Meta-model provides, in a few words, guidelines for model definition.

The introduction of the meta-model idea has introduced the meta-case tools. A standard case tool supports a fixed notation hard coded in the tool: a change in the methodology requires a change in the code of the tool and this requires high costs and a lot of time. Meta-case tools, based on the meta-model, allow separating the notation from the methodology definition, so a change in the methodology

Copyright © 2009, IGI Global, distributing in print or electronic forms without written permission of IGI Global is prohibited.

will reflect in the tool with a few changes (or without change) in the code. In order to include a meta-model in a Meta-Case tool, it is important that the meta-model addresses three important requirements. A meta-model must be:

- *Complete:* it must cover all of the primitives that methology represents.
- *Extensible*: meta-model must follow the methodology evolution so it will be possible to adapt the meta-model in a simple way without redefining it from scratch.
- *Semantic*: meta-model must express all the semantic of the methodology primitives to give the right meaning to each element.

To avoid confusion between meta-model and model, we explain the MOF™ (meta-object facility) approach to meta-model proposed by OMG™. MOF™ architecture is very helpful because it allows separating, in a simple way, the concept of the meta-model from the concept of the model: a model will be an instantiation of the meta-model.

MOF™ approach is based on a four-level architecture. It allows defining a language for the methodology representation and using this language for the model definition. The four-level architecture proposed by OMG™ is very helpful to separate the different levels of abstraction.

As shown in table 1, at the M3 level (the meta-meta model level) the MOF™ language that is the abstract language used to describe MOF™ meta-model is defined. The M2 level MOF™ approach allows defining the meta-model. MOF™ is object-oriented and strictly connected to UML® notation that is used to express MOF™ meta-model. The main MOF™ elements are classes, associations and packages; moreover, to express model rules, it is necessary to define constraints. MOF™ does not force the use of a particular language but suggests the object constraint language (OCL) (OMG, 1997). Starting from the meta-model defined at M2 level, the designer of a particular methodology using meta-model (guidelines for methodology) designs his/her model. Finally, M0 level represents data of a specific model.

Using an idea similar to the MOF™ idea, in this work, we propose the use of a language different from that proposed by OMG™: the language is the ontological language OWL. In this way the meta-model defined at M2 level is made up of classes that represent the primitives of the methodology and properties that link together methodology concepts (using the same semantic of the methodology). At M1 level there is the model obtained by adding individuals to the concepts and relationships defined at the M2 level. At the M0 level, it is possible to add data for the specific model.

Copyright © 2009, IGI Global, distributing in print or electronic forms without written permission of IGI Global is prohibited.

Thanks to this approach, it is possible to obtain several advantages. The most important advantages are:

- *Meta-model semantic*: OWL allows defining a semantic represented through classes and properties that represent the characteristics of the classes. Thanks to the architectural choice, this semantic will be inherited in the model.
- *Semantic relationship*: OWL and ontology allow defining ad hoc relationships.
- *Standard description of the model*: by using OWL, it is possible to obtain a machine- readable description of the model that software agents may read in a univocal way. OWL is supported by W3C®.
- *Graphical representation*: ontological languages are based on a text and not on a specific notation, so it is possible to provide both the meta-model and the model with a specific graphical representation based on the methodology and not on a general representation.

The description of the model in ontological language will be the input of a well-specified software generator that allows obtaining all of the code of the application related to the model. The idea of using an ontological language to represent a model that will be the input of a code generator, was created from the authors of this work, but the idea has been validated in scientific panorama as shown in Cardoso (2007).

Table 1. MOF and ontological approaches compared

Approach Level	MOF	Ontological
Meta-meta model (M3)	MOF-Language	OWL-language
Meta-Model(M2)	Classes, associations packages	Ontological classes and properties
Model(M1)	Derived classes, associations, packages	Instances of classes and properties
Data(M0)	Data	Data

Copyright © 2009, IGI Global, distributing in print or electronic forms without written permission of IGI Global is prohibited.

ONTOLOGY REPRESENTATION OF BPMN

We introduce here the approach followed in order to obtain the meta-model of the BPMN™ notation. A similar approach will be described for the IDM methodology and for the methodology that links together BPMN and IDM as it will be clear later on.

The definition of the meta-model is, in a few words, the formal representation of a knowledge base: the knowledge is the methodology that we will apply.

The ontology design methodology selected to define our knowledge base is the methodology proposed by Stanford University; this methodology is simple to apply and to understand. Following the different steps proposed by the methodology and due to the non-existence of an existing ontology to define BPMN™, the first step is to define a set of terms that, for BPMN, are the primitives of the notation. In the following phase, the semantic relationships between terms have been defined by object properties and datatype properties. Finally, some individuals of interest have been created allowing provision of more details about concepts.

In our approach, we develop BPMN™ meta-model following different steps:

- Analysis of BPMN™ specification in order to extract the main concepts: each concept is defined as ontological class.
- Analysis of BPMN™ in order to extract details of each concept defined in the previous step: each concept is modeled as ontological sub-class tied to the main classes.
- Analysis of BPMN™ in order to extract concepts that support the concepts defined in the previous steps. Each concept is defined as an ontological class.
- Analysis of BPMN™ in order to extract properties that allow providing a semantic to concepts previously defined. It is important to define both object properties that allow linking together concepts, and data type properties that are a simple type.
- Analysis of BPMN™ in order to identify some concepts that it is not possible to model by classes and properties that must be modelled as instances of classes and properties.

In the BPMN™ ontological meta-model, we define two main types of classes: concrete and abstract classes. Concrete classes are classes where it is possible to insert instances when defining a model. Abstract classes are used only to define BPMN™ concepts, but these classes cannot contain instances of a specific model. Each abstract class has at least one concrete class where it is possible to define instances.

Copyright © 2009, IGI Global, distributing in print or electronic forms without written permission of IGI Global is prohibited.

Following the notation specification, in the meta-model definition, there are four main concepts:

- *Swimlane*: this concept has been defined to make a generalization of pool and lane. *Pool* and *lane* are concrete sub-classes (of type "specialization") of the abstract class wwimlane. The concept of pool, following the BPMN™ definition, allows defining an actor (a person or/and a machine) of the process. A pool may contain a lane, flow object (defined below) or nothing. The ontological class lane meets the concept of lane defined by BPMN™ and it is defined to allow the definition of a lane within a pool.
- *FlowObject*: according to the BPMN™ specification, the ontological abstract class FlowObject is defined as a super-class that contains three subclasses: activity, event and gateway. The Activity, Event and Gateway classes, that are concrete classes, are linked with their super-class with a "specialization" relation. Both activity, gateway and event have a sub-class that allow defining the specific characteristics defined in the BPMN™ specification. As an example to define three different type of events (start, intermediate, end), we define three different sub-classes of the class event.
- *Artifact*: following the BPMN™ specification, the ontological class artifact allows defining information not tied to the process flow. Ontological class artifact (an abstract class) contains three concrete sub-classes: annotation, data object and group.
- *Connecting object*: according to BPMN™ notation, connecting object is defined as a super-class that contains three different sub-classes: SequenceFlow, MessageFlow and Association Flow.

The abstract class GenericBusinessProcessObject is a generalization of the classes SwimLane, FlowObject, Artifact and ConncetingObject. In the abstract class there is a definition of some properties (datatype properties) common to each subclass. Properties of this abstract class are:

- *categories*: in BPMN™ specification it has documentation purpose; in the meta-model it is a datatype property of type "text."
- *documentation*: as categories, it is a datatype property of type "text"
- *name*: it is a text data type property that allows defining a unique name in the business process diagram for each generic business process object.

Properties defined in the abstract classes cannot contain instances, but thanks to the class-sub-class relationships, property will be inherited by sub-classes until the sub-classes will be concrete.

Copyright © 2009, IGI Global, distributing in print or electronic forms without written permission of IGI Global is prohibited.

To the four classes previous defined, we add another two classes to define general concepts:

- *Business process diagram*: it is a concrete class; it contains general information about design such as author, creation date and so on. Following the BPMN™ specification, a business process diagram is made up of several pools.
- *Process*: this concept has been defined to contain the process design that is all of the BPMN™ elements that allow defining different steps in the process execution design. Process is a concrete ontological class and has three ontological sub-classes of type "specialization."

Starting from the main BPMN™ concept translated as ontological classes, we define properties (object properties) that link main concepts together.

The use of object property in the BPMN™ ontology is a little different from the traditional Semantic Web. An example is useful to understand this interesting aspect. Each process may be composed by different generic business process objects and it is not required to define in each process all of the generic business process objects defined in the BPMN™ specification. If each generic business process object is defined only by its name, a solution may be to define in the class "process" several properties (datatype properties), each one of the generic business process. The generic business process is a more complicated concept: it has several sub-classes and each of them has its own properties. To solve this problem in the meta-model that we developed, we adopt an object property that has generic business process object which has the class process as the domain and the class generic business process object as range. The OWL code is shown

```
<owl:InverseFunctionalProperty rdf:ID="hasGenericBusinessPro
cessDiagramGraphicalObject">
    <rdfs:range rdf:resource="#BusinessProcessDiagramGraphi
calObject"/>
    <rdfs:domain rdf:resource="#Process"/>
    <rdf:type rdf:resource="http://www.w3.org/2002/07/
owl#ObjectProperty"/>
  </owl:InverseFunctionalProperty>
```

In this way, it is possible, when defining the model starting from the meta-model, to define several instances of the property generic business process object; each of them defines a specific business process object with its own properties. Starting from this example, we define, in the same way, the property "hasSwimlane." This property has the ontological class business process diagram as the domain and the ontological class swimlane as the range. Finally, we define the property

Copyright © 2009, IGI Global, distributing in print or electronic forms without written permission of IGI Global is prohibited.

Figure 1. Main classes and relationships

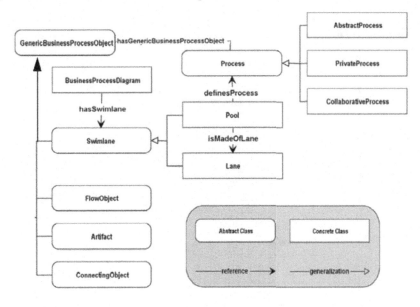

"isMadeOfLane" to state that each pool (class pool is the domain of this property) may contain one or more lane (range of property).

Starting from previous considerations, the core classes and main relationship of the ontology meta-model are represented in Figure 1.

Some special cases have been faced during the development of the BPMN™ ontology meta-model.

A pool, according to BPMN™ specification, may contain both a lane and a generic business process object (different from wwimlanes) (Figure 3). The problem is how to model this concept: does it make two different object properties or the same? The best solution, following the ontology idea, is to provide the same object property because the semantics of the relationship is the same. We define the object property "belongsToPool" with only one class as the range (the ontological class pool) and the domain as the union of the other classes: flow object, artifact and connecting object. In this way, the same property, depending on the context, is used to express both the fact that a Lane belongs to Pool and to lay Flow Object, Artifact and Connecting Object to the specific pool.

Additional Classes

In order to cover all of the BPMN™ complexity, during the BPMN™ meta-model development, we define concepts modeled as ontological classes that are not clearly defined in the BPMN™ specification.

Copyright © 2009, IGI Global, distributing in print or electronic forms without written permission of IGI Global is prohibited.

Figure 2. Ontological property belongsToLane and belongsToPool

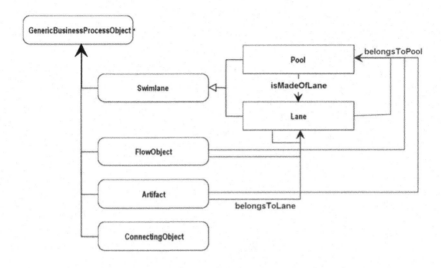

Figure 3. Ontological class trigger

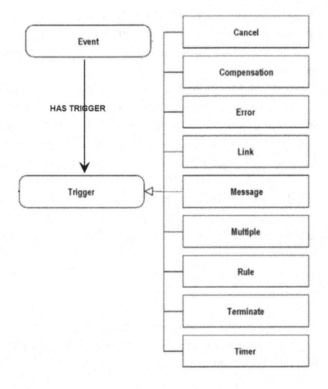

Copyright © 2009, IGI Global, distributing in print or electronic forms without written permission of IGI Global is prohibited.

As an example, we consider the class trigger. We observe that a trigger is the mechanism that allows an event to start, so a trigger is lain to the events that allow it to start. BPMN™ specification defines some properties for a trigger; for instance, if a trigger is of type timer, it has the property timeCycle that defines the duration of the event and timeDate that defines when the event starts. We link the ontological class "trigger" with the event by the property "hasTrigger." The class trigger is made up of several sub-classes, each of them, according to the BPMN™ specification, expresses a special type of trigger (Figure 4).

FROM META-MODEL TO MODEL

By creating the individuals of the classes and properties for each concept, it is possible to obtain a well-defined business process model.

Ontology Representation of Web Application Design Methodology

The observation made up until now allow to realize a meta-model in OWL ontological language and to obtain a specific model adding individuals. According to the same idea, the meta-models related to the other design methodologies considered in this work have been realized.

In order to not weigh down the reading, we do not get into the technical details that brought to the realization of the meta-models related to the IDM methodology; nevertheless, it is observed that the realized meta-model reflects all the peculiarities of the methodology beginning from the separation of the design aspects (it exists a meta-model for IDM and one for P-IDM) and describes all the primitives of modeling contemplated by the methodology. Of course, the existing semantic connections between primitives have been respected; the obtained meta-model, in conclusion, represents a knowledge base for the methodologies that it represents.

In the realization of the meta-models related to the IDM methodology, it is chosen to respectively build two separate meta-models for IDM and PIDM: the two designs, as underlined in Chapter III, concern two well-separated aspects of the Web application design: on one hand the design of the contents and on the other hand the design of the pages in which the contents are inserted. The two designs can live independently from one another; in fact, even though they exist some rules of mapping that allow easily having the passage from one to the other, P-IDM can use, as definition of the information content and of the semantic relationships between them, not only IDM but whatever information contents design methodology; therefore, it is possible to use the information model of W2000 as methodology to

Copyright © 2009, IGI Global, distributing in print or electronic forms without written permission of IGI Global is prohibited.

structure the information and to pass subsequently to P-IDM to point out as this information they will be shown to the end user.

Meta-Model Integration

The design of a complex Web information system, as it will be clearer in the following chapters, integrates, in some cases, the know-how coming from the user experience design and the know- how coming from the business processes representation.

In the phase of integration, the ontologies are particularly useful: at a technological level the integration consists, in fact, to merge, in an appropriated way, the meta-models of BPMN™, IDM and P-IDM realized in times and for different purposes. In a well-specified point of this work, it has been important to link together the meta-models to realize other meta-models that they succeeded in understanding all of the peculiarities of the meta-models of origin, and that they added those coming from the methodological guidelines provided, as it will be exposed subsequently.

To do this, it is really suitable the mechanism of import of ontologies that allows to gather in a unique ontology several ontologies, and, therefore, in our case different meta-models. Of course in some cases it has not only been necessary to connect among them, with the addition of appropriate object properties, the relative meta-models but also to add, according to the observations coming from the methodological guidelines, some new concepts.

Wanting to maintain once more the separation between the design of the information and that of the pages, two meta-models have been realized: one that integrates the meta-model IDM with the specific BPMN™ and anything else, and another that integrates the meta-model PIDM once more with the specific BPMN™.

This last strategy will be clearer subsequently in the reading when the methodological guidelines will be introduced.

CONCLUSION

Methodologies are without a doubt essential for the development of a project from the solid foundations. If undisputed it is the effectiveness of the methodologies, even more important it is the presence of a set of tools that not only facilitates the designer in the application of the methodology but also in the possibility to see, in brief times, a first realization of its project.

The first step to face in this challenging project is without a doubt converting the ideas contained in the methodology in a language close to the computer allow, through a model-driven approach, the realization of the tools and the necessary outputs to first, validate the design and subsequently to get the final application.

Copyright © 2009, IGI Global, distributing in print or electronic forms without written permission of IGI Global is prohibited.

The adopted approach in this work to make the realized design machine-readable is the ontological approach; surely, such an approach is innovative in comparison to the "traditional" XML transformations completed up until this moment and it introduces several advantages: first, the possibility to assign, according to an ontological approach, a semantic meaning to the modeling primitives that can be connected to each other in a native way. The ontological approach, thanks to the mechanism of import that is particularly effective, allows to gather in a unique knowledge base the knowledge of domain (the meta-models) that have been conceptualized in different moments and with different goals and to amalgamate with a relative simplicity the concepts coming from different meta-models.

Finally, thanks to the use of the ontology, it is possible to dispose of a semantic net that can easily be managed and that can easily be updated with the purpose of introducing, if it was necessary, new primitives of modeling.

The ontological representation described in this paragraph has been realized thanks to the aid of an editor of ontologies realized by Stanford University. The tool, known as "protégé," is one of the best and most used in the international scientific area.

We describe in the following parts of this work a special purpose editor that we design and implement that allows using the methodologies such as BPMN™, IDM, PIDM and exporting in an ontological format the obtained design.

REFERENCES

Cardoso, J. (2007). The semantic Web vision: Where are we?. *IEEE Intelligent Systems, 22*(5), 84-88.

Corcho, O.R., Mariano, F., Gómez-Pérez, A., & López-Cima, A. (2005). Building legal ontologies with METHONTOLOGY and WebODE. In: R. Benjamins, P. Casanovas, J. Breuker, & A. Gangemi, *Law and the Semantic Web,* (pp. 142-157). Springer-Verlag.

Gröninger, M., & Fox, M.S. (1995). Methodology for the design and evaluation of ontologies. *Proceedings From IJCAI'95, Workshop on Basic Ontological Issues in Knowledge Sharing.* Montreal Canada.

Mariano F. L., Gómez-Pérez, A. & Juristo, N. (1997). Methontology: From ontological art towards ontological engineering. *Proceedings of the Symposium on Ontological Engineering of AAAI,* (pp. 33-40). Stanford Universusty, CA.

Noy, D., & McGuinness, D. (2001). *Ontology development 101: A guide to creating your first ontology.* (Tech. Rep. KSL-01-05 and Stanford Medical Informatics

Copyright © 2009, IGI Global, distributing in print or electronic forms without written permission of IGI Global is prohibited.

Technical Report SMI-2001-0880) Stanford University: Stanford Knowledge Systems Laboratory.

OMG. (1997). *Object constraint language specification, (version 1.1). Recommendation.*

Uschold, M., & King, M. (1995). Towards a methodology for building ontologies. *Workshop on Basic Ontological Issues in Knowledge Sharing, held in conjunction with IJCAI-95.* Montreal, Canada.

W3C. (2004). *OWL Web ontology language reference.*

W3C. (2004). *RDF vocabulary description language 1.0: RDF schema.*

W3C. (2004). *RDF/XML syntax specification W3C recommendation.*

Copyright © 2009, IGI Global, distributing in print or electronic forms without written permission of IGI Global is prohibited.

Section II
The Methodologies

The coverage of this section represents the most important aspect of the book. Here, the two methodologies, for the internal and the external users, are presented. As will be detailed in the section, we make a difference between these users. Those internal use mainly the function of intranet to perform their daily activities driven essentially by the data and by the flow of BPs; while, the external users to perform their task, use mainly the Web. This kind of users is an integrating part of the Company when they use the BPs oriented to provide services to the customers. To approach the first category, the methodology is based on the BPs flow and provides a guideline to map each task with a Portlet. It seems very similar to the use of Workflow engines; however, the approach is quite different. In fact, our starting point is very pragmatic: the business experts design the BPs without considering the implementation details, and then an IT expert can refine this BPs according to the developers needs. The final model is used by the tool that performs the automatic generation of the Portlet. When the BPs change, it is possible to automatic generate the new application. The methodology for the other category, the external users, is very different because it requires an effective integration between the design of BPs and the design of the user experience. The integration occurs between the P-IDM model and the BPs creating a new model called P-IDM Process. Every methodology is presented using a simple case study that helps the reader to better understand each step; immediately, after, a more complex and real case study is used to apply the methodology. Finally, although the requirements elicitation is not part of our research, it is interesting to deal with this argument for the completeness of coverage. For this reason in the Chapter V it is presented a brief introduction to the requirement analysis.

Chapter V
The Design Vision

INTRODUCTION

From the considerations made in the previous chapters, it emerges that the design of the complex Web information system must consider in a separate way two most important aspects of Web application: on one hand, the definition of the business processes, and on the other hand, to identify an optimal way to define what information is remarkable and how to present this information to the final user.

Only after the definition of these two designs made up in a separate way is it possible to go on with the integration activity, linking together the problems of both. At this point of the job, a consideration arises: it is possible that in a Web application, the only information about the business processes can be enough for structuring with an engineering approach the Web application. The same approach, however, is not practicable for the Web applications for which, contrarily, it is necessary to also associate some other information that can be also completely different in comparison to those tightly connected to the business processes, but that they result essential so that the application is indeed useful for the end user.

Copyright © 2009, IGI Global, distributing in print or electronic forms without written permission of IGI Global is prohibited.

A BRIEF INTRODUCTION TO THE REQUIREMENT ANALYSIS

This section briefly introduces the bases of the requirement elicitation. It is based on two approaches: AWARE to describe the requirements of the Web application, and a modeling technique able to extract and analyze the business process goals. Furthermore, at the end, we introduce an example (the supply in a mill company) where these approaches are applied.

The Requirement Elicitation Bases

This paragraph describes the requirement elicitation approach based on Axel van Lamsweerde's goal-oriented requirements engineering, developed inside the KAOS project (Dardenne, van Lamsweerde, & Fickas, 1993). The approach is based on the experience of UWA project (UWA Consortium, 2001).

Using the work performed by Yue (1987), KAOS approached the requirements engineering problem from a new point of view: the *goal-oriented* approach. The basic idea of this new approach is explicating the why of the requirements. Quoting van Lamsweerde, "[before goal-oriented requirements engineering] the requirements on data and operations were just there; one could not capture why they were there, and whether they were sufficient" (van Lamsweerde, 2000). Van Lamsweerde's goal-oriented requirements engineering approach has three levels of modeling: (i) the meta level (to describe the domain-independent abstractions). The model contains the concepts of goal, requirement, object, entity, and so on; (ii) the base level (to model the domain-dependent abstractions, such as service, telephone, bandwidth, etc.). The meta-level model provides the guidelines on how to conduct a requirements engineering activity. For example, since a goal and requirement are linked by an operational link, every concept in the base level, that is an instance of a meta-level requirement, must be linked to an instance of a meta-level goal by an instance of a meta-level operational link; (iii) the instance level to model specific instances of the domain-level concepts.

This goal-oriented requirement's engineering is universally accepted in the academic community worldwide; thus, it is used as the base of our approach. In order to improve the relationships between a software artifact and the surrounding world, the work of Michael Jackson's *World and Machine* (Jackson, 1995) is used. It represents a cornerstone in understanding the relationships between a software artifact and the surrounding world.

Starting from this point of view, in Figure 1 and 2, the overall requirements engineering meta-model of AWARE approach is shown: the elements and their relationships, whereas the latter emphasizes the inheritance relationships between them.

Copyright © 2009, IGI Global, distributing in print or electronic forms without written permission of IGI Global is prohibited.

A stakeholder is someone or something that has an interest in the system. The stakeholder concept is extremely generic (practically anything can be a stakeholder); there, the definition is very vague. A stakeholder could be (but is not limited to): the end users of the system, the developers of the system, the buyers, the managers (i.e., people who, again, will not use the system, but who manage people who do).

The task to model the stakeholders is of utmost importance, in order to manage the conflicts between the goals of different stakeholders or for the requirements traceability.

The stakeholder is different from an actor in UML® (Booch, Jacobson, & Rumbaugh, 1998) terms: the UML® actor models someone or something interacting with the system; instead, a stakeholder does not necessarily interact with the system. For example, a manager will probably be involved in the test of the system running during a commercial demo, but he/she will never interact with it. For these reasons, often the managers are modeled as stakeholders, because they actually have an interest in the system.

A *goal* is a high-level, long-term objective *owned* by one or more stakeholders. In other words, given the nature of the applications at play, a user-centered approach was employed. In the user-centered approach, the center of the world is the user of the system. In this approach, every goal can be traced back to its owners. As emphasized in the meta-model in Figure 1, a stakeholder may own an arbitrary number of goals, but it must own at least one. From this point of view, the AWARE approach is like the UML® one: an actor must be associated to at least one use case and a goal must be owned by an arbitrary number of stakeholders but must be

Figure 1. The overall meta-model

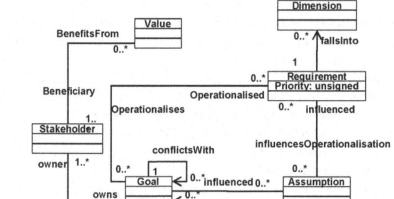

Copyright © 2009, IGI Global, distributing in print or electronic forms without written permission of IGI Global is prohibited.

Figure 2. The inheritance view of the meta-model

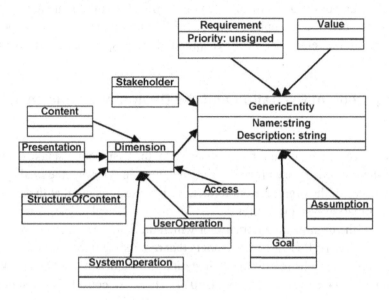

owned by at least one. In fact, a goal that interests noone is a non-goal, and should therefore be removed.

A goal has a specific value for its stakeholders. The actual value delivered represents the why of the ownership, and is strictly dependent on both the goal and the stakeholder.

In order to be strictly compliant with the UML® (semi-formal) semantics, the value is not modeled as a link attribute; in fact, a link attribute means that there must be exactly one instance of the link class for each pair of instances of the associated classes. Considering this a bit too restrictive, in the approach the value is represented as a pair of normal relationships between Goal and Value, and Value and Stakeholder respectively. In addition, a redundant association between Stakeholder and Goal represents the ownership. In this way, the flexibility is improved, and it is possible to represent the goals shared between several users but with different values.

High-level goals (defined as the ultimate desires of stakeholders) have to be refined into lower-level goals. The refinement process is necessary because a high-level goal is too abstract, too much at high-level of abstraction and too long-term to be used by designers. Therefore, it has to be refined into lower-level goals.

The refinement process helps to find the conflicts. A conflict is a relation between two goals/requirements, that the two cannot be fulfilled together. The conflicts must therefore be solved or the designers will not know what to do. A conflict must be

Copyright © 2009, IGI Global, distributing in print or electronic forms without written permission of IGI Global is prohibited.

solved as soon as possible, and in any case before the operational step (see below), that is, before any of the goals involved in the conflict are turned into actual, low-level requirements. The examples of the AWARE requirement elicitation approach are presented in the remainder of this chapter and in the specific case study of the book.

The Requirement Elicitation and the Design of an Information System

During the development of an information system, the designer must take the business (and then the enterprise processes) into account. In this way, the final system fulfils the needs of the organization; in fact, we have to consider that the development of information system requires the resolution of technical problems and a good knowledge of the organization domain for which the information systems will be realized. In literature, there are many papers that remark the important to make the process design before the requirement elicitation techniques (Yu, 1995;Kavakli & Loucopoulos, 2004; Regev & Wegmann, 2004). However, considering that during the design of an information system, people must be involved, applications and business process, new requirement elicitation techniques are created in order to take into account all of these factors. Thus, there are several methodologies able to derive the goals from the business process design (De la Vara, 2006; González & Sánchez Díaz, 2007). In the following paragraphs, we introduce this technique (used in the following as a bridge between the AWARE goals and business goals).

The technique has three stages: in the first one, the business strategies are described by a set of statements (about the organizational mission, the strategic goals, etc.); in the second stage, the business infrastructure is designed using process map, role model, and so forht. In the third stage, the most important one, the business process goals are extracted and analyzed. These goals are the bases of the requirements. A definition of goal in agreement with the AWARE definition is used in this state: a goal is a high-level objective or state that must be reached. From this point of view, each process have an associated goal that must be reached by a specific user during its execution; also, the sub-goals are operational goals and could be considered as milestones within the process. The output is a set of use cases that the system must fulfill to satisfy the enterprise needs.

In the last stage, the approach is based on the creation of a goal's tree for the definition of the business goals. The tree is based on the structural patterns of the BPMN™ diagrams (OMG, 2006). The process is the high-level goal that could be refined using the events with triggers and tasks of BPMN™ represented into the tree. The elements of the tree are labeled in order to define the "automated goal," the "manual goal," the "ceased goal" (when the element is ceased because the in-

Copyright © 2009, IGI Global, distributing in print or electronic forms without written permission of IGI Global is prohibited.

formation system carries out the task or goal autonomously), and the "automatic goal" (the tasks that the information system perform automatically). At the end, after the tree creation, a use case model can be derived from it.

Starting from this technique, we use it not to derive the Web application goal, but to make a mapping between the goal analysis (made with AWARE) and the business process design in BMPN™ notation. In order to improve the explanation, in the following paragraphs a complete example of requirements elicitation is presented.

Example: The Supply Chain in a Mill Company

The example is about the supply process of raw material in a mill company. In detail, the analyzed process manages the arrival of purchased wheat in the mill plant: the planning of the wheat load, the chemical analyses on each arrival and its storage in specific silos categorized according to wheat quality and country of origin.

The scheduling process provides the arrival plan of the wheat load in a specific time and sequence in order: (i) to reduce the stored quantity, (ii) to optimize the storage units of silos and (iii) to avoid too many deliveries at the same time. Every day, the scheduler traces the number of wheat load, their quality, and the company gates that will accept the load (all of this information will be used to properly store the wheat).

According to the contracts, the schedule supervisor agrees with the supplier about the arrival in order to maximize the efficiency of the silos: each wheat supply could be delivered with more loads in different days (within a specific period established in the sale contract). The charge of wheat transport could be assigned to the supplier (in this case the wheat is directly delivered to the plan sometimes without a specific supervisor agreement) or could be assigned to the mill company (in this case the buyer contacts a carrier company).

When a wheat load is scheduled, a preliminary check is made in order to verify the delivered quantity and the quality. If the quality check is positive, the load is weighed and unloaded; in detail, the loaded truck is weighed, then it is unloaded (the wheat is tipped in a pit) and at last the empty truck are re-weighed in order to establish the weight of the load. The truck balance is one for the mill company.

If the preliminary quality check is negative, a specific process to manage legal argument is activated. In detail, the mill company serves the supplier with the notification of non-compliance loads about the quality established in the contract. All the needed tasks to reach an agreement are activated: the mill company can accept the load with a rebate or in extreme cases can refuse the load.

If the contract of supply plans more than one delivery and the preliminary check is negative, the supervisor can activate the legal argument but accepts the low quality

Copyright © 2009, IGI Global, distributing in print or electronic forms without written permission of IGI Global is prohibited.

load waiting to check the quality on the following deliveries; the contract quality is calculated not on the single delivery but as the average of the entire supply. In addition to the preliminary check, during the unloading of the truck, a wheat sample is taken in order to make the chemical analyses and carefully check the quality. The chemical analyses are made outside the mill company; thus, this process is not considered a specific sub-process and is not described in the following. The wheat unloading is made in a pit from which the conveyor belts store it in the silo units.

The unloading is made following the instructions of the store supervisor. The instructions are reported on the unloading document that contains also the silo units in which the wheat must be stored. Using the domain analysis, in the following paragraphs the requirement elicitation is presented. The analysis describes the three stakeholders and their goals.

1. The arrival supervisor. His/her tasks are to trace the incoming wheat loads, to check their quality and to establish the specific silo unit to store it according to the store supervisor (Figure 3). Hence, the system has to provide the stakeholder with a clear view of the arriving wheat loads (highlighting expected quantity and quality) and of the free silo units. The supervisor has to define the order of the arrivals and to sign the completed deliveries. If the quality of the wheat load is low, the supervisor has to report it into the system; in detail, he/she has to activate the legal argument process, to reject the load if the quality is too much low, or to rebate the wheat price. These tasks have several requirements such as signaling the low-quality load and describing

Figure 3. The requirement of the arrival supervisor

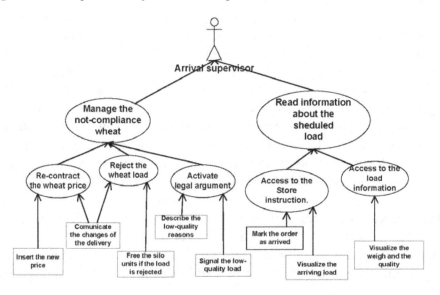

Copyright © 2009, IGI Global, distributing in print or electronic forms without written permission of IGI Global is prohibited.

the cause of the low quality. If the wheat load is rejected, the supervisor has to free the reserved silo units, or if the price is rebated, he/she has to insert the new price into the system.

2. The store supervisor. His/her tasks are to address the load to the specific silo units and to activate the conveyor belts to store the wheat (Figure 4). To make these operations, the supervisor needs the information about the free silo units, the raw wheat reserve and the reserve of floor. When the wheat arrives at the plant, the supervisor has to: (i) establish the silo unit to store it, and (ii) communicate to an arrival supervisor the pit in which the trucks have to unload the wheat; furthermore, he/she needs the information about the scheduled arrivals. These goals have several requirements: to view the quality and the quantity of the arrived wheat, to view the free pit to unload, and to view the free silo units.

3. Supervisor of the arrival plan. There is one supervisor of the arrival plan (Figure 5) for the entire mill company. His/her main tasks are: to check the plan status and to access to the wheat purchase orders. The first task has the following requirements: to view the arrived orders that need to be unloaded, to view the purchase contracts, to establish a date for the delivery and a plan to unload the wheat. The second task has the requirement of viewing the free silo units.

Figure 4. Requirement for the store supervisor

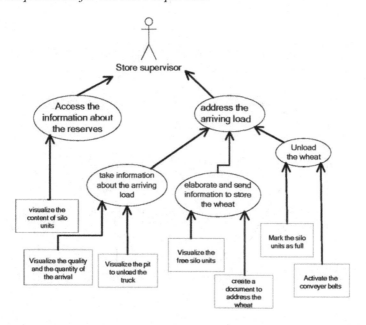

Copyright © 2009, IGI Global, distributing in print or electronic forms without written permission of IGI Global is prohibited.

The requirement to access to the wheat order could be detailed with the requirement to manage the wheat transport and, thus, to view the available transport companies and to choose the type of the truck. To view the available transport, companies could be detailed in viewing all of the transportation companies and to assign a transport to a specific company. The choice of the type of the truck has the requirement to trace all of the information about the unloading operation.

According to the requirement elicitation technique described above, we build the goal tree for the definition of the business goals. The entire process is a goal that will be detailed using all of the information about itself and also its sub-processes. All of the tasks that are not directly connected with the information system are not considered in the tree creation. The sub-processes are sub-goals that are composed of one or more stages. Several tasks play a part in fulfilling the same main goal; in this case, they are linked between themselves with the aggregation symbol "AND." These tasks are developed in sequence or simultaneously or are tasks that in BPMN™ notation are in input or in output to a "parallel gateway." In the cases in which the BPMN™ has "exclusive gateway" or when a "sequence flow" has more than one branch, the tasks are connected to the parent through the OR symbol.

In the first stage, the main goals are extracted and defined from the process; then, the tasks and the sub-tasks (that need to fulfil the main goals) are described in the tree. Thus, it is possible to classify the goals that are not involved in the definition

Figure 5. Requirement of the arrival planner

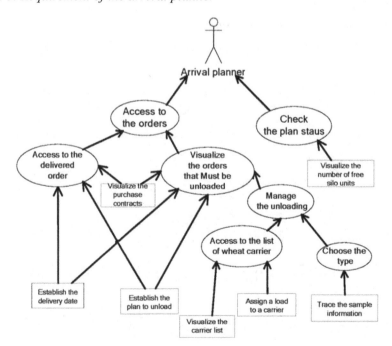

Copyright © 2009, IGI Global, distributing in print or electronic forms without written permission of IGI Global is prohibited.

of the operational requirements. After the definition of the goal tree, it is possible to associate the specific goal derived from the Web application requirement analysis. In the following figures, we report the complete BPMN™ diagrams of the process. In the first diagram, the two main phases of the process are the planning of the arrivals and the trace of the orders.

The planning of the arrivals causes the analysis of the free silos and free silo units and the request of the scheduled contracts. The access to the contracts means the access to the orders delivered by a supplier (that not require the transport) or to the orders that required the definition of the carrier; in this last case, means that the mill needs to sign a carrier, otherwise the association between the silo units and the wheat load is made.

The output of this sub-process is the plan document (one of the two main goals of the entire process).

The trace of the arrival needs to be weighed, unloaded and the checked for quality. The weighing goal and the unloading goal are composed in the store phase in which conveyor belts are activated and the wheat weight are registered. Each wheat example is marked using RFID technologies.

After the definition of the goal tree, in the following figure it is possible to see the association between the goals derived from the process and the goal derived from the Web application analysis.

Figure 6. Process of the arrival of purchased wheat

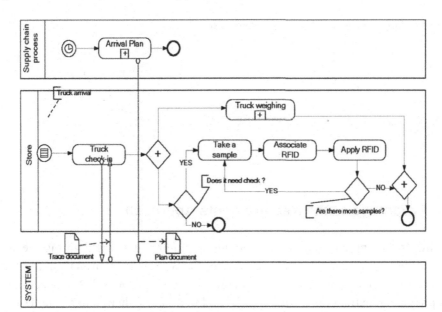

Copyright © 2009, IGI Global, distributing in print or electronic forms without written permission of IGI Global is prohibited.

Figure 7. Sub-process of the arrival scheduling

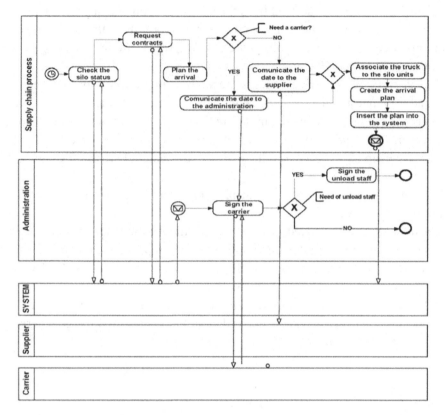

Figure 8. Sub-process of the wheat weighting

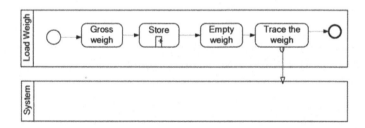

The Advantage of the Requirements Approach

The illustrated approach allows describing the requirements highlighting the association between the requirements derived by the Web application analysis and the requirements derived by the business process. Starting from the BPMN™ diagrams, it is possible to extract the business goals and to describe them into a tree. Using

Copyright © 2009, IGI Global, distributing in print or electronic forms without written permission of IGI Global is prohibited.

Figure 9. Sub-process of the "wheat store"

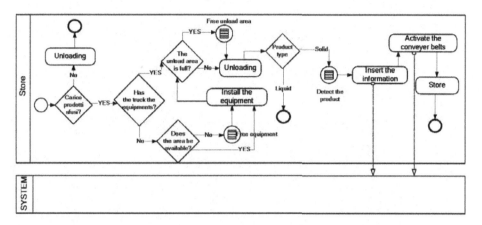

Figure 10. Sub-process of the weigh and quality check

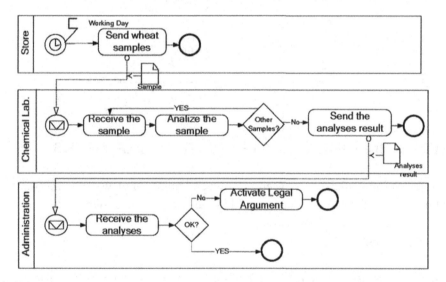

the built tree, it is possible to introduce the requirement of the IT experts. This association allows the alignment between the business design and the IT design; in this way, it is certain that the analysis of the IT expert will support the business process. Also, the integrated representation helps the IT designer to customize the final system in order to support better the enterprise process.

Copyright © 2009, IGI Global, distributing in print or electronic forms without written permission of IGI Global is prohibited.

Figure 11. The goal tree derived by the BPMN diagram of the process of the arrival of purchased wheat

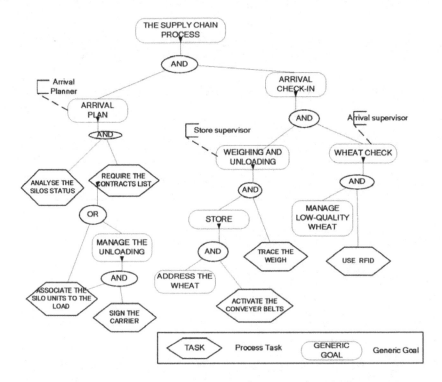

SEVERAL INFORMATION SYSTEMS TYPES OF USERS

The information system can be seen from several points of view depending on the final user that is the stakeholder involved in the information system.

External User

For the external user of the information system, the information system itself is a contact point between the users and the company, and for this reason, they want to see in the information system all of the information strictly related to the company in order to know and to evaluate it.

The company for its point of view, not only uses the Web platform as a visiting card towards the user, but also as a tool to put the customer in contact with the company directly involving it in the execution of some well-precise steps of the business processes. You should not only think about the Web sites of electronic commerce in which a consumer has involved in the business processes with the goal to insert all those necessary information to the completion of the purchase,

Copyright © 2009, IGI Global, distributing in print or electronic forms without written permission of IGI Global is prohibited.

Figure 12. The association between the process goal and the web application goal

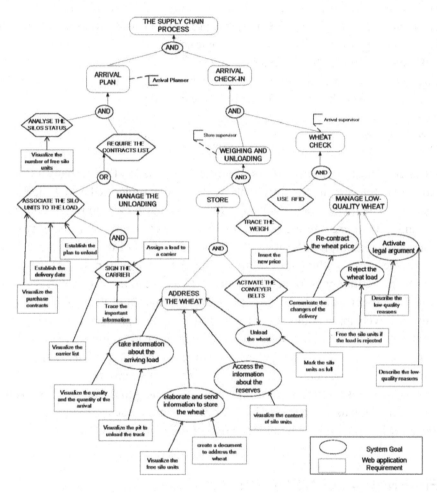

but also to the companies that, through the Web, transfer part of their activities to the customer.

The immediate advantage of this business politics, adopted more and more not only by the big companies but also from the small and medium size ones, allows, on one hand, improving their own inside business processes (making the task to perform different steps of the business processes directly fall on the customer, where it is possible to free inside resources in order to move them on other types of activity); on the other hand, it allows notably increasing the quality of the offered service and therefore always attracting a greater number of customers.

The external users, therefore, are customers that must be searched and must remain faithful and the Web application is a powerful retention tool for old custom-

Copyright © 2009, IGI Global, distributing in print or electronic forms without written permission of IGI Global is prohibited.

ers, therefore the company is forced to not only invest continually for identifying new services to offer to the customer, but also to offer these services in a way much simpler and effective as possible. It is in this typology of Web applications that the logics of management of the user experience are woven with those of management of the business processes. The created complexity produces the necessity to not leave the expert completely free to write some code in which the business processes are directly wired, but rather to think to a methodology of design that drives the designer in the difficulty task of fusion of the two know-how.

Internal User

For the internal user, the information system, both that used by the company intranet or through the Internet, it is an inimitable work tool that replaces the "old" desktop applications. The inside company user, after a first phase of training oriented to understand how to execute the own tasks inside the company, exclusively works with the input and output information of the several steps of the business process that he/she performs without the addition of another information that, as we have seen in the preceding paragraph, are particularly useful to the external user. As a proof of this observation, there is the birth and affirmation of the portlet applications that are Web applications that have the tendency to reproduce on the Web the "metaphor desktop" or rather, they allow the final user to configure his/her own work environment: the final user will insert on his/her own desktop (virtual desktop) all of the useful applications to carrying out his/her daily activities.

All this brings us to think that the applications oriented to the inside user do not need a design of the user experience but the only business process design, carefully detailed, allows reaching the implementation of the final application.

REFERENCE ARCHITECTURE

Starting from the considerations made up in the previous paragraph, it is necessary to follow two methodological approaches completely differently depending on the user to which the Web application is oriented: the external or internal user of the company.

Two typologies of very different types of users require two different approaches.

In Figure 13, there is a first architecture to which we will refer in the following parts of this job.

Copyright © 2009, IGI Global, distributing in print or electronic forms without written permission of IGI Global is prohibited.

Figure 13. Overview of a general architecture

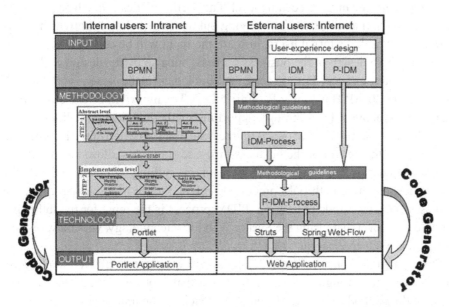

The proposed architecture is made up of four levels: an initial level (named input level); one methodological that represents the heart of the present job; one more exquisitely technological, and finally the final output.

In regards to the internal users that use the information system almost exclusively through the company intranet, the only input required is the BPMN™ design of the business processes to implement the final Web application. We specify that, of course, it is not said that the internal users must access the information system exclusively through the company intranet, but it is possible, if the company allows this, that the users use another access channel also leaving the completed considerations unchanged.

It is clear that, since the design of the business processes made up by the business expert is very often not enough alone to allow the realization of the whole Web application because it lacks several pieces of information that are not of competence of the business expert, the methodological level drives, according to a methodology conceived in this job, to a refinement of the initial business process design up to come to a business process design more possible close to the requirements of the IT expert. The methodology of refinement, that will be the object of Chapter VIII, is made up of two steps; the first step allows obtaining the so defined "workflow BPMN™" design or, rather, a design of the business process close to the implementation requirements and in a second step the methodology drives the designer in the transition from the workflow BPMN™ to a specific technology of reference. We have chosen to use the portlet technology that, in Figure 12, has been represented

Copyright © 2009, IGI Global, distributing in print or electronic forms without written permission of IGI Global is prohibited.

in the technological level. The output, the portlet application, is clearly bound to the technology selected in the preceding level. The portlet application will be provided, therefore, to the internal users for carrying out their normal daily activities.

In regards to the external users, instead, the input will be constituted not only by the BPMN™ design of the business process, but also by the design of the user experience made up according to ad hoc methodologies (in the present work we have chosen IDM / PIDM [Bolchini & Paolini, 2006]). The input will be elaborated then in the methodological level through opportune methodological guidelines, better defined in the Chapter VI, that they will integrate first the design of the information contents with the design of the business processes (and this allows obtaining the IDM process design) and, in a second moment, everything will meet in the PIDM process design where both IDM process design and, once more the design of the business processes, are kept in mind. PIDM process is the input for the following technological level that, using the Spring Web Flow technology, will allow obtaining the final Web application.

The transition from the methodological aspect to the final Web application could be made up through code generation tools that opportunely read the model in output at the methodological level and allow reaching the final application without the intervention of the programmer people. This transition will be described in details in Chapter VI as it regards to the part related to the external user; for the internal user, we have yet to obtain any result, and it is not ready to be presented in this work.

An important thing to underline is that the format of interchange that allows transiting from the methodological level to the technological level in both the approaches the ontological language OWL (W3C, 2004) through which, as underlined in the preceding chapters, the meta-model of the single methodologies have been defined.

DIFFERENT EXPERTS BEEN INVOLVED IN THE DESIGN AND REALIZATION OF THE SYSTEM

The design of a system, in which is kept in consideration both the aspects tied up to the business process logic and those (if they exist) tied up to the design of the user experience, requires the presence of two separate professionalisms that work together constantly cooperating. We can individualize two different typologies of experts that have directly been involved in this project: business experts and IT experts.

The first ones, the *business experts*, know (or they analyze) the company in which they operate.

Copyright © 2009, IGI Global, distributing in print or electronic forms without written permission of IGI Global is prohibited.

The business experts have the direct contact with those whom perform his/her own job inside of the company every day, and as a fundamental goal they have to create, in every moment, the best conditions that allow the company to increase the real billing-reducing times and costs. It is essential, to provide to the business experts, once they know how to execute the business process, the possibility of analyzing its performances and eventually to intervene with the goal of converging on the logics of the business process with the inside and market demands of the company.

On the other side, the *IT experts* are those people which worry about constantly adapting the information system to the demands of the company noticed by the business expert. They deal, therefore, with the technological aspect, and they are called to understand the applications of the business expert to translate them in application logic.

The first fundamental problem that is set to this point is tied up to the difference of existing language among these two typologies of professionals. The first ones, the business experts, are interested in a high-level analysis of the working of the company; the second ones, the IT experts, are interested, instead, in all of the technical details related to the business processes.

FLEXIBILITY OF THE INFORMATION SYSTEM

Very often, the existing semantic gap between business experts and IT experts is translated in a methodological gap: the business experts analyzing the business processes individualize possible points to intervention with the goal to improve the company work, they advance proposals, and they pass their business processes design to the IT experts that, if not expressly driven by an appropriate methodology of design, incur into the error to directly cable the logic of the business processes in the application logic.

This makes the final information system, particularly rigid, a simple change to the flow of the business processes could also be reflected in an intervention of software maintenance that could be very complex and, in consequence, requiring an expensive effort in terms both of time and costs. To avoid this, very often there is the tendency to not effect the intervention of maintenance incurring into the serious error to adapt the business processes to the information system and not the information system to the business processes as instead would be desirable.

The flexibility of the information system, of the highest importance in the modern companies, either of big dimensions or of middle to small dimensions, results so a fundamental element for the success of the company itself; therefore, it is important

Copyright © 2009, IGI Global, distributing in print or electronic forms without written permission of IGI Global is prohibited.

to think to this requirement and, de facto, it requires a radical change of the actual architectures of the information systems.

FOUR LEVEL ARCHITECTURE FOR THE MODERN WEB INFORMATION SYSTEM

From the considerations made up in the preceding paragraphs, the true hard core of the design emerges that realization and maintenance of the information system is on the definition, the design and redesign of business processes, and the success of the underlying information system depends on the possibility of sharing ideas, founding on a common language among the involved experts. To succeed in facing this problem, it has immediately emerged that the typical three levels of architecture of a modern information system are not enough alone to manage such levels of complexity.

It is necessary, therefore, to *add a further level that allows to separate the logic of the business process from the application logic*. In this way, creating a level that focuses in a special way on the management of the business process, both the business experts and the IT experts have a *common base* on which to be able to operate for sharing their own ideas.

The three levels currently present in the modern information systems are:

- *Data Level* constituted by a centralized or distributed database
- *Application level* where there is the business logic and where data coming from the underlying level are managed
- *Presentation level* that allows the end user to interact with the business logic

To the traditional three levels of architecture, we add in this job a fourth level, *the level of the business process* to be used as a link among the two typologies of experts involved in the phases of analysis, design and redesign of the business process. In the specific one:

- The business experts can focus on the management of the business process and if necessary, can intervene on the business process with the goal of modifying the operational formalities of the company. Thanks to the separation of the levels, a change to the business processes will immediately reflect on the application that implements the business processes without asking for an overall re-design or re-implementation. With the proposed architecture, a change in the business processes will immediately reflect a change in the application

Copyright © 2009, IGI Global, distributing in print or electronic forms without written permission of IGI Global is prohibited.

Figure 14. Detailed view of a information system four-level architecture

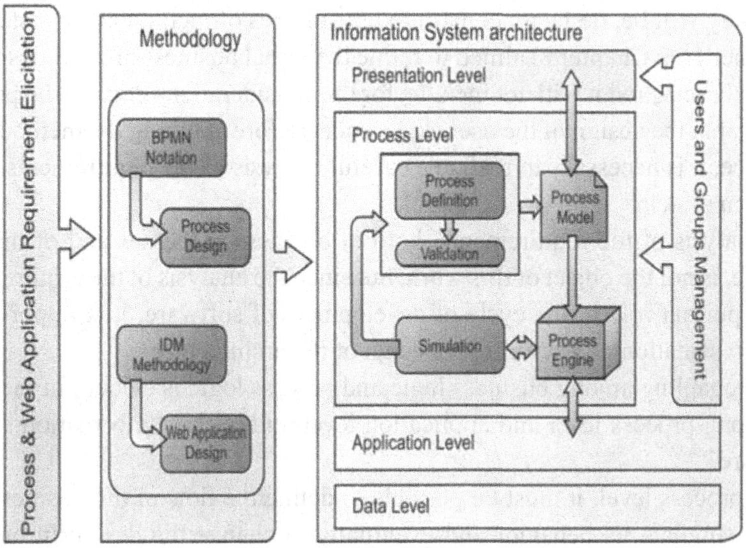

because a change in the business process flow will implicate a change to the management of the business logic and not a change to the business logic. In this way, the final application and the entire information system will become particularly flexible.

- From the IT experts point of view, it the management of the code will be simplified: a change in the business logic implicates a change at the application level and not a change of the flow of the business process or of the presentation aspects.

The tight cooperation between business expert and IT expert is of course in the process level. Business experts and IT experts work in the same level but with a different point of view. In the overall information system design and development, it is clear that the business expert will focus on the process level but the IT experts must work at the application and data level. If we consider IT experts and also the designer of the information system, they work also at the process and the presentation level.

In conclusion, this tight cooperation has a result that a change in the flow of the business process will implicate only an intervention to the process level and not a change in the business logic; on the contrary, a change of the formalities of carrying out a determined task of the business process will implicate a change of the business logic without passing for a change of the business process itself. Figure 14 provides a detailed view of the proposed architecture.

Copyright © 2009, IGI Global, distributing in print or electronic forms without written permission of IGI Global is prohibited.

As it clearly appears in Figure 13, the four levels of architecture of the information system are "fed" from a suitable methodology of design. Of course, the methodology will be, de facto, constituted by a series of methodological steps (as specified better in Chapter 8) aimed to refine the initial business process design for the internal users, and it will not include, for the considerations done in the preceding paragraph, the design of the user experience. Before applying the methodology of reference, it is necessary to realize a careful analysis of the requirements of the information system.

The analysis of the requirements, both of business processes and of the user experience, is not the object of this work, but since the analysis of the requirements has an important role in the cycle of development of software, it is important to give a representation of it within the design of the architecture.

The uncoupling among business logic and process logic is evident in the separation among process level and application level within the "information system architecture."

In the process level, it must be possible to define the flow of the business processes, to simulate its behavior and eventually to change the design in order to answer to the change in requirements of the companies; it has to be possible to define the actors and the tasks of every business process, while in the application level, it has to be possible to implement every task (and therefore it is logical) to individualize the strategies and the technologies to solve *purely technical problems and not conceptual.*

FROM THE METHODOLOGY TO THE TOOLS

The only architecture, equipped also by an appropriate methodology (both useful to realize applications for the internal user of the company and for the external user) is not enough to provide a useful tool to the designer of the information system and/or to whom will use the information system.

It is important then to realize a set of tools that drives the designer both in the definition of the business process and in the application of the methodological guidelines that bring from the business process definition to the final Web application.

To reach this goal, as illustrated in Figure 2, the designer will be endowed by a set of tools realized ad hoc such as a process editor that will allow obtaining in output the model of business process in a selected formal language (OWL). The editor will provide full support to the BPMN™ notation, and it will be designed with the goal of allowing its use by people less experienced in the use of the notation. The tool of design will provide in output a formal representation of the business

Copyright © 2009, IGI Global, distributing in print or electronic forms without written permission of IGI Global is prohibited.

process (based on an ontological model) where all of the information related to the business process will be stored.

The business process model will be input for a process engine tool that will allow, once some points are defined, analyzing the performances of the business processes before it has been put into production. Finally, the process engine is the point of contact with the application level occupying to individualize, in every instant, the appropriate business logic that allows the user to continue with the execution of the business processes.

THE BENEFITS OF THE APPROACH

The proposed approach, both as it regards to the architectural and the methodological aspects, provides several benefits to the designer and to the final user of the Web information system.

First of all, we propose a methodological approach in order to consider the business process as *protagonist* in the overall information system life cycle: business processes are not for us just a requirement made up in the first phase of the design and never considered in the following phases, but they are valid tools to define the activities flow in the company and to be integrated directly in the final application. The approach considers two separate types of users and for each one, there is a specific methodology oriented to solve specific needs and this is surely a benefit; thinking about the needs of the final user is always a good practice of design.

In regards to the methodology oriented to the external user, as it will be clearer, the main advantage is that the integration between business process and user experience is very simple but, at the same time, very effective; the main benefit is that business experts and IT experts may work separately and each one can apply its own competencies without any constraints. As it will be clear, the integration between these two designs allows covering many open issues coming from the integration between business process and user experience.

In regards to the methodology oriented to the development of a Web information system for the internal user, although there are many BPM tools that solve this problem, the approach is quite different and in our opinion more correct. Furthermore, for this type of user, business experts and IT experts may work separately on their own competencies. Business experts design the business process as it is in the reality without considering implementation details, while the IT experts, starting from the business experts design, will be driven in the refinement; the refinement will have a first phase made up in cooperation between business experts and IT experts and in a second phase is exclusively in charge of the IT experts.

Copyright © 2009, IGI Global, distributing in print or electronic forms without written permission of IGI Global is prohibited.

In this way, the benefit is that the designer is sure that the final application is close to the business processes as realized by the business experts.

Finally, if we refer to Figure 13, we can see that it is possible to generate the code in automatic way thanks to the representation of model through a formal language both for the internal user and for the external user.

This fact, together with the consideration that the business process, as protagonist for the design and implementation of the Web information system, will assure a high-level of flexibility to the overall Web information system; a little change in the business process will be immediately traceable in the information system. Indeed, to change the business process means to change the design of the Web information system and thus, the model of the information system. Aince according to the DSM idea it is possible to generate the code immediately, the new code that allows the information system to adapt to the new business process will be obtained in a few minutes and this is a real benefit of our approach.

Another benefit of the approach is the possibility of immediately validating the design with the customer.

It is clear that whatever application domain is considered, the proposed approaches are valid. The methodologies here proposed, in fact, are not oriented to a well-specific application domain:

- In regards to the internal user, the approach starts from the BPMN™ design, and it carries on using the same notation, so since the notation is useful for about all the application domain, also our approach is useful in the same way.
- In regards to the external user, the approach is also generic because it comes from a design methodology for very general Web application, and so it is applicable to all of the application domains.

CONCLUSION

Delineating the architecture of a work is surely a fundamental aspect much complex to face. The considerations mentioned in this chapter have been the result of following iterations: the initial analysis, in fact, did not distinguish among the different typologies of users (internal user or external user) starting from the presupposition that a Web application has to have the same characteristics for both. Subsequently, by a more detailed analysis, we observe that the two typologies of users have some very different peculiarities, and therefore, they need two separate methodological and technological approaches. The same consideration has been given for the definition of the architecture of the information system. In this architecture, valid

Copyright © 2009, IGI Global, distributing in print or electronic forms without written permission of IGI Global is prohibited.

for both typologies of user, it has been of the highest importance to consider a way to render explicit the business processes. Initially, the architecture was a tree-layer architecture in which the application level and the business process level were fused together. To avoid cabling the implementation logic in the business process logic, we have subsequently, decided to separate the two levels obtiaining, in this way, a greater flexibility to the information system and providing to whom is directly interested in the definition and analysis of the business process the possibility of having some useful tools on which to be able to operate.

In conclusion, the proposed architecture is particularly useful, flexible and innovative.

REFERENCES

Bolchini, D., & Paolini, P.(2006). Interactive dialogue model: A design techinique for multichannel applications. *IEEE Transaction on multimedia, 8*(3), 529-541.

Booch, G., Jacobson, I., & Rumbaugh, J. (1998). *The unified modeling language user guide.* Boston, MA: Addison-Wesley Readings.

Dardenne, A., van Lamsweerde, A., & Fickas, S. (1993). Goal-directed requirements acquisition, *In Science of Computer Programming, 20,* 3-50. Amsterdam: Elsevier North-Holland Inc.

De la Vara, J. L. (2006). *Requirements models derivation from organizational models.* MC Thesis. Valencia: University of Technology.

González, J., & Sánchez Díaz, J. (2007). Business process-driven requirements engineering: A goal-based approach. *Proceedings of 8th Workshop on Business Process Modeling, Development and Support in conjunction with Caise 07.*

Jackson, M. (1995). The world and the machine. *Proceedings of the 17th International Conference on Software Engineering,* (pp. 283-292). New York, NY: ACM Press.

Kavakli, E., & Loucopoulos, P. (2004). *Goal modeling in requirements engineering: Analysis and critique of current methods.* Information Modeling Methods and Methodologies, 102-124. Hershey, PA: Idea Group Publishing

OMG. (2006). *Business process modeling notation specification.*

Regev, G., & Wegmann, A. (2004). Defining early IT system requirements with regulation principles: The light switch approach. *Proceedings of the 12th IEEE International, 6*(11), 144- 153. IEEE Computer Society Press.

Copyright © 2009, IGI Global, distributing in print or electronic forms without written permission of IGI Global is prohibited.

UWA Consortium. (2001). *General definition of the UWA framework*. (Tech. rep. EC IST) UWA project (IST-2000-25131).

van Lamsweerde, A. (2000). Requirements engineering in the year 00: A research perspective. *Proceedings of ICSE '2000 – 22nd International Conference on Software Engineering, Limerick*, (pp. 5-19). New York: ACM Press.

W3C. (2004). *OWL Web ontology language reference*.

Yu, E. (1995). *Modeling strategic relationships for process reengineering*. Doctoral thesis. Toronto, University of Toronto.

Yue, K. (1997). What does it mean to say that a specification is complete?. *Proceedings of IWSSD-4 – the Fourth International Workshop on Software Specification and Design*. Monterey, USA. IEEE Computer Society Press.

Copyright © 2009, IGI Global, distributing in print or electronic forms without written permission of IGI Global is prohibited.

Chapter VI
Web Application Process–Oriented Design for External Users

INTRODUCTION

There are several problems to face in the definition of the methodology of design object of this chapter.

In regards to the internal users of the company that mainly use the information system through the company intranet, the principal problems to face is adjusting to a design of the business processes made up by the business experts to a design oriented to the specific demands of the IT experts without changing the underlying representation that is the BPMN™ (OMG, 2006) representation of the business processes.

While in regards to the methodology oriented to the design of Web applications useful for the users external to the company, the problem is more complex because it is of the highest importance to link together the know-how coming from two worlds that, until today, have not had common points but whose integration is an element of success for the birth and for the affirmation of new information systems.

In the present chapter, they will be faced, therefore, the problems inherent to the methodological level of the delineated architecture relative to the external user of the company. The problems for the internal users will be discussed in Chapter VIII.

Copyright © 2009, IGI Global, distributing in print or electronic forms without written permission of IGI Global is prohibited.

The fusion of the IDM (and PIDM) (Bolchini & Paolini, 2006) methodology of design of Web application with the representation of the business processes made up using BPMN™ notation introduces several problems that can be faced by the designer in different ways according to the typology of application to design. It is for this reason that it is not wanted to constrain the designer to a rigid design methodology that forces his/her design choices, but the aim is only to provide some methodological guidelines useful for the designer from which he/she can freely move away in order to make a design according to the needs of the specific application domain.

One of the main reasons that has brought us to delineate some methodological guidelines, surely less rigid and formal than a real methodology, resides in the fact that the models to be integrated, being produced by different professional figures, can give life to different formalities of representation, without considering that the same business processes and the applications introduce details and specific behaviors that need a personalized treatment with the purpose of obtaining an effective integration. A methodology, to be such, has to keep in mind all of the particular cases, but the most frequent risk is that such detailed level brings to the renouncement of some essential aspects of the business processes or of the Web application. In some cases it is possible, in fact, that the business processes assumes a preponderant role, or that the business processes are not very represented, and therefore, its temporal and logical constraints are not respected.

The methodological guidelines, instead of a well-defined design methodology, allow adapting in a faster and elastic way the various cases that can be introduced, in how much they represent directives of modeling that unite the characteristics of universality and opening to those of formality and authoritativeness.

Before illustrating the methodological guidelines of integration, we see what problems there are to face.

METHODOLOGICAL GUIDELINES: A BRIEF OVERVIEW

The last goal of the methodological guidelines is to integrate in an opportune way the know how up to the present moment consolidated, coming from the design of the information related to the Web applications (made up through IDM design methodology) with the know-how coming from the design of the business processes and, accordingly, the resulting know-how coming from the design of the user experience (made up through PIDM design methodology) with the design of the business processes.

For this reason, in the definition of the methodological guidelines, it is assumed to already have been available:

Copyright © 2009, IGI Global, distributing in print or electronic forms without written permission of IGI Global is prohibited.

- the IDM conceptual and logical designs of the Web application (the user experience)
- the page design (PIDM design)
- the design of the business processes (BPMN™ design)

In the special case, we assume that the design of the business processes is made up with a level of granularity how much detailed possible: a task does not have to hide to its inside a set of activities that could be represented as sub-process. If the BPMN™ design is unsuitable for the application of the methodological guidelines, it is necessary to realize a first phase of refinement of the design that consists in dividing in atomic activities those activities with a high level of granularity.

The logical way to be faced for realizing the design of the final complex Web information system that include, therefore, both the problems related to the design of the information and those related to the design of the business processes, are represented in Figure 1.

There are several motivations that bring forth the methodological guidelines of integration starting to think about on one hand, from the design of the Web application and on the other hand from the design of the business processes. First of all, since every type of design asks for the *specific competences*, it is important that professionals with different competences are occupied in a separate and independent way in order to design every aspect. Besides, it has been found that the attempt to integrate Web application and business processes fails if the integration does not happen starting from the two separate designs: it is impossible to make reference

Figure 1. From separated design to the final WIS design

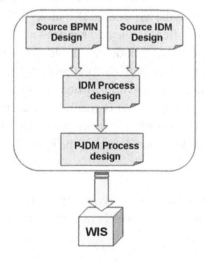

Copyright © 2009, IGI Global, distributing in print or electronic forms without written permission of IGI Global is prohibited.

only to the business processes and to draw the integrated model skipping the modeling of the information unities or contrarily to have available the only design of the Web application to insert the business processes inside the hypertext.

We observe, besides, that the base provided by the two designs allows having a clear picture of the complexity of the Web system to realize, of the differences, of the dependences and of the relationships among the two perspectives.

In the optics of the realization of a process-oriented WIS (Web information system), it is essential to be able to allow the traceability between the two designs; in a few words, it is important to understand in the integrated design what parts are coming from the design of the business processes and what, instead, are coming from the design of the information as they are enjoyed by the end user. In this way, it is possible to quickly individualize how the final application behaves because of a change brought in the design of the business processes and/or a change brought in the design of the user experience.

Design Alignment

In Chapter V, we have demonstrated two different typologies of experts that interact with the goal to complete the design of a process-oriented WIS: the business expert and the IT expert. Of course, the different goals that the two typologies of experts aim to reach bring as an immediate consequence to a strong discordance among the design of the business processes made up by the business analyst and the design of the business processes that instead it is necessary to the designer of the Web application. In the specific one, the design made up by the business expert could introduce some details that are not particularly important for the IT design; in the same way, there could be some details that the business expert does not hold remarkable, but that they could be fundamental for the IT designer.

For instance, the business designer could also insert in the design of the business processes some tasks that, after all, they do not need a Web interface to be able to be executed (task completely automatic or completely manual). The IT designer, from his/her point of view, could need information more detailed about the business processes (what, for instance, are the information on the input data and output data of every task) that the business analyst typically does not provide.

For such reasons, a first operation to make before applying the methodological guidelines consists of the deepened design of the business processes. The study is oriented:

• To individualize possible completely automatic task
• To individualize possible completely manual task and not automatic

Copyright © 2009, IGI Global, distributing in print or electronic forms without written permission of IGI Global is prohibited.

- To require, if necessary, input and output information for every task: typically, the business experts do not provide this level of detail.

At this point, having available a well-detailed BPMN™ diagram, we describe the other problems to face before moving to the definition of the methodological guidelines.

Integration Problems: Open Issues

Before moving on to a detailed description of the methodological guidelines, it is opportune to underline the problems that we notice (open issues). The solution of these problems will constitute, then, the foundations to better define the methodological guidelines that will follow.

Cohabitation in the Integrated Design of Several Types of Information

In a traditional Web application, the disposition of the information is not causal: every part of the Web page is realized subsequently to a well-precise structuring of the contents among which the user can navigate. The navigation, also being free, is driven by the designer that, through semantic relationships, drives the final user through the various contents avoiding that it loses him/her among the information. In the moment in which the designer needs to also consider the presence of the business processes, the discourse is more complicated because:

- The information to which the final user can access can also be information that is functional to the business processes or, rather, information that the final user would not see if there was no specific business processes to drive the logic of the application.
- The navigation inside the Web application is not more driven exclusively from semantic relationships: the presence of the business processes heavily constrains the navigation seeing to it that the final user, when he/she decides to begin a business process, has, close to the free navigation, a well-precise sequence of steps driven from the business process.

More precisely, in regards to the information contents, we can distinguish three typologies of information:

- Information consumed by each task of the business process: for instance, the input data (and output data) of every task.

Copyright © 2009, IGI Global, distributing in print or electronic forms without written permission of IGI Global is prohibited.

- Information strictly related to the business process but not involved in the specific instance of the business process: we think about the fact that the final user could be interested in visualizing information related to some instances of the already finished business processes. In this case, information is connected to the business process, but after all, they must be treated as information not belonging to it and among which the final user can navigate with a free navigation. For this information, therefore, it is important to design its navigation through semantic associations.
- Hypermedia information that is does not belong to the business process: you may think about marketing information that is not connected to the specific business process, but that is support for it and that must be introduced to the final user together with the information of the business process. The final user can read both the information of the business process and the hypermedia information within the same session.

The three typologies of information previously defined, are not between them separated: the hypermedia information can coincide with the data connected to the business process but not involved in the specific instance of the business processes; it is also possible that the same information can be introduced to the final user, depending on the state of the business process (active or concluded) as information of input or information of output. The information of output, when is related to the instances of a business process already terminated, coincides with the information strictly correlated to the business process but not involved in a specific instance of the business process.

An important observation to make is that the IDM design must include all of the input and output information of every task of the considered business process.

Figure 2. Different typologies of information involved in the Web application

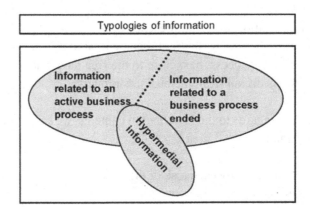

Copyright © 2009, IGI Global, distributing in print or electronic forms without written permission of IGI Global is prohibited.

It is important to suppose in fact, that the designer of the Web application, also not knowing the details of the dynamics of the business process, knows the information involved in it, and he/she can structure this information in a way that is much more close to the demands of the end user. We assume, then, that the information tightly connected to the business process is only a subset of all of the information involved in the Web application. A strong discordance among the two typologies of information implicates a possible error in the design of the Web application.

Cohabitation in the Design of Several Types of Navigation

Another open problem, approached only partly from the design methodologies that have the goal of integrating the design of the business process with the design of the user experience introduced in Chapter III, concerns the navigation among the information. It is important to observe that the pages destined to the execution of the various tasks of the business process, and therefore the information produced or used by the business process, are connected among them according to a predetermined logic from which it is impossible to get further: *the final user can decide to go out from the business process execution but the final user cannot change the order with which the various tasks are performed*. The traditional pages destined to contain and to introduce static information, therefore not business process information, are tied up among them so that can be reached, and it is possible to navigate through them depending on the momentary interest of the final user through the links that are thought for the purpose of capturing the final user attention: in the hypermedia applications is, therefore, the final user that leads the navigation and to do this, he/she is supported by a suitable design of the application.

In the same Web application cohabit, therefore, two different typologies of links (and therefore two different typologies of navigation): the process links and the semantic links that must opportunely be managed in the application design phase.

The fact that the data of the business process are tied up among them according to a logic defined by the business process, does not limit the liberty of the final user to a simple and passive compilation of form; the user has the possibility to go out from the business process that he/she is performing and undertake extra navigation not related to the business process and to be able to return from the suspended activity leaving to the application the task to manage the state of the business process.

Process State

The typologies of information that can be individualized in the Web application are differentiated among them, within the same Web application, according to the state of the business process. During the execution of a task of the business process, the

Copyright © 2009, IGI Global, distributing in print or electronic forms without written permission of IGI Global is prohibited.

final user could decide to temporarily go out from the business process in order to consult, for instance, information of marketing or to consult information related to the instances of the business process already concluded. Of course, continuing with the execution of the business process, the final user has to be able to take back from the point in which he/she had left the business process. This problem must be solved at the design level and not only at the implementation level: the state of the business process heavily engraves on the design of the access structures of the Web application in order to guarantee the final user to continue with the fruition of the available information and to continue with the execution of the business process' task once the user comes back to the abandoned business process.

To clarify the concept, we can think about the scenario of an online purchase of a product. The final user, in the navigation through the pages related to the proposed articles, puts in the shopping cart some articles of interest and then the user reaches the phase of payment. It is possible, for instance, that during this phase the final user wants to navigate toward other pages to know the conditions of payment or other products on sale; several possibilities will be open: after the navigation that currently brings the user out of the execution of business process, it is essential that the user can exactly take back the business process from the point in which had been interrupted. For such a reason, it is necessary to provide to the user all of the *access structures* that, depending on the business process state, will be activated in order to give the possibility being able to re-enter in the business process. The new type of access structures allows to solve:

- The uncertainty of the final user respect to the operations that he/she can complete when he/she comes back from the extra-process navigation in this situation
- The possible insubstantiality of the state of the objects - if during the extra-process navigation (or rather, the navigation that lead the user to go out from the business process in execution), they have been added products, the shopping cart must be updated when the user returns to the business process execution-
- The insubstantiality of the business process state - how long the business process can remain in the suspended state? –

These aspects are of the highest importance, but the actual Web application design methodologies do not take into consideration these aspects, but they leave them in the hands of the developers with all the consequences of the case.

Copyright © 2009, IGI Global, distributing in print or electronic forms without written permission of IGI Global is prohibited.

Business Processes and Web Pages

Another aspect to consider and that it directly strikes again on what the end user perceives is the design of the Web pages that will enclose the information and navigational structures previously designed. In this aspect of the design, it is important to decide, for each specific case study, whether to destine to the business process, or to a part of it, one or more pages of the Web application. It does not exist, however, a fixed rule that allows understanding how many pages to assign to every task; this depends on the level of granularity of the design of the business process previously realized. Sometimes the execution of a task concludes itself in a unique page, other times more pages are still necessary to allow the final user to complete a task; it is also possible that a task does not ask for the intervention of a well-precise actor, but that it is directly performed by the computer without the intervention of the human; in such a case, any correspondence will not be had between a task and the Web pages.

Type of User Involved in the Web Application

In the BPMN™ design, the various involved actors correspond, de facto, to a pool or to a lane inside the pool. In the IDM, PIDM design methodologies, instead, many separate designs as the final users interested to the application are will be had. It is not said, however, that the final user identified in the BPMN™ design correspond with those individualized in the design of the user experience and this because in BPMN™ it is possible to represent with some pools and/or lanes unreal actors of the Web application, that is actors that have been involved in the business process but the formalities of execution of the relative tasks are not of interest. In the substance of the BPMN™ design, it is possible that there are some black boxes that, of course, are not of interest for the Web application. These actors can represent both actors external to the context of the business process and abstract actors that perform an important role in the business process (for example an external application that provides some results useful to complete a business process).

There does not exist, therefore, a general rule to individualize, starting from the BPMN™ design, the actors of the Web application or the BPMN™ actors starting on the user experience design; all depend on the good sense of the designer.

IDM PROCESS: METHODOLOGICAL GUIDELINES

Before listing the methodological guidelines that lead to the integration among the design of the logical design made up with IDM and the design of the business

Copyright © 2009, IGI Global, distributing in print or electronic forms without written permission of IGI Global is prohibited.

process made up with BPMN™, we point out some key points on which to focus the attention.

We underline that in order to give greater emphasis to the fact that the gotten design is the fusion of the design IDM with the design of BPMN™, the resultant design has been denominated *IDM process.*

Dialogue Act of Input and Operation Act

Considering only the IDM design, without referring to the design of the business process, the dialogue acts are nothing else other than the elements that, in the respective topics where they are defined, they pick up some information: the only interaction required to the final user is the selection of the following steps of navigation among those proposed in the design. The dialogue acts, represent, therefore, a tool of fruition of information; for this reason, they have to be considered when it is necessary to introduce the concept of "task" proper tp BPMN™. When the concept of task takes over, since the information related to it can be input or output information (remember that output information are read only), the dialogue acts can also be used to insert some information; in such a case it is essential to make a distinction among input dialogue acts and read-only dialogue acts. The border among these two kinds of dialogue acts is marked by the *state of the business process.*

With the goal of creating a connection among the BPMN™ design and the IDM design, we introduce the concept of operation act. This concept in reality already exists in the IDM methodology, but in this work, the concept has been well formalized. The operation act represents, in fact, the formalization of a well-precise activity that the final user can execute inside the application. An operation act represents, therefore, an elementary operation, and we can say that:

- If the BPMN™ diagram has a level of granularity that allows representing in every task only one elementary operation, there will be a direct correspondence among BPMN™ task and IDM operation act; otherwise, to every BPMN™ task, it is possible to associate more operations act. It is clear that this correspondence is individualized if and only if the task asks for an intervention from the final user in the application.
- If the task is completely manual and/or completely automatic, it will not be possible to individualize such connection.

The connection among the various operations acts, realized through the process links (what we will detail subsequently better), follows the connection among the relative tasks of the BPMN™ design.

Copyright © 2009, IGI Global, distributing in print or electronic forms without written permission of IGI Global is prohibited.

Labeling the links that bring to an operation act the name of the operation act of destination, we are sure that the operation act represents the operation contained in a well-precise task (and therefore in a well-precise state), and that it is possible to reach it only from the specific task that comes before.

Process Link and Semantic Link

The process links, as stated in the preceding paragraph, are useful to address the requirement of traceability between the business processes design and the user experience design. Of course, in the final design, the semantic links will also appear because they come from the IDM design (relevant relation). In the final design, therefore, the coexistence will be between links of business processes and semantic links. The first ones, connected to the state of the business processes, allow performing the different steps; the second ones allow realizing a simple semantic navigation, the same one that would be had if there was no integration with the business processes in the design.

An important observation to make is that there cannot exist relationships coming from the business processes that cannot be navigable to the outside of the business processes context.

In other words, the process links should be a subset of the links of the whole application: this observation is justified by the fact that the information contents involved by the business processes, are numerically inferior in comparison to those introduced by the IDM design of the Web application. Thanks to the experience in this field, we can affirm that this assertion is right in most cases; really, in fact, there could be few cases in which the refinement of the business process introduces some information that is not considered as a topic or a content dialog act during the design of user experience.

This allows us to say that a strong discordance among the two types of link points out an error of design that can come from the business processes design or from the Web application design.

Instance of a Kind of Topic

Thinking about the particular situation in which a business process is started (the start event), it will involve some topics inside the IDM design. Clearly, on that topic, it is essential to create an ad hoc access structure that allows starting the business process. The start of a new business process coincides, clearly, with the instance of a new topic (in which at least a dialogue act is not read only, but it is possible to write in). Therefore, it is important to correspond to a start event of the diagram

Copyright © 2009, IGI Global, distributing in print or electronic forms without written permission of IGI Global is prohibited.

BPMN™ an access structure that allows the user to start the business process. The corresponding element in the IDM diagram takes the name of *introductory act*.

Stop and Resume of a Business Process

An important aspect, not to be underestimated for the frequency with which it is verified, is the possibility of the final user going out into any moment from the area reserved to the business process in order to navigate through the information not related to the business process but semantically connected to it. At the end of the user's navigation, the final user that wants to take back the business process wants to resume in the point where he/she had interrupted his/her process execution. *The user can do this thanks to a special link that holds trace of the last completely performed task and therefore the following one in the sequence of the business process.* Such links represent particular access structures that want to facilitate the use of the application without setting any constraints: in effects, a Web application that constrains the potentialities of the final user preventing to navigate through determined pages, loses usability and dynamism.

For these reasons, in the IDM design integrated with the design of the business process there will be so many access structures as are the tasks where the final user can navigate: particularly such access structures will exactly be situated on the topic related to the dialogue act which the operation act corresponds (this will be subsequently detailed better).

IDM Process: Methodological Guidelines

After an accurate analysis of the individualized problems, we now list the methodological integration guidelines to which have come, and that answer adequately to the open issues previously proposed.

In order to improve the reading and understanding of these methodological guidelines, we provide a chronological order with which the designer, in a theoretical line, will apply them. However, this order does not absolutely have to constrain the designer that is free to return more times on every methodological guideline and that can decide to apply these methodological guidelines according to a different order from the introduced one.

Before definings the methodological guidelines, we explain a simple case study very useful to understand the application of the methodological guidelines.

Copyright © 2009, IGI Global, distributing in print or electronic forms without written permission of IGI Global is prohibited.

Introduction to a Simple Case Study

We refer to a filing paper company. The company wants to design a Web application to support the business process of filing, that is, the location of the documents that will arrive in the warehouse in the boxes. The business process involves three different actors (Figure 3):

- the person responsible
- the warehouseman
- the customer

The person responsible is who manages the request coming from the customer. He/she will generate a list where there will be all of the information useful to the warehouseman to put the box in the ledge.

The warehouseman will locate the boxes in the ledge. The list provided by the person responsible will contain all of the detailed information useful for its task.

The customer requests the service of filing to the company. After the filing is complete, he/she may require access to his/her own documents. As highlighted in

Figure 3. Design BPMN™ of the considered process

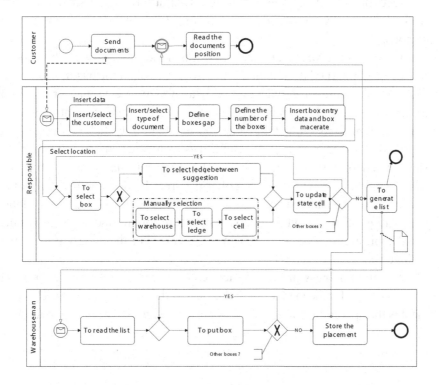

Copyright © 2009, IGI Global, distributing in print or electronic forms without written permission of IGI Global is prohibited.

the previous sections, it is important that the BPMN™ design of the business process and the IDM design are made up by two different experts. In the next figure, there is the BPMN™ design of the business process.

In Figures 4, 5 and 6, we define the IDM design made up for each actor in the business process.

After the business process design and the user experience design for all of the actors is shown, we will focus on the actor "responsible." This actor is selected because the relative design is simple, and at the same time, completed in order to help with the explanation of the methodological guidelines.

Methodological Guidelines

1. **Types of users:** in the IDM methodology, a diagram is realized for every final user, while in BPMN™ a final user can be represented either through a pool or through separate lanes in the same pool. It is possible to have, potentially, an IDM diagram for every pool or lane of the BPMN™ diagram. Clearly, the correspondence is not one to one because a pool of a BPMN™ diagram could also interest an actor (you know, for instance, that in BPMN™ it is possible to represent in a pool an actor external to the company with which the company interacts) not involved in the same Web application. The example here considers that the three pools will have a separate IDM process diagram. As we said in the previous section, we will consider only the pool of the person responsible.

2. **Analysis of the information contents:** it is important to establish what information of the IDM design intervenes in every task of the business process. A same task can involve dialogue acts related to different topics or can refer to the same topic. The analysis of the information contents continues with the distinction among input dialogue acts and read-only dialogue acts. If not expressly suitable in the IDM design, it is also necessary to introduce the slots related to every dialogue act. The slot represents the atomic information while the dialogue act gathers together different homogeneous information unities. In the considered process, for example, both the dialogue act "data" of the "request" topic and the dialogue act "description" and "location" of the "box" topic are involved in the business process. The dialogue acts are input dialogue act.

3. **Start of the business process:** a new element to represent inside the IDM process design has been identified: the start of the business process. This element is the operation strategy (⇧): points to the operation act corresponding to the *first task* of the business process where the operation will be executed. An operation strategy corresponds, therefore, to the start event of the pool (or

Copyright © 2009, IGI Global, distributing in print or electronic forms without written permission of IGI Global is prohibited.

Figure 4. Design IDM for the person responsible

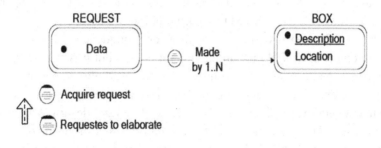

Figure 5. Design IDM for the warehouseman

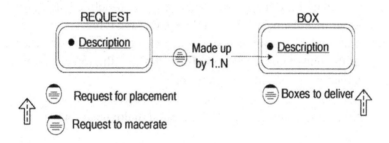

Figure 6. Design IDM for the customer

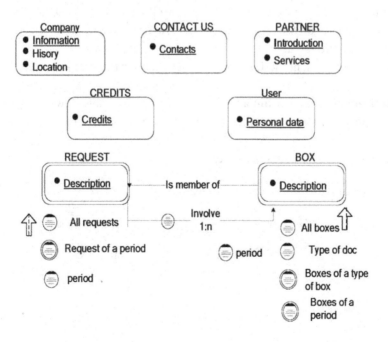

Copyright © 2009, IGI Global, distributing in print or electronic forms without written permission of IGI Global is prohibited.

lane) correspondent to the actor for which the designer is making the design. The case study here considers that the business process starts in the operation act "start new request" related to the kind of topic "request."

4.   **Analysis of the tasks:** we have said that a correspondence can be individual-ized among a BPMN™ task and an operation act, but it is true also that an operation act is not always tied up to a particular dialogue act in the IDM design. For example, considering the task "it sends message," it would not be able to connect to any dialogue acts of the relative IDM design. An operation act corresponds to this task (that it could be translated in terms of Web ap-plication in a button "it sends") that however it must not be connected neither to some dialogue acts nor to some topics. Therefore:

*   If an operation modifies or it creates value for a well-defined dialogue act, the operation act must be positioned on the edge of the topic.
*   If an operation does not involve any dialogues act, the operation act must be located at the outside of the last modified topic or the topic that introduces semantic relationships with the operation.

The operation act is connected to the interested dialogue act with a line called *"relation."*

In the case study here presented, we observe, in regards to the business process, that the task "to update state cell" and "to generate list" are automatic tasks: they will not appear in the final IDM process design. We observe that all of the other BPMN™ tasks modify, or create values for a well-defined dialogue act so all of the operation acts are on the edge of the topic. The operation act is connected with a relation to the dialogue act.

In Figure 7, we present the IDM process design after the first four steps.

5.   **Definition of an operation act:** If the task has a message flow that goes out, it is important to be represented besides the proper operation of the task, also

Figure 7. Design IDM process after step 4

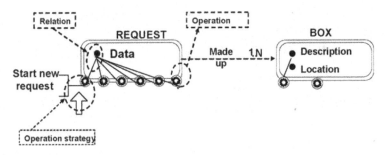

Copyright © 2009, IGI Global, distributing in print or electronic forms without written permission of IGI Global is prohibited.

the dispatch of the message as operation act: this is able not to be situated on the edge of the topic, from the moment that it doesn't tightly interest the data of the topic, but simply connected to the operation act related to the same task of the message.

Only when on the same task there are messages incoming flow and message outcoming flow, from and to the same user, the message exchange is not represented as operation act. In this case, in fact, it is assumed that the task has been represented only to represent a message exchange, and it deals with a task of type "service" that it does not have a correspondent in the graphic interface of the Web application.

The same way that the messages flows, the sequence flow must be considered; it connects two or more lanes of the same pool: if there are tasks or other elements that have a sequence flow directly out coming toward another lane, it is important to represent, besides the operation proper of the task, the operation of dispatch of the message to another user positioning the operation act out of the relative topic as seen in precedence.

In order to support whatever operation that is defined in the business processes, some properties that allow describing details and behavior of the operation act has been defined. The concept of operation act already existed in IDM design methodology; however, here this concept has been more structured (Table 1).

You observe that the property "type" contains exactly the different typologies of tasks allowed in the BPMN™ notation.

In the case study presented here, because each BPMN™ task is a single operation, each task corresponds to a single operation act.

We present in Table 2 one of the operation acts defined in the case study and present the details here.

6. **Gateways:** the designer may decide if insert or not in the IDM design the gateway.

Without the introduction of the gateways, an exclusive decision is designed as two or more process relation outcome from an operation act and once more specifying, among the attributes of the following operations acts, the pre-conditions and the type of gateway.

In the case in which the business processes are made up by more consecutive gateways without intermediate operations, the first useful task will be represented by an operation act that has more values related to the attribute pre-condition and more values related to the attribute gateway. Since an operation act source of more process relations represent, whether an exclusive gateway or an AND gateway, the reader of the diagram would not be able to understand the real meaning of

Copyright © 2009, IGI Global, distributing in print or electronic forms without written permission of IGI Global is prohibited.

Table 1. Definition of operation act

PROPERTY	DESCRIPTION
Name	Name of the operation act
Process	Name of the related process
Task	Name of the relative task
Type	Service: Provide some type of service by Web Service or others automatic application. It may be: InMessage, OutMessage, Implementation, Owner
	Receive: It waits for a message coming from another actor of the business process. It may be: Message, Instantiate false, Implementation, Sender
	Send: Send a message to another actor. It may be: Message, Implementation, Receiver
	User: It specifies if the operation has been made up by a human with a software application. It may be: Performers, InMessage, OutMessage, Implementation
	Script: It allows to indicate that the operation is executed by a business process engine that understand a script
	Manual: Manual operation made up without the help of a software or without a business process execution engine
	Reference: It refers to other activities already defined with the same behaviour
Pre-Condition	A pre-condition will be defined in order to verify that the operation is valid in the context where it is executed
Output	The result of the operation. It will indicate if the operation has been completed or if the operation has as output a well defined document
Gateway	It defines the types of gateway that come before the task to which operation act refer
Kind of topic	Kind of topic involved in the operation
Dialogue act	Dialogue act involved in the operation
Slot	Slot involved in the operation

the representation if not deepening the knowledge of it up to the attributes of the operations act. We believe, therefore, that it is suitable to limit the presence of the gateways on the design of the logical IDM to the exclusive gateway, but we do not force the designer to rigidly followthis suggestion leaving ample space to decide if the specific business process needs a more specific treatment.

If it is important to use the gateways in the design of the application, it is suggested to use the same symbol of the business process and to mark the process relations coming out. The use of the pre-condition in the operation acts that follow any type of gateway remains valid.

In the case study presented here, we represent the gateway in the design: there are only two gateways for the user "responsible" and the representation of the gate-

Copyright © 2009, IGI Global, distributing in print or electronic forms without written permission of IGI Global is prohibited.

Table 2. Details of the operation act "select warehouse"

PROPERTY	DESCRIPTION
Name	Select warehouse
Process	Main process
Task	Select warehouse
Type	User
Pre-Condition	Data on the box
Output	Warehouse selected
Gateway	Before the task there is the XOR gateway
Kind of topic	Box
Dialogue act	Location
Slot	All the slot of the location

ways make the design clearer. In Figure 8, it is possible to see the two gateways of the business process inside the integrated design.

7. **Process link:** In order to allow the coexistence inside the Web application design of business process links and of semantic links, we introduced a process link that connects among them the operations acts proposing the process flow inside the integrated design. The process link is labeled with the name of the operation act of destination and their graphic representation is a straight and continuous line. Generally, a process link connects among them two operation acts, but it may happen that a process link has as source as destination a gateway (admitted that is decided to represent the gateway in the design). In this case, the sequence flow of the BPMN™ design that connects a task to the gateway corresponds, in the integrated design, to a process link without label while the sequences flow that starts from the gateway and finishes to an operation act is represented with a process link labeled with the name of the operation act of destination. An operation act can have more target process link; in such a case, two process links will be have the same label (because they take the name of the operation act of destination), but they will have an OR gateway that points out the flow to undertake. It is evident that the process links allow following, inside the integrated design, the flow of the business process.

In the example here presented, process links and semantic links coexist: the only one semantic link is the "made up by" between "Request" and "Box" topics and the other are process links. The semantic links allow the navigation between information when the person responsible does not execute any process but want to see information about an instance of business process already complete. We

Copyright © 2009, IGI Global, distributing in print or electronic forms without written permission of IGI Global is prohibited.

Figure 8. IDM process after step 7

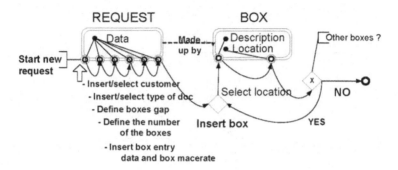

can observe that process link have the same name of the target operation act that represents the BPMN™ task. For example, the process link that links together the first and second operation act of the topic Request has the same name of the first task of the responsible actor (Figure 8).

8.   **Intermediate strategy:** The BPMN™ design provides the possibility to position an intermediate event among two connected tasks linked together by a sequence flow.

The intermediate event is translated, in the IDM process diagram into an intermediate strategy (⇑) that it is positioned with the arrow toward the process link to which it refers (obviously the process link will connect the two operation acts corresponding to the tasks among which the intermediate event is set).

The intermediate strategy is positioned only on the process-related relation as it regards the intermediate event type message or timer. For the other types of intermediate events (error, cancel, compensation and rule), they produce a new flow that manages them. In such a case, it is obligatory to point that out on the intermediate strategy positioned on the process relation that has as a target the operation act.

In the example that we follow, there are no intermediate events for the user "responsible" so the intermediate strategy is not in the PIDM design.

9.   **Access structures:** In a previous section, we observed that when the final user executes a task in the business process, he/she could be interested in abandoning the flow of the business processes to do a free navigation. The final user must clearly be able to exactly take back the business process in the point in which he/she had left the business process. To allow this, we introduce for every operation act that uses the application, an opportune access structure.

Copyright © 2009, IGI Global, distributing in print or electronic forms without written permission of IGI Global is prohibited.

The application will have to trace the last task performed to give the possibility to exactly take back the execution from the following task to the last performed to the user completely.

The access structure that allows doing this is an *introductory act* that represents the first access structure, and therefore it is inserted in correspondence to the operation act corresponding to the first task that the user has to perform for beginning the business process; for the other operation acts, it is introduced, instead, a group of introductory acts.

The motivation for which a *group of introductory acts* is inserted, instead of an introductory act, in correspondence to the operations act following to the first one, depends on the fact that there can be, for a same actor, more instances of same business processes suspended in a determined point.

Obviously, if the designer who analyzed the problem is sure that in a determined instant a user could have suspended a unique instance, he/she will not be bound to insert a group of introductory acts, but he will insert just an introductory act.

The access structures, inserted in the design phase to provide the possibility of activating a business process or resume it once interrupted, are dynamic access structures in the sense that they are not always active, but they became active when the user interrupts the execution of the business process. For this reason, with the goal to distinguish, in the phase of design, the traditional access structures from the others, we recommend to represent them with a different notation (Table 3)

In this example, we add a group of introductory acts for each operation act here defined (see Figure 9). We observe that in the design there are the same introductory acts of the IDM design, and we add also the group of introductory act related to each operation act. We observe, also, that the introductory act "start new request" that is related to the start event already exist in the IDM design.

This is not an error. The IDM designer, when he/she defines the user experience, highlighted the importance of the topic request and the importance to start the user experience from this point. The IDM designer does not know the business process but he/she gathers from the study of the user experience that it is important to add this access structure.

Table 3. Notation to represent introductory act

	IDM	IDM-Process
Introductory act	⊜	⊜ᴾ
Group of Introductory act	⊜	⊜ᴾ

Copyright © 2009, IGI Global, distributing in print or electronic forms without written permission of IGI Global is prohibited.

Figure 9. IDM process after step 9

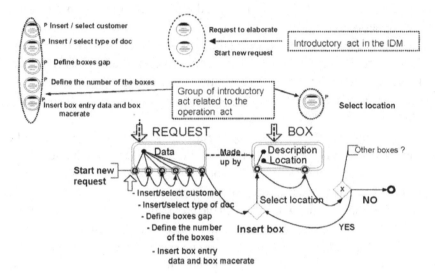

10. **Sub-processes:** It is possible to leave in the integrated design the notation of a sub-process and to explode it in a separated design. In this case, the sub-process is represented with an operation act labeling the process relation that reaches it with the name of the sub-process followed by the sign "+." In the case study presented here, the "select location" is an embedded sub-process. The IDM process designer decides to define the "select location" sub-process in a separate diagram (Figure 10) and adds a "+" label to the "select location.. In order to make a complete case study, we define in the next figure the IDM

Figure 10. IDM process of the embedded sub-process "select notation." For a legibility reason, we prefer not to show the topic "box" but the operation act are on the border of this topic.

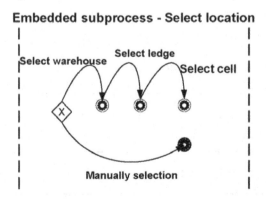

Copyright © 2009, IGI Global, distributing in print or electronic forms without written permission of IGI Global is prohibited.

process of the "select location sub-process." In order to obtain this design, it is possible to follow the same steps defined here.

11. **End event:** A simple end event that is a BPMN™ end event, but without inside markers, does not have a correspondent in the integrated design. In the case in which the end event is present inside markers, the same representation of an intermediate event is used, or rather the presence of the end event is pointed out on the process relation. In Figure 9, it is possible to see the end event of the business process represented.

Table 4. Summary of methodological guidelines for IDM process

Summary of methodological guidelines for IDM Process (part 1 of 3)			
Step	Input	IDM Process	Output
1.Definition of types of user	BPMN design, IDM Diagram	Individualize which pool or lane of the BPMN diagram will have a separate IDM Process diagram	A separate diagram for each user
2. Analysis of the information contents	BPMN tasks and IDM Dialogue act	Analysis of the dialogue acts and, if not present, adding the slots for each dialogue acts.	First integration between dialogue act and BPMN tasks
3. Process start	BPMN design	Introduction of the process strategy corresponding to the start event	The integrated design for each user has the process strategy that defines where the navigation will start.
4. Analysis of the tasks	BPMN design	1.The operation act may be on the edge of the topic interested. 2.The operation act may be outside the last topic of interest or to the topic that presents semantic relationships with the operation 3.Link together the operation act and the dialogue act with a direct edge named "relation"	The integrated design has all the operation acts corresponding to the BPMN task. Each operation act may be on the edge or outside a well defined topic. Operation acts are related with the dialogue acts through a relation

Copyright © 2009, IGI Global, distributing in print or electronic forms without written permission of IGI Global is prohibited.

Table 5. Summary of methodological guidelines for IDM process

Summary of methodological guidelines for IDM Process (part 2 of 3)			
5. Definition of the operation act	Integrated design obtained in the step 4 and BPMN design	To define all the properties strictly related to the operation act	A set of table (one of each operation act) with the detail of each
6. Gateway	Integrated design obtained in the step 4 and BPMN design	Gateway can be inserted in the IDM diagram or can implicitly be considered in the related operation acts	The integrated design may have the gateways. It is possible to improve the table defined in the step 5 and to add information about gateway
7. Process relation	Integrated design obtained in the step 6 and BPMN diagram	Process relations cohabit with semantic links and allow to link together operation acts following the process flow. Process relation is labeled with the name of the target operation act.	The integrated design is made up, now, of the process link: it is possible to have a direct mapping between BPMN and the integrated design
8.Intermediate strategy	Integrated design obtained in the step 7 and BPMN diagram	Intermediate strategy represents an intermediate event of a type message or timer. It is represented by an arrow oriented to the corresponding process link	If the BPMN design for the considered actor has an intermediate event, in the integrated design there will be an arrow oriented to the corresponding process link.

Copyright © 2009, IGI Global, distributing in print or electronic forms without written permission of IGI Global is prohibited.

Table 6. Summary of methodological guidelines for IDM process

Summary of methodological guidelines for IDM Process (part 3 of 3)			
9. Access structure	Integrated design obtained in the step 7 and IDM diagram	An introductory act defines the start of the business process, a group of introductory acts is related to the operation acts and allows to resume a suspended business process	For each operation act there will be in the integrated design a group of introductory acts.
10. Sub processes	Integrated design obtained in the step 9 and BPMN diagram	They are designed as different sub-process and are represented with an operation act. The process relation that brings to this operation act is labeled with the sub-process name and the symbol "+"	A separate integrated design for the sub-process: the new IDMProcess design will be made following the same methodological guidelines here explained.
11. End Event	Integrated design obtained in the step 10 and BPMN diagram	Optionally, the designer may represent the end event	The integrated design may have the end event in order to define the end of the business process

Summary

In the next tables (Tables 4, 5 and 6), there is a summary of the most important methodological guidelines provided.

PIDM PROCESS: PRELIMINARY OBSERVATIONS

Starting form the IDM process design, made up using the methodological guidelines already defined, it is necessary to make the PIDM process design that is the integration between the PIDM design and the design of the business processes. In this transition, it is opportune, first of all, to safeguard the directives imposed by the same methodology IDM for the passage to PIDM, already described in preced-

Copyright © 2009, IGI Global, distributing in print or electronic forms without written permission of IGI Global is prohibited.

ing chapters. Subsequently, it is essential to face the problems that have brought to the methodological guidelines previously described according to the concepts of PIDM with the goal of get some methodological guidelines coherent with those already provided for PIDM process.

Dialogue Act and Screen

In IDM process, there is an important distinction among input dialogue act and read-only dialogue act: the nature of the dialogue act is influenced by the state of the business process.

Since an IDM dialogue act is translated in a screen for PIDM, such correspondence must be maintained in the passage from IDM process to PIDM process. Of course, in this case, further observation needs:

- The screens corresponding to read-only dialogue acts that limit them to contain and to expose information without giving the possibility to operate on them
- The screens corresponding to input dialogue acts that will have to provide the possibility of also adding in the design input forms

The same data require, therefore, *two different representations*: the first limits it to introduce the information that the final user can only read, the second allows the final user to insert values, to update or to cancel those existing. In PIDM process, this is translated respectively to use a screen and content or screen and input form. In both cases, the designer is free to assign to every dialogue act that are read-only or input, one or more screens.

Task and Screen

At this point, since also for PIDM process it is important to maintain the requirement of the traceability, or rather it has to always be possible to individualize in the PIDM process design the flow of the business processes, it is essential to understand whether to associate a task and screen. In order to associate a task and screen, there are two problems:

- Should a task be represented from one or more screens?
- It is possible to represent the same set of screens for a concluded task and for a process task?

The first problem comes directly from the correspondence among dialogue acts and screens: the operation acts in which a task decomposes it are connected to input

Copyright © 2009, IGI Global, distributing in print or electronic forms without written permission of IGI Global is prohibited.

dialogue act. To represent an operation act means, therefore, representing a dialogue act because it supports well-defined operations. However, the representation of a dialogue act, that is read-only or input, can be realized with one or more screens based on the requirements of the application on the business process design and on the needs of the designer.

Besides, it had to consider the distinction between concluded tasks and active tasks and the possibility of assigning to both the same set of screens; this behavior has the advantage of limiting the total number of pages of the application, but it has the disadvantage of using screens useful for the business processes, but poor in regards to the information content from the point of view of the final user.

Suspension and Resumption of the Business Process

Surely, a fundamental problem, but often underestimated by the methodologies of design of Web applications that has focused on a business process, is managing the suspension and resumption of a business process. In IDM process, the problem has been faced introducing some ad hoc access structures. In the case of PIDM process, the application has to define that the templates of the pages that the user visits after the exit from the business process contain some links that lead him/her to the task or to the tasks left in a suspended mode belonging to one or more business processes. The templates, of which PIDM occupies it in a specific view, assume, therefore, an important role in the management of the navigation and of the state of the business processes since they remember the following tasks to present to the final user according to the flow of the business processes. The templates hide a mechanism oriented both to store the information related to the tasks, for instance those correctly performed, those incomplete and those complete, but consequently also the pages to be proposed to the final user in the logic of the business processes, keeping in mind the possible decisional branch or point where the flow become parallel.

Business Process State

The preceding observations have demonstrated that the concept of state of the business processes has a fundamental importance in the realization of the diagram and in the following understanding by an external reader. To associate every screen that participates in the business processes, the relative state allows coherently connecting screens that follow each other so that the operations realized by each are consistent with the operation related to the adjacent screens. It has been, therefore, necessary to introduce only for the process screen, a property that preserves the name of the task that is performing. The property is physically positioned on the screen, and it

Copyright © 2009, IGI Global, distributing in print or electronic forms without written permission of IGI Global is prohibited.

is possible that more screens contemporarily contain the same task and therefore the same property. To visualize the state of the business processes on the interested screen, it has, besides, the further advantage of allowing a faster visual mapping between business processes and application, and therefore it allows answering to the requirement of traceability.

P-IDM Process: Methodological Guidelines

An IDM diagram turns it into different PIDM views according to a defined mapping; in the same way, a IDM process diagram turns into a series of PIDM process views: to the PIDM view has been added also a specific view named *Process view* to hold trace of the presence of the business processes in the P-IDM Process design.

In the following parts of this chapter, we can see for each view, some methodological guideline.

Structural View

Step 1: Every topic of the IDM process design generates different structural views in which an abstract screen with the same name of the topic is represented. In the case study already presented, for the responsible actor, we will have two separate structural views, one for the topic "request" and the other for the topic "box."

Step 2: If the topic contains operation acts, surely all or parts of the dialogue acts of the topic are input dialogue acts. To individualize input dialogue acts, it is enough to verify if in the attribute "dialogue act" of the operation act there is a reference to the related dialogue act to which the operation act makes reference. If a dialogue act is not mentioned, then none of the operation acts connected to the relative topic are read-only. In the case study presented here, each dialogue act has a content related to the screen and the input form one of each operation act.

Step 3: Every dialogue act, that is, input dialogue act or read-only dialogue act, corresponds to a content aggregated to the screen from the topic of which the dialogue act depends. It is possible that the designer wants to divide the content of a dialogue act in more contents: it is suggested then to aggregate to the main screen content with a first part of the data and to link this content, without direction, to a second screen and the related content with the remaining information. You watch out to correctly specify the fields of the contents that have to *exactly correspond* to the dialogue act slots. In the case study, there is only one content for each dialogue act while there are several input forms, each for one operation act.

Step 4: Every operation act involves the input dialogue act to which is connected, besides the representation through content; it has to have another representation of it with one or more screens and input forms. The screen related to an opera-

Copyright © 2009, IGI Global, distributing in print or electronic forms without written permission of IGI Global is prohibited.

tion, and therefore to a part or to a whole task, has in its graphical representation a "P" on the left and a field with the state of the business process corresponding to the name of the task from which the operation act derives. In the case where it is impossible to go up again to the task that has originated the operation act (if, for instance, the operation act is preceded by a gateway), the field of the state can be omitted. The input forms that represent the input dialogue acts modified by the operation act have to contain, all and alone, the useful fields to the operation and these are the values related to the attribute "slot" of the operation act. For possible other data that is wanted to make visible, but not modifiable, on the same screen, it is possible to aggregate to the screen a content specifying the fields to be showed. In the case study here presented, there is, for each dialogue act, a process screen where the state of the business process is defined.

In Figure 11, we can see the process screen "insert/select type of doc" with the input form. Inside the process screen, the "state" will define the task from which the operation act derives. In the process screen, it is possible to define the dialogue act related to the operation act with a relation.

Step 5: An operation act that is not connected to any topics (for instance, an operation act that deals with sending a message to another user) it is translated, in PIDM process, in a screen and input form. It is possible also to use a second screen for the receipt of the answer (even if this is not anticipated from IDM process). These screens as those servants to step 4, are screens of a business process, and therefore they must be labeled with one << P >> and they will contain the attribute related to the state of the process. In the example shown here, there is no screen connected to any topics.

Step 6: From the point of view of the application it does not have sense to make explicit the questions that the final user is set for selecting the activities to complete, while it has sense point out if an action of the final user can be made only following to come true of a specific condition. Assignment of the designer remains to decide however whether to represent the gateways on the P-IDM Process design.

- If the business process is relatively simple, it is possible not to bring the gateways in the application design, but it is necessary, from an implementa-

Figure 11. An example of process screen and input form

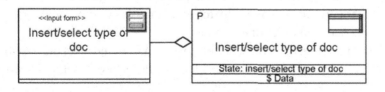

Copyright © 2009, IGI Global, distributing in print or electronic forms without written permission of IGI Global is prohibited.

tion point of view, that the links that bring to the pages that represent tasks checked by the gateway include the control that conditions are verified because that screen can be visualized and performed. In effects, when the gateway performs a decision, exclusive, inclusive, complex or a parallel ramification, the information of which we need concern only which out coming flows are active because this decides the navigability or less on some screens and this information is contained in the attributes of the operation acts.

- If it is important to represent the gateways into the application design, then we have to distinguish among the various types of gateway:
  - XOR decision: it is possible to present this gateway as a screen with input form in which the final user has called to select one of the offered options: it has to be then the application that dynamically decides the next page to present to the final user according to the effected choice. A consequential screen from a gateway is still a screen of process flow, and is marked therefore from a <<P>>, and it has to be tied up from process link, eventually typified, to the screens that can be reached through the gateway. If the flows outcoming from the gateway refer to a different kind of topic and therefore to different structural view, to duplicate the screen-gateway in both the view and without bringing the process link for the other entity.
  - XOR merging: if the XOR merging comes from a XOR decision, any control on the incoming flows is not necessary because the flow will have been filtered based on the user decision; if the XOR gateway is used for linking the flows coming from an exclusive gateway, it is necessary to add a screen that controls which of the two or more flows can continue.
  - OR decision: it is possible that more flows are active when the user exit from a gateway; the modeling most useful to this situation is a guided tour through the screens that realize the parallel flow; the guided tour drives the final user through a series of steps that is, in a few words, the sequence of the tasks of the parallel flows out coming from the gateway. Since it deals with a non exclusive decision, that is, a true condition that does not exclude the evaluation of the other conditions, an initial screen is necessary for the guided tour in which the controls of the flows effect it to cross; for instance, every condition could be modeled as an input form that asks the final user to select those true. For the expert user (of the Web application that he/she is using), the guided tour is a choice alternative to the possibility to autonomously cross the walks according to a personal order of execution.
  - OR merging: the representation that keeps in mind all of the possibilities uses a screen that checks that all of the flows have been performed, and

Copyright © 2009, IGI Global, distributing in print or electronic forms without written permission of IGI Global is prohibited.

it eventually suggests the remaining activities to the final user. It is possible, in fact, that an OR merging synchronizes consequential flows from OR decision or AND synchronizing which are represented by guided tour or they are autonomously performed by the final user; in both cases we cannot be sure of the result, and therefore a further control becomes necessary.

- ○ AND synchronizing: it is a simplification of the OR decision considering that it does not need to verify what conditions are verified, but it creates only parallel flows. You represent therefore with guided tour without the initial screen of control.
- ○ AND joining: it is suggested the same representation of the OR merging.

In the case study defined here, the gateway is represented as a screen. For example, if we think to "select location" sub-process, the related design will be next in Figure 12.

Step 7: The screens coming from operations cannot be connected to any other screens if the following operation to the represented one *happens on another topic*. If one same operation is represented by more input forms aggregated to the screen,

Figure 12. An example of XOR gateway

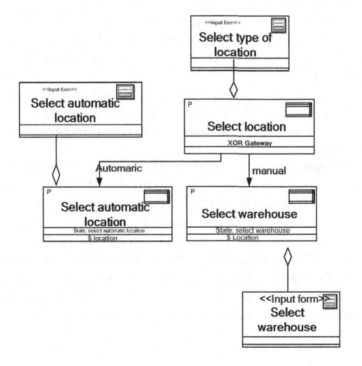

Copyright © 2009, IGI Global, distributing in print or electronic forms without written permission of IGI Global is prohibited.

these last ones have to be connected from generic-oriented process links. If two consecutive operations exist on the same topic, the corresponding screens have to be connected with oriented process links in the direction pointed out by the process relation that has to target the second operation act.

In the case study, the operation act "insert box entry data and macerate data" and the operation act "select box" are in two different topics, so there are no connections between these two process screens.

Step 8: If an *intermediate strategy* is present among two operation acts that are found on the same topic, the corresponding screens have to be connected by *intermediate links,* and it is opportune to comment the intermediate links adding a textual comment related to the specific type of intermediate event inheriting this information from the attribute "type" of the intermediate strategy. If the two operation acts among which there is an intermediate event, they are found on a different topic, it is important to represent the screen-input form set in every structural view without necessity to connect to any other screens. We observe that, in the case in which the operations among which an intermediate event exists, relative to the types just seen, and ends on the same topic, the corresponding screens are tied up from link that, in reality, the application does not give the possibility of navigating from the moment between one and the other one that it had to attend to the arrival of a message or an expiration. It exists, therefore, a *not concretely navigable link* but that he/she explains it for the semantic value that is attributed to it.

In the case study, there is no intermediate link.

Step 9: Since it is possible that the IDM process design does not bring all of the gateways present in the business process, it is necessary to check that every operation act has one or more pre-conditions, as much as the gateways that the flow that reaches it cross.

Step 10: If an operation act has two or more process relations out coming or incoming, this is an index of the presence of a gateway; the attributes of the operation acts point out the values (can also be multiple), in correspondence of "pre-conditions" and "gateway."

Step 11: An operations strategy (in IDM it defines the starting point of the business process) does not have any correspondent in the PIDM process diagram from the moment that it is impossible to follow the course of the operations on an only diagram, but it fragments it into more structural view.

Step 12: An end event does not have any correspondent in the PIDM process diagram; it is possible that the designer of the application wants to suggest to the final user that the business process is concluded and wants to propose some possibilities of navigation, through a specific screen, that therefore it does not re-enter among those related to the business process.

Copyright © 2009, IGI Global, distributing in print or electronic forms without written permission of IGI Global is prohibited.

The two structural views after the application of the 12 steps are presented in Figures 13 and 14.

Figure 13. Structural view for the topic "request"

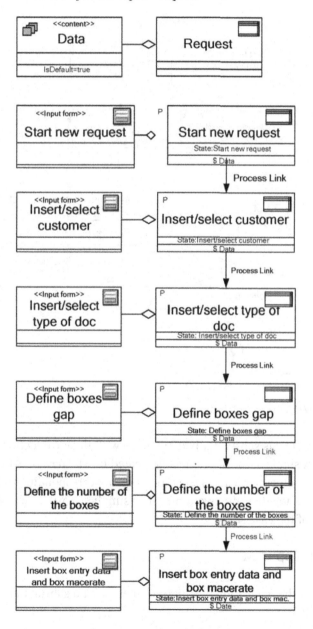

Copyright © 2009, IGI Global, distributing in print or electronic forms without written permission of IGI Global is prohibited.

Figure 14. structural view for the topic box

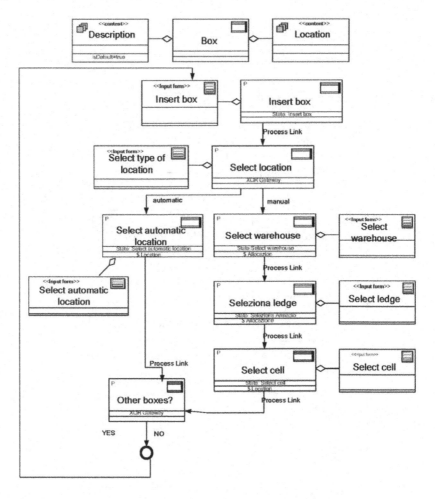

Association View

The association view is substantially unchanged with the introduction of the business process. A single association view is created in which every kind of topic is represented as a screen with an association content corresponding to the relevant relation that links together the two topics. For simplicity, we do not show the association view of the case study.

Navigational Map view

Furthermore, for the navigational map view, there are no substantial variations in comparison to PIDM:

Copyright © 2009, IGI Global, distributing in print or electronic forms without written permission of IGI Global is prohibited.

- **Step 1:** For every kind of topic, there is a navigational map view. You create a screen for the access to the kind of topic.
- **Step2:** Every introductory act corresponds to an access content whose name is equal to that of the introductory act. The access content has to be aggregated to the screen of access to the kind of topic and connected through collection link to the screen of the kind of topic.
- **Step 3:** A group of introductory acts is represented as sequence of access content and screen with access content aggregated. The first access content is aggregated to the screen of access to the kind of topic and tied by a collection link to the belonging screen to its same sequence. The second access content has to be connected through a collection link to the screen of the kind of topic.

Of course, in the case study presented here, there are both the access content related to the introductory act of the IDM design and the access content related to the introductory act here introduced to support the business process. We present here only the navigational map view for the topic "request" (Figure 15). We observe that for the access content related to the new request, there is only an access content (that is related to the introductory act), for the access content related to the other BPMN™ task there is the access content related to the screen and to another access content because it comes from a group of introductory acts that allows the user to start again a specific instance of the business process.

Template View

The template view is created partly from the IDM process design and is partly built on the base of the demands of the application when they emerge during the design of the user experience. The methodological guidelines proposed are:

Step 1. Each topic has its own template view in which a screen template is created with the name of the same topic: if there already exist another screen template, the last has to be aggregated to be more general. In the case study presented here, we define a template for the topic request (Figure 16).

Step 2. To create a layout content with the name of the final user that will use this part of application and connect it to the screen template, seen at step 1, through aggregation. You connect the layout content to the access screen realized at step 1 of the view of the navigational map with a direct link that terminates on the screen. In this case study, we define the layout content for the responsible user (Figure 17).

Step 3. All of the screens of the navigational map view have to be connected to the screen template through tie of specialization: this assures that all the screens have the necessary links to allow the navigation through the pages of the applica-

Copyright © 2009, IGI Global, distributing in print or electronic forms without written permission of IGI Global is prohibited.

Figure 15. Navigational map view

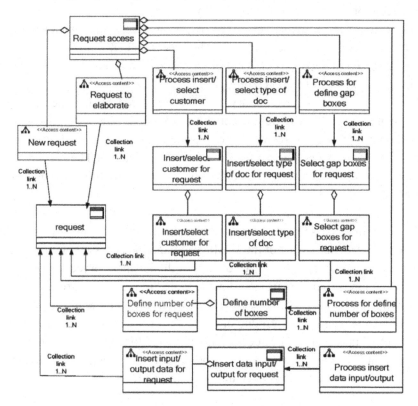

Figure 16. Screen template for the topic request

tion. If the screens that specialize on the screen template are not a too elevated number, it is possible to bring them on a single diagram, otherwise it must have a screen template and layout content in every view drawing the opportune connections in every sketch.

It is noted that all of the access structures to the application defined in the navigational map view have been implicitly made available from the moment that the access screen to the kind of topic enters to belong to the template of all the pages.

In this case study, we add all of the process screens to the screen template; they will be activated based on the business process state (Figure 18).

Copyright © 2009, IGI Global, distributing in print or electronic forms without written permission of IGI Global is prohibited.

Figure 17. Screen and layout content

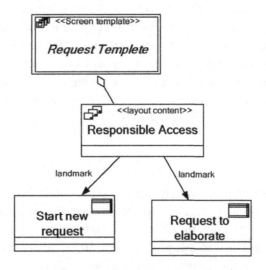

Among the other access structures, of particular importance are those related to the tasks of the business process. For a greater usability of the application and a complete support to the business process, the links to the screens of business process are had to dynamically activate every time the final user, for any reason, has gone out from the area reserved to the business process to perform extra navigation: such links allow to return to the task left in a suspended mode.

Figure 18. Template view for the topic request

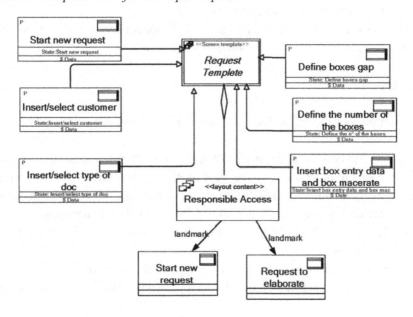

Copyright © 2009, IGI Global, distributing in print or electronic forms without written permission of IGI Global is prohibited.

The activations of the links over that dynamics, must carefully be defined in order to not taking the risk to allow the access to a task that requires for the execution of other operations before its turn. You, for instance, could think about a screen that represents an operation that in the business process, is found after an intermediate event of a type message; since the operation requires that another actor of the business process has sent a message, such a link must either be deactivated for avoiding being selected or has to contain the same controls of the normal connections among the pages, as specified in the structural view.

Process View

To give the possibility of representing, in a unique view, all of the screens belonging to the business process and, therefore, to address to the requirement of traceability of the business process design in the integrated design, the business process view has been introduced. The business process view allows understanding as the flow of the business process moves through the various screens.

The introduction of the business process view is particularly useful when the business process develops itself passing from a topic to the other, for which the single structural view is not able to adequately represent the connections among the screens of the business process.

All of the screens of the business process and the possible present connections among them are grouped in only one view: process link may link together process screens.

Clearly, if the business process interests only one topic the view of the business process coincides with the structural view.

In this case study, there are two topics, so the process view is different from the structural view. In Figure 19, there is the process view for the case study.

Summary

A brief summary of the methodological guidelines proposed is presented here.

- Maintaining how much defined in PIDM, also in PIDM process, the design is fragmented in more view. To the view of PIDM (structural view, association view, navigational map view, template view), a further view has been added: the process view. Nevertheless, in the case in which the business process refers to only one IDM topic, the view of the business process coincides with the structural view.
- In the structural view, the concept of input form has been added; the input form must be aggregated to the relative screen when the dialogue act is input

Copyright © 2009, IGI Global, distributing in print or electronic forms without written permission of IGI Global is prohibited.

Figure 19. Process view

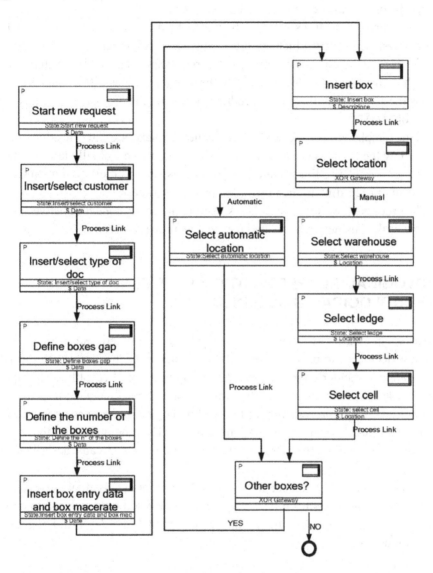

dialogue act (and therefore, it implies that the final user can edit its fields). Input forms coexist with the contents which could refer to the same slots of the inputs form. It is important, nevertheless, to point out what slots must have looked out upon (for reading or for writing) the final user. The screens that admit input form are related to the business process, and therefore they are marked by one << P >> and by the indication of the state of the business process or rather of the relative task to which refer.

Copyright © 2009, IGI Global, distributing in print or electronic forms without written permission of IGI Global is prohibited.

- The process links connect among them a screen of a business process following the order imposed by the same business process.
- The intermediate links connect between them a screen corresponding to operation act among which an intermediate strategy is set.
- The introductory act and the groups of introductory act are added to guarantee to the consumer to be able to access to the business process, if left interrupted, has the same semantic of the introductory act and the groups of introductory act of PIDM.
- In the templates view the screens of business process are introduced in order to allow the final user to access the business process eventually left in a suspended mode. The links related to the process screens must be dynamically activated according to the flow of the business process.
- The process view, if it exists, allows making the correspondence between the flow of the business process and the various process screens.

ONTOLOGICAL REPRESENTATION OF THE METHODOLOGICAL GUIDELINES

In order to supply a tool to support the methodological guidelines previously exposed, it is necessary to provide a formal representation of the same; such formal representation, as underlined in Figure 2 of Chapter IV, will constitute the input for the four levels of architecture of the information system. To reach this goal, we used an ontological representation of the methodological guidelines opportunely integrating the ontological representation of the BPMN™ notation with the ontological representation of the IDM—P-IDM methodologies already described in Chapter V.

Also, we define an ontological meta-model that comprehends all of these methodologies: to do so it has been necessary to introduce some new elements (new classes and new properties) to the originally meta-model in order to link together these methodologies.

Meta-Model Integration – IDM Process

In order for the reading not to get heavy, we present only the logical steps followed in order to integrate the IDM, PIDM and BPMN™ meta-models already defined.

To be able to distinguish among input dialogue act and read-only dialogue act, the datatype property has been introduced, in the integrated meta-model, *typeOf-DialogueAct* of type string with LIDM as domain; DialogueAct has as admitted

Copyright © 2009, IGI Global, distributing in print or electronic forms without written permission of IGI Global is prohibited.

values 'Input' and 'ReadOnly'; such values allow distinguishing among an input dialogue act and one read-only dialogue act.

While the read-only dialogue acts can only be navigated, the input dialogue acts contain one or more slots to allow the final user to insert values. It is therefore necessary to insert a new class slot that allows preserving the desired values and the object property has slot with the domain *IDM:DialogueAct* and range *IDMProcess: Slot;* in this way, it is possible to individualize what slots belong to what dialogue acts. We observe that the new class slot inserted in the integrated meta-model was already present in the PIDM meta-model, producing an apparent conflict in the integrated meta-model PIDM process that includes it.

The two classes 'slot' are equal from the conceptual point of view, but not from the point of view of the properties, and at the moments of their use, therefore, not being possible to unify them, it is important to make possible their coexistence in order to allow PIDM and IDM process models to maintain their independence.

With the proposed solution (or the use of the namespaces), the two classes 'slot' have the possibility of coexisting in the meta-model PIDM process without producing problems of integrity; in fact, the 'namespaces' guarantee the oneness of the key used for accessing the corresponding instances.

Recognizing the double nature of the dialogue act introduces us to the IDM concept of *operations*.

For the operations modeled as operation acts have been necessary to introduce a link between these operations and the task that has produced them. This bond is made possible by the object property *generateOperationAct* with domain *BPMN: Task* and range *IDM:OperationAct*. For greater flexibility of the meta-model, it is opportune to also insert the inverse object property *generatedByTask* with domain *IDM:OperationAct* and range *BPMN:Task.*

To model the business process, links have been necessary to insert, in the meta-model, the concept of process relation. Such a concept has been introduced with the purpose of containing the operation acts source and target of the relationship; to its inside, the objects property "source" and "target" have been introduced that have as range the concept of operation act.

To model the possibility of suspending a business process in order to take back later, has been introduced the object property ***lastPerformedTask*** with domain *BPMN:Process* and range *BPMN:Task*, that allows to hold trace of the last task performed completely.

The mapping among a BPMN™ lane and a type of user of the Web application has been realized through the object property *mapSwimlane* that has the domain *IDM:L-IDMDiagram* and range *BPMN:Swimlane*. For greater flexibility of the meta-model, it is held opportune to insert the inverse object property *mappedOnL-IDMdiagram* with domain *BPMN:Swimlane* and range *IDM:L-IDMDiagram*.

Copyright © 2009, IGI Global, distributing in print or electronic forms without written permission of IGI Global is prohibited.

The concept of operation strategy and, therefore, the individualization of the dialogue act, corresponding to the start event of the business process, is realized in IDM process through the datatype property of type boolean *operationStrategy* that has as the domain both *IDM:OperationAct* and *BPMN:Gateway.*

The connection among operation act and dialogue act is realized in the integrated meta-model through the object property *involveDialogueAct* with domain *IDM: OperationAct* and range *IDM:DialogueAct.*

Of course, support has been provided also to the operation act that, structured in the definition of methodological guidelines, has also been furthermore structured in the definition of the ontological meta-model here defined. The class that represents the operation act has been completed, therefore, with the opportune properties (ObjectProperty or Datatype property) mirroring the definition previously given.

Besides, among the operation acts created, we have to distinguish those that modify a specific IDM topic from those that do not involve any topics, but, for their execution, they need to interact with the Web application. These last ones are the operation acts that are represented outside, and not on the edge, of a topic. In the integrated meta- model, this distinction is obtained through the datatype property of type boolean *alterTopic* that allows understanding f the operation act interacts with the dialogues act (and therefore it alters the topic) or less.

The integrated meta-model traces the connection from and toward *gateway* through the following objects property:

- **gatewaySource** (object property) has as domain *IDMProcess:ProcessRelation* and as range *BPMN:Gateway* that indicates (if present) the source gateway of the process relation.
- **gatewayTarget** (object property) has as domain *IDMProcess:ProcessRelation* and as range *BPMN:Gateway* that indicates (if present) the target gateway of the process relation.
- **linkedByProcessRelation** (object property) has two domains: *IDM:OperationAct* and *BPMN:Gateway*, and it has as range *IDMProcess:ProcessRelation*. This relationship allows pointing out what link of business process is connected to the dialogue act and what link of the business process is connected to the gateway it will be brought then inside the process relation if gateway and operation acts are target or source for the link.

If the gateways are used in the design of the application, the methodological guidelines suggest using the same symbol used in the business process design and to mark the process relation out coming through a label that is introduced in the integrated meta-model through the datatype property label of type string with the domain *IDMProcess: ProcessRelation.*

Copyright © 2009, IGI Global, distributing in print or electronic forms without written permission of IGI Global is prohibited.

The use of the pre-condition in the operation acts that follow any type of gateway remains valid in any case.

To manage the process relation, it is inserted in the class ProcessRelation of the integrated meta-model the objects property: *operationActSource* and *operationAct-Target*, both having as domain *IDMProcess:ProcessRelation* and as range *IDM:OperationAct*; these allow individualizing the operation act target (if it exists) and the operation act source (if it exists) of the process relation.

The label of the links indirectly solves the problem of the state of the business process: the potential reader of the design can individualize the exact flow of the business process to less than some elements that do not appear in IDM process and whose presence is revealed only by the attributes of the operation acts involved.

If the business process uses the intermediate event of a type message or timer, this last used as delay, the methodological guidelines impose to position an *intermediate strategy* in correspondence to the process relation that ties the two operation acts related to the tasks preceding and following the event.

In the meta-model, the *intermediate strategy* has been modeled through the class *IntermediateStrategy* that owns the following objects property:

- **generatedByIntermediateEvent** (object property) has as domain *IDMProcess:IntermediateStrategy* and as range *BPMN:IntermetiateEvent*. For greater flexibility of the meta-model, it is held opportune to also insert the inverse object property *generateIntermediateStrategy* that has as domain *BPMN:IntermediateEvent* and range *IDMProcess:IntermediateStrategy*. The proposed solution allows connecting the intermediate strategy with the intermediate event that has produced it.
- **applicatedToProcessRelation** (object property) has as domain *IDMProcess:IntermediateStrategy* and range *IDMProcess:ProcessRelation*. For greater flexibility of the meta-model, it is opportune to also insert the inverse object property hasIntermediateStrategy that has as domain *IDMProcess:ProcessRelation* and as range *IDMProcess:IntermediateStrategy*. This solution connects the intermediate strategy with the process relation to which must be applied.

An end-event does not necessarily have a correspondent in the design of the application unless it does not have any inside markers; in this case, the same representation of an intermediate event uses it. The presence of the end event in the integrated meta-model is obtained through the object property *endEventTarget* that has as domain *IDMProcess:ProcessRelation* and as range *BPMN:EndEvent*.

In Figure 21, there is an overview of the integration made up for IDM process.

Copyright © 2009, IGI Global, distributing in print or electronic forms without written permission of IGI Global is prohibited.

To facilitate the reading of the diagram and the individualization of the namespaces of affiliation (BPMN™, IDM and IDM process) of every class, it is opportune to associate to every class an icon that was representative of the namespace of affiliation, as Table 7 illustrates.

In the realization of the diagram, the followings conventions are being applied (Figure 20).

For every class, a rectangle is used and divided in two parts: the superior part contains the information on class and its possible subclasses; the inferior part contains information on the datatypes property inserted for the integration and possible datatype and object property and therefore existing before the integration and belonging to the class. For every class following information there is:

- the name of the origin class
- the icon to represent the class where it belongs
- the symbol ▶ that indicate the presence of subclasses; in the diagram, just the subclasses that have involved in the integration will be described, and the other

Table 7. Icon to identify the affiliation

Icon	Descrcription
✖	The select icon brings some utensils of job with the purpose to represent the operation made up in the business process development.
♣	Namespace IDM: the select icon intends to represent the information content of the web application.
♠	Namespace IDMProcess: the selected icon intends to represent the elements of bond among the entities of the business process and the information content of the web application.

Figure 20. Convention in the realization of the diagram

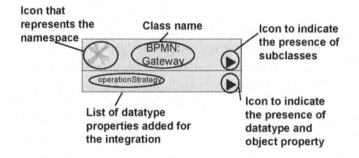

Copyright © 2009, IGI Global, distributing in print or electronic forms without written permission of IGI Global is prohibited.

Figure 21. Overview of the IDM process integration meta-model

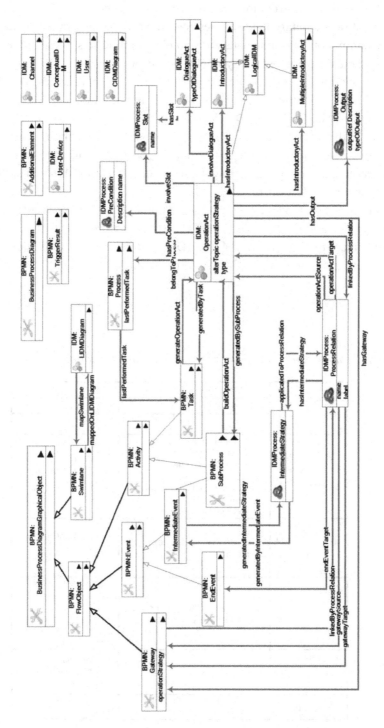

Copyright © 2009, IGI Global, distributing in print or electronic forms without written permission of IGI Global is prohibited.

ones stay unexploded since the objective of the diagram is to put demonstrate the elements inserted for realizing the integration.

- a list of the datatype properties inserted for the integration; if the class in examination has some datatype and object properties, these are not brought into the diagram, but the symbol▶ points out their presence
- the relationship is-to (father-child) between class and subclass is represented with the following arrow that departs from the child class and sit arrive on the class father━━━━━▷
- in the diagram, the object properties are inserted for realizing the integration through an arrow that departs from the class domain, and it arrives on the class range; on such an arrow the name of the relationship is inserted as the following is described: ━━━━mappedByContent━━━━▶.

You can observe that, in the diagram, the new classes are inserted for realizing the integration and all of the classes of first level, in comparison to the class THING of every meta-models (BPMN™ and IDM), while those of the following levels (subclasses) are brought only if involved in the integration.

Table 8. Comparison between open issues and possible solutions

OPEN ISSUES	PROPOSED SOLUTIONS	
	IDM PROCESS	P-IDM PROCESS
Cohabitation of several typologies of information	✓ The information in the topics IDM would be able not to be useful for the execution of a task (marketing information) ✓ It is important to distinguish input information from those of output (pure visualization).	✓ The screens can also aggregate besides the contents the inputs form.
Cohabitation of several typologies of navigation	✓ Process link links together operation acts	✓ Process link links together Process Screen.
Process state	✓ Definition of the operation act ✓ Add ad-hoc access structures	✓ Link to the process screen in the template view ✓ Add properties to indicate the state of the process screen
Business processes and web pages		✓ A task may be distributed on several web pages.
Types of user	✓ There isn't a mapping rule	✓ There isn't a mapping rule

Copyright © 2009, IGI Global, distributing in print or electronic forms without written permission of IGI Global is prohibited.

CONCLUSION

The methodological guidelines proposed to allow a complete design of complex information systems for the external user for which it is necessary to face, on one hand, the problems tied up to the Web, and therefore to opportunely design the information to introduce and the navigation between them, and on the other hand, to design the business processes always fundamental within the information systems.

The methodological guidelines proposed in the preceding paragraphs address the open issues individualized in this same chapter both for the methodological guidelines that lead to the IDM process and for the methodological guidelines that allow getting the PIDM process.

Table 9. Comparison between process-oriented Web application design methodologies

	OOHDM extension	WEBML - extension	UWE- extension	IDM Process - PIDM Process
Traceability of the business process in the final design	**	*	***	***
Support for the stop and resume a business process	* Use of a process anchor	-	***	***
Support to the process state	* Use of a process anchor	-	***	***
Support to the execution of the multiple business process	**	-	-	***
Explicit business process model	-	***	***	*** Is the starting point for the methodology application
Separation between business process and navigation process	-	-	***	*** Business process and navigation model are in only one design but clearly separated
Support to the free navigation	***	**	***	***

Copyright © 2009, IGI Global, distributing in print or electronic forms without written permission of IGI Global is prohibited.

The following table (Table 8), reassumes the formalities with which, respectively in IDM Process and in P-IDM Process, an answer was given to the open issues.

We underline that the methodological guidelines continue to assure the traceability, understood as the possibility to individualize in the integrated design IDM process and PIDM process the flow of the business processes with the purpose to address the requirement of flexibility of the modern information systems.

You known as the requirement of traceability has been maintained in IDM process introducing the operation strategy, the processes link and the intermediate strategy, and in PIDM process through the process screen that admits input form and the process links that connect between them different process screens.

Of course to this it is added the business process view that represents a 1 to 1 mapping with the design of the business process in the case in which the business process interests more topics of a same design. For the sake of simplicity, in Table 9, we present the same comparison between the extension for the business process methodologies already presented in Chapter II, and we compare also the IDM process and PIDM process presented here.

REFERENCES

Bolchini, D., & Paolini, P.(2006). Interactive dialogue model: A design technique for multichannel applications. *IEEE Transaction on multimedia, 8*(3), 529-541.

OMG. (2006). *Business process modeling notation specification.*

Copyright © 2009, IGI Global, distributing in print or electronic forms without written permission of IGI Global is prohibited.

Chapter VII
A Case Study for External Users

INTRODUCTION

The case of study in examination has the goal of realizing a Web application to support an operator of a tourist agency that wants to realize a tourist package according to the requirements of the customer. The operator has to organize the trip starting from the purchase of the flights or the railway ticket up to the booking of the service of car rental, of taxi, of the hotel or other tourist features. The proposed solution has to be that much closer to the demands of the user relative to the destination, to the dates and to the range of price that he/she will have pointed out.

The operator, to get the more proper solution of trip:

- looks among the suppliers of services (fly companies, hotel, restaurants, etc.) those that are able better to satisfy the needs of the customer;
- proposes to the customer the solutions;
- when the operator identifies the pool of elements that better satisfy the requirement, he/she books on behalf of the customer;
- once the confirmation from the supplier is received, the operator receives the payment from the customer;

Copyright © 2009, IGI Global, distributing in print or electronic forms without written permission of IGI Global is prohibited.

- After payment (cash or through credit card) is successfully received, the operator will send the confirmation to the suppliers.

The customer has to specify his/her preferences without constraints of pre-arranged solutions: it will be then the operator of the Web agency to take care to combine, according to the expressed demands (schedules, places of departure and arrival, price range, etc.) the results obtained by the various suppliers of services and to propose to the customer the found solutions. Once the customer has chosen the solution, the operator will purchase all of the necessary resources on behalf of the customer. The communication between the operator and the customer and between the operator and the supplier uses the Web as a preferential means. Finally, we observe that, for as it has been introduced, the process could be considered a process oriented at the inside users of the company, but it is studied here applying the methodology for the external users. This because, despite the operator works according to imposed directives (as it normally does in an intranet) he/she has large degrees of freedom in the selection of the price, of the most proper supplier and of the useful combination of the variables to make the travel package. In order to take decisions the operator needs of a navigation different from those that it would have in a classical intranet (for instance, before probably consulting the suppliers that operator, probably, will identify what offers best services at affordable prices for that specific customer); it is for this reason that it is preferred to use the methodological guidelines oriented at the external users.

Details of the Considered Process

In the application of the methodology, we have taken into examination a sub-process of the whole process realized by the operator. The sub-process is: "determines the availability of the necessary resources" particularly meaningful to the goals of the application of the methodological guidelines because in the sub- process, they are present tasks, intermediate events type message, intermediate events type timer used as delay, gateways of a different kind and start event that allow to fully use the methodological guidelines.

The considered sub-process receives as input the list of the stops and the services required for each stop, with the relative time constraints and the desired character-istics; according to the types of services and the preferences of trip, the operator initially determines the list of the suppliers to contact, that we suppose is in number equal to N. For each supplier on the list, the operator compiles the list of the resources of which to check the availability, pointing out for every element of the list, the constraints required by the customer; this list is forwarded to the supplier

Copyright © 2009, IGI Global, distributing in print or electronic forms without written permission of IGI Global is prohibited.

so it can elaborate it. The operator, at this point, is waiting for a detailed answer by the supplier.

The supplier, at the reception of the list, uses its system of back-office and it prepares an answer that will have to contain all the required elements, with the relative availability and the possible alternatives that the supplier intends to propose to the customer, through the Web agency.

If the answer from the supplier does not arrive within a default timeout (specific for every supplier according to the technology of the back-office system and to the interface), the operator will hypothesize that the supplier there has no availability of the required resources.

At the end of the receipt of the answers from all the suppliers, the operator, founding on the availabilities expressed from the suppliers, elaborates the solutions of trips appropriated for satisfying the requirement of the customer. It is necessary to underline that the activities of cooperation toward the different suppliers are not to tightly consider in a sequential way: such representation is used just for expositive clarity. The 'point of synchronization' is to immediately put before the elaboration of the solutions of trip that is a task for which it is necessary to have all the answers of the different suppliers. In Figure 1, the diagram of the sub-process is shown, modeled using the BPMN™ (OMG, 2006). This shows the operations performed by the operator to determine the availability of the resources of trip.

The IDM (Bolchini & Paolini, 2006) diagram realized by an IT expert is shown in Figure 2. Every dialogue act is characterized by the relative slots that here we do not recopy for brevity.

Figure 1. Design BPMN of the sub-process determine the availability of the necessary resources

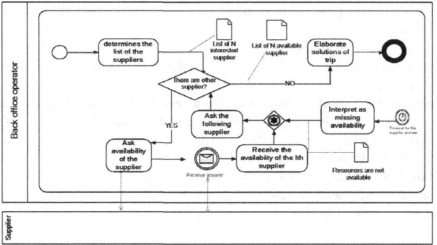

Copyright © 2009, IGI Global, distributing in print or electronic forms without written permission of IGI Global is prohibited.

Figure 2. IDM design of the application

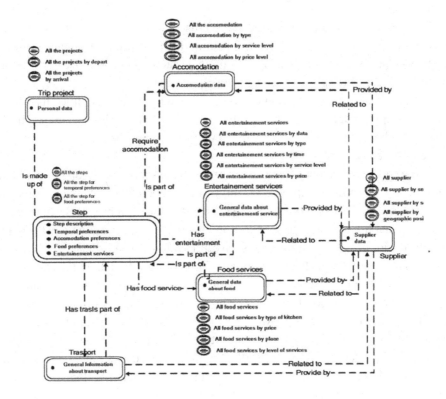

APPLICATION OF THE METHODOLOGICAL GUIDELINES IDM PROCESS

We now apply the proposed methodological guidelines with the goal to aim the IDM process design.

Step 1: User's types. Since we report to the operative user (in the BPMN™ diagram represented as a lane inside the pool Web travel agency), we realize the IDM process diagram related to this user.

Step 2: Analysis of the information contents. In the chart that follows, we can see what topics are involved in the drawing of the process. In this case, all the tasks of the process originate operation acts because they require the intervention of the operator in the Web application.

Step 3: Start of the process. The process starts through the operation act "determines the N interested suppliers" related to the kind of topic "stop." The operation strategy is drawn in the relative operation act.

Copyright © 2009, IGI Global, distributing in print or electronic forms without written permission of IGI Global is prohibited.

Step 4: Analysis of the tasks: An operation act for every operation that asks for the support of the application is created. The operations that modify or somehow use the information of the kind of topic are positioned on the edge; those that do not refer to any slot or dialogue act of any topics are positioned at the outside. Since in this case study all of the operations are interested somehow in the relative topics, the operation acts are all suitable ones on the edges.

Step 5: Definition of the operations act: We consider the task determines the N interested suppliers. It is decomposed in two separate operations acts positioned on two different topics related to the operations of elaboration of the data distinguishing the stops desired by the customer and individualization of the suppliers that own the suitable characteristics for the stops at issue. In the charts that follow, it puts on in evidence that every operation act coming from the same task it refers two different topics (and the relative dialogue acts).

An analogous discourse does it for the operations acts related to the other tasks of the process.

There are, besides, operation acts not directly connected to a specific IDM topic: we report to the operation acts that represent the operations of sending and receiving messages. Such operation acts are connected among them through process relation respecting the flow of the process.

Step 6: Gateway: The gateways are reported on the IDM process diagram exploiting the possibility offered by the methodological guidelines to represent them. In the process in examination, there are two types of gateway that are reported in the relative IDM process.

Table 1. List of the topics related to every task

Task		Topic
Name task	**Actor**	
Determine the N interested suppliers	Operator	Stop, Supplier
Consider the following supplier in the list	Operator	Supplier
Check the availability to ith supplier	Operator	Supplier
Receive the availability from ith supplier	Operator	Supplier
Interpret as missing availability	Operator	Supplier
Elaborate solutions of trip	Operator	Stop, Mean of Transport, Service Lodging, Service Food, Entertainment, Supplier

Copyright © 2009, IGI Global, distributing in print or electronic forms without written permission of IGI Global is prohibited.

Table 2. Attributes of the operation act "Determine the N interested suppliers-Stop"

ATTRIBUTE	VALUE
Name	Determine the N interested suppliers
Process	Determine the availability of the necessary resources
Task	Determine the N interested suppliers
Type	Service
Pre-condition	/
Output	List of the characteristics that the suppliers have to satisfy
Gateway	/
Kind of topic	Stop
Dialogue act	Stop Description, time Preferences, Preferences of Lodging service, Preferences of Food service, Preferences of service entertainment
Slot	Slot of Stop Description: Address, Place, City, Province, Region, Country, Type of stop, Nature of stop. Slot of time Preferences: the least arrival date, the least arrival Time, the highest arrival Date, the highest arrival Time, the least departure date, the least departure Time, the highest departure Date, the highest departure Time, the least Time of stop, the maximum Time of stop. Slot of Preferences of Lodging service: Type Lodging, Service Level, Number people, required Optional. Slot of Preferences of Food service: Type of Structure, Number of seats, Type of cooking, service Level, Date of reservation, Time of reservation, required Optional. Slot of Preferences of Entertainment service: Type of event, Event Dates, Event Time, Number of seats, required Optional, Service Level.

Copyright © 2009, IGI Global, distributing in print or electronic forms without written permission of IGI Global is prohibited.

Table 3. Attributes of the operation act "Determine the N interested suppliers- Supplier"

ATTRIBUTE	VALUE
Name	Determine the N interested suppliers
Process	Determine the availability of the necessary resources
Task	Determine the N interested suppliers
Type	Service
Pre-condition	/
Output	List of the potential suppliers
Gateway	/
Kind of topic	Supplier
Dialogue act	Data supplier
Slot	Name of the supplier, Type of offered service, geographical Location, Contacts, service Level

Step 7: Process relation: The process relation has been introduced with the goal of allowing the direct mapping between the drawing of the process and the P-IDM. Particularly the guidelines are respected for the definition of the processes relation in presence of gateway: if the next element after an operation act is a gateway, we connect the operation act to the gateway with a not labeled process relation, and we connect the gateway to the following operation act with a labeled process relation. For instance, the gateway "there are suppliers to contact?" has two incoming flows and two out coming flow, *ask availability to ith supplier* and *elaborate solutions of trip.*

Step 8: Intermediate strategy: The selected sub-process has two intermediate events, one of the type message and one of the type timer. According to the integration guidelines, the presence of the intermediate event of a type message has been modeled inserting an intermediate strategy in correspondence of the process relation that goes out from the operation act preceding the event. In fact, after the operation act *ask availability to Ith supplier*, the process relation that finishes on the operation act *receive the availability from the supplier*, is accompanied by an intermediate strategy. The presence of the intermediate event type timer has been modeled inserting an intermediate strategy in correspondence of the processes relation that goes out from operation act preceding the event that makes to activate the timer. In fact, after the operation act *message to the ith supplier*, the process relation that finishes on the operation act *interpret as missing availability*, it is accompanied by

Copyright © 2009, IGI Global, distributing in print or electronic forms without written permission of IGI Global is prohibited.

an intermediate strategy. You observe that in the corresponding BPMN™ diagram does not exist this explicit bond among the sending of the message to ask for the resources to the Ith supplier and the task *interpret as missing availability*, however, in the context of IDM process it is held opportune to consecutively consider the two corresponding operations act.

Step 9: Access structures: An introductory act for the first task of the sub-process that allows the creation of a new instance of the kind of topic and a group of introductory acts for every other operation act connected to the relative topic has been created.

Step 10: Sub-process: In the case study in examination, sub-processes do not exist.

Step 11: End event: It is chosen not to report the end event in the diagram.

The correspondent IDM process design is shown in Figure 3.

Figure 4 points out, in miniature, the correspondences among the BPMN™ design, the IDM design and the resultant IDM process.

Application of the Methodological Guidelines: P-IDM Process

After having obtained the IDM process model, we now apply the guidelines that lead us to get P-IDM process. We analyze the different views that will compose the final P-IDM process design.

Structural View

Step 1: To realize the diagram of the structural view for the kind of topic *Supplier*. First of all, the kind of topic is represented through a generic screen assigning the same name of the kind of topic to the screen.

Step 2: The considered kind of topic has only a dialogue act that is as input; this can be proven checking the attribute dialogue act of all the operation acts that refer to the supplier or, directly from the drawing observing that the dialogue act is connected from relation to the operations act.

Step 3: For the dialogue act of the *supplier* there has been created a content that is joined to the screen produced at step 1: *supplier data*. It is not necessary to divide the slots of the dialogue act in more contents. In the content, the slots of the dialogue act from which it derives are defined: for example, the content *Supplier Data* has the slots *Name of the supplier*, *Type of offered service*, *geographical Location*, *Contacts* and *Service Levels*.

Step 4: To consider the first operation act, determine the N interested suppliers: this is connected to the dialogue act of the kind of topic and, therefore, a screen and an input form is created maintaining the same name of the dialogue act. To

Copyright © 2009, IGI Global, distributing in print or electronic forms without written permission of IGI Global is prohibited.

Figure 3. IDM process design

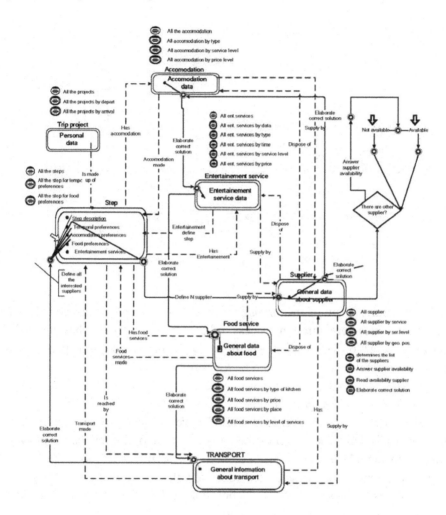

the created screen, the P of process and the name of the operation act are added. Besides, the created screen goes to compose a guided tour that the operator follows for the elaboration of all the necessary information for the composition of the solutions of trip.

Step 5: Because the integration guidelines allow it, we decided to represent in P-IDM process the gateways, as on the IDM process drawing.

The exclusive gateway *there are suppliers to contact?* allows performing the count of the suppliers consulted to check the availability of their services in line with the preferences pointed out by the customer.

Copyright © 2009, IGI Global, distributing in print or electronic forms without written permission of IGI Global is prohibited.

Figure 4. Mapping among design IDM, BPMN and IDM process

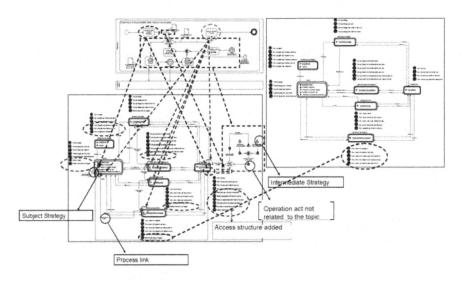

The structural View of the *supplier* shows the screen *there are suppliers to contact?*; it comes here, through process link, from the screen that has allowed to determine the list of the suppliers interested by the preferences of trip, related to the operation act *determine the N interested suppliers*, and also from the screen in which the following interested supplier is considered, related to the operation act *consider the following supplier in list.*

The screen *there are suppliers to contact?* drives through process link, if all the suppliers in a list have not been consulted, to the screen for the application of availability of ith supplier related to the operation act *ask availability to first supplier*; if all the suppliers of the list have been consulted, the screen *there are suppliers to contact?* drives to the screen for the elaboration of the solutions of trip related to the operation act *elaborates solutions of trip.*

The event-based gateway *feedback availability of first supplier*, it comes here, through process link, from the screen of *receipt of the availability of the ith supplier*, related to the operation act *Receive the availability from first supplier*, and from the screen of *missing availability of the ith supplier*, at the expiration of the timer related to the operation act *Interpret as missing availability*. The screen gateway elaborates the information that comes to appraise if the supplier has given an answer (positive or negative), or if it has not given any feedback in the established time, the attitude to be considered is a negative answer; after such evaluation the screen conducts, through process link, to the screen in which the following interested supplier is considered related to the operation act *consider the following supplier in list.*

Copyright © 2009, IGI Global, distributing in print or electronic forms without written permission of IGI Global is prohibited.

It is possible to observe that the connection among the screens related to the operation act and the consecutive gateway is done using a generic process link. Vice versa, the other process links have been labeled for explaining their function.

Step 6: In relation to the *supplier,* two intermediate strategies exist; one is due to a message intermediate event located among the operation act *message to first supplier* and the operation act *receive the availability from first supplier*: the intermediate strategy is reported on the P-IDM process drawing through an intermediate link among the process screens correspondent to the specified operation act. The second intermediate strategy is due to a timer intermediate event located among the operation act *message to first supplier* and the operation act *interpret as missing availability*: the intermediate strategy is reported on the P-IDM process drawing through an intermediate link among the screens of process correspondent to the specified operation acts.

Figure 5 shows the structural view of the *supplier* for the *operator.*

Association View

The view of association for the operator has been built in the following way:

Step 1: For every kind of topic there has been created a screen.

Step 2: For every relevant relation coming out from a kind of topic there has been built association content, aggregated to the screen of the same topic with the name of the link. For instance, *stop* aggregates the association contents *has lodging, has food, has entertainment* and *reached with,* connected to the screens *lodging service, food service, entertainment service* and a *transport,* respectively.

Step 3: The association contents have been then connected to the kind of topic of destination through association link. We see the resultant drawing in Figure 6.

View of the Navigation Paths

The view of the navigation paths visualizes the access structures of the application to the relative pages of a kind of topic. Consider again the *supplier.*

Step 1: It is created a screen of access to the kind of topic called *access supplier.*

Step 2: It is represented an introductory act as access content that has the same name of the access structure from which it derives. For instance, the introductory act *all the suppliers* becomes an access content with the same name. Every access content has to be aggregated to the screen *access supplier* and tied by a collection link to the screen *supplier.*

Step 3: To represent the group of introductory acts, it proceeds in the way described through the following example: *all the suppliers for type of service* becomes

Copyright © 2009, IGI Global, distributing in print or electronic forms without written permission of IGI Global is prohibited.

Figure 5. Structural view for the kind of topic supplier

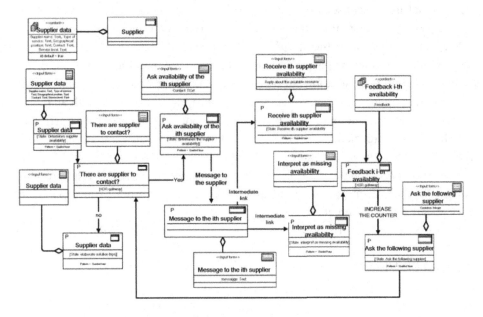

Figure 6. Association view of the application for the operator

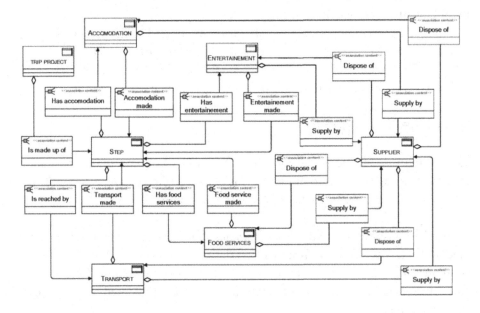

Copyright © 2009, IGI Global, distributing in print or electronic forms without written permission of IGI Global is prohibited.

the access content *types of service of the suppliers*; this access content is aggregated to the screen *access supplier* and tied through collection link to the screen *Suppliers for type of service*. An access content is aggregated to the last created screen and tied, through collection link, to the *supplier*. The same procedure is repeated for every group of introductory acts of access to the kind of topic.

The result of the above operations is shown in Figure 7.

Templates View

The view of the templates allows having visibility of the access structures without which the application would lose usability and dynamism.

Step 1: It is created a screen template with the name *supplier*.

Step 2: It is created a layout content with the name *operator index*: this is aggregated to the screen template *supplier* and tied up to the screen *access supplier* through a link that points at this last screen.

Step 3: All the screens of the structural view and the navigation paths view are reported on the current diagram and tied up to the screen template *supplier* with relationships of specialization.

In this way, all the pages that specialize in the screen template will have visibility of the access structures contained in the screen *access supplier* to which the layout content is connected. The view of the templates is shown in Figure 8.

View of Process

To realize the view of process for the user *operator,* it has been reported on a unique diagram all the screens of process, related both to tasks and to gateways, of all of the kinds of topics involved in the sub-process, *project of trip*, *stops*, *lodging service*, *entertainment service*, *food service*, *transport* and *supplier*, connecting them through process links.

The resultant drawing is that shown in Figure 9.

CONCLUSION

The application of the methodological guidelines, described in Chapter 6, has led to good results: starting from the separate design of the user experience and of the business processes, it has been possible, in fact, to get a complete design of a process-oriented Web application. The resultant design is detailed enough, and it constitutes a solid base for the following implementation phase that can be realized both manually and by the way of special tools of code generation.

Copyright © 2009, IGI Global, distributing in print or electronic forms without written permission of IGI Global is prohibited.

Figure 7. View of navigation paths of the kind of topic supplier for the operator

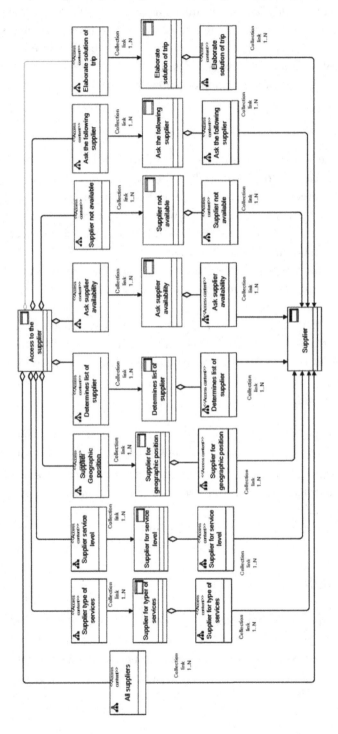

Copyright © 2009, IGI Global, distributing in print or electronic forms without written permission of IGI Global is prohibited.

Figure 8. Template view of the kind of topic supplier for the operator

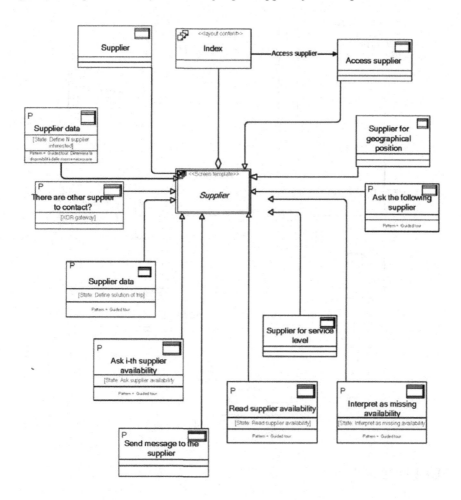

Copyright © 2009, IGI Global, distributing in print or electronic forms without written permission of IGI Global is prohibited.

Figure 9. View of process of the Web application travel agency for the operator

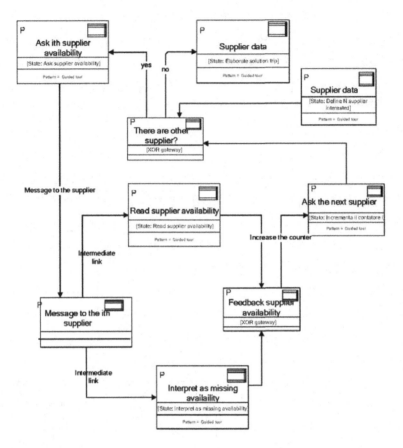

REFERENCES

Bolchini, D., & Paolini, P.(2006). Interactive dialogue model: A design techinique for multichannel applications. *IEEE Transaction on multimedia, 8*(3), 529-541.

OMG. (2006). *Business process modeling notation specification.*

Copyright © 2009, IGI Global, distributing in print or electronic forms without written permission of IGI Global is prohibited.

Chapter VIII
Web Application Process–Oriented Design for Internal Users

INTRODUCTION

As more times underlined within this book, when the application is turned to the inside, users of the company that do not need information of contour in comparison to those necessary for the carrying out the task of the process, the alone design of the process is enough to come up to the final application. It is necessary, however, to submit the initial design to a transformation that allows making it suitable to the requests of whom will have called then to implement the application. In this process of passage from a high-level design (what is that aim to define the business processes) up to the final implementation of the application, of course, both the business experts and the IT experts are involved, each of them needing different levels of detail. The business experts, understanding the problems present in the company, try to delineate its underlying processes in a clear and unambiguous way; to do, the use of the BPMN™ notation (OMG, 2006) is a great help. Among the receivers of the documents produced by the business analyst there are the IT experts that will have to realize the final application on the base of such documentation.

The business experts, for the role they have, do not worry about the specific functional requirements of the final application, and they do not think in a structured

Copyright © 2009, IGI Global, distributing in print or electronic forms without written permission of IGI Global is prohibited.

way about the final application. The schema of the realized process, as it is right, does not keep in mind the particular implications that it will have on the application. The only analysis of the process realized by the analyst of business surely is not enough to aim the realization of the final application to support the process, but it subsequently goes refined up to come to a level of detail suitable to such purpose.

The identification of the functional requirements of the application and the basic application modules are, instead, the most important competences of IT designers. These elements are determined, carefully examining the model provided by the business experts having as a goal to specify the functional characteristics of the application to make them available to the end users and identify the data classes that must have managed from the information system, necessary to the application for its operation.

The business experts and the IT experts work, therefore, with different goals, and it usually happens that the model of process realized by the business expert has been very different from those required to satisfy the needs of the IT designers. The business experts, in fact, put also in evidence tasks that, practically, they do not have a confirmation in the application such as, for instance, tasks purely manuals, or they tend to represent different elementary operations using just one task, or it still does not exactly provide for the input and the output information of every task belonging to the process.

In this perspective, the open issues, identified during the definition of the methodological guidelines proposed in Chapter VI really do not exist because the design of the user experience is practically nonexistent.

It is particularly important, however, to provide some methodological guidelines that give the possibility to pass, in a structured way, from the high-level design realized by the business experts to a more detailed design that, as input, can be used for the implementation.

The methodology of refinement proposed is composed of two steps, each of which is set at a different level of abstraction (Figure 1). In the first step, more methodological than technological, the BPMN™ design is subject to a refinement process up to come to the definition of the workflow BPMN™ or rather of a drawing of a realized process using the same notation BPMN™, but that it represents all of the necessary details to the following phase of implementation.

The second step focuses, instead, on an implementation level and, taking as input the workflow BPMN™ realized in the first step, it allows determining the applicative modules that will constitute the final application.

At this point, according to the actual tendencies of the technology, we have preferred to use the portlet technology as reference technology to pass to the real implementation. Really, the methodological guidelines provided in the step 2,

Copyright © 2009, IGI Global, distributing in print or electronic forms without written permission of IGI Global is prohibited.

Figure 1. Overview of the proposed methodology

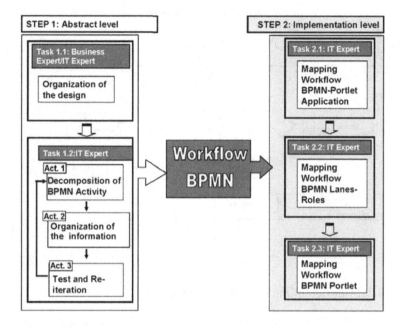

despite that they are modeled on such technology, they are also valid on any other technology of reference.

We now will describe in detail the different steps of the methodology.

Introduction to a Simple Case Study

In order to present the methodology in the best way, we introduce here a simple case study already presented in Chapter V. In order to help the reader with the reading of the case study, we present in Figure 2 the design BPMN™ of process concerning the arrival of purchased wheat. In the special case, we refer to the sub-process presented in Figure 3 (the sub-process "arrival plan").

In the case study, we do not explain the details of the considered case study: a reader may refer to the case study of Chapter V. The sub-process of "arrival plan" is presented in Figure 3.

STEP 1. ABSTRACT LEVEL

The first step, more methodological than technological, is composed of two tasks: the first one can be performed by either the business expert or the IT expert, but it

Copyright © 2009, IGI Global, distributing in print or electronic forms without written permission of IGI Global is prohibited.

Figure 2. Process of the arrival of purchased wheat

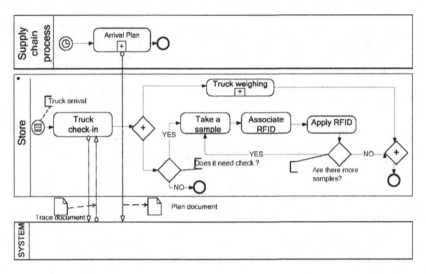

Figure 3. BPMN design of the sub-process arrival plan

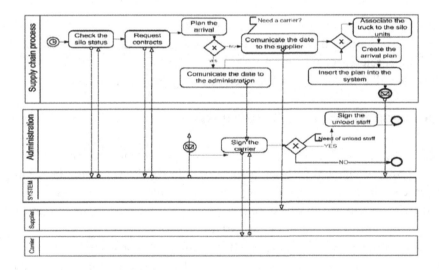

is generally arranged by both; the second task, that is composed of three activities, is mainly performed by the IT expert using the suggestions provided in this job.

Task 1.1 Reorganization of the Design

The refinement can be realized both by the IT experts and the business expert, and it consists of producing diagrams that introduce a modular structure and enough

Copyright © 2009, IGI Global, distributing in print or electronic forms without written permission of IGI Global is prohibited.

clarity regarding the flow of the activities, or at least delineate with precision the macro-activities, to easily pass to the following phases. The problems that typically emerge from a study of the diagrams produced by the business analyst are:

- *Level of detail*: the diagram produced by the business analyst could introduce some parts very detailed or parts delineated too much in a generic way. For instance, some activities specified as task in reality could require a very articulated series of operations that the analyst of business is not interested to represent in the details, but such details are essential for the software designer.
- *High degree of dependence among the tasks of a same diagram*: the diagram could introduce tasks tightly connected each other sharing the same data; in this case it could be convenient to gather the tasks in a single sub-process that will be managed then by a specific applicative module, increasing so the modularity and the reusability of the software modules of the final application.
- The model neglects the data objects used by the activities (or it does not define them in detail), that are crucial because the primary resource managed by any information system is the information, and therefore the data.

To obviate to these issues and, therefore, to come to a drawing of process, that will be input for the second task of this step, it is essential:

- To identify and to point out as sub-process the activities that imply a set of more graininess operations meaningful for the process, and that they have been neglected for needs of clarity, or because intentionally not analyzed in a more detailed way. If the sub-process is particularly important and requires an effective support by the information system, it is necessary to provide a further diagram of a kind private business process, which puts in evidence, at least broadly, the flow of the activities skipped in the first diagram. In the case study here presented, there is not this problem but the BPMN™ designer has been very detailed: instead, in the case study there are many tasks that will be grouped in a sub-process in order to make the design clearer.
- To identify tasks strongly correlated in terms of time and place, or that use the same data, especially in the case in which these data are not used by other activities of the process, and to gather them in a unique sub-process, to make the diagram more structured, with the effect to make the final application more modular, when an independent applicative module is associated to the sub-process. Although the business analyst has been very detailed in the BPMN™ design, he/she put in separate tasks operations that share the same data and

Copyright © 2009, IGI Global, distributing in print or electronic forms without written permission of IGI Global is prohibited.

lead to one output. In this step, it is important to group together these activities in order to re-organize the design: it is possible to see in the next figure that many tasks have been grouped in a single sub-process. For example, tasks "check the site status," "request contracts" and "plan the arrival" has been grouped in the sub-process "show contracts" (Figure 4).

We notice that the BPMN™ design on the bottom of Figure 4 is more complicated than the portion of design in the top but these design choices are very useful for the IT expert that will implement the application. It is clear that the IT expert and the business expert must work together in order to obtain this new design more suitable for the IT experts needs.

- To put into evidence the more important data objects used in the process, not to absolutely skip the data whose presence is essential in the information system. If we refer to Figure 4, we can see in the bottom that more data objects are represented in order to better explain the data that will be used in the information system. For example, the data object "scheduling document" is presented in the new diagram in order to explain that it is important to provide information about scheduling in an explicit way. This information will be output for the "make scheduling document" sub-process.

Figure 4. The refinement of the BPMN design – Task 1.1

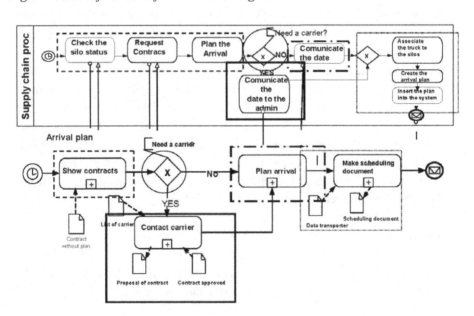

Copyright © 2009, IGI Global, distributing in print or electronic forms without written permission of IGI Global is prohibited.

Task 1.2 Refinement

Generally, it is possible to identify two aspects that address the process of refinement of the diagrams:

- The decomposition of the activities, allows identifying tasks that represent function with which the users of the system can directly interact; they could be eventually reusable.
- The structuring of the data objects in the BPMN™ diagrams allows to identify the elementary informative objects used by the process.

Activity 1: Decomposition of the Activities

The first operation to be completed for getting a BPMN™ diagram more detailed (workflow BPMN™) is to verify if the activities described in the process have dignity to be represented inside an application; the business analyst, in phase of modeling of the process, could also describe purely manual activities, such as making a phone call or sending a fax. Then, to get a proper model for the development of the final application, it is necessary to verify if inside each process there exist some tasks that do not ask for support from the information system. *Such tasks will have to be ignored.*

Another fundamental passage is to identify a possible decomposition of the tasks; in fact, the tasks identified by the business analyst, considered elementary activities, could not be such for the application, in the sense that they could require the implementation of more elementary features.

For each task present in the original BPMN™ diagram, it is necessary to consider that:

- If the task corresponds to a purely manual activity, it does not have a confirmation in terms of application, and therefore the task must be discarded by the design of the application or marked as such, and accordingly ignored in the following phases. The case study here explained has the goal of making as automatic as possible the considered business process, so there are no tasks that will be ignored.
- For each identified task (among those remaining after the process of selection realized to the preceding step), it is necessary to consider if it is homogeneous in terms of time and place (it can immediately be performed in a unique site by an only operator). In the case study here explained, we group as sub-process more tasks, in this step it is important to define which tasks will be homogeneous in terms of time and place and to define these tasks as single tasks.

Copyright © 2009, IGI Global, distributing in print or electronic forms without written permission of IGI Global is prohibited.

- For each sub-process and for each task it is necessary to consider if it depends only on the data objects in input and in output indicated, or if it also uses other information that have not been put into evidence. If there are other data, then they must be pointed out, using the data objects and if the new data objects make to emerge tasks not introduced in the diagram, they must expressly be reported. In this step, the analysis of the tasks has been made for the case study here presented: all the data objects have been defined in the step 1, but in this step, because we refine the sub-process, we add for each task the right data object useful to perform the task.

Activity 2: The Information Structuring

Another aspect to be taken into consideration during the definition of a drawing of the process more closely to the implementation, is the management of the information. In fact, while in the processes, particular emphasis is set to the flow of the activities; in the design of the application it is fundamental to structure the information or rather the data in input and in output to the activities of the process.

The structuring of the information is, therefore, a very delicate point in the passage from the drawing of the process to that of the final application.

The information in the BPMN™ is represented by the data objects; every activity, task or sub-process, it uses the data objects that can be gathered in input sets (for the data in input to the activity), output sets (for the data produced by the activity). Besides in BPMN™ it is possible to represent the IORules (that allow representing the rules of transformation from the input to the output). In the construction of the model workflow BPMN™, it is necessary to define precisely these elements.

In the case study presented here, we add details about each data object presented in the BPMN™ diagram of Figure 4. We explain in Table 1 the details of each data object.

The arrows will indicate if each data object is an input set or an output set.

Activity 3: Test and Reiteration

Finally, it is necessary to verify that the new model built starting from the initial diagram puts into evidence all of the necessary elements for the definition of the application modules and for the design of the data-base. The verification consists of examining the identified tasks, and to verify that they represent function of the application externally visible and usable directly by the users; otherwise, it must reiterate starting from the activity 1.

The final design, after the application of the previous steps shown is in Figure 5. It is important to highlight, for example, that in the activity 1 and 2 the "contact

Copyright © 2009, IGI Global, distributing in print or electronic forms without written permission of IGI Global is prohibited.

Table 1. Details about each data object

Data Object	Elementary information
Contract without plan	Arrival company Supplier Data Contract Data Lot data Scheduled Quantity Delivery condition
List of carrier	Carrier data Company data Truck data
Proposal of contract	Number of carrier needed Number of truck needed Delivery data Destination company
Contract approved	Contract approved
Data	Truck data Carrier data
Scheduling document	Estimate delivery date Truck status Supplier data Lot Estimated quantity Destination company

carrier" sub-process does not have the "show list of transport company" as a task but in the reiteration phase the IT expert in order to better explain the importance of the selection of a carrier from the list, add this task with the relative data object.

It is possible to see that each task is homogeneous in terms of time and place and that each task has its own input and output data object.

The output of step 1 is the workflow BPMN™ that can be used as input for step 2 of the methodology. Before explaining the second step in the detail, it is necessary to make some considerations.

FROM THE WORKFLOW BPMN TO THE REALIZATION OF THE PORTAL

Step 1, that allows defining the workflow BPMN™, has general validity, and it can be applied independently by the specific implementation technology that will be chosen in the following phase. Starting from the workflow BPMN™, it is possible to choose among different alternatives to reach the implementation of the final application all equally valid ones. It is possible, for instance, to realize a stand-alone application that implements the business process or to realize a Web application

Copyright © 2009, IGI Global, distributing in print or electronic forms without written permission of IGI Global is prohibited.

Figure 5. Workflow BPMN of the considered case study

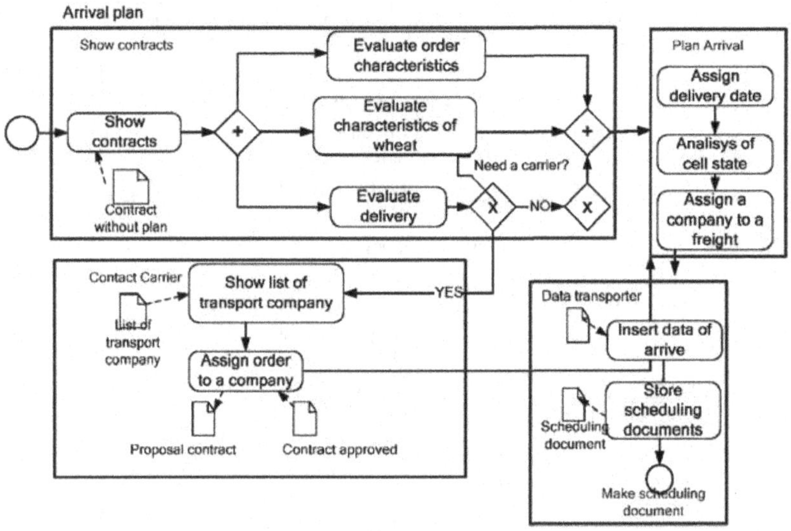

managing the user experience in an appropriate way, and therefore, putting the end user in condition to operate in the best some ways.

To aim to realize a Web application whose users will mainly be the inside users of the company, it is desired to give the possibility to be able to use a suitable operational dashboard to the user, better if it is customized according to its own needs.

The choice of the portlet technology with the purpose of realizing a company intranet process-intensive has been suggested by numerous characteristics that the technology introduces and that well suit it for our purposes.

First of all, the choice of the technology is related to an important remark (Diaz & Iñaki, 2005) according to which the difference between WA and portlet originates from different planning and from different users' target. The use of the portlet is very suitable in the intranet environment; in fact, the users are the same employees of the company, each with a well-precise and defined role that see the portal as a tool in which they operate performing their assignments (often repetitive). In a portal, the users, as in a desktop environment, have all of the information they need also passing through other applications that can be or applications that implement other business processes or applications that simply provide the user with useful information to the carrying out of the processes (you may, for instance, think about the possibility of constantly having news about the Stock Exchange prices for a bank employee).

Copyright © 2009, IGI Global, distributing in print or electronic forms without written permission of IGI Global is prohibited.

In the portal, it is possible to integrate either existing applications or to realize new applications (for instance, to support a process that is inserted ex novo within the information system).

The user, during the normal progress of his/her job, could be forced to pass through different applications and, without having a portal, it would pass in different contexts with the necessity to do a login to more applications finding itself, every time, with different graphic layout with a consequent disorientation and therefore difficulty to operate (above all for low technical users). The portals offer, therefore, a single point of access to the company information system for each user involved in the system. The possibility of customization offered by the portals drives the user, instead, to realize his/her own operational dashboard that, as a desktop environment, allows him/her to have constantly available everything he/she needs.

While the Web applications are self-sufficient enough, a portlet is deployed into a container (the portal framework) and rendered with another portlet; therefore, it must be inserted into a well- precise context that, with a good design of the portlet container, is exactly the context in which the user operates providing to it all and only the information it needs for the performing of the own tasks without the necessity to get information from external applications.

Last, but not least, a portal is made of a portlet, each of which support a well-defined service and not a whole process: it is the portal to realize a mechanism of "orchestration" that by putting together according to a certain well-precise logic the various portlets, it builds the process in which the user has involved. Clearly, this fact is fundamental in the perspective of the reuse of the code: being an autonomous entity and not tied up to the specific context, portlet realized that one determined process can also be reused for other processes simply identifying the portlet that implements a well-precise task.

A further motive that pushes us to the use of the portlets is the actual phase of standardization that are following through the specific JSR 168 in which are defined, besides the fundamental definitions of portal, portlet and portlet container, the standard API to create the portlet, the rules of integration between portals and portlet. According to this standard, a portlet can be reused in whatever portal (what it agrees to the same standard). Currently, it is in compilation time the version 268 of the JSR.

STEP 2. IMPLEMENTATION LEVEL

Step 2 of the proposed methodology is, therefore, more operational: the application of this step drives the design of the final application (portlet-based) that will faithfully answer to the requirements imposed by the drawing of the process.

Copyright © 2009, IGI Global, distributing in print or electronic forms without written permission of IGI Global is prohibited.

Task 2.1: Mapping of the Processes

For each process and each independent sub-process delineated using the notation BPMN™, it is necessary to create separate portlet-applications that communicate between them through the common techniques of communication among the Web applications or more, inside the same organization, through the access to a layer of persistence shared as a database.

It might be the case in which the process presents independent sub-process, which according to the established BPMN™ notation, they have no global data shared with the process father, even if the process parent is able to use/provide data from/to an independent sub-process. The independent sub-process can have more pools, and can be, therefore, treated as a distinct portlet-application (one for each independent sub-process). An exception to such a rule is the case in which an independent sub-process is referenced in a unique process father: in such a case it is not obligatory to create a separate portlet application.

You note that if a process is modified to its inside, but does not change the messages exchanged with the other processes with which it interacts, the changes do not strike again on the other processes: equally, the portlet-applications determined with the described rule are independent, and the updating of a portlet-application will not interest the other portlet-applications.

If we refer to Figure 3, we notice that in the application there will be two portlet applications, one for the supply chain manager and one for the manager. Each portlet application will be delivered to the specific actor.

Task 2.2: Mapping of the Lanes

Every lane corresponds to a role inside the process, and it must be associated with a role of the portal, and therefore, to the relative security constraints inside the system of management of the permissions provided by the portal. The lanes also cover a fundamental role to determine the pages of the portal. In fact, considering every process, it joins to every lane present in the process a page in the portal. So, if one certain professional figure inside an organization performs tasks related to more processes, there will be more pages of the portal related to the corresponding role.

If a role has competences in more processes, there will be more pages of the portal related through the security constraints to that role; the security constraints determine what pages of the portal are visible to each user, and therefore, what links are available in the navigation bar.

If a certain user has to abandon an activity of a process to intervene on another process of its competence, he will pass to another page of the portal without doing

Copyright © 2009, IGI Global, distributing in print or electronic forms without written permission of IGI Global is prohibited.

the logout. In this way, the state of the interrupted activity is saved even if a recording has not been affected in the database or the rescue in the layer of persistence of another type used by the application, and the process can become active again before concluding the session of a job.

Because in the design of the considered business process lanes always overlap with pools, each portlet application (defined in task 2.1) has its own role.

Task 2.3: Decomposition of the Application in Modules: Identifying the Portlets

At this point, it is needed to determine the portlet present in every portlet-application. The portlet are the fundamental application modules and eventually reusable of the application. Each sub-process or atomic task identified in the drawing of the process workflow BPMN™ is mapped into a portlet: since a same sub-process or task can be present in different lanes that, in turn is mapped (task 2) in a page of the portal, the same portlet can belong to more pages of the portal.

The criteria individualized for decomposing the application in modules are the following:

- Every identified embedded sub-process corresponds with a portlet. Furthermore, to the "isolated" tasks that do not belong to a sub-process corresponds to a portlet. Therefore, if we refer to Figure 5, it is possible to have four portlets, one for each sub-process: "show contract," "plan arrival," "contact carrier," "make scheduling document."
- To every task that implicates the visualization of a data object, by the user it corresponds with a form of visualization inside of a portlet. If we refer to Figure 5, for example, we will have a form of visualization in order to visualize "contract without plan" or "list of transport company" or the "proposal contract."
- To every task involved in the insertion of data by the users, which they will go to fill a data object as output of the task, it corresponds with a form of data insertion inside a portlet. In order to provide the user of the considered case study with the possibility of filling the data object,we will have the data entry form for the "contract approved" and/or for the "scheduling document."
- To every fork/join defined in the BPMN™ design (a gateway of any type with its own rows to follow) where is required the selection by the user, it corresponds with a portlet where each task is defined in order to allow the user the selection of one (or more depending on the special gateway in use) rows in the process flow. In the case study here considered, we will have a portlet in order to allow to the user the possibility of determining whether or not the

Copyright © 2009, IGI Global, distributing in print or electronic forms without written permission of IGI Global is prohibited.

delivery needs a carrier (after the evaluation task performed).

- If the task provides neither the visualization nor the insertion of the data, it represents an inside function of the system and, therefore, it will not have some confirmation from the point of view of the presentation of the application. Manual activities are been discarded in phase of refinement of the diagram (step 1-activity 1).

COHERENCE BETWEEN THE FLOW OF THE PROCESS AND THE SUPPORT APPLICATION

We described in task 2.3 that to each task or embedded sub-process correspond with a portlet; it is obvious that the portlet must be inserted in an operational context conforming to the flow of the process, and therefore it is necessary to manage the activation of the portlet in a way consistent with the flow of the process.

Regarding the gateways, they represent points in which the flow of the process can undertake alternative or parallel runs. The gateways, according to the BPMN™ notation, can be type fork or type join. The gateways check the flow of the activities, and therefore, also in this case they determine the activation of an application module, and therefore of a fragment of the page, coherently with the modeling of the process.

The gateways type fork can be data-based or event-based. Regarding the gateways data-based, it is necessary to verify a condition that depends on the data of the process, and therefore it has to be valued on the data-object present. In regards to the gateways event-based, since the events generally have to be recorded from the information system, the condition must be verified regarding the information that certifies the event. A particular case is that for which the run to be undertaken depends on a decision of the user.

Regarding the events, they can be a type message, timer or rule. The events type message represents the sent or received messages by a process, and as such they have to be recorded from the information system; so the event associates data inside the information system. Regarding the events type timer or rule, they remind specific conditions that it is necessary to check at an implementation level, performing the opportune action to achieve the result.

ONTOLOGICAL REPRESENTATION OF THE METHODOLOGY

As it is obvious, it is possible to provide only an ontological representation of the first step of the methodology (and therefore of the workflow BPMN™ obtained in

Copyright © 2009, IGI Global, distributing in print or electronic forms without written permission of IGI Global is prohibited.

output) being the second step a set of practical rules that cannot be contained in some language. Since nothing is used if not BPMN™, the ontological representation of the notation, opportunely detailed in the preceding chapter, is enough for the representation of the workflow BPMN™. Chapter IV described a detailed treatment.

THE DEFINITION OF THE LAYOUT

We know that in order to obtain the final application starting from the model, it is important to provide some information about the final layout; for example, it is important to define if a specific field of input will be edited directly from the user or if the user will just select one field from a check box or a drop down list and so on.

It is of the highest importance to specify the information field structure at a design level and this task is of competence of the IT expert. Although these are considerations, the structure of the input and/or output fields is out of BPMN™ competencies, so in order to preserve the compatibility between the ontological BPMN™ meta-model and the BPMN™ specification, we think to add this information in another level of design, the layout design. This level of design will be, in a few words, the same workflow BPMN™ where the information about layout will be added. For example, the information structure of the input field will be as in the Table 2.

CONCLUSION

The methodological guidelines provided relatively to the realization of an information system oriented to the internal users, result as well structured, and they allow showing the importance that the business processes assumed in the definition of such information system.

Once more, in fact, according to the modern techniques of design of the information systems that are exalted in the definition of these guidelines, the design of

Table 2. Input field structure

Name	Type	Input/output	Modality	Control
Name of the field	Text, numeric, Date, etc.	Specify if the field is of input or output	Input from keyboard, radio, combobox and so on	Specify here the check required from the field

Copyright © 2009, IGI Global, distributing in print or electronic forms without written permission of IGI Global is prohibited.

the process assumes a central role considering that it is the only design on which both business expert and IT expert work each with its own purposes.

The refinement of the design, proposed in step 1 of the methodology; it seems appropriate to fill the existing gap among the two different professional figures.

The choice, in step 2, of the portlet technology for the implementation of the final application adjusts it, instead, to the modern technological trends; the portlet, in fact, is very suitable for the realization of an information system according to the needs of the internal users.

The realized technological choice leaves space to an easy integration of the information system with useful external applications to the performing of the jobs of the user inside to the company.

REFERENCES

Diaz, O., & Paz, I. (2005) Turning Web applications into Portlets: Raising the issues. *Proceedings of the 2005 Symposium on Applications and the Internet (SAINT'05)*, (pp. 31-37). Trento, Italy.

OMG. (2006). *Business process modeling notation specification.*

Copyright © 2009, IGI Global, distributing in print or electronic forms without written permission of IGI Global is prohibited.

Chapter IX
Case Study for Internal Users

INTRODUCTION

The case study taken into examination to validate the proposed methodology relative to the inside users of the information system is a process regarding a public local administration that involves citizens, professionals and companies; it rules the payment of an annual tax that the citizens pay to the public local administration.

The tax is calculated assuming the value of the building estates that the contributor owns; particularly, the calculation is done assuming the typology of building and its value, using the rates defined by the local administration, and the data of the owner.

The case immediately introduces it as a case strongly oriented to the logic of process and for which the operator, which in this context operates by the business intranet, does not have necessity of particular navigation, but it only has to limit itself to performing the orders of service.

For this case study, therefore, the problem to choose the better methodology to apply is not present, but that proposed for the internal users immediately seems the most suitable.

Copyright © 2009, IGI Global, distributing in print or electronic forms without written permission of IGI Global is prohibited.

DETAILS OF THE PROCESS

The citizen can fill out the form to be able to make the due payment both person-ally and turning to advisors that perform the calculation in place of it. Of course, in the calculation of the tax the citizen or the advisor will be supported by the application.

The citizen can fill out the form without using the application, in such a case, an advisor entrusted by the public administration will insert and transmit the data pointed out by the citizen itself.

The business expert realizes a first design of the process using the BPMN™ notation (OMG, 2006). The produced diagram introduces a general vision of the process, putting in evidence the different involved actors and the relationship among them (Figure 1).

Figure 1. BPMN design of the process realized by the business analyst

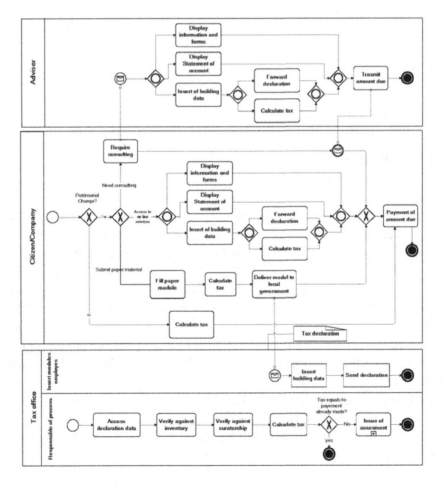

Copyright © 2009, IGI Global, distributing in print or electronic forms without written permission of IGI Global is prohibited.

Application of the Methodological Guidelines: Step 1

Having available enough of the complete design of the process, we now apply the methodological guidelines relative to the inside users of the company.

Task 1.1 Organization of the Design

To realize a first level of structuring of the diagram produced, it will subsequently be refined then to reach the level of workflow BPMN™; we observe that:

- Some tasks imply a meaningful series of activities at finer granularity, particularly the insertion of the data on the buildings estates (task developed from the citizen or from the advisor) and the execution of the verifications on the declarations (task developed by the manager of procedure), surely, they carry out of not banal operations that must be supported by the application and that have not put into evidence. These tasks, therefore, must be shaped as sub-process and further BPMN™ diagrams type private business process must have realized showing the flow of the unspecified activities.
- The portion of flow that describes the activities shared among the various advisors responsible of the compilation of the forms and the citizen or the company, and that substantially it represents the set of services accessible online by the external users of the system, more than as a flow of parallel activities, it is opportune to represent it as an ad hoc flow: the user is free to determine the execution order of the tasks.
- The operations of *insertion of the data of the building* with the purpose to submit the declaration and the insertion of data to calculate the tax are deeply different: first of all, the calculation of the tax could be a service offered to the generic users without effecting the login, while, regarding the transmission of the declaration, this operation must have be done only behind authentication and with precise controls on the provided data. Besides, for a contributor, the calculation of the tax can almost totally be automated, if there are no variations. So, the two operations must be distinguished.
- *Insertion of the data* and *submission of the declaration* can be united in a unique sub-process, type independent, since it does not share data with its father, and it does not depend on other processes for the start, since it will be inserted into an ad hoc flow. Besides, this sub-process is not banal, and it is particularly important, and therefore, it requires the support of the information system. So, it must be specified with a diagram type private business process before passing to the design and implementation of the application of support.

Copyright © 2009, IGI Global, distributing in print or electronic forms without written permission of IGI Global is prohibited.

• The verifications conducted with the databases of the inventory and of the curatorship could be performed either in parallel or without a precise order, and also they imply not banal operations, and they require the support of the information system. So, these tasks become, de facto, a sub-process.

At the light of these considerations, a more structured diagram has been produced (Figure 2) from which to get, with the task 1.2 the workflow BPMN™:

Task 1.2 Activity 1 Decomposition of the Activities

We now focus on the sub-process *Online compilation and submission of the form* that repeats itself in more lanes of the process described in Figure 1. We suppose, for brevity, that this sub-process was already restructured according to the task 1.1, and it is, therefore, as in Figure 3.

Figure 2. Design of the process restructured according to the task 1

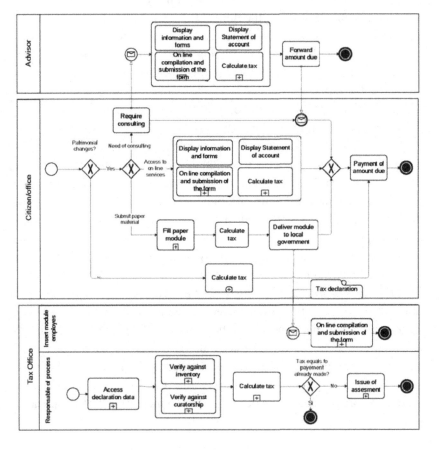

Copyright © 2009, IGI Global, distributing in print or electronic forms without written permission of IGI Global is prohibited.

When applying the guidelines provided for activity 1, it is necessary, first of all, to verify if the identified tasks correspond purely to activity manuals, but this it is not the case of the above model where every activity requires an interaction with the information system.

The second criterion to be verified is the homogeneity for time and for place of the tasks; furthermore, this criterion nevertheless results satisfied in the considered example, since the whole process of online compilation and submission of the form is brief, and it is performed through a single computer.

Figure 3. Diagram of the process "online compilation and submission of the form": it refers to a single actor: for space reasons it has been separated in three parts connected by an intermediate event type link

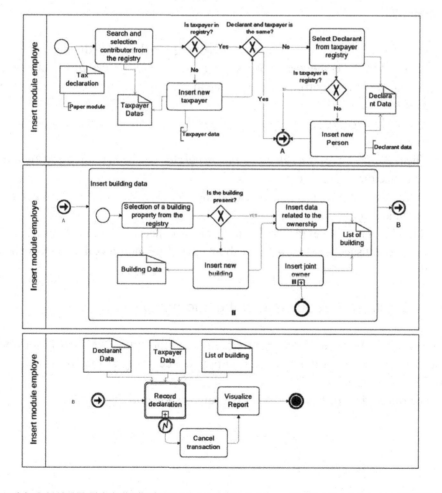

Copyright © 2009, IGI Global, distributing in print or electronic forms without written permission of IGI Global is prohibited.

The third criterion tequires verifying that the identified tasks do not use other information besides that signaled by the individualized data objects. In this case, the criterion is not satisfied, in fact:

- In regards to the operations of search and selection in the registry, both of subjects and of the building estates, they use the list of the results that is not present in the diagram;
- Furthermore, the operation of insertion of the joint owner uses the information on the subjects and the data on the ownership that is not underlined by the model of the process.

All of these informative objects must be put into evidence and the tasks with which they are associated eventually have to be decomposed.

So, at this point it is necessary to decompose the tasks and the data objects that do not satisfy the above criteria. Particularly the segmentation has been performed as it follows:

- The task of *search and selection from the registry* has been divided and also included in the embedded sub-process *points out the contributor* and *points out the declarant*, putting into evidence the data objects with the result of the search.
- The task *selection of a building property from the registry* has been refined;
- The task *insert the data related to the ownership* has been refined putting into evidence the opportune data objects;
- Some tasks that represent a check on the data have been inserted to correct possible errors;
- It has been put into evidence the data objects concerning the declaration, and that the transactional sub-process about the online submission of the form has been specified better.

Task 1.2 Activity 2 Structuring of the Information

In this activity there are been inserted, in the opportune BPMN™ tasks, the information in terms of input set and output set according to the considerations introduced in activity 1.

The produced workflow BPMN™ diagram is shown in Figure 4.

Copyright © 2009, IGI Global, distributing in print or electronic forms without written permission of IGI Global is prohibited.

Figure 4. Workflows-BPMN related to the sub-process online compilation and submission of the form

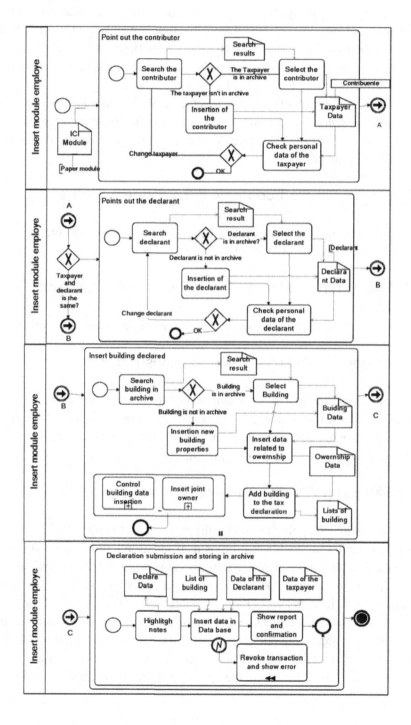

Copyright © 2009, IGI Global, distributing in print or electronic forms without written permission of IGI Global is prohibited.

Task 1.2 Activity 3: Control and Reiteration

Now it is necessary to perform a further evaluation of the identified tasks, and to verify that they externally correspond to visible function and directly usable by the users. In the diagram, the only two non-atomic activities that need to be detailed are *control building data inserted* and *insert joint owners* that we have provided for subsequently detailing (we do not report them for brevity).

The BPMN™ diagram of Figure 4, together with the diagrams that detail the *control building data inserted* and *insert joint owners*, represent, therefore the workflow BPMN™ or rather the input for step 2 of the methodology that leads to the realization of the portal.

Application of the Methodological Guidelines: Step 2

At this point, with having the workflow BPMN™, it is possible to progress with step 2 through the various proposed tasks.

Task 2.1 Mapping Workflow BPMN to the Portlet Application

In our case we only have a process and therefore a single portlet application.

Task 2.2 Mapping Workflow BPMN to Lanes-Roles

Since it has been considered only the lane related to the employee of the *tax office*, there will be just one role to define in the user management system of the portal. A special page of the portal will be associated to this role that assembles the portlets related to the sub-processes and to the identified tasks.

Task 2.3 Mapping Workflow BPMN to Portlet

Now, it is necessary to apply the rule for the mapping of the portlets that provides associating a portlet for each sub-process or if identified an atomic task. In this case, we observe that the embedded sub-processes *point out the contributor* and *point out the declarant*, have the same sequence of activities, and they consider the same data classes. It seems opportune, therefore, not to realize two portlets with the same functionalities but just one that opportunely parameterized in regards to names of the data objects, in one case, related to the contributor, and in the other, related to the declarant, can be used for covering both the functionalities, simply creating two "portlet entities" with the opportune parameters inside the page.

Copyright © 2009, IGI Global, distributing in print or electronic forms without written permission of IGI Global is prohibited.

Another consideration concerns the tasks *subject insertion* and *building insertion*. Since the task *subject insertion* is referenced in more sub-processes, such as the insertion of the contributor, of the declarant and of the joint owners, and, besides, considering that involves the insertion of a series of information, related to the registry data, the residence data and other additional information, it is preferred to realize for this task a separated portlet, and not to integrate the same functions three times in three separate sub-processes. In regards to the task *building insertion,* the same decision has been taken, since being an operation of insertion in a registry; also it could be reused in other processes.

Applying the guideline for the determination of the portlets, and appraising the considerations exposed in precedence, the portlets, the masks and the forms have been organized in the following way:

- Portlet for the search and selection in the registry of the subjects (contributor or declarant): it corresponds to the sub-process *point out contributor* and *point out declarant*, and according to the tasks present in the model, it includes the following elements:
  - Form for the insertion of the parameters of search (e.g. *name, last name* and *C.F.*);
  - Form to visualize the list of the results and the selection of the subject of interest;
  - Mask for the visualization of the complete data of the subject.
- Portlet for the insertion of a new subject: it corresponds to the task *insertion of a new subject* and includes the form for the insertion of the data related to citizen or to a company.
- Portlet for the search and selection from the registry of the building properties: it corresponds to the sub-process *insertion building declared,* and it includes the following forms, that correspond to the tasks included in the sub-process:
  - Form for the insertion of the parameters of search
  - Form for the selection of the building estates interested by the declaration
  - Mask of visualization of the data of the selected building estate
  - Form to point out the data of ownership
- Portlet for the insertion of a new building estate: it corresponds to the task *insertion new building property,* and it includes the form for the insertion of the data about the address, the cadastral data and those on the value.
- Portlet for the visualization of the data on the declared building estates: it corresponds to the sub-process *control building data inserted,* and it includes the form for the visualization of the data present in the list of the declared

Copyright © 2009, IGI Global, distributing in print or electronic forms without written permission of IGI Global is prohibited.

building estates, with the related joint owners, and eventually the removal of the building estate if the data are wrong.

- Portlet for the insertion of the joint owners: it corresponds to the sub-process *insertion of joint owner,* and it includes the following elements:
  - ○ Form for the insertion of the parameters of search of the joint owner (*C.F.*)
  - ○ Form to visualize the list of the results and the selection of the subject of interest
  - ○ Mask for the visualization of the data on the selected building estate
  - ○ Form for the insertion of the data on the ownership
- Portlet for the insertion of the data of declaration and submission: it corresponds to the sub-process *declaration submission and storing in archive,* and it includes the following elements:
  - ○ Form to insert the data on the declaration, particularly the year, the city and the date are inserted in an automatic way, the user has to insert the additional notes, and the number of the protocol that is produced instead during the submission;
  - ○ Routine for the execution of the transaction on the database, for the updating of all the interested tables and eventually the management of a rollback;
  - ○ Mask for the visualization of a report of confirmation or an error message according to the positive or negative result of the transaction.

CONCLUSION

The application of the methodology oriented to the internal users of the company has given good results: it allows, in fact, to realize, starting from a high-level design and with an opportune interaction with the involved professional figures, a design of the final application in terms of Portlets and forms inside each Portlet. Starting from this design, it is possible to realize, in a manual or automatic way, an application that faithfully follows the flow of the process.

In this work, it is already manually developed, the portlet application that allows validating the design realized in the case study above described, and to follow, passing among the various portlets, the flow of the process.

The selected configuration for the development and the deployment of the application has been the following:

Copyright © 2009, IGI Global, distributing in print or electronic forms without written permission of IGI Global is prohibited.

- Phase of development
  - ○ **Application level:** IDE Sun Java™ Studio (http://developers.sun.com/ prodtech/ javatools/jsenterprise/index.jsp), since among the free or low-cost software for the development of Web applications, it is the only one that provides a module oriented to the development of a portlet, the portlet builder, which also provides a specific support for the debug.
  - ○ **Presentation level:** the presentation layer is not of pertinence to the Sun Java™ Studio, for which it is necessary to equip it with another environment, possibly visual, for the design of the fragments of code JSP™ or HTML corresponding to every portlet.
- Phase of deploy
  - ○ **Portal server:** for the deployment of the selected portal server is JetSpeed 2™ (http://portals.apache.org/jetspeed-2 /), since it is the open source reference implementation regarding the conformity to the jsr-168s.

REFERENCES

OMG. (2006). *Business process modeling notation specification.*

Copyright © 2009, IGI Global, distributing in print or electronic forms without written permission of IGI Global is prohibited.

Section III
Automatic Code Generation
and the Tools

This section deals with the other relevant aspect of this book: the automatic generation of the final application. As discussed in the preface, the challenge of our research concerns to realize Information System that can easily adapt themselves to the continuous changes of the way the Companies perform their activities. We said that the Information Systems must adopt a "contingent" perspective according to the vision of Companies as "open systems"; furthermore, also the research in this area is going to emphasize the modeling obtaining the final applications in an automatic way. To aim this goal, we developed two different tools to obtain the outcome starting from the models using the most common OpenSource Frameworks. In this section, the problems faced going from the model to the final application are described; furthermore, the architectural and the technological aspects of the code generators are presented. Another fundamental tool, to allow a real usage of our research is the capability to use an intelligent editor to design the models. An editor is very useful if it let the designer to concentrate his/her attention about the problem to be solved instead to think about the graphics notation or the methodological guidelines. The configurable editor which we present allows the designer to do this; it permits to design BP using the BPMN™, or to design a Web Application using IDM or to merge these two aspects according to our methodology hiding the complexity and driving the designer in an effective way. Finally, a case study will show too the reader the outcome of our research.

Chapter X
From the Model to the Code Generator

INTRODUCTION

Surely, the design phase is one of the most important in the whole information system life cycle. The design phase allows realizing of the information system according to an engineering approach that by abstracting itself completely from the implementation details, it can adequately focus itself on the design aspects allowing for provision of a clear and precise methodological guideline to the developers. In this way, a high level of quality is guaranteed to the information system that will be not influenced by ad hoc decisions made up by the developers; decisions that, in the greatest part of the cases, are deprived of a suitable methodological support, and that inevitably bring to a diminution of the total quality of the project.

All of the details of the design phase have been underlined in the first part of the job and have been provided both approaches from the methodological point of view (specialized for the different typologies of users that will use the information system) and case studies oriented to understand the real applicability on the field of these methodologies.

At this point, it is essential to provide a technological aspect to the book thinking that the design methodologies are useful up until when they simplify the job of

Copyright © 2009, IGI Global, distributing in print or electronic forms without written permission of IGI Global is prohibited.

the designer: in the moment in which the design methodology adds complexity it is immediately abandoned by the designer.

During an accurate analysis of the designer requirements, it is evident that the tools that he/she needs are primarily of two types:

- Tool of graphic design
- Tool of automatic code generation

The tools of graphic design must have realized in order to simplify how much more possible the application of the methodologies of design previously exposed and to get, of course, a graphic representation conforming to the primitives of those methodologies.

In parallel, it is essential to have a tool that allows, starting from a machine readable representation of the gotten models, automatic production of the whole necessary code to obtain an application very close to that final application. To avoid that, this effort is not suitable, as it will be clearer subsequently, the generation of code will not be elegant in itself, but it will use some advanced technologies that will allow obtaining an application that, if on one hand, answers to the design choices, and on the other hand is a good base that can be used for the following development.

THE SUPPORT TOOLS

A methodology of design not adequately supported by a tool it is a little effective and this is very more true how much anymore methodology is complex, or rather it holds in consideration more aspects as in the case of the methodology PIDM process that it unites different aspects going from the design of the business process and up to the definition of the pages through which the business process will be performed by the final user.

To ask a designer to remember all of the methodological guidelines that allow obtaining from an IDM design the relative P-IDM process means, in concrete terms, forcing the designer to distract his/her attention from the real design problems with a consequent diminution of the quality of the final product. In the long run, the designer will refuse to use this methodology of design landing in the best hypotheses toward the realization of a well structured design of the information system or directly passing in the development phase, realizing an application without a good design support.

In order to provide support to the designer, it is necessity to realize an integrated tool that on one hand supports him/her to use the methodology and on the other side supports him/her in the following phases of export of the model in machine readable

Copyright © 2009, IGI Global, distributing in print or electronic forms without written permission of IGI Global is prohibited.

format and consequently in the automatic code generation. The generated code is very useful in the following phase of the development of the information system.

THE MACHINE READABLE DESIGN

If the designer has the experience with the methodology, it is possible to not consider the problems coming from the methodology learning, but the problem related to the following transformation of the design in a machine readable format is not overcome. The transformation of the design in a machine readable format is very helpful in the following code generation phase.

In this book, we adopted (see Chapter 3) an ontological format for the representation of the models. It could be thought about as using a common editor of ontology, such as Protégé (http://protege.stanford.edu) to represent the design in OWL format (W3C, 2004). Protégé is, today, a good open source editor of ontology in the international panorama, but in this job, it is surely few advisable. Using the editor Protégé to represent the model of a specific Web application would actually be necessary:

- To graphically represent the design of the Web application using, if held opportune, a visual editor that the same designer chooses
- To transfer the design to the ontology editor Protégé in order to add the individuals to the meta-model related to the methodology in use. In a few words this consists of manually adding individuals to the concepts that define the meta-model with the relative object property and datatype property.

This solution if on one hand it leads the designer to use a tool for the design, that, probably, he/she knows well, and therefore he/she does not need a phase of preliminary training, on the other hand it could be an elevated possibility of errors due to the "manual" transfer of the design in the editor Protégé. It is very useful, then, to have an integrated environment where it is possible to operate the diagram of the Web application and its translation in ontological format without the designer wasting more time and with an elevated level of precision that only an automatic tool can give.

Even though sharing the idea that the graphic design, especially in the projects of big dimensions, is essential in order to guarantee the sharing of the models in the work team, it is also necessary to have the model of the design in machine readable format to allow not only the exchange of the design among the components of the team of design, but also between the team of design and the computer. The element of communication between human and computer is the "translation" of the design in

Copyright © 2009, IGI Global, distributing in print or electronic forms without written permission of IGI Global is prohibited.

a machine readable language, and since the computer is not able to reason, neither formal errors nor inaccuracies of any type are admitted.

CODE GENERATOR

The graphic representation and that in machine readable format of the designs surely is not an activity unto itself, but it is finalized to the obtainment of a first draft of the information system design that works well and it is particularly useful to discuss with the customer in order to understand the designs (even if simple). The customer, in fact, is not able to fully understand the design but he/she is more and more skilled to directly use the Web application obtained directly from the design to verify the real operability of it. The designer cannot, therefore, abdicate to a tool that starting from the design is both able to automatically produce the whole necessary code to a Web application very close to that real and, on the base of which, he/she is able to validate the design choices.

Besides, the rapid growth of the complexity of the information system design and its subsequent development is only manageable through structured and engineering approaches.

To improve the quality of the applications, an information system designer must not only adequately manage the interrelated aspects of the information and navigation, but above all, the multi-user and multi-device requirements and the increasing needs for personalization. Although such aspects have been the object of studies (Brusilovsky, 1996; Oreizy et al., 1999), their high cohesion to their mutual implications has brought about the birth of new approaches in modeling that are often completely detached from the implementing technology and are exclusively focused on the conceptual aspects. Besides such specific demands, it must be noted that the methodological and technological panorama of the Web application is highly variegated. Just as there are well-defined design models and technologies available for the development of standard applications (for instance, in the case of an object-oriented design where suitable tools of development exist leading directly back to the design architecture used independently from the language used), there are also several design methodologies and implementation techniques in the case of Web application, which are often incompatible.

Such incompatibility results in the specific design methodologies being intentionally disconnected from the specific implementation technique in order not to restrict the designer in the architectural choices that must be made in the subsequent phase of development. In the world of the Web application, there is a clear separation between "conceptual" type methodologies and techniques and/or development technologies. Conceptual type methodologies are those that focus on the analysis of

Copyright © 2009, IGI Global, distributing in print or electronic forms without written permission of IGI Global is prohibited.

single aspects and on their interactions without considering the ways in which the design will then be implemented. The techniques and the development technologies focus on the implementation aspects and on their problems. The resulting design is notably improved since it is developed on the real demands of the application and not on the possibilities offered by the technology, even if the application is not directly connected to its realization.

Besides such problems, as in all software development projects, it is necessary to adequately manage the relationship between the various stakeholders; often, the customer (i.e., the application expert who knows precisely what he needs from the Web application) has difficulty understanding the choices of the designer because he does not know the language used (UML® [Booch, Jacobson, & Rumbaugh, 1998] or some other forms of representation), and in the case of conceptual modeling, does not find the pages and links he expects from a Web application directly available in the model. In such situations, at the beginning of the project, the buyer is led to accept the model; he/she will then ask for continuous and substantial changes only in an advanced phase of development, when seeing the pages and the means of navigating through them, he has a clear perception of the final result. In other words, the real requirements of the application are rendered explicit only in the advanced phase of development making the initial work of the designer of little use and resulting in increased costs and timescale. The conceptual model must be understood not only by the customer, but also by the developer who must deliver it within the specific implementing technology. In fact, it must be considered that if the conceptual model has its own generic value, before being referred to as a base for development, it must be enriched with that information directly related to the implementing technology, which for good reasons has been intentionally ignored in the design phase. In other words, the developer has a certain degree of flexibility but must be supervised by the designer in order to avoid breaking away from the agreed objectives either intentionally (as a consequence of technological choices) or accidentally (through a misunderstanding of the model).

To solve such communicative problems, it is fundamental that the production of a first mock-up application prototyping the most important aspects of a Web application (and in general information system) with the least investment of time and resources. In fact, in accordance with the definition of Bochicchio (Bochicchio & Paiano, 2000), the prototype mock-up helps the designer to control and to check the model of the WA and to share it with the customer and the developers. Even if the first version of the prototype rarely meets the customers' needs, it helps the designer to encourage feedback from the user that can be incorporated into the redesign phase. Such a process of revision generally facilitates software creation that is in the long run, very satisfactory, rather than software that simply "meets the requirement." Creating a prototype involves the development of a scale version

Copyright © 2009, IGI Global, distributing in print or electronic forms without written permission of IGI Global is prohibited.

of a complex system, which is the substance of a Web application, to acquire demanded critical knowledge to build a complete system (Szekely, 1994). Although an enormous effort can be expended to realize a prototype for a product that could be eliminated during the final phase, it proves to be a fundamental step and represents a wise investment as it avoids expensive re-works during subsequent phases.

In other words, the development of a mock-up of a final application through prototyping is economic and secure and allows all the stakeholders—buyer, designer and developers—to verify and buy-in to the model.

State of the Art

Only a few years ago, when methodologies and design tools were unavailable, the creation of a prototype in software engineering was considered to be the only way for a designer to express his/her own ideas and constituted a real phase of analysis. Since the prototype had to be created for a specific application, to reduce costs and the development timescale, the designer would often reuse parts of existing applications, jeopardizing the quality of the final application which resulted in a mere melting pot of already existing modules. This prototype is of scarce support to the developer, resulting in too much approximation (very far from the final product) or limited flexibility (being the first version of the application); moreover, the needs of the buyer were marginalized in respect to the process itself.

With the introduction of Web application design methodologies, the creation of the prototype has become model-driven: rapid generation of the application prototype is realized through the integration of environments and appropriate design tools (Zhang & Chung, 2003); often, the prototype is created using a code generation tool that translates the application model into software structures that implements the application and that could be completed in order to produce the final product.

A project near to the prototyping problems is ARANEUS (Atzeni, Masci, Mecca, Merialdo, & Sindoni, 1998). The design is based on the information that must be visualized. The data, and the applications, are described by a page-oriented model: the "ARANEUS Data Model" whose principal construct is the scheme that describes the structure of a set of homogeneous pages. The basic idea of Araneus is that the HTML pages can be seen as objects endowed with an identifier (the URL) and some attributes (one for every important data point) that can be either simple or complex. In this way, the WA is a collection of page schemes connected through links. To interrogate the data present within the data model, Araneus uses a language named ARANEUS view language (AVL) that, being based on the concept of navigational expression (Mendelzon, Mecca & Merialdo, 1999), allows the capture of the navigational aspects of the system. AVL is based on the presence of

Copyright © 2009, IGI Global, distributing in print or electronic forms without written permission of IGI Global is prohibited.

a data entry point (typically the home page) and on the possibility of "navigating" through the data to get to that which is considered interesting.

Another approach is the WebML system constituted by WebRatio (www.webratio. com), a modeling and generation case tool, which uses the notation ER as a high-level conceptual specification to formalize the requisites of the data and the Web modeling language (WebML) for the functional requirements. The support given to the ER model is rather conventional, except for a few limitations that make the data mapping easier thanks to a standard relational database. WebML proposes adapting the techniques of the logical modeling to the distinctive characteristics of the Web applications. It includes primitives to manage aspects such as the structuring of the application in different hypertexts (called site views), that meet the demands of classes of heterogeneous users providing navigational interfaces to access the information, to manipulate it and to activate services.

The approaches described above place a specific navigational engine alongside the model that, using the information of the design through a language owner (such as WebML for WebRatio or AVL for Araneus), allows realization of a working prototype of the application. Such solutions suffer from numerous problems: every change to the methodology, for instance, requires all modules of the system to adequately support the new constructs or the new primitives. Furthermore, the prototype can rarely be used as a starting point for the final product because it is based on a specific technological solution and on an engine of navigation that is proper for the generation of the prototype but one that is hardly suitable for use in a real environment.

Alongside these approaches, UML® the industry de facto standard for the representation of models, has been enhanced to directly support the specific elements for the Web (Conallen, 1999). Such extensions, that do not describe a design methodology, but which include the primitives as pages, screens, links, and so forth, exhibit limitations when they are used for describing the model of a specific methodology. As a consequence of such difficulties, not all methodologies use a UML® notation.

Many of the examined prototyping environments have been based on well-consolidated methodologies but the resulting environments and infrastructures are difficult (if not impossible) to be reused in other contexts. In fact, the graphic editor used to draw the model is created ad hoc; the description of the model for the prototyping uses a non-standard format that can be used only by the specific engine that will interpret it producing the prototype. In other words, the editor, the description of the model and the engine build a closed environment. Furthermore, the created prototype is not very effective in the design phase since the engine that produces it will hardly be robust enough to effectively manage a real task. More-

Copyright © 2009, IGI Global, distributing in print or electronic forms without written permission of IGI Global is prohibited.

over, in the case in which the mock-up is to be evolved into a final application, the changes required are so great as to make the job excessively expensive.

Code Generator for External Users

If the generation of code is essential in order to get a first prototype of the Web application and alone includes the problems related to the design of the user experience, even more complex is the discourse when the problems related to the business processes are added.

The problems that we face in the methodology of design oriented to the external users of the information system, and that which have been discussed in Chapter 6, are the same in the phase of analysis and development of a tool of generation of code. You can observe, in fact, that the difficulties which are present from linking together the know-how coming from the business processes design with that coming from the Web applications design are the same ones present in the realization of the tool of generation of code: in the produced application it is, in fact, necessary to hold under control the flow of the business processes, and in the meanwhile, to find for the final user the possibility of freely navigating among various information connected to the business process: to this problem we add the necessity to provide for the final user the right structures of access to the information, following the methodological guidelines defined in the design phase.

In the generated Web Application, the final user that uses it has to be free to undertake a business process, to suspend it and to eventually take it back in a second moment or to undertake multiple business processes. All of this is in line with the tasks assigned to the final user in the design of the business process: the final user can perform only and exclusively the tasks allowed by his/her role. Only having an application produced that it pushes it up to this level of functionality, it could be possible to use really the output not only for demonstrative purposes but also as a good base for the following implementation/completion.

The realization of a tool of code generation must contain different technologies keeping in mind that it is necessary to recreate both the structure of the data necessary for allowing the final user to use the applications, and the necessary infrastructure to give the possibility to access the business processes and to store their state.

The system has to be able, for instance, to distinguish the links of business process from the semantic links; the first ones that lead the user to perform a sequence of pre-defined steps, the second ones that allow the user to freely navigate among the information without a well-precise order but are always driven by an underlying logic coming from a careful analysis of the information contents. Of course, the Web application produced has to be able to appear to the user just the tasks and the information of his/her competence without trespassing in those of other users.

Copyright © 2009, IGI Global, distributing in print or electronic forms without written permission of IGI Global is prohibited.

The starting point for the development of the tool of generation of code is the P-IDM process design. P-IDM process, in contrast to IDM process, in fact, preserves all of the necessary information for the realization of the pages of the Web application.

CONCLUSION

The necessity of a suitable technological support, both in the phase of design and in the following phases of automatic generation of code, has been more times underlined during the treatment of this chapter. It misses only observing the essential passage among design and generation of code realized through the representation of the design in an opportune ontological language. Such translation is made up through an opportune tool introduced in the chapters that will follow that finds itself on a meta-model previously realized (the meta-model describes the proposed methodologies). The tool allows adding individuals to the meta-model in order to store the design of a specific Web application.

REFERENCES

Atzeni, P., Masci, A., Mecca, G., Merialdo, P., & Sindoni, G. (1998). The araneus Web-based management system. *ACM SIGMOD Record, 2 (2)*, 544-546.

Bochicchio, M., & Paiano, R. (2000). Prototyping Web applications. *Proceedings of the 2000 ACM symposium on Applied computing,* (pp 978-983).Como, Italy.

Booch, G., Jacobson, I., & Rumbaugh, J. (1998). *The unified modeling language user guide.* Boston: MA: Addison-Wesley Readings.

Brusilovsky, P. (1996). Methods and technique of adaptive hypermedia. *User modeling and user adaptive interaction, 6*(2-3), 87-129.

Conallen, J. (1999). Modeling Web application architectures with UML. *Communication of the ACM, 42*(10), 63-70.

McConnell, S. (1998). *Software project survival guide.* Microsoft Press.

Mendelzon, A., Mecca, G., Merialdo, M. (1999). *Efficient queries over Web views.* Araneus Project Working Report.

Oreizy, P., Gorlick, M.M., Taylor, R.N., Heimbigner,D., Johnson, G., Medvidovic, et al. (1999). An architecture-based approach to self-adaptive software. *IEEE Intelligent System, 14*(3), 54-62.

Copyright © 2009, IGI Global, distributing in print or electronic forms without written permission of IGI Global is prohibited.

Szekely, P. (1994). User interface prototyping: Tool and techniques. *Proceedings of the Workshop on Software Engineering and Human Computer Interaction.*

W3C. (2004). *RDF/XML Syntax Specification W3C Recommendation.*

Zhang, J., & Chung, J (2003). Mockup-driven fast-prototyping methodology for Web application development. *Software: Practice and Experience, 33*(13), 1251-1272.

Copyright © 2009, IGI Global, distributing in print or electronic forms without written permission of IGI Global is prohibited.

Chapter XI
Technological Choices

INTRODUCTION

Referring back to how much was described in the preceding chapters, we introduce in this chapter the technological choices made up in order to address the requirements to realize a tool of support to the designer applying the proposed methodologies, and that it allows to export, according to the selected design choices, using the ontological language OWL (W3C, 2004), the realized design., We also want to provide in this chapter a technological scouting related to the choices made up for realizing the code generator.

As it will be clearer subsequently, two different technologies will be used for realizing the generation of the code; the first one predominantly focused on the generation of code for the Web applications that do not have an underlying business process, and that they do not require, therefore, the management of the relative problems. The second technology has been selected instead, to also keep in mind the business processes.

TECHNOLOGICAL CHOICE FOR THE REALIZATION OF THE EDITOR

The choice of the technology made up for the realization of the design tool to support the methodology is a very hard task because the technology must allow the

Copyright © 2009, IGI Global, distributing in print or electronic forms without written permission of IGI Global is prohibited.

realization of a tool easy to use that, in the meanwhile allows to manage the whole intrinsic complexity of the methodologies previously defined. The technological choice in this job is Eclipse™ Platform.

The Eclipse™ (//www.eclipse.org/) project was originally created by IBM® in November 2001 and supported by a consortium of software vendors. The main goal of the project is the realization of a software development platform that is very modular and extensible. Eclipse™ is entirely written in Java™, and it is available therefore for all platforms.

Despite that Eclipse™ was developed as a development environment for Java™ projects, really its elevated modularity allows its use as an environment of generic development: other programming languages as C and C++ are supported (also thanks to the plug in CDT™, "C/C++ Development Tooling"™), XML and PHP. However, the great flexibility of such a platform has allowed realizing plug-in (Eclipse Visual Editor™) for the graphic design of the graphic interfaces of the Java™ applications, making the Eclipse™ environment a RAD (rapid application development) environment.

The modularity of Eclipse™ platform is made up through the architecture introduced in Figure 1 in which it can be seen how all of its components are plug-in.

The core of the architecture is the platform runtime, that represents the kernel of Eclipse™ through which the operation of the environment and the start of the plug-in contained in it are guaranteed. The workbench module defines the whole work area with which the user interacts; this area is made up through the modules devoted to the graphics and those devoted to the manager of events (JFace and SWT). The workspace represents the work area that is the part of file system that Eclipse™ uses to save the projects and the configuration files.

Help system and team support defines other functionalities available in order to provide support for the realization of documentation (contextual help) and for the execution of the work in team (through CVS or concurrent version system).

The modules just described provide some base functionality to the platform, while the two modules showed on the left, Eclipse JDT™ (Java™ development tools) and Eclipse PDE™ (plug-in developer environment), provide some specific functionality.

The first one is made up by a set of plug-ins useful to provide all the functionality of a Java™ IDE (integrated development environment): they add to the workbench functionality of editing, compilation, execution and debugging of Java™ code.

The second is the module thanks to which it is possible to realize further plug-ins for the platform.

The Eclipse™ platform is therefore a layered architecture made up of four levels, as it is possible to see in Figure 2.

Copyright © 2009, IGI Global, distributing in print or electronic forms without written permission of IGI Global is prohibited.

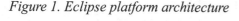
Figure 1. Eclipse platform architecture

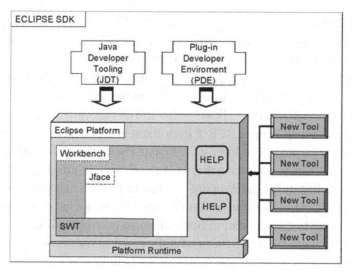

Of course, at the base of the architecture there is the Java™ virtual machine that allows the development of a multi-platform application; on the Java™ virtual machine is based the Eclipse™ platform and on this all of the tools that allow to develop Java™ applications.

It is evident that the Eclipse PDE™ level is the key of the extensibility of the Eclipse™ framework. It allows providing new functionality thanks to the creation of new plug-ins, operation that can be performed through semi-automatic procedure (wizard) whose output is a new Eclipse™ project, in the workspace of reference, composed by all the necessary parts for the realization of the plug in.

The definition of a plug-in asks to follow a well-precise scheme of implementation, with the creation of different configuration files and the organization of the packets according to pre-arranged package.

Figure 2. Four layer architecture of the Eclipse platform

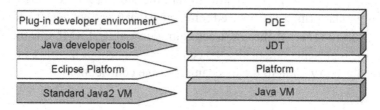

Copyright © 2009, IGI Global, distributing in print or electronic forms without written permission of IGI Global is prohibited.

PLUG-IN DEVELOPMENT ENVIRONMENT

The Eclipse Plug-In Development Environment™ allows for easy creation of some plug-ins. The plug-ins, so realized, can be integrated inside the same platform, where they will have to cohabit with the other plug-ins already installed, proper of Eclipse™ or of third parts. They add to the platform new functionality, but undoubtedly they will not have the opportunity to customize the environment in its wholeness.

From the version 3.0, in the Eclipse™ platform an innovative characteristic has been introduced, called Eclipse RCP™ (rich client platform), thanks to which it is possible to export a plug-in of Eclipse™, together with the desired plug-ins, and obtaining a stand-alone application that works very well. In this way, not only it is not necessary to install Eclipse™ in order to have a product that works well, but it will be possible to entirely customize the environment removing or modifying any contribution given to the application from other unwanted plug-ins.

The resultant application uses the two fundamental modules of Eclipse™: a core and UI, from which it gets the base functionality of Eclipse™.

The gotten product is characterized by an elevated configurability: it exploits the same mechanisms at the base of Eclipse™, extensions and points of extension, that allow for contributing, to personalizing or eliminating new functionality to the Eclipse™ environment.

An "extension point" is defined by a plug-in, and it represents an entry point for those functionalities or services exposed to the outside, usable from any other plug-in. A plug-in extension point can be seen therefore how an interface exposed to the other plug-ins that is used with the definition of new extensions.

An extension allows, therefore, to add functionality to the final product: for instance, through the extensions all the components that will go to realize the final user interface (the workbench), defining views, perspectives, wizard, actions, elements of the menu bar and still more, can be built.

The definition of extension points or a new extension happens entirely using XML configuration file, interpreted by the core of Eclipse™ in order to build and to introduce the final product.

The Plug-Ins, the Extensions and Extension Points

A plug-in for the Eclipse RCP™ platform (but the same applies obviously, to the only Eclipse™ platform) is a structured component that describes itself to the central system, the run-time kernel, through a configuration manifest XML file: the plugin. xml. This file represents practically the central component of the plug-in because it describes the entry point to the mechanism of the contribution.

Copyright © 2009, IGI Global, distributing in print or electronic forms without written permission of IGI Global is prohibited.

To create a new plug-in is exploited the highest level of the architecture Eclipse™, the Eclipse PDE™ (Plug-in Development Environment), that offers a set of wizard for the creation of an empty plug-in or with example code.

These procedures, that follow the user along all the phases of its realization, have the purpose of building a structure of basic components composed by three configuration files, plugin.xml, MANIFEST.MF and build.properties, and by a build path to which a plug-in class is associated.

Starting from this configuration, it is possible, therefore, to feed the plug-in with new functionalities: this is made through the mechanisms of extensions and points of extension feasible, whose job it is to put in communication the plug- in matter with others existing plug-ins.

An extension is, technically, the declaration of a contribution, with which it is possible to inform the system that a well-defined functionality, which already exists inside other plug-ins, has been requested inside the plug-in under examination, in order to re-use this functionality in some way.

An extension point, in fact, is substantially a point of hook-up to a well-defined plug-in. It represents an interface that the central system has to be able to implement, with the goal of providing, to anyone who wishes them, the new functionalities offered by the corresponding the plug-in.

At the base of the operation of an extension point, there is a configuration file (scheme) XSD, through which it is necessary to describe what information must be provided in order to correctly extend a well-defined plug-in.

Graphic User Interface Analysis

The graphic user interface (GUI) of Eclipse™ is very advanced introducing an elevated usability and customization possibility.

One of the points of strength of the whole GUI is that it offers the user the possibility to open, to close, to move and to reorganize the panels (views) that they constitute it. There are several panels, and their disposition can be defined by the end user in a complete autonomy. In this way, it is possible to improve the experience of the user with the application and, consequently the user can increase his/her productivity.

A fundamental concept of the platform is that of perspective: a perspective can be thought as the configuration of the workbench that is the list of the open panels (complete of position and dimension), the active keyboard shortcuts and all those other information typical of the GUI of the application. Eclipse™ allows the creation of different perspective, a rapid passage between them, the automatic opening of one of them in certain situations as well as the automatic rescue of the perspective at the exit from the program.

Copyright © 2009, IGI Global, distributing in print or electronic forms without written permission of IGI Global is prohibited.

In Figure 3, an example of the work area is described, with a brief description of the main sections.

It is important to point out that:

- The menu bar and the tool bar, from which the principal functionalities of the tool are accessible
- The perspective bar, with which it is possible to choose, among those of default and those saved by the user, the perspective of visualization of the workbench
- The resource navigator, it allows to visualize the content of the work space; particularly, it represents a real "explore resources" through which is possible to operate on the files and on the folders that build the workspace used by Eclipse™
- The editor view, or the principal work area of the application, inside which it is possible to edit the content of the Java™ files and not other views

Besides this, the environment offers a set of driven procedures (wizards) that they help the user during the execution of the most complex operations, informing him/her about the errors committed through feedback during the performed operations.

Figure 3. The workbench of Eclipse

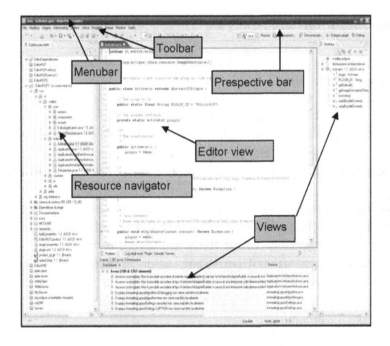

Copyright © 2009, IGI Global, distributing in print or electronic forms without written permission of IGI Global is prohibited.

Hereafter, an example of such a mechanism is described: during the realization of a new Java™ class, Eclipse™ informs the user that the selected name for the class is not written in the correct format (Figure 4).

The Motivations of the Choice

The choice of Eclipse™ for the realization of the editor of support for the methodology is due to the modularity of its architecture: based on a plug-in schema, it is possible to create and to add a new plug-in, customizing the product with the addition of new features.

The decision to use Eclipse RCP™ as underlying framework of the whole architecture that we will realize, have several advantages, particularly in terms of usability, re-use and extensibility of the final product. There are two possibilities for the realization of the general framework:

- The usage of Eclipse™ extension points
- The modification of the Eclipse™ plug-ins.

Figure 4. Example of Wizard for the definition of a class

Copyright © 2009, IGI Global, distributing in print or electronic forms without written permission of IGI Global is prohibited.

The second point is made possible thanks to the availability of the source code of Eclipse™ platform. The elements, connected to the framework will have the possibility to exploit at the best the intrinsic mechanisms of the Eclipse™ platform, getting, in such a way, some advantages for the final CASE tool. These mechanisms are:

- Using the advanced graphic user interface of Eclipse™
- Software usability
- Re-using the software: the development as a plug-in provides a high modularity level of the final product and this is a point of favor for the re-usability of the software
- Extensibility of the software: to this is added the possibility to define, inside the plug-ins, some extension points, that allow to subsequently extend its functions, fully exploiting the power of the framework Eclipse™

It is not essential to use together the whole set of Eclipse™ plug-ins, rather it is possible to tightly use only those necessary. This characteristic of Eclipse™ allows, as for any standalone application, studying the graphic user interface for the application to realize and to entirely design the user experience. It is possible to use the views of Eclipse™ and all of the components, basic or advanced, that take part to its operation, getting so a usable advanced user interface that also the final user can customize according to his/her own needs. Additionally because a plug-in is an Eclipse RCP™ application, it can easily be expandable, inheriting from the extensions points' philosophy all the advantages related to the modularity and to the re-use of the code.

Besides this, Eclipse™ has several characteristics already implemented and ready to use, which may be re-used composing among them depending on the final goal. There are several of these characteristics already present; some examples may be:

- the presence of a project explorer, that allows exploring the content of the work area and to operate with its elements making all those operations typical of a resources explorer
- simplified creation of useful procedures for the export and the import of resources
- possibility to totally customize the menu bar, the tool bars and the contextual menus
- possibility to realize complex operations driving the final user with the use of wizards, in which the management of the errors and the synchronization with the file system are very simple

Copyright © 2009, IGI Global, distributing in print or electronic forms without written permission of IGI Global is prohibited.

- possibility to realize typologies of editor corresponding to different file extensions: the opening of a file in the project explorer allows the automatic opening of the relative editor
- customization of the GUI through the addition of new panels called "views"

This is only at least part of the potentialities offered by this framework. It allows, besides, the contemporary opening of different editor windows, an operation that will be useful, for instance, to guarantee the integration among the different methodologies that will be supported by the editor.

The Eclipse™ platform founds all its architecture on the mechanism of the contribution, not possessing to its inside any built-in function; in other words, every part of it is made up through a plug-in (there are around 60 for the project Eclipse-JDT™, for instance) which are activated or deactivated based on the user needs (according to the logic "Contributions are only loaded when they are needed" lazy loading rule).

The core of this architecture is the Runtime Kernel (or Eclipse™ platform run-time), a low- level module designed in order to manage thousands of plug-ins contemporarily, whose goal is to provide only the necessary services for the integration of high-level software tools, that are able, therefore, to bring new features to the existing structure.

Under the idea that "everything is a contribution," the addition of new features to the base architecture is notably simple: the designer must follow theconsolidate methodological guidelines.

The Eclipse™ platform seems, therefore, seems to be well suited for the modularity of which methodology to be supported is composed. The methodology of design, as exposed in the preceding chapters, is very modular and every part of the methodology can be used in different contexts in a separate way regarding to the other parts.

You, for instance, think about the requirements of a business analyst that could be interested in designing the business processes independently from the design of the user experience that, in the greatest part of the cases, it is of competence of a different designer. The modularity of Eclipse™ allows then to realize two different editors for these two different professional figures, but depending on the requirements, it is possible to do a perfect integration of the two editors gotten opportunely putting together the relative ones plug-in, equipped by another plug- in which the relative methodological guidelines are implemented.

Copyright © 2009, IGI Global, distributing in print or electronic forms without written permission of IGI Global is prohibited.

Technological Choice for the Realization of the Code Generator for Web Application

Within this work, we realized two different tools of model-driven code generation. We speak about tools of generation of a model-driven code because the generation is driven from a model made up through a specific design methodology. Particularly, the first tool of generation is oriented to the generation of a Web application that did not contain to its inside business processes, and the second is oriented to the generation of a Web application that contains to its inside also business processes.

The first tool of generation of code takes as input the machine readable description of the design made up through the methodology P-IDM (where there are also the layout information using the layout model as stated in the conclusions of Chapter 3), while the second has as input the representation machine readable of the design made up through P-IDM process methodology.

Of course, the choice of the technology strongly depends on the motivations that push to use the selected technology: when the input will be a model made up through the methodology P-IDM the focus is on the aspect of presentation of the contents and navigation between them; instead, in the case in which a model is made up through the P-IDM process methodology the focus has to be on the management of the business processes and therefore on the possibility to present to the final user the tasks coherently with the business process flow previously defined.

In the following section, we will provide a brief introduction about the selected technologies. We underline that, during the design and implementation of the tools of generation made up through the classical tools of the software engineering oriented to the object oriented programming, we take into account the particular technology selected in order to get in output a Web application compatible with such a technology.

In the next chapter, we will present a design of the tools.

State of the Art of the Model Driven Code Generator

The problem of the model-driven generation of Web Applications has been faced in different frameworks that, avoiding to the developer to write repetitive code, they allow to reduce the times of development and to get a complete application starting from the model. It is had to notice that the model used for producing such code is a logical model (that is tightly tied up to its implementation), and it does not support in some way the job of the designer that will require, instead, high-level tools to analyze and to conceptually design the application.

The most meaningful frameworks that face this problem are:

Copyright © 2009, IGI Global, distributing in print or electronic forms without written permission of IGI Global is prohibited.

- Model-driven development environment (MDE), produced by Metanology (http://www.metanology.com/); it is a tool of integrated development that allows the creation of Web-based application on J2EE™ and on some correlated technologies (Apache Struts™, Enterprise JavaBeans™) starting from models made up in UML® language (Booch, Jacobson, & Rumbaugh, 1998). MDE is made up of different forms: MDE for UML® (for the design), MDE for Apache Struts™ (it produces the whole code to perform an application based on Apache Struts™), MDE for EJB™ (it uses the technology Enterprise JavaBeans™ for the access to database and to other resources) and MDE for J2EE™ (it completes the configuration of MDE for Struts and MDE for EJB).
- Java™ Application Generator (JAG) (http://jag.sourceforge.net/), made up by the Finalist IT Group (http://www.finalist.com); it is an open-source J2EE™ generator of applications that uses Apache Struts™ and EJB™. In contrast to MDE, it is not model-driven, but it facilitates (starting from a modeling performed with any technique) the assignment of the implementation writing the whole necessary repetitive code. JAG, is much diffused particularly to implement the "Model" of Struts (in the following sections there will be greater details on Struts).
- Karapan Sapi (http://www.javanovic.com/); it is also a generator of Web applications based on the Apache Struts™ framework. Its purpose is to produce repeated common code in different parts of the application.

Many of the examined environments use, or they found them on the framework Struts that for its characteristics it receives a lot of success, especially in the industrial world since it is used as environment of fruition for broadly multi-channel web applications contemporarily enjoyed by thousand of users.

The Apache Struts™ Framework

Apache Struts™ is an open-source framework that belongs to the project Apache™ (http://www.apache.org) released under ASL (Apache Software License) license that also allows the use, the change or re-use of the source code for commercial purposes; the only one condition is that in the license of the produced software, the terms of copyright related to the source distribution of Apache Struts™ are reported. Struts is based on the design pattern model-view-controller model 2, thought in order to facilitate the development of Web applications since it clearly separates the aspects of visualization of the Web application from those of control and elaboration; besides, Struts is the environment where all of the bests practices, experiences and

Copyright © 2009, IGI Global, distributing in print or electronic forms without written permission of IGI Global is prohibited.

patterns, related to problems of design and implementation converge, and they are concretized in infrastructures and code.

The Struts operating is based on two configuration files:

- web.xml that is the deployment descriptor present in all the Web applications according to the J2EE™ architecture. This file establishes the modality of operation of the application in the operational environment; it contains information about the names of the servlets, the paths of the pages, and so forth.
- struts-config.xml describes the dynamic behavior of the Struts environment. In this file it is possible to define what Java™ class (extension of the class action of the project) it will manipulate a particular request.

The action servlet is the servlet provided by the project with the function of controller. In the file web.xml there is a reference to it that specifies what URI has to elaborate while the file struts-config.xml establishes the behavior of the controller. In the detail, the controller included in Struts uses the class provided by the Struts project org.apache.struts.action.ActionServlet that works using the map of the actions described in Web-INF/struts-config.xml, operating on the URI that have extension (of default) "*.do".

The file struts-config.xml is divided in three sections:

1. Form-beans section (the tag is <form-beans>) it specifies the forms beans that are used in order to store and to verify the information coming from a form of a HTML page.
2. Global-forwards section (the tag is <global-forwards>) that it establishes in the case of success of an action to what generic page has to be forwarded.
3. Action-mapping section (the tag is <action-mappings>) it defines what action (or classes) that is possible to activate in order to perform a well-specified request.

After this necessary premise on the configuration files, it is possible to examine in Figure 5 how the Apache Struts™ framework works.

In Figure 5, the flow of the activities is represented through numbers:

1. Request: The Struts controller servlet (ActionServlet), defined by default and unique, deals with to intercept every HTTP request with extension "*.do.".
2. Fill with request data: the ActionServlet instances (or re-use) the form bean related to the URL of the request; the form bean has properties that coincide

Copyright © 2009, IGI Global, distributing in print or electronic forms without written permission of IGI Global is prohibited.

Figure 5. Struts architecture

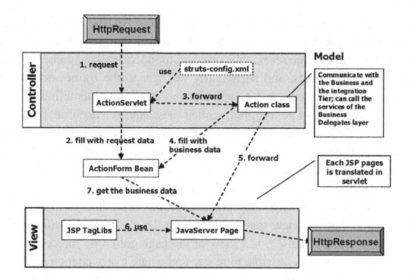

with the fields of the HTML form populated with the data contained in the form.

3. Forward: the ActionServlet occupies itself, therefore, to pass the control to the "Action;" in this way the Struts controller servlet associates an application to a class, that is, it maps the actions passing through the file struts-config.xml (use). The class written by the developer (as extension of the class org.apache.struts.action.Action) contains the code to elaborate the specific request so that to make the opportune operations.

4. Fill with business data: a class action can use the form bean defined in the point 2 (the association happens in the file struts-config.xml). A form bean is a class that extends the form bean ActionForm previously activated, of which it is possible to manipulate the data.

5. Forward: typically, the action takes the data from the model of the MVC architecture, it prepares the data for the visualization (usually creating some beans), and it passes the control to the side "View."

6. Use: the view can be constituted by several technologies (JSP™, XML, XSLT, etc.); it is possible to usually be preferring to use JSP™ pages considering that Apache Struts™ makes available the opportune package that simplifies their creation.

7. Get business data: the JSP™ page asks for the data from a bean.

8. Response: the view is the HTTP response.

Copyright © 2009, IGI Global, distributing in print or electronic forms without written permission of IGI Global is prohibited.

The Framework Apache Tiles™

As it is evident from a description even though brief of Apache Struts™, there is not in this framework any facility for the definition of the graphic aspect of the Web application. Insofar the research is oriented to individualize another compatible framework with Struts, and particularly we refer to the framework Apache Tiles™ (that implements composite view pattern). It allows assembling the page through the composition of its fragments called tiles. Tiles is a document assembly framework used for resolving the problem of layout and of content re-use, and it is perfectly integrated for completing in an effective way the side "view;" in fact, Apache Tiles™, originally created as an autonomous project in the Jakarta Commons project, is now included and distributed with Apache Strut™ framework.

The framework tiles, as written in precedence, has been thought to implement the concept of composite view that, according to the available definition on the site of the Sun Microsystems™, is a view of the page gotten by the composition of other sub-views that it is possible to re-use and where every change performed in the sub-view automatically reflects itself on every composite view that uses it. A composite view is, as it says the same literal translation, a view made up by different fragments, whose dynamic re-composition creates the final view; these fragments, then, will be parts of other views and can be included realizing a high level of modularity and re-use of several parts among different pages.

The concept of the composite view is made up in tiles through the definition of the tiles and of a XML file (tiles-defs.xml) that describes as such fragments that have to be assembled among them. The tiles are the blocks that define the presentation layer; considering, for instance, the case of a page where situated are menus, header, footer, body, a tile will be defined for each area. The layout (in substance a JSP™ page, because the framework tiles operate only with this technology) it allows, according to the description of the file, preparing the tiles inside a page. Tiles allow differentiating the output for delivery device integrating the packet "dimensions" that it provides to add, inside struts-config.xml, the configuration properties of the file tiles-defs *. xml of tiles; in this way it is possible to specify different "tiles-defs *. Xml" (and therefore different layouts) according to the capability of the device.

The disposition of the tiles inside the page is not static; in fact, through the parameters (called attributes), it is possible to modify at run-time the tiles that compose the same page; for instance, in the case in which it is hard to recall a menu in a page, its definition will be a type "<tiles:insert attribute = "menu" />" where the parameter menu will be specified at run time; therefore, according to the user, it will be possible to activate a valid menu for its role. These attributes are local to the page in which they are defined, avoiding conflicts with tiles of different pages, allowing the re-use of the same tile among separate pages. It is hard

Copyright © 2009, IGI Global, distributing in print or electronic forms without written permission of IGI Global is prohibited.

to notice that in the definition of the pages ("basic definition") it refers only to the logical name of the tile; while, the association between logical name and physical page is effected in a section of the tiles-defs.xml file. For instance, the definition of the homepage will be:

```
<definition name="homepage" path=" homepage.jsp">
    <put name="menu" value="menu.jsp">
    <put name="header" value="header.jsp">
        .....
```

The use of tiles allows the realization of the principles of inheritance and encapsulation for the dynamic pages; in fact, it is possible to declare one "basic definition" from which to derive other definitions.

Technological Choice for the Realization of the Code Generator for Process-Oriented Web Application

In the technological choice related to the realization of a tool of generation of code for a process-oriented Web application, the research is directed toward frameworks able to manage in a simple and efficient way the business process flow.

Despite all of the advantages shown by the framework Struts in the generation of Web applications, that did not contain inside business processes, soon we were aware that such framework did not adequately support the business processes. The attention is moved then on a framework that considers, in a native way without particular artifices, the business processes. We selected the Spring framework™ (ww.springframework.org) and particularly the framework Spring Web Flow. The Spring framework™ is an open source project released under the terms of the Apache Licence.

Spring is a layered Java/J2EE™ application framework.

Spring is the most complete lightweight container, providing centralized, automated configuration and wiring for the application objects. The container is non-invasive, capable of assembling a complex system from a set of loosely-coupled components, POJO (Plain Old Java Object), in a consistent and transparent way. The container brings agility and leverage, and improves application testability and scalability by allowing software components to be first developed and tested in isolation, then scaled up for deployment in any environment (J2SE™ or J2EE™).

In order to support a pluggable transaction, a common abstraction layer for transaction management makes it easy to demarcate transactions without dealing with low-level issues. Generic strategies for JTA (Java™ transaction API) and a single JDBC™ data source are included. In contrast to plain JTA or EJB™ CMT

Copyright © 2009, IGI Global, distributing in print or electronic forms without written permission of IGI Global is prohibited.

(container managed transaction), Spring's transaction support is not tied to J2EE™ environments.

A JDBC™ abstraction layer that offers a meaningful exception hierarchy (no more pulling vendor codes out of SQLException), simplifies error handling, and greatly reduces the amount of code you will need to write. You will never need to write another block to use JDBC™ again. The JDBC-oriented exceptions comply with Spring's generic DAO exception hierarchy.

Integration with Toplink™, Hibernate™, JDO™, and iBATIS™ SQL Maps: in terms of resource holders, DAO implementation support, and transaction strategies. First-class hibernate support with lots of IoC convenience features, addressing many typical hibernate integration issues. All of these comply with Spring's generic transaction and DAO exception hierarchies.

AOP (aspect-oriented programming) functionality, fully integrated into Spring configuration management. It is possible to AOP-enable any object managed by Spring, adding aspects such as declarative transaction management. With Spring, you can have declarative transaction management without EJB™ even without JTA, if you are using a single database in Apache Tomcat™ or another Web container without JTA support.

A flexible MVC Web application framework, is built on core Spring functionality. This framework is highly configurable via strategy interfaces, and accommodates multiple view technologies like JSP™, Apache Velocity™, Apache Tiles™, and so forth. Note that a Spring middle tier can easily be combined with a Web tier based on any other Web MVC framework, like Apache Struts™, or Tapestry™ or WebWork.

All of Spring's functionality can be used in any J2EE™ server, and most of it also in non-managed environments. A central focus of Spring is to allow for reusable business and data access objects that are not tied to specific J2EE™ services. Such objects can be reused across J2EE™ environments (Web or EJB™), standalone applications, test environments, and so forth, without any hassle.

Spring's layered architecture provides a lot of flexibility.

Spring Web Flow

The fundamental characteristic of Spring Web Flow (SWF) is to allow a management suitable of the flow of logical elaboration made up from more steps (called page flow). SWF allows, in fact, realizing a XML configuration file in order to describe the steps of which the flow of the business process is composed. Spring Web Flow integrates other Web frameworks as a dedicated controller framework. It is, in a few words, a self-contained, emendable page flow engine. Based internally on a finite state, machine allows developing focused controller modules that guide the

Copyright © 2009, IGI Global, distributing in print or electronic forms without written permission of IGI Global is prohibited.

users through their role in a business process. The most important thing is that the semantics of the process is defined directly by the designer.

A flow definition consists of a set of states that defines the business process (Figure 6) while a flow execution represents a runtime instance of a flow definition.

In traditional Web applications, page flows are not explicit—they are not first class citizens. Take a wWeb application built on Apache Struts™, for example. To implement a page flow in Struts, most developers build on what the framework provides them: actions and views. In this case, a single action is associated with a specific request URL. When a request comes in at that URL, the action is executed. During execution, the action performs some processing and then selects an appropriate result view for display. It is that simple.

Therefore, to implement a multi-step page flow in Struts, individual actions are chained together through the various views. Action URLs to process different events like "back" or "submit" are hard-coded into each view. Some form of ad hoc session storage is used to manage a flow state. Redirect after post is used to prevent duplicate submissions, and so forth.

Although this is a simple and functional approach, it has a major disadvantage: the overall page flow of the Web application is not clear from looking at the action definitions in the struts-config.xml file. It is impossible to forest – the flow – from the trees – the many action and view definitions. Flexibility also suffers since actions and views cannot be easily reused.

Spring Web Flow comes allows to represent the page flow of a Web application in a clear and simple way, and reuse it anywhere, including environments like Struts, Spring MVC, Tapestry, JSF, and even Portlets.

Spring Web Flow offers several advantages:

- The page flow in a wWeb application is clearly visible by looking at the corresponding Web flow definition (in an XML file or Java™ class).
- Web flows are designed to be self-contained. This allows seeing a part of your application as a module you can reuse in multiple situations.

Figure 6. Possible states of a business process

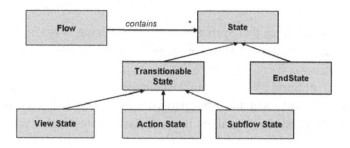

Copyright © 2009, IGI Global, distributing in print or electronic forms without written permission of IGI Global is prohibited.

- Web flows capture any reasonable page flow in a Web application always using the same consistent technique. You are not forced into using specialized
  controllers for very particular situations.

Finally, a Web flow is a first-class citizen with a well-defined contract for use. It
has a clear, observable lifecycle that is managed for the development automatically
as a result is very easy to use.

Spring Web Flow is composed of a set of states (displaying a view or executing any action, etc.). Transition of the flow from one state to another is triggered
by an event. This continues until the flow completes and enters the end-state. The
important Spring Web Flow states are:

- The start-state, when a flow is created the initial state of the flow is defined
  by the start-state attribute in the Webflow.
- An action-state executes an action and returns a logical result on its completion. The next to which the flow will be transitioned will depend on the result
  of this state
- A view-state when entered pauses in the flow and returns the control to the
  client/user and the flow is resumed on the user/client event which resumes the
  flow and triggers the transition to the state depending on the user/client input
  or decision.
- A decision-state is used to determine the next state in the dynamic way or
  at runtime. If our next state depends on some attributes or properties (i.e., if
  users are not logged then redirect them to login page).
- A sub flow-state is used to represent independent flows which are not dependent on the main flow. A sub flow is created as a child of main flow (parent
  flow). When a sub flow is called, the parent flow is suspended until the child
  flow completes. This helps to maintain the application as a set of sub-modules
  (sub flows) which can be used multiple times. The sub flow can be a child of
  another sub flow or of the root flow.
- End-state means the end of the flow. When a flow enters the end-state the
  active flow session is terminated. If the end-state of the root flow is entered,
  the resources associated with it are cleaned up automatically.

It is important to notice that Spring Web Flow, as Spring, it is a layered framework, packaged, and it allows the use of the only parts which need in the specific
application.

The approach of Spring Web Flow in the management of the flow represents, in
concrete terms, the implementation of the pattern inverse of control, and it guarantees
a greater flexibility and clarity making the code easier to test and to reuse.

Copyright © 2009, IGI Global, distributing in print or electronic forms without written permission of IGI Global
is prohibited.

The system allows capturing the logical flow of the Web application as a container of forms that it is possible to re-use in different situations. This flow drives a single user through the execution of the business process, and it is possible to consider this flow as a conversation with the final user.

To be able to use SWF, it must use at least the followings base components:

- The framework Spring Web Flow
- The classes with the base utilities internally used by the framework: spring-core
- The framework necessary for the data binding internally used: spring-binding
- A simple façade of logging internally used: commons-logging

It is evident that the Page Flow of Spring Web Flow allows perfectly modeling the business process view defined in the methodology PIDM because it represents as Web pages all the screens of the business process, and it allows understanding as the flow of the operations it moves through them.

CONCLUSION

A panorama on the technologies used in the following parts of this work is of the highest importance to understand it.

In this chapter, we consider three technologies of the highest importance in order to develop the support tools for the designer. The technological choices have been dictated by the implicit requirement of the tools that we are building. Particularly, relative to the realization of the tool of design, a highly extensible and configurable technology is selected in order to allow a complete support to the complexity of the methodologies that the tool will have to support. The possibility of customizing the selected framework allows distributing only the part of editor that interests the particular designer. If the designer is interested in designing oriented to the internal users, he/she will not have the necessity to also have the editors IDM and PIDM therefore, the customization of the selected framework, will allow distributing only the BPMN™ editor that will be used.

Likewise, in the choice of the technology useful to the realization of the tool of generation of code, a clean distinction has been made between the technology that allows a correct management of the navigation among Web pages and the graphic structuring of the same one (the Apache Struts and tiles frameworks) and the technology that allows a suitable management of the business process separating it from the remaining logic (Spring Web Flow).

Copyright © 2009, IGI Global, distributing in print or electronic forms without written permission of IGI Global is prohibited.

The two following chapters focus on the design and implementation of these tools.

REFERENCES

Booch, G., Jacobson, I., & Rumbaugh, J. (1998). *The unified modeling language user guide*. Boston, MA: Addison-Wesley Readings.

W3C. (2004). *OWL Web ontology language reference*.

Copyright © 2009, IGI Global, distributing in print or electronic forms without written permission of IGI Global is prohibited.

Chapter XII
Tool to Support the Design Methodology:
A Configurable Editor

INTRODUCTION

In order to provide support to the designer in the design of the whole complex Web information system, it is essential to provide a suitable tool that hides the intrinsic complexity of the methodology supporting the designer in the application of the same that is often complex, and the tool has to be able to translate the design made up in a machine readable format to be able to use this design in the following automatic code generation of the Web application according to a model-driven approach.

In this chapter, we introduce the design and implementation of the editor made up mainly of the architecture presented (and based on Eclipse™ Platform as illustrated in the preceding chapter) and on the methodological steps of integration among the several editors for the design and implementation of these guidelines.

REQUIREMENTS

We now describe in detail the requirements on which the following design and implementation of the editor is founded.

Copyright © 2009, IGI Global, distributing in print or electronic forms without written permission of IGI Global is prohibited.

First of all, we highlight that the tool that we want to provide is not a simple editor that supports the proposed methodology but a customization tool in which to make all of the editors meet allowing realization of the intermediary designs provided by the methodology and that provides the possibility of the designer to work with more designs at the same time. Besides, the tool has to be easily extensible in the sense that has to be simple adding new editors to support possible extensions of the methodology.

For this reason, we do not simply deal with an editor, but we speak about a base framework inside which to make the different editors meet.

Starting from the framework, and through well-defined configurations, it has to be possible to get the desired standalone editor: it will integrate, according to the particular requirements, one or more editors in order to support the methodology. The final product, starting from the framework opportunely shaped, will take the name of CASE tool. We want to guarantee an easy and elevated customization of the final product: the CASE tool has to be able to be built on the framework with simple passages. In this way, it will be possible to easily get the CASE tool that differs, for instance, for the number of integrated editors or activated features. It must be simple to add or to modify languages of modeling or methodological guidelines for the CASE tool.

The CASE tool must also allow design of a Web application applying in everything or partly the methodologies previously exposed. Although a project plans, as principle, the use of different methodologies of design, the design of the application must also have been made possible with only some of these. For instance, the designer has to be free, if he/she desires to directly create a P-IDM or P-IDM Process diagram.

The CASE tool will have to allow the creation of a project, correspondent to the design of the Web application. Within the project so made, it will be possible to draw different categories of diagrams and more diagrams for category. It is fundamental, therefore, that the usability of the final application has to be guaranteed to be an intuitive and easy to use environment to the designer; particularly, the integration among the different modeling must be easily, allowing the passage from modeling the other (when possible) in a simple and fast way.

A very important requisite is the implementation of the methodological guidelines of integration that allow the transition from a methodology of design to the other; this requisite involves the communication among the editors of the CASE tool. The complexity of the methodological guidelines must, nevertheless, be completely hidden to the final user.

The designer has to be able to work on more editors contemporarily and has to have the possibility of realizing or completing a well-defined diagram eventually using elements of other open diagrams; in this case, the application has to perform,

Copyright © 2009, IGI Global, distributing in print or electronic forms without written permission of IGI Global is prohibited.

in a way completely transparent to the final user, the operations of translation among the different typologies of design (semi-automatic export), according to the rules described in the methodological guidelines of integration. Besides this, it has to be able to perform, when possible, the transformation also starting from a whole diagram (it will speak, in such case, of automatic export).

In order to realize the automatic generation of a prototype of the application starting from the design of the business process, it is necessary that the final application is able to produce an ontological machine readable file related to the design, which will be used by the generator of code for the creation of the prototype. In the last analysis, the realization of the ontological file consists of adding the individuals to the meta-model already defined (specific for a particular methodology). The meta-model of the methodologies has already been discussed in Chapter III.

DEFINITION OF THE SOFTWARE ARCHITECTURE

The problem to be faced is very complex: on one hand it is necessary to design and to realize a framework that allows for entertaining the many editors that compose the methodology; on the other hand, it is necessary to design and to realize the various editors as well as the methodological guidelines that allow to pass from one design to another as allowed by the methodology. After having selected Eclipse™ as the technological platform that appears to support at the best these requisites, it is necessary to think about an architecture that found itself on this platform and that uses all of its characteristics.

The choice has been realized among two alternatives:

* Definition of a new framework
* Re-use of the existing framework

Definition of a New Framework

The first analyzed solution consists of the realization of the framework ex novo, but is also always based on the selected platform. The choice would bring forth a very tall level of complexity because it is necessary to realize ex novo all of the functions that the framework should make available to the many editors and the methodological guidelines. You, for instance, think about the base functions related to the graphic user interface (GUI) that it would need to realize (even though being facilitated by the already code present in the Eclipse™ platform) or to all the APIs that the framework should make available to the editors and to the methodological guidelines.

Copyright © 2009, IGI Global, distributing in print or electronic forms without written permission of IGI Global is prohibited.

The ex novo realization of the framework, if on one hand it allows to exactly obtain the framework desired, then on the other hand it behaves like a notable design and implementation and, as every project, would require a lot of time to perform the test and the improvement of all of the functions that the framework makes to the superior levels before arriving at a mature and stable release available.

Re-Use of an Existing Framework

The second considered hypothesis is to fully exploit the framework that already exists in the selected technologic platform and to build on this platform a further level that personalizes it on which to lean than the several CASE tools that support the methodology.

The selected platform will constitute in this architecture the base framework, as shown in Figure 1. This platform will have to provide some base features, allowing particularly a simple management and customization of the GUI, as well as the addition of new functions.

The realization of the CASE tool would not be different from the preceding case: it will be necessary to use the same technology of the framework, and we will proceed realizing, according to the specifications dictated by the framework, the editors, the methodological guidelines and eventually the other functions of the case.

For the realization of the editors, the re-use of existing libraries to manage the realization of the necessary palette can be useful to the several editors to realize the support to the methodology.

The choice to re-use a framework brings with itself several advantages: the first is a possibility to use a diffused and well-documented framework which is the Eclipse™ framework and that is consolidated during the years reaching high levels of stability, an elevated number of features, good modularity and usability, and that, at the same time, has a mechanism for the extensibility.

Figure 1. Architecture of a CASE tool

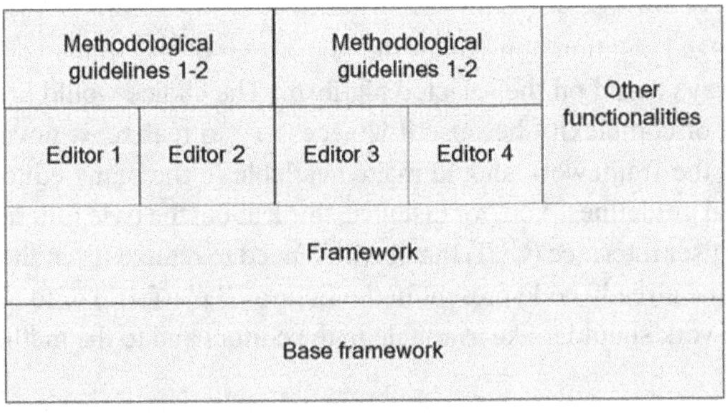

Methodological guidelines 1-2		Methodological guidelines 1-2		Other functionalities
Editor 1	Editor 2	Editor 3	Editor 4	
Framework				
Base framework				

Copyright © 2009, IGI Global, distributing in print or electronic forms without written permission of IGI Global is prohibited.

Selected Solution

Of course, after considering the requisites of extensibility and customization and considering that the product has to present itself as an essential and irreplaceable tool for the designer and, therefore, has to be found on a stable and consolidate base, the most proper solution is to re-use an existing framework, in particular the Eclipse RCP™.

Undisputed, in fact, are the consequential advantages coming from the use of the Eclipse RCP™ platform in order to answer to the above requirements. First of all, there is the possibility to use a stable and well-documented base framework; besides, it is possible to extend the framework through the technique of the contributions. Finally, thanks to the RCP system, it is possible to exactly export the plug-in useful in a particular moment providing the end user with a product that releases it from the development environment. This last feature is particularly interesting because it would allow providing the end user with one or more editors depending on the particular methodology in use.

The final architecture of the software can be structured according to the scheme described in Figure 1 and where, starting from the lower part, there is the base framework, constituted by the base Eclipse RCP. Immediately above, there is the Framework that provides new functions, more specific and advanced, to those provided by the underlying level.

Finally, the highest levels are made up by all of the single modules that, exploiting the APIs made available by the underlying levels, they realize indeed the features of the final CASE Tool; in a few words, they implement the specific editors for each methodology and the methodological guidelines of integration between these methodologies.

DESIGN OF BASE FRAMEWORK

We will describe here the features that can be re-used by the final product, and that they can realize, together with the above level, the interface of integration for the following modules.

The Re-Usable Plug-In

The plug-in of the base framework that we intend to define deal, above all, with building aspects proper to the GUI of the system.

Copyright © 2009, IGI Global, distributing in print or electronic forms without written permission of IGI Global is prohibited.

The analysis of the existing components gives us the possibility to consider re-usable the plug-in *org.eclipse.ui* and *org.eclipse.core.resources* extending in particular:

- *org.eclipse.ui.editor*, to allow the construction of the editors inside the GUI
- *org.eclipse.ui.perspectives*, to allow the realization of different views of perspective related to the same work area
- *org.eclipse.ui.view*, for the construction of the generic panels of visualization (views) inside the GUI
- *org.eclipse.ui.newWizard*, to allow the realization of driven procedures multi-steps (wizards)
- *org.eclipse.ui.editorAction*, to allow the addition of the actions, related to the editor, internally to the toolbar and to the menu bar of system
- *org.eclipse.ui.bindings*, to manage the shortcut to the existing actions
- *org.eclipse.core.resources*, to allow the use of the project exploration and its functions

Besides these, we plan to re-use the modules whose goal is only functional to the execution of the software; we deal with the plug-in *org.eclipse.core.runtime*, for which it is important to extend:

- *org.eclipse.core.runtime.applications,* to guarantee the execution of the rich client application
- *org.eclipse.core.runtime.products,* to realize the concept of software product necessary to the correct working with the rich client application realized

The Customized Plug-In

The study made up on the platform in examination has involved very closely the analysis of the graphic user interface that it provides by default; re-using the standard plug-in provided by Eclipse™; in fact, has been possible to notice as some of the components (those that realize parts of the user interface) are not proper for the present implementation.

In some cases, we face the problem to have an excessive number of tools in comparison to the ones due, being these directly inherited by the framework.

In this situation, therefore, it is necessary to eliminate from the user interface all the unwanted contributions that can uselessly weigh down the application, and can confuse the final user.

Copyright © 2009, IGI Global, distributing in print or electronic forms without written permission of IGI Global is prohibited.

This can be done working directly on the code at the base of the plug-in at question, *org.eclipse.ui.ide*, disarming the contributions in excess or replacing them with new ones.

Design of the Framework

We now face the design phase of one of the most important and delicate parts of the whole architecture presented in Figure 1: the framework module.

The goal is to design an intermediary module that addresses the requirements of the highest levels of this architecture and that can provide new and more advanced features to those already introduced by the underlying base framework.

As we have seen in the previous section, in fact, the base framework, and therefore the base Eclipse RCP™, has allowed to introduce several advantages in terms of extensibility of the final product: the introduction of the advanced concepts such as plug-in, extension and points of extension allow to potentially widen to the endless the whole software architecture.

What we intend to make now, is, instead, to design, starting from a base so built and exploiting all the potentialities of it, a software layer that allows the maximum possible customization to the whole architecture guaranteeing an easier integration of the superior modules through advanced functions.

These functions can be entirely new, or they can simply constitute some simplifications of functions already existing and introduced by the lowest level; in every case, these will be created in order to allow directly an integration of the superior modules in the architecture (the editors) with the lower effort possible.

Everything aims to offer an intermediary level that will be able to provide a simpler view of the underlying architecture (the base framework), usable from the greater part of the module at superior levels. The modules for which an advanced customization is required can directly access, however, the base framework.

In a panorama so defined, therefore, it will need to design the framework not starting only from the analysis of what the whole architecture will have to offer to the end user, but focusing on what it is necessary to provide at the superior levels.

In this way, the analysis that will be performed will have as a starting point the study of the use cases related to the true actor of the architecture of the framework, that is the module of the editor.

Because the whole architecture is based on the Eclipse RCP™ platform, it is true that the great importance of the realization of the framework as a plug-in of Eclipse™: in this way it can perfectly integrate in the architecture, intervening with contributions of several kinds.

Copyright © 2009, IGI Global, distributing in print or electronic forms without written permission of IGI Global is prohibited.

Framework: Use Case Diagram

In this paragraph we define the diagram of the use cases related to the only actor of the framework module, the *module editor* (Figure 2).

From the diagram in Figure 2, we highlight the prerogatives of a generic editor module: it first has to contribute to the realization of the graphic user interface and to provide the designer with the main work area (panel editor), the panel with properties of the elements and the panel of the overview related to the diagram (the bird-eye view).

It can also *provide actions to the menu*, so defining the actions that can populate the inside menus of the framework, and to *define new wizards*, through which to make the driven procedures for the creation of a new diagram (obligatory) and that for the export of a diagram in OWL ontological format (W3C, 2004) (when necessary).

Besides this, the editor module *defines a new type of diagram*: to every editor belonging to the architecture it must be associated with a particular typology of design and, therefore, a particular typology of file (with the related extension); in this way the framework will be able to open the corresponding editor according to the particular type of file.

Finally, the editor module can notify the user, in order to centralize the mechanism of notification of the notices that could be introduced to the final user during the normal use of the application.

Figure 2. Use case diagram for the framework module

Copyright © 2009, IGI Global, distributing in print or electronic forms without written permission of IGI Global is prohibited.

Class Diagram

We now describe, starting from the diagrams of the use cases just defined, the diagrams of the conceptual classes related to the framework module that we intend to realize.

In this analysis the principal intent is not to internally centralize the whole logic of the architecture inside the framework, but to provide an interface that makes the operations of integration of the superior modules friendlier. In this way, we are been able to determine as, in some cases, the use of the mechanisms of extension and points of extension, made by the base framework, they were enough to provide the correct support. Whereas, instead, the operations to be performed are more complex, we decided to intervene, realizing a plug-in of support suitable to guarantee a simpler integration among components.

Use Case "Provide Panel to the GUI"

According to what was said before, the editor module, that will have to compose part of the CASE tool, must provide the framework with the three panels described above (panel editor, panel properties, panel overview). A way to allow their design is, then, to exploit the potentialities provided by the Base Framework available, particularly using the mechanism of the points of extension.

In regard to the main panel, which is related to the central work area, the point of extension *org.eclipse.ui.editor* is used, through which it is necessary to build the class that realizes the panel extending the abstract interface *IEditorPart*.

For the panels of the properties and overview, instead, it proceeds, extending the plug in *org.eclipse.ui.views*, through which the classes useful to build the panel will have to extend, this time, the abstract interface *IViewPart*.

In this context, however, we must face an additional problem introduced by the intrinsic dynamism of the panels of properties and overview; the content of these panels, in fact, can change depending on the operation of the selection of elements and of the activation of the editors inside the tool, because they are panels always fixed, and they are replaceable by the editors in use. All this means, therefore, that it is important to provide a mechanism of notification of the modification of the inside selection of the diagram, in order to update the content of the properties panel at every selection of an element inside of the panel; besides this, it is also necessary for a mechanism of notification around the active editor inside the work area; it finally needs to guarantee the persistence of the work area saving the inside disposition of the panels every time the tool is closed. In this case, it will be necessary to perform some preliminary operations to guarantee a correct initialization of the two panel overview and properties.

Copyright © 2009, IGI Global, distributing in print or electronic forms without written permission of IGI Global is prohibited.

In regards to the first of the three introduced problems, the best solution seems to be the use of the design pattern observer: it defines a dependence on one to many among objects, so that if a subject changes its state, all the objects dependent from it are notified and automatically updated. The applicability of this design pattern, therefore, is very useful, because the editor needs to notify other objects (the two panels) without knowing their characteristics; in this way it will be possible to guarantee a high level of modularity among the editor module and the framework besides.

In Figure 3, the resultant diagram of the classes is represented.

By analyzing the components that realize the diagram, we can immediately individualize the application of the design pattern observer: the class *EditorSubject* covers the role of subject, which knows its own observers providing them an interface able to associate and to dissociate them; the class *EditorObserver* is the observer that provides an interface able to notify the observers of the changes of the subject; *AbstractEditor* represents the concrete subject, that contains information around the selection inside of a diagram and notification to the observers when something changes; *OverView* and *PropertiesView* finally cover the role of the concrete observers, that they store a reference inside of the concrete subject, and they implement the interface of notification of observer in order to maintain their state consistent with that of the subject.

For the remaining parts, we observe first the existence of an abstract class *AbstractEditor*, that it provides a base implementation of the editor, inheriting an

Figure 3. Class diagram for the use case "Provide panel to the GUI"

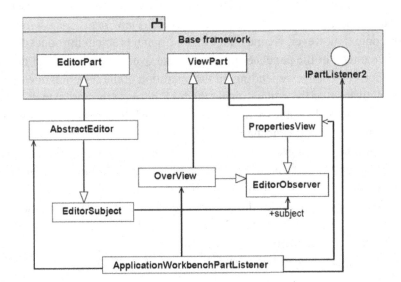

Copyright © 2009, IGI Global, distributing in print or electronic forms without written permission of IGI Global is prohibited.

implementation of a class *EditorPart* (of the base framework), and introduces new fundamental features (such as the mechanism of notification of the panels in case of change of inside selection). Using as a point of reference this abstract class, instead of directly implementing *IEditorPart*, the editor module can exploit these features in a native way.

The classes *OverView* and *PropertiesView* represent two *ViewParts* or the two views that will be available inside of the GUI making use of the class *Perspective*. Their contents can be provided by the module editor, through the class that extends *AbstractEditor*.

Finally, the class *ApplicationWorkbenchPartListener*, exploiting the functions of the base framework (through the listener *IPartListener2*) allows to remain in listening of all the events of the Workbench (such as opening, closing, activate, deactivate, etc. the editors). In this way, every time that a variation of the selection will be intercepted inside the work area, the two panels of properties and overview can be notified, that can redraw themselves according to the new selection.

Use Case "Provide Action to the Menu"

Besides contributing in terms of panels, the module editor can also provide actions to the underlying levels, adding elements to the menu bar, to the toolbar, and so forth. All of this, once more, can be made using the features provided by the base framework or by the framework.

In fact, in the Eclipse™ platform, two typologies of actions exists: those classics, that characterize a particular editor realized and those more general (as the operations cut, copy, redo and undo) and that can be implemented by the various existing modules.

In the first case, an editor module can decide to include a new action inside the toolbar using the features proper to the base framework: it will be necessary to use the point of extension *org.eclipse.ui.editorActions* and to provide a class with the implementation of the operation to perform. In this way, every editor can choose what operations to include and what not to incluce.

The more general interface allows the module editor to contribute to the implementation of the actions common of the GUI. In this case, it is the framework itself that provides the proper tools for the module editor, creating a whole abstract action to which to make internally graphic elements correspond to the menu bar and the toolbar. It will then be the assignment of the single editor to provide a complete implementation for such actions (class *Contributor*) adding the correspondent graphic elements to the work area.

The base framework provides that the actions will be defined inside a subclass of *ActionBarAdvisor ApplicationActionBarAdvisor*.

Copyright © 2009, IGI Global, distributing in print or electronic forms without written permission of IGI Global is prohibited.

Figure 4. Class diagram for the use case "Provide action to the menu"

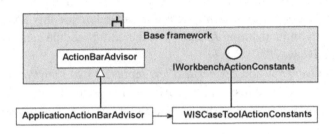

The diagram of the classes that results is shown in Figure 4.

Use Case "Define New Wizards"

The definition of a wizard is, under certain points of view, comparable to the definition of an action because, as this last, it provides the addition of new components to the GUI of system (in terms, once more, of menu bar and toolbar or of panels of dialogue that follow the final user along the one or the other operation).

In the case under analysis, there are two driven procedures of interest: one for the creation of a new diagram and one related to the operation of export in OWL ontological format.

In the first case, every editor necessarily has to implement this procedure, for which it has to be requested by the user to insert the information regarding the name of the file and the destination, in order to get an empty diagram on which to work.

In the second case, only the possibility to realize this procedure not being necessary for all the typologies of design must be provided.

Just for this last case, the framework can help by simplifying the realization of a similar wizard and exploiting, in particular, the mechanism of the extensions and the points of extension.

To achieve this goal has been developed, inside the framework, a new point of extension. It is used by each module editor, and it offers them the possibility, among the other things, to define an implementation of the operation of OWL export. This implementation must be provided as a concrete subclass of the class *AbstractOwl-ExportRunnableWithProgress*, defined in the framework.

Likewise, inside the same point of extension the editors have to previously give an explicit reference to a *newWizard*: only in this way can the framework hold a trace of these, adding elements to the GUI where necessary.

The class diagram regarding the wizard for the export in OWL and for the creation of a new diagram is described in the Figure 5.

Copyright © 2009, IGI Global, distributing in print or electronic forms without written permission of IGI Global is prohibited.

Figure 5. Class diagram "Define new wizards"

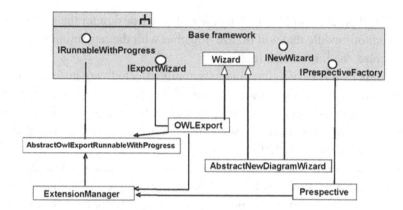

Use Case "Define a New Type of Diagram"

The definition of a new type of diagram is important in order to allow the univocal association between editor and typology of diagram. A deep study of the Base Framework has brought to track down, as best possible solution the re-use of the plug-in *org.eclipse.ui* making use, in particular, of the point of extension *org.eclipse. ui.editors.*

In fact, by extending this point of extension, it is possible to describe the association through the definition of some important information: the name of the editor, the icon to associate it, the extension of the files associated and two important classes (one that implements the interface *IEditorPart* and the other *IEditorAction-BarContributor*, as it will be clearer after).

In this way, the system is instructed around what editor to open according to the specified extension.

Use Case "Notify Advice to the User"

The last use case in examination analyzes the mechanism used by the architecture for the management of the messages of notice to introduce to the user. The framework, in fact, provides that every editor module supply these messages (both simple notice and errors), in order to be able to exhibit them in a unique format (using the GUI of the Eclipse platform).

This characteristic, together with a lot of others, is made possible thanks to the use of only one utility class present in the framework, *Util*, that will be adopted by all the editors in order to realize the containing dialogue boxes and the information of interest.

Copyright © 2009, IGI Global, distributing in print or electronic forms without written permission of IGI Global is prohibited.

Design of the Module Editor

In this , we will proceed with describing the necessary design for the implementation of the editor module that will realize, together with the remaining modules of the architecture, the final CASE tool.

This design, as it is easy to imagine, is actually affected very positively by the choices made up at this moment: the definition of the architecture that has as a point of strength, the extensibility and customization, it immediately involves an easy realization of the superior modules, following the mechanism of the "contribution" introduced by the Eclipse™ platform.

From a point of view where every realized module provides new features to the central system, every editor it will constitute, in concrete terms, a plug-in for the platform, to use features of the framework and the base framework (mechanisms of extension and points of extension) in order to contribute to the realization of the final application.

We will introduce here the design of only one of the editor modules: the design will result in the implementation of the remaining editor modules.

The architecture introduced here, in fact, would theoretically allow the integration of a number of base editors, independently from the way according to which these are realized; this choice, therefore, is exclusively a practical choice and allows building a set of modules that differ among them only for the characteristic parts.

To achieve this goal, we propose only the design of the editor of support to the P-IDM methodology.

The realization of this editor has made advanced use of the JGraph libraries that provide unlimited potentiality as it regards the design of graphs and flow chart while the use of the platform GraphPad confers several advantages in terms of modularity of the architecture.

The main goal, in fact, is to adapt its structure for the mechanism of the "contribution" introduced by the base framework, to be able to realize a module that contributes, as a plug in, to the final architecture that it will go to realize.

The Use Case Diagram

In the definition of the use cases for the editor module, we chose to describe two general diagrams, one for the actor User and the other for the actor Framework; this has been done because if on one hand must be considered the requirements proper of the User, for which the editor has to provide some features, on the other hand, it is important to consider also the requirements proper of the base architecture, for which the editor has to provide some characteristics.

Copyright © 2009, IGI Global, distributing in print or electronic forms without written permission of IGI Global is prohibited.

This aspect is of the highest importance in the optics to reach a complete and rigorous design of the product: the use cases related to the final user introduce, in fact, the characteristics proper to the editor, that will bring to design the inside features that it has to provide to the user designer; the use cases concerning the framework will allow instead, to design the typical aspects of existing interface among the base framework architecture, the framework and the editors modules.

Only contemporarily analyzing them, therefore it will be possible to get a complete picture of the components that realize the whole module, that will result composed by classes, that take care of the working of the editor and by classes devoted to the communication with the underlying platform.

Use Case for the Stakeholder "User"

The following diagram of use cases (Figure 6) describes what the requirements that an editor of P-IDM diagrams (but the same would be true for any other typology of editor) has to provide to the user that wants to design a Web application.

The user that uses the editor has the goal of drawing a diagram for the typology of design in examination, to view it or to perform its export.

For the first use case, draws diagram, the final user has the possibility to perform the typical operations of editing inside of the panel of principal work area: insert element, necessarily choosing it from the notation toolbar inside of the same editor, change element, moving it or reorganizing it, define element property mak-

Figure 6. Use case diagram for the "user" stakeholder—the editor module

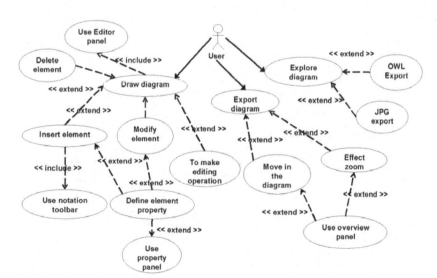

Copyright © 2009, IGI Global, distributing in print or electronic forms without written permission of IGI Global is prohibited.

ing use of a panel, specifically made up to this purpose, and delete element. The operations of insertion and change can be facilitated particularly, thanks to the aid of operations common to the editors, such as cut/paste and undo/redo (use case of effects actions of common editing). For the second main use case explores diagram, instead, the final user has the possibility to use a panel of navigation (a bird-eye view) in order to quickly move in the diagram and to easily perform operations of zoom (effects the zoom).

The last use case, that is export diagram, describes the wish of the user to export a well- defined diagram in image format JPG or in ontological format OWL.

Use Case for the User "Framework"

The following diagram (Figure 7) describes the interactions that exist among the considered editor and the second level of the software architecture, the framework.

This diagram describes as the stakeholder framework, substantially has the necessity to get from the editor module only the components that define the Graphic User Interface that is the panels useful for the visualization of the information and the necessary wizard.

In this way the framework *asks for the panels* containing the work area (inside which it must necessarily be the notation toolbar for the design of the elements of the methodology): the panel related to the representation of the properties of the elements of the design and the panel of overview. Besides this, the framework *asks for the wizard* useful to realize the most complex actions as the realization of a new diagram file and to export the same in OWL format. This configuration, even

Figure 7. Use case diagram for the use case related to the stakeholder –editor module

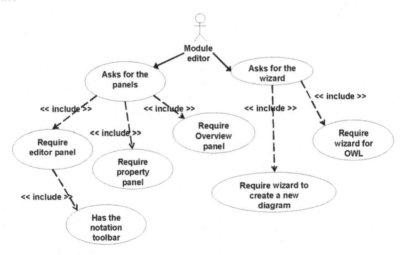

Copyright © 2009, IGI Global, distributing in print or electronic forms without written permission of IGI Global is prohibited.

if superficial, does not have to deceive; in fact, although the editor can provide the framework with well more than these components (you, for instance, can think about the actions in the visualization of the menu bar), only for these elements are eventually required by the framework itself. In other words, the framework cannot require that all of the components useful to the correct operation of the system are provided because it is not said that an editor effectively implements them.

Class Diagrams

We describe now the high-level class diagram made up for the realization of the editor module.

Use Case "Design Diagram" - Stakeholder User

We define here the class diagram related to the use case draw diagram defined for the actor user. At this time, the classes that guarantee the correct execution of the operations of addition, change and elimination of the elements of the diagram are designed, providing, at the same time, a vision of the main classes that characterize the heart of the editor module.

As already said in previous sections, the P-IDM editor that we intend to realize is based on a GraphPad, a set of components (panels, toolbar, etc.) that refer to only one class that has the work to manage a standalone application. The phase of design made up in order to suit this technology for the specific ones required by the underlying platform, has made it necessary to have to build a class diagram described in the Figure 8.

In this configuration, the most important class is the *GPGraphpad*, which represents, in concrete terms, the panel containing the main work area. To its realization two main panels contribute, described by the classes *GPDocument* and *GPBarFactory*: the first one builds the real work area, while the second represents the panel containing the notation toolbar, to whose inside the buttons for the design of the elements related the specific notation (P-IDM, in this case) find place.

The classes that allow for making the operations of design inside the panel *GPDocument* are *GPMarqueHandler* and *GPGraph*: the first one includes in it all the logic necessary to adding elements inside of the real work area, the second allows the use of all the potentialities offered by the graphic libraries JGraph.

The classes *GPGraphModel* and *DefaultGraphModelFileFormatXML*, respectively, deal finally with providing a formal representation of the realized model that is useful in all those circumstances in which it is necessary to work at a level of information of diagram, and to realize the operations of open/store of the model in a XML file.

Copyright © 2009, IGI Global, distributing in print or electronic forms without written permission of IGI Global is prohibited.

Figure 8. Use case diagram related to the use case "draw diagram"

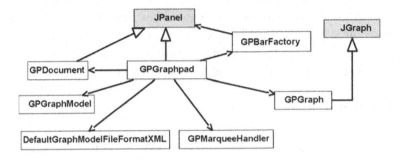

Use Case "Explore Diagram" User Actor

The use case here exploded describes what classes are necessary in order to realize the operations of navigation inside of the diagram: we are speaking, therefore, about the realization of the overview panel, through which it is possible to have a global vision of the edited graph and to make operations of zoom.

The classes involved in these operations are shown in Figure 9.

The class *GPOverviewPanel* describes the panel inside which is drawn, making use of the class GPGraph, the global view of the present diagram inside of the main panel (GPDocument); this panel deals with notifying the class GPOverviewPanel whenever there will be changes to the area of visualization of the diagram, in this way it can be updated accordingly.

Use Case "OWL Export": User Actor

A feature that must be provided to the user that makes a P-IDM diagram must be the export of the diagram in OWL format.

For this reason, a software interface must be built that, starting from the model that describes the diagram in examination, effects the translation of it starting from a well-defined ontology.

Figure 9. Class diagram related to the use case "explore diagram"

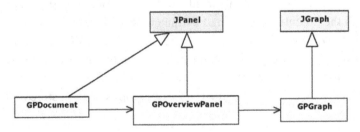

Copyright © 2009, IGI Global, distributing in print or electronic forms without written permission of IGI Global is prohibited.

This interface is defined by the classes showed in the Figure 10.

In this diagram, the mechanism of export is developed by the class *OWLExport*: it uses the class *GPGraph* to load the information related to the model of the diagram in use, starting from which it loads all the properties of the elements in it. Besides it uses the class *DiagramPropertySheet* to get the properties related the same diagram. From here, using some functions of the package *edu.stanford.smi. protegex.owl* useful for building the classes and the properties that realize an OWL ontology, it makes available the desired file.

Use Case "Ask for the Panel": Framework Actor

The use case in examination envisages that the framework asks the realized plug-in the panels what will have to populate the GUI.

To be able to make this, it is important to realize a structure of the classes using the concepts of extension and extension points, contributing, therefore, to the platform according to the specifications dictated by these mechanisms. In this way, it has to be necessary, as we saw in the paragraph of design of the framework, to use the point of extension *org.eclipse.ui.editors* for the editor panel, in which must be described important information such as the name of the editor, the extension of the file and a class that implements the abstract class *AbstractEditor*.

The use of this class, besides, it allows for centralizing the management of the panels of properties and overview: extending *AbstractEditor*, in fact, the features can be implemented through which to make available these panels, that will correctly be updated thanks to the applying of the design pattern observer previously seen.

In such optics, it is possible to define a class diagram so built.

In this diagram (Figure 11), the principal class is *PIDMEditor*: this represents, practically, the point of contact with the underlying module framework, extending the abstract class *AbstractEditor* belonging to the same framework. This class has therefore the task to provide the central panel that realizes the work area of the editor to the lower level, described by *GPGraphpad*, together with the panels of

Figure 10. Class diagram related to the use case "OWL export"

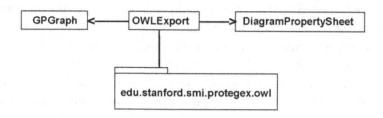

Copyright © 2009, IGI Global, distributing in print or electronic forms without written permission of IGI Global is prohibited.

Figure 11. Class diagram "Ask for the panel"

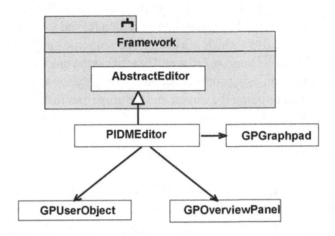

the properties and overview realized using, respectively, the classes *GPUserObject* and *GPOverviewPanel*.

Use Case "Ask for the Wizard": Framework Actor

The realization of the use case "Ask for the wizard" concerns, as seen, the design of the driven procedures for the generation of a new diagram and that relative to the export of the same in the OWL format.

In the first case, the module editor has to use a point of extension at the base of the base framework, *org.eclipse.ui.newWizard*, through which the platform of the contribution that is wanted to add is informed. Doing this, it needs to provide some important information: the name of the wizard (what will appear in the relative dialogue box), the icon representing the wizard itself, the category defined inside of the framework (or the category to which the wizard will belong, in the specific case *newDiagrams*) and a class that, implementing the abstract class *AbstractNewDiagramWizard*, builds the driven procedure. Besides this, the module editor must use a point of extension of the framework, named *it.unile.wiscasetool. editors*: this must be done because every editor, that necessarily has to realize this driven procedure, has to contribute to the menu of realization of the new diagram, specifically realized. To do this, while creating the extension, it provides the univocal identifier of the editor (the ID described during the phase of creation of the editor, extending *org.eclipse.ui.editors*), and the univocal identifier of the created wizard. In the case of the wizard of export in OWL format, instead, the only use of the point of extension realized in the framework is provided. This operation of export, not realized by all the editor modules, will have to appear inside of the

Copyright © 2009, IGI Global, distributing in print or electronic forms without written permission of IGI Global is prohibited.

menus of the export provided in the project explorer inside of the platform, and it is planned, therefore, that should be performed starting from the selection of a file of diagram (with extension .pidm, in this case). It will be necessary, therefore, to describe what class will perform this operation, that will have to extend the abstract class *AbstractOwlExportRunnableWithProgress* without implementing, therefore, the pages that realize the driven procedure (the class implements only the necessary features to create the file .owl starting from the .pidm file).The class diagram is shown in Figure 12.

Starting from the left, the class *NewDiagramWizard* allows the realization of the pages that compose the guided procedure in order to create a new P-IDM diagram, extending the abstract class *AbstractNewDiagramWizard* and founding itself on the specific imposed by the Eclipse™ framework.

The class *OwlExportRunnableWithProgressFromFile*, deals instead with realizing the necessary operations to the export the P-IDM diagram, in ontological language. This is made possible using the class *DefaultGraphModelFileFormatXML*, which deals with the loading of the information from the file related to the diagram in examination. From here it is possible, through the class *GPGraph*, to realize the final model that will be used then by the class *OWLExport* to allow its translation in OWL format.

Methodological Guidelines for the Integration

The methodological guidelines are on the fourth level of the architecture, above the editor modules. The main goal is to put in communication the several editors, in

Figure 12. Class diagram for the use case "Ask for the wizard"

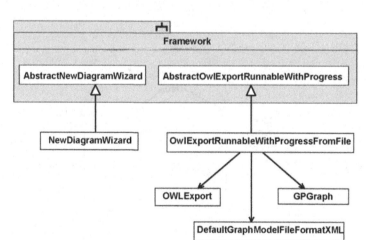

Copyright © 2009, IGI Global, distributing in print or electronic forms without written permission of IGI Global is prohibited.

order to provide a support for the different methodological guidelines of integration present inside of the methodology.

In this section, we focus on the transition between IDM and P-IDM (you can compare with Chapter III for further details on this mapping): the design of the module that we present here can be replied for the other methodological guidelines in the methodology.

The design of the module starts from the analysis of the use cases considering the actor user, that is who can adopt the final CASE tool to design the Web application.

Use Case Diagram for the Actor User

With regards to the application of the methodological guidelines, a use case diagram has been identified for the actor user of the final system, described in Figure 13.

There are two different use cases: to make the integral export and to make the partial export of the diagram.

The first one happens when the user decides to use the editor in order to create a P-IDM diagram starting from a L-IDM diagram previously modeled. In this case, he/she will make use of a wizard defined by the framework, accessible from the contextual menu situated inside of the project explorer.

In the second case, the user makes a partial export. With this we intend that the user creates "manually" the new P-IDM diagram starting from a portion of selected L-IDM diagram. This operation can be made in two ways: in the first one, the user selects one or more elements inside the IDM diagram and drags them inside of a P-IDM diagram (or, he/she uses the drag and drop feature); in the second one the user makes a copy of some elements of a IDM diagram, and paste inside of a P-

Figure 13. Use case diagram for the module "methodological guidelines" – actor user

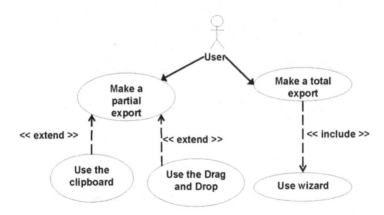

Copyright © 2009, IGI Global, distributing in print or electronic forms without written permission of IGI Global is prohibited.

IDM diagram. In both cases, the system must take care to intercept the event and to manage it, effecting a conversion of the selected elements, as provided by the methodological guidelines.

Class Diagrams

Make the Integral Export

The integral export of a file consists of the interaction of the user with the project explorer. In this way, a wizard for the export of the modeling according to the methodological guidelines will have to be integrated in the GUI.

The activation of this wizard by the user will happen through a click with the right key of the mouse inside of the project explorer, on a file corresponding to a L-IDM diagram. From the contextual menu, it has to choose the item exports and subsequently methodological guidelines. You can choose the export in a new P-IDM diagram.

The wizard will ask the user for the name of the new diagram and the position inside of the work area. Once the wizard ends, it will set out the operation of real export that will provide the creation of the new file in the work area and the opening of the corresponding diagram.

All of this involve sthe necessity to define, inside of the present module, an extension of the point of extension *guideLinesExport*, defined by the framework. This point of extension provides that the module methodological guidelines defines a class that implements *AbstractGuideLinesExportWithProgress* and, at the same time, indicates the starting point design and the conclusive design attended by these methodological guidelines.

The class so defined, called *ExportRunnableWithProgress*, has the assignment to start the real export, performing besides the preliminary and conclusive operations and managing a progress monitor that is a bar of advancement of the operation.

The real export operation can be performed by a class exporter on purpose thought: its concrete implementation for the export from L-IDM to P-IDM will communicate with the two editors, and it will complete the operations of translation using the features offered by other two classes:

- *L-IDMModel*, that provides simple methods for reading the source diagram
- *P-IDMModel,* that provides, instead, methods useful to design new elements in the target diagram

These classes can provide only these features operating with the basic library of the respective editors, in this case *jgraph* and *graphpad*. For this reason, the

Copyright © 2009, IGI Global, distributing in print or electronic forms without written permission of IGI Global is prohibited.

introduction of two further classes is useful, *LIDMUtils* and *PIDMUtils*, which respectively provide a simpler interface to *LIDMModel* and *PIDMModel* with these libraries.

In Figure 14, the final class diagram is represented.

Make the Partial Export

As already described, the partial export consists of the use of the drag and drop among editor, or by the clipboard. Therefore, the first step to make a partial export consists of "putting in communication" the several editors, activating the drag and drop.

The drag and drop can be activated at different levels that are in this order: Eclipse™ level, SWT or Java Virtual Machine™. We decided to activate the drag and drop at a lower level, or of Java Virtual Machine™, since in this way in the future, it will be possible to put in communication editors independently from the particular technology with which they are realized.

Once the drag and drop are activated, it is necessary to intercept the events dropped on the single editors, submitting then the real management of this event to the module methodological guidelines.

In the case under analysis concerning the editor P-IDM, the drop is intercepted in the class *GPGraphUI*. At this point, it is necessary to design an interface among the module editor and the module methodological guidelines (levels 3 and 4 of the architecture).

Figure 14. Class diagram for the integral export using the methodological guidelines

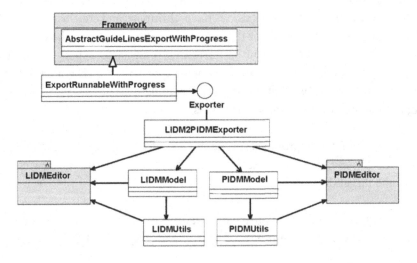

Copyright © 2009, IGI Global, distributing in print or electronic forms without written permission of IGI Global is prohibited.

The selected mechanism to do this, is that of the *delegation*, a mechanism often used in software engineering, at the base of the systems able to be the re-used. The event is totally managed by the modules methodological guidelines: using the design pattern observer, all of them, it will have to worry to record itself as observer of the events dropped for a good, specific editor. For instance, the module methodological guidelines *L- IDM2P-IDM* it will have to record itself as observer of the events dropped close to the module Editor P IDM.

All of the methodological guideline modules recorded at an editor will be notified from drop events, and they will be, depending on the editor that generates the drag event, to decide whether to intervene depending on the application. It will play the mechanism of delegation, according to which this module can directly intervene on the target diagram drawing the new elements. In practice, when a drop event occurs, the editor "passes itself" to the module methodological guidelines that will manage the partial export, and lastly, this can use all of the features which it requires.

The last knot to be loosened is the protocol for the recording of the observers or the mechanism with which a methodological guideline module can record itself on an editor module. The best solution consists of the use of the mechanism of the extensions/points of extension of Eclipse: in the editor module, a point of extension will be defined, *dropListener* and the single module methodological guidelines can extend this point of extension recording itself in this way, at compile-time, on the editor.

The editor module will obviously need an *ExtensionManager* very similar to that already seen for the framework, in order to determine, to every drop event, the list of the observers (that is the methodological guidelines modules) recorded on the editor.

In Figure 15, the resultant diagram of the classes is shown.

AN EXAMPLE OF USE

In the treatment of this chapter, we do not point our attention on the design of the various editors that will compose the methodology, but we focus our attention on the design of the core (framework) on which lean both the various editors realized and the methodological guidelines of integration defined in the methodology.

The many editors that compose the CASE tool are, in concrete terms, implemented following the design described concerning the P-IDM editor and with more attention to the graphic aspects of every editor.

We introduce here some screenshots related to the real use of the CASE tool.

Copyright © 2009, IGI Global, distributing in print or electronic forms without written permission of IGI Global is prohibited.

Figure 15. Class diagram for the partial export of the methodological guidelines.

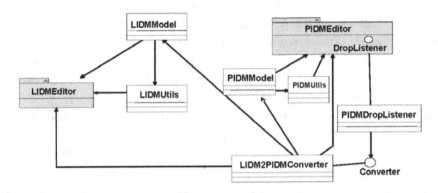

First Start

At the first start of the application, a default work area is created inside of the main folder that contains the application itself, where all the created projects will be stored.

Once the work area is defined, the application will start. Figure 16 shows as the application introduces itself at the first start.

Besides the classical menu bar on the top, and the toolbar, there are four main elements:

- *Work area*, greater and central, initially in gray
- *Project Explorer*, on the left, it allows the management of the work area

Figure 16. Main window of the application at the first start

Copyright © 2009, IGI Global, distributing in print or electronic forms without written permission of IGI Global is prohibited.

- *Properties*, on the right corner allow to visualize, and to modify the properties of the element selected in the active diagram
- *Overview*, it allows to have together a vision of the diagram, as well as to quickly move the point of view and to increase or to decrease the level of zoom

The Work Area

The first operation to make in order to be able to use the application consists of creating at least one project. This operation can be made in several different ways: from the toolbar, from the menu bar or through the contextual menu of the *ProjectExplorer.*

It is started in a wizard where it is required by the user the name to be attributed to the project.

Once the project is created, it will introduce inside of the project explorer.

It can be observed as many empty diagrams will be automatically created, one for every typology of available design. To open one of these and to begin to draw will be enough to do double click on its name, to select the item "open" from the contextual menu that appears and right click on its name, or to drag the diagram in the work area.

The project explorer allows using the diagrams as if they were files, cancelling them, renaming them, moving them, copying them and cutting and pasting them. Inside of every project it is also possible to create folders and to organize the diagrams as the user prefers.

Draw a Diagram

The operation of designing a diagram happens internally to the principal work area. This, once the file to open from the project explorer is selected, introduces it as shown in Figure 17.

The side bar, inside of the work area, allows the insertion of the elements of the specific typology of design; this can typically be done in two ways:

- Selecting the element in the notation toolbar and defining position and dimension of it with the mouse inside of the work area
- Selecting a particular element from the notation toolbar and clicking on the already existing element in the diagram, in the case in which there is the necessity to realize composed elements

Copyright © 2009, IGI Global, distributing in print or electronic forms without written permission of IGI Global is prohibited.

Figure 17. Main window of the editor when editors are open

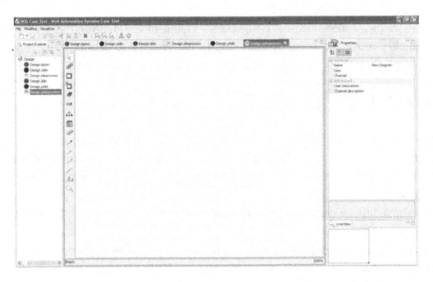

In the case of an IDM diagram, for instance, the realization of an element "dialog act" inside of a "single topic" or a 'kind of topic" happens according to the second technique: by selecting from the notation toolbar the element "dialog act," it will be possible to add it to a "single topic" simply by clicking on it; to every additional click, in particular, it will correspond to the addition of a further element, correctly positioned depending of the precedent.

It is, besides, possible to make use of the classical operations of cut/copy/paste and undo/redo, usable directly from the menu bar and toolbar or respectively using the classical keys of rapid choice CTRL+T/C/X and CTRL+Z/Y.

Design of a BPMN Diagram

In order to illustrate as the realized editor allows to hide the intrinsic complexity of the methodologies of design that it supports, we define here (Figure 18) an example of use making reference to an imaginary business process using the BPMN™ notation (OMG, 2006) (it is possible to refer to Chapter II for details on the notation). As it can be observed in Figure 18, the panel that contains the tools of design for BPMN seems not to support the entire notation. In reality, this choice has been dictated by the requirement to simplify how much more possible the use of the notation. Observing well, in fact, the toolbar represents only the base concepts of the notation that is lane, task, events, gateway and flow without going down in the specializations of each element; they will be defined depending on the context and on the particular requirement of the final user.

Copyright © 2009, IGI Global, distributing in print or electronic forms without written permission of IGI Global is prohibited.

To clarify better, we, for instance, suppose to draw the message flow that connects the task 1 of the first pool with the task 2 of the second. From the study of BPMN, it is evident that the interconnection rules among several elements forbid the use of a sequence flow to connect these two elements imposing instead using a message flow. The tool of interconnection is unique so the rules of interconnection are wired in the editor facilitating in this way the use of the notation by the designer.

Another meaningful example can be found again in the use of the events. Despite that the notation provides three different typologies of event (start, intermediate, message) and for each different inside icons every usable to model well precise situations, in the toolbar only a symbol of event is present. To understand better in Figure 18, we can see an overview of possible type of "events" and the related icons that will be used inside (the same is for other BPMN elements). Our effort in the design and implementation of BPMN editor has been oriented to support user design: the right stereotype depends on the user. For example, if the user chooses an event from the palette (the palette shows only a circle without start, intermediate or end distinction) it became automatically a start event without any icon inside. If the event becomes a target for a sequence flow and the same event is a source for another sequence flow, it automatically became an intermediate event (without icon inside). In the same way, if the event is targeted for a sequence flow, and it is not a source for any other sequence flow, it became an end event (without an icon inside).

In regards to properties of each BPMN element, in the design and implementation of the BPMN editor our efforts have been oriented to provide the user with

Figure 18. The BPMN editor

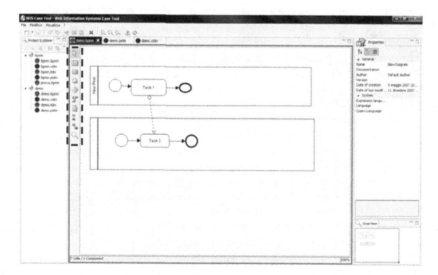

Copyright © 2009, IGI Global, distributing in print or electronic forms without written permission of IGI Global is prohibited.

the capability to insert a property, using a property form show on the right of the screen.

The editor allows a business user to reach the detail level necessary to achieve his/her goal; at the same time, IT experts may read in the first step all the process design and then read all process details in the property form. Some details unknown to the business user (e.g., implementation details) may be added from the IT experts in the same business process design where business experts work.

Therefore, the user could, for instance, position directly an end event in the design without worrying himself/herself about the particular typology of end event. In a second moment, when it will have clearer ideas on the design, it will be able to redefine the element and to set the relative properties by the property panel (Figure. 19).

We can obtain what is shown in Figure 20.

Of course, here we described just some examples; all the complexity of the BMPN notation is hidden to the final user.

THE ADVANCED FEATURES

The Graphic User Interface

The graphic interface is broadly customizable by the user: every panel can simply be moved dragging its title in a new position. For instance, a user could be accustomed

Figure 19. Modify the property from the property panel

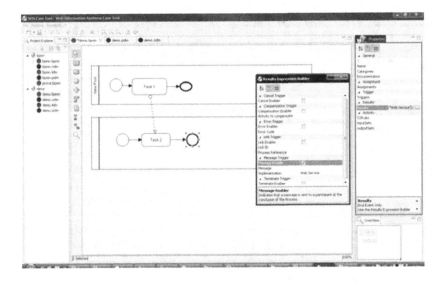

Copyright © 2009, IGI Global, distributing in print or electronic forms without written permission of IGI Global is prohibited.

Figure 20. BPMN design of the end event of type message

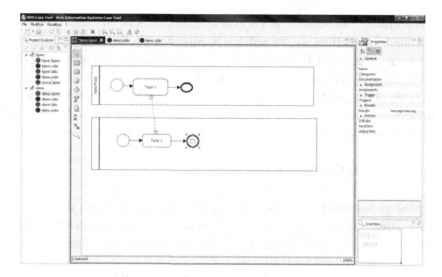

to having the panel of overview down on the left. By moving the panel, it will go to that position and this preference will be memorized by the application and used to every following start of the same one.

This characteristic is also valid for the editors, and in this way the final user can visualize more diagrams contemporarily.

This is useful not only because it allows the final user to design a diagram according to another previously drawn, but also because it is possible to drag elements among different diagrams.

Interesting and often useful feature is that to allow the enlargement of a panel, as, for instance, a diagram, doing double-click on the title of the same panel.

This allows maximizing the dimensions of the same panel (all the other panels will disappear from the GUI), having so a greater work area. To make the other panels reappear will be enough to again do double-click on the title of the panel.

Drag and Drop

As described in the previous paragraph, one of the most interesting characteristics of this application is the possibility offered to the final user to drag elements between diagrams.

Contemporarily having two open diagrams, for instance two L-IDM diagrams, the user can select and drag any element as a kind of topic, from a diagram to the other.

Copyright © 2009, IGI Global, distributing in print or electronic forms without written permission of IGI Global is prohibited.

The result of the moving is the creation of the same element, and of all its children, inside of the target diagram.

This operation can be made not also among diagrams of the same type: if the methodological guidelines are defined, it is possible to make the passage among two different types of diagram. For instance, this is provided for the passage from L-IDM to P-IDM: the drag of a kind of topic in a diagram P-IDM involves the creation of a screen father correspondent to it, and of a screen to it connected for every dialogue acts present to its inside; all of this to notably simplify the job of the designer that uses the methodology, following the methodological guidelines.

Methodological Guidelines

Whereas some methodological guidelines for the transition from a design to the other are defined, as among the models L-IDM and P-IDM or between P-IDM and P-IDM process, it is possible to define over that the mechanism of drag and drop a real global export of the source diagram.

Using the contextual menu of the project explorer, it will be possible to export a diagram using some methodological guidelines activating a wizard.

It will be enough to provide the wizard with the required information (name and position of the target diagram) and, click to the end key, will be started the procedure of export, completely automatic, that will finish with the creation and the opening of the new diagram.

Export in OWL

The operation of export in OWL of a diagram, when available, is realizable in two ways:

- Through the key OWL export in the toolbar
- Through the contextual menu of the project explorer

In the first case, a classical dialogue box will appear to save the file in the desired location.

In the second case, instead, a driven procedure will be introduced (wizard) through which it will be possible to perform the export. In both cases, the final user will have to provide the wizard with the required information (name and position of the target OWL file). When this is done, the start of the procedure of export will involve the appearance of a dialogue box with the information about the advancement of the operation, in order to give to the final user the possibility of following the whole procedure.

Copyright © 2009, IGI Global, distributing in print or electronic forms without written permission of IGI Global is prohibited.

CONCLUSION

In this chapter the attention is set on the configurability and extensibility of the support tool for the designer in the design of Web application. We highlight that the configurability is a main element because it allows providing the designer with the most proper tool according to his/her needs. For instance, supposing that the designer wants to apply the methodology of design for internal user, just the BPMN™ editor will be provided to the designer; while, if the designer wants to apply the methodology P-IDM process, the CASE tool will be equipped by the editors BPMN™, IDM, P-IDM and P-IDM process with the relative methodological guidelines. The tool has been realized with the goal of completely disguising the whole complexity of the methodology that supports and the whole consequential complexity coming from the application of the methodological guidelines. Particularly useful is the addition in the architecture of the level that allows management of the methodological guidelines for the integration between several methodologies; in particular, the tool includes the methodological guidelines for the integration that allow the following methodological passages:

- From IDM to P-IDM
- From IDM and BPMN to IDM process
- From IDM process, P-IDM and BPMN and P-IDM process

The methodological guidelines here implemented are coherent with the methodological guidelines proposed at the methodological level, and they allow obtaining a complete design of the Web application with or without the design of the business process depending on the requirement of the user. Another important element is the possibility to export, according to the ontological meta-model defined in this work, the realized designs.

The final CASE tool, complete of all the editors provided for the methodology, allows particularly both the export in machine readable format of the BPMN™ diagrams and of those IDM/P-IDM, and of the diagrams IDM process/PIDM process. The elevated configurability and extensibility of the framework leave space to the possible addition of new editors and new methodological guidelines if we want to subsequently extend the underlying methodology.

The accurate design of the framework also leaves space for the possibility to integrate inside of the CASE tool the functionality of automatic generation of code that will be introduced in the detail in the following chapter.

Copyright © 2009, IGI Global, distributing in print or electronic forms without written permission of IGI Global is prohibited.

REFERENCES

OMG. (2006). *Business process modeling notation specification.*

W3C. (2004). *OWL Web ontology language reference.*

Copyright © 2009, IGI Global, distributing in print or electronic forms without written permission of IGI Global is prohibited.

Chapter XIII
Code Generators

INTRODUCTION

In this chapter, the design and the development of the code generating tools based on the technologies (described in Chapter XI) are presented. In detail, the chapter describes the development of the tools that manages P-IDM design as a Web application input model (the design does not take care the presence of the process level); also, it describes the tool that considers as input model the P-IDM process design. It is clear that the two designs will be represented using the ontological language OWL (W3C, 2004).

In the description of the tool that uses the P-IDM model as input, the main focus is on the page composition (based on the framework tiles) (http://www.apache.org) and thus, the focus is on the final graphical aspect of the generated application. In the description of the tool that uses the P-IDM process, the main focus is on the aspect related to navigational aspect; the navigation is driven by the process and so the tool description is mainly oriented to show the process flow configuration.

CODE GENERATOR FOR IDM METHODOLOGY-OVERVIEW

The IDM methodology (Bolchini & Paolini, 2006), besides being a conceptual type, allows the designer to specify the model at two levels of detail: the Conceptual IDM

Copyright © 2009, IGI Global, distributing in print or electronic forms without written permission of IGI Global is prohibited.

(which also serves to describe general aspects in an informal way) and the Logical IDM (which allows the addition of the detailed information to the model).

It is clear that, the more complete and detailed the design, the more accurate the final Web application obtained through code generator will be. In order to understand the behavior of the system in the case where the model of the application to be generated is not at a detailed enough level, it is appropriate to introduce Engelberg's (Engelberg & Seffah, 2002) classification. This states that, using the level of fidelity (Isensee & Rudd, 1996; Jung & Winter, 1998), the tools and methods of prototyping are divided into three levels:

- The tools and methods appropriate for the initial design are found in the low-fidelity level. These tools are very powerful in conducting the initial analysis of the requirement and in helping to conceptualize and to conceive the high-level interfaces. These tools often support raw drafts of the interface either with manual drawings or with graphic tools.
- The prototyping tools used after the initial design are found in the average fidelity level. These allow the creation of a more detailed design for verifying the usability of the application. In fact, they enable the definition of detailed information on the navigation, functionality, contents and layout.
- In the high-fidelity level the prototyping tools, which enable the creation of a realistic simulation before the final version is produced, are found. Such tools are oriented to the developers, and they are often created for general-purpose development. Due to the effort required, these tools are not usually "rapid" even if the expression RAD (rapid application development) is broadly used in the field.

The code generation environment cannot be strictly classified in any of the levels above since the quality of the produced application is dependent on the quality and the completeness of the design. In fact, it is possible to also produce a prototype when the design is not complete. The developed system presented in the following sections, if during the generation of the prototype finds information missing in the model (for instance the dialogue act of a topic), actives a mechanism of "fall-back" that sets a label to the information place not specified.

The basic idea assumes that if the information is not important in the phase of design, it is not even in the phase of publishing. Typically, to generate a code it is important that the greatest part of the P-IDM design extended with layout design is present, but it is possible to skip the definition of all the details in the L-IDM design. Thanks to the "fall-back," it is possible to also get a prototype of the Web application during the first phases of the design providing an excellent starting point for discussing the specifications of the application with the buyer.

Copyright © 2009, IGI Global, distributing in print or electronic forms without written permission of IGI Global is prohibited.

Furthermore, the system that we propose allows a prototype to be produced at two levels of detail: in the first, denominated scaffold, the pages are produced taking into account only the information contained in the model. The output is a Web application that allows navigation among the structures of the model, providing the designer with a useful tool for the immediate verification of the developed task (see Figure 1). In the second level, the pages are populated with information contained in a dedicated database. The output is a complete Web application that can be taken as reference for the development of the final product.

In detail, the process of model-driven prototyping considered has the following phases:

1. Design of the application model using the IDM methodology. In this phase, the principal actor is the Web application designer that designs the application based on the buyer requirements.
2. Completion of the model with the P-IDM design and the layout model. In order to obtain the application, the designer must enrich the model with application specific information. The main actor is again the Web application designer who uses the editor to establish the position of the contents into the page and the structure of the application page.
3. The model is exported in OWL format. The model of the application is now available to the code generator environment.
4. Generation of the prototype. In this phase, starting from the OWL model, both the code and the necessary infrastructures necessary to use the generated code are produced. Besides, being a usable prototype with two levels of detail, it is possible to divide it into two sub-phases: creation of the scaffold and creation of the final application.
5. Population of the database instances. This phase is only required if we want to use a complete prototype (second level of prototyping). It is concerned with

Figure 1. Prototyping process

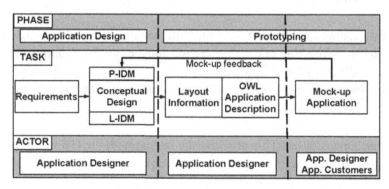

Copyright © 2009, IGI Global, distributing in print or electronic forms without written permission of IGI Global is prohibited.

the creation of data, which will be visualized by the end user, in the relational database created during the "generation of prototype" phase.

6.   Creation of the look and feel. In this phase, in which the main actor is the graphic designer, the Web pages are completed with the insertion of the graphic aspects such as colour, images, and so forth.

Code Generator for IDM Methodology-Details

The tool of code generation based on the IDM methodology (in particular on the P-IDM design of the Web application extended with layout design) uses the architecture defined in the frameworks Apache Struts™ and Tiles™ (http://www.apache. org) in order to produce the final application. The tool works configuring the above frameworks generating all the needed infrastructures to navigate the pages. Keeping in mind Chapter XI in relation to the frameworks Apache Struts™ and Tiles™, to create the final application it is necessary:

*   To configure the Struts framework through the creation of struts-config.xml file; in order to create this file that define the action objects (that specify the operation to do) the tool has to elaborate the information coming from the IDM model and from the information of the layout model in order to detect the navigational links that are described in both the two models.
*   To configure the tiles framework through the generation of tiles-defs.xml files. In this case, only the information of the layout design is elaborated in order to define the tiles derived from the structures of screens, frames and contents.
*   To create the physical JSP™ pages that contain the information slots of the P-IDM design. These pages derive directly from the logic pages of the design.
*   To create the code for the action classes (to allow the navigation) and for the JavaBeans™ (to allow at run-time to use in the page the information stored in the database). These classes must be compiled and are part of the whole infrastructure; the compiling operations are made automatically after the code generation phase.

In Figure 2, the complete schema of the entire architecture is shown. The figure shows both the architecture of code generation and the run-time application of the Apache Struts™ and Tiles™ frameworks.

The architecture is composed of different areas each with some specific purposes:

*   *Design Environment*: This provides the system with the OWL model of the application. This environment (the framework based on Eclipse RCP™ plat-

Copyright © 2009, IGI Global, distributing in print or electronic forms without written permission of IGI Global is prohibited.

Figure 2. Architecture of the code generation tool

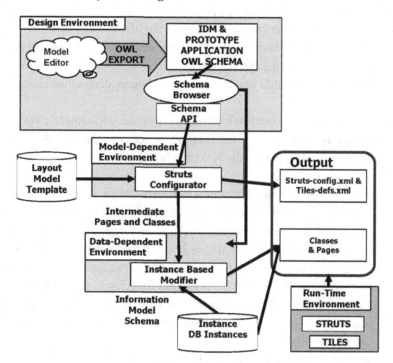

form) has been presented in the previous chapter. In this context, we refer only to the IDM design that is made up of the design of the information structures in terms of *topics* made up of *dialogue acts* and linked together by *relevant relations*. The design is made up also by the P-IDM that allows defining the screens that made up the Web application and the layout IDM design that adds some information helpful for the layout such as the position of each frame in the page and the position of each information content in every frame.

- *Model-Dependent Environment* is used to configure the static part of the Apache Struts™, which is to configure the framework for those parts that can be directly drawn from the model. The main module is the Struts configurator. This gets the information of the model structure from the Schema API and allows it to create the *struts-config.xml* file (used for navigation through pages) and *tiles-defs.xml* file (for the configuration of tiles so that pages are correctly composed), some intermediate classes useful to allow navigation coherent with that specified in the *struts-config.xml* and some intermediate pages that will contain only visual elements that the user can observe. At this level of prototyping, the pages will only show content of an informative type coming from the model. The same name, Struts configurator, is associated with the idea of converting the application model, navigated through the Schema

Copyright © 2009, IGI Global, distributing in print or electronic forms without written permission of IGI Global is prohibited.

API, in a configuration suitable for the framework. More exactly, the Struts configurator uses the followings parts of the model:

- ○ the structure of every page to create the file *tiles-defs.xml*
- ○ the navigational links to create the file *struts-config.xml* that establishes the behaviour of the application
- ○ the navigational links also to generate the intermediate action classes.

Finally, to complete the configuration, it is necessary to generate the physical pages organized as containers of informative structures, that are the topics and dialogue acts in accordance with the IDM methodology.

- The *Data-Dependent* environment is concerned with the configuration of all that information which must be loaded at run-time of the generated Web application, enabling views of the data in the generate pages. The main module is the *Instance-Based Modifier* that uses as input the intermediate pages, which, at this level, just contain static informative structures, and intermediate classes generated to allow navigation. Its principal function is to complete:
  - ○ the intermediate classes (used only for navigation) with the information retrieved by the model, turning them into action classes that extract data through interfacing with the Instance DB
  - ○ to produce and populate the beans with the data values
  - ○ to replace the static informative structures in the pages with the necessary code to visualize the instances contained within the beans

The output of the module is a complete, usable mock-up application usable through the Apache Struts™ and Tiles™ frameworks.

- *Run-Time Environment*: it is composed of file compatible with the two frameworks. Tiles, through the file tiles-defs.xml, reconstructs the pages according to the structure defined within using the physical pages, populated by the data released by the instance-based modifier, as elements. The Struts project *Action Servlet* uses the struts-config.xml file to sort the actions (also produced by the instance-based modifier) and to pass the control to the following view. In Figure 3, the sequence diagram of the run-time environment is presented.

Two repositories are available to complete the architecture: the layout model template (a relational database that contains references to the visualization template to create the page) and the instance DB. The instance DB is a relational database divided into two sections: the first, the *Information Model DB Scheme*, is related to the informative objects contained within the L-IDM model extracted by the

Copyright © 2009, IGI Global, distributing in print or electronic forms without written permission of IGI Global is prohibited.

Figure 3. Start of the generated application

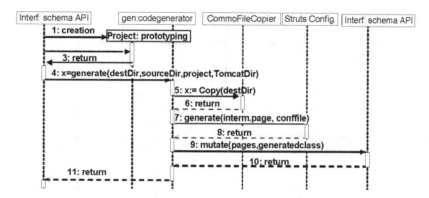

OWL file. The second is the *Information Model Instance DB*, which is related to the instances of the above informative objects.

Design of the Struts Configurator Module

In Figure 4, it is possible to see the module architecture of the Struts configurator. It is composed of two sub-modules:

- The *Intermediate Results Generator* has as a main goal to generate the intermediate infrastructures using as input the model information through the Schema API. The module creates: the page structures, the page content (the static information structures) based on the IDM model, the navigational link and the intermediated classes that activates these links.
- The *Configurator Generator,* instead, using the model information, creates the page structures and the links that must be inserted into the *tiles-defs.xml* and the *struts-config.xml*.

Not taking into account the schemas of the classes, that is difficult to describe without an interactive tool (or case tool), in Figure 5 is presented the UML® (Rumbaugh, Jacobson, & Booch, 2004) sequence diagram of generation of the intermediate pages. At first steps, the object "page creator" requires to the SCHEMA API (the API that allow the generation of the code) the schema of the layout model (based on these schemas the JSP™ page that has to contain the topics will be created); in the same way for each frame, the page that has to contain the dialogue acts will be created. After the creation of the container pages, the visualizations for each user for each page of the application are requested to the SCHEMA API. Each visualization is rendered through a specific JSP™ code (called "placeholder") that

Copyright © 2009, IGI Global, distributing in print or electronic forms without written permission of IGI Global is prohibited.

Figure 4. Architecture of module Struts configurator

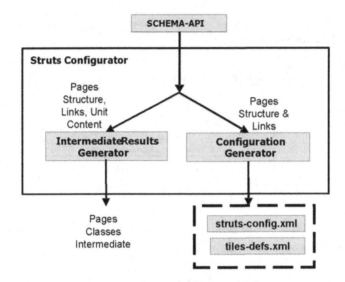

will be shown to the final user when he/she will request the specific page. After the creation of the placeholders, the system takes in the specific information needed to generate the application such as the position of the dialogue acts in the final pages. This information generates the common page template for all the application.

The output of this module allows seeing a prototype of application (application scaffold).

"Instance Based Modifier" Architecture

The "instance-based Modifier" module creates the complete working prototype starting from the intermediate prototype produced using the Struts configurator. In particular, it modifies the static JSP™ pages, and it generates new Java™ classes that allow using dynamic data (stored into the instance DB) into the modified pages.

In detail, to generate a Web application means:

- To read (using the SCHEMA API) the model to generate the Web application
- To generate the action class (used by the Struts controller) that will manage the entire application flow: pages and their data to display
- Build the generated classes
- To modify the intermediate JSP™ pages, generated by the Struts configurator; these pages must be adjusted to use during the run-time phase the beans (that contain the data instances gotten from Instance DB)

Copyright © 2009, IGI Global, distributing in print or electronic forms without written permission of IGI Global is prohibited.

Figure 5. Sequence diagram of the generation of a page

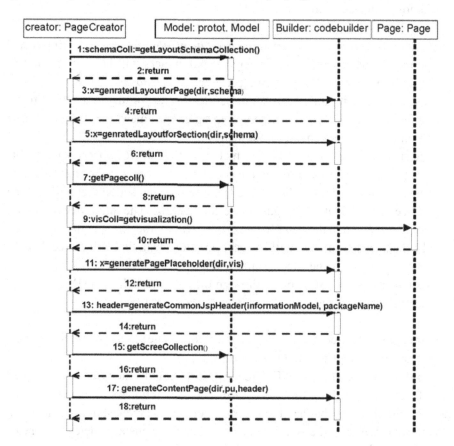

- To modify the struts-config.xml to insert the generated action classes in order to the Struts controller can use them

Thus, before to describe the detail of infrastructures that the module has to generate, it is necessary to analyze the general application architecture. Based on this architecture, analyzing the behavior and the features of each class it is possible to define what the generating application tool has to create.

Architecture of the Generated Application

In order to use the Web application obtained by the code generator, a Web server, on which the Apache Struts and Tiles™ frameworks are installed, is necessary. In the model it is expected that a page will have different views dependent on the user

Copyright © 2009, IGI Global, distributing in print or electronic forms without written permission of IGI Global is prohibited.

and the device. Every time the end user requests a page, or rather its view of the data, the following steps are performed:

- Struts activates an ActionForm (named "*itemChooserForm*") that intercepts the request parameters. In this way the parameters will be available not as strings but as properties of the object *itemChooserForm*.
- Struts activates its controller ActionServlet that, according to the file "struts-config.xml" (generated by the prototyping environment), activates the right action for the management of the request.
- The specified action uses the parameters of the "*itemChooserForm*" for its own processes. For example, in the case where a page template must display a specific instance (identified by an ID) it will be the action that will recall a service of the business delegate (described below). The latter, depending on the ID contained in the *itemChooserForm*, will extract the specified instance. The instance parameters will be inserted into a bean that will be recalled by the page to display the specific information.
- Visualization of a JSP™ page, through the aid of Apache Tiles™. Ready for a new end-user request.

Figure 6 shows the sequence diagram of the homepage request in order to clarify the behavior of the application during run-time.

According to the end user's HTTP request, with the extension ".do" (intercepted by the framework engine), the server (through the ActionServlet) activates the action of initialization, that has the task to intercept the request and to include it in its properties. Again, the ActionServlet activates the business delegate service that restores the information present in the DB to display it in the requested pages

Figure 6. Sequence diagram of home page request

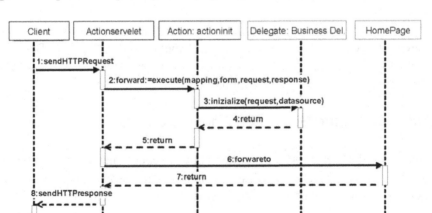

Copyright © 2009, IGI Global, distributing in print or electronic forms without written permission of IGI Global is prohibited.

activating the *collbeans* (whose description is below). The action returns the JSP™ page (or a fragment of it in the case that it is a tile) to the ActionServlet that executes the forward. The result of the forward is inserted in the http response that is sent to the client.

In order to make the prototype as flexible as possible, the generated code implements different design patterns:

- "bean": This design pattern has been used as a container of information of the IDM model. The "bean" is a class with "set" and "get" methods that allow it to easily manage the information that must be displayed in the JSP™ pages. If there is a need to show more information than the generated Web application displays, you need only to extend the class including the new information and modifying the pages or tiles. In particular, it is very useful to store data related to the introductory acts; the beans used to store data about the collections (definite by a group of introductory acts) will name using the term "*collbeans*".
- "ActionForm": It is the design pattern used by Struts to contain the parameters of the end user requests (previously indicated with "*itemChooserForm*"). Such object has been extended to also contain the information related to the guided navigation (in the case of navigation in a guided tour this will also contain the instances of the preceding and following elements, etc.).
- The design pattern "business delegate" (used in Web application to make the application independent from the data storage technologies): It is used to create the class that accesses the data and manages the instances of the instance DB.

Based on this pattern, Figure 7 shows the final configuration of the Web application as a set of generated classes without showing the interactions with the Struts and tiles infrastructures (that make it more difficult to understand the diagram).

It must be noted that the structure of the instance DB conforms to the representation of the data in the IDM methodology, while the data are inserted to every new code generation. According to this design, even the DB access class (that considers the data according to the semantic structure of the IDM methodology) is not dependent on the prototype. To guarantee the greatest flexibility for data access in every case, the "business delegate" design pattern (implemented in the class "business delegate") is used. This guarantees great flexibility in the use of external data sources to whomever wishes to extend the prototype toward the final application.

Copyright © 2009, IGI Global, distributing in print or electronic forms without written permission of IGI Global is prohibited.

Figure 7. Final configuration of generated Web application

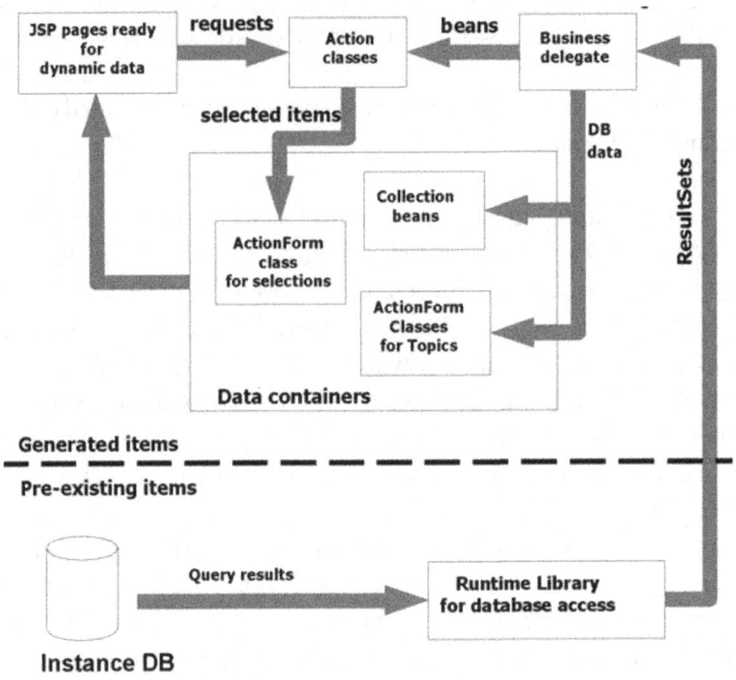

CONCLUSION ABOUT CODE GENERATOR FOR P-IDM

The design of the code generator environment proposed the creation of a system using Apache Struts and Tiles™, a set of frameworks widely used in the manufacturing world.

Apache Struts™ implements the model view controller (MVC) design pattern while Apache Tiles™ is a document assembly framework (that implements composite views of J2EE™). Tiles is used for solving problems relating to the reuse of layout and content through the breakdown of the page into fragments (tiles) and then the reconstruction of them. It originated as an autonomous project in the Jakarta Commons project and has now been incorporated with Apache Struts™ (in Version 1.1).

Considering the concepts of the IDM methodology, according to which the modeling has been affected, the notion of page corresponds to the intuitive idea of a Web page and presents a structure, in most cases, of a union of frame that are composed of contents. The same definition provides for a high level of modularity and reusability. The existing parallelism among the information design of IDM methodology and the concept of composite view is evident: a frame is a frag-

Copyright © 2009, IGI Global, distributing in print or electronic forms without written permission of IGI Global is prohibited.

ment or a sub-view of a page and content is a sub-view of a frame. The model of a generated page is a composite view, in which the contents hold the content of the page. For a greater explanation of how the tiles framework succeeds in efficiently representing a Web application prototype, please refer to the example given in the case study in the next chapter.

It is possible to use the application generated in two different environments: the first is the scaffold while the second can display dynamic data. The creation of the first level provides for the generation of HTML pages (tiles and tile containers), classes (the necessary actions to allow navigation within the Apache Struts™ framework) and of the tiles-defs.xml and struts-config.xml configuration files. The second level deals with creating the complete Web application starting from the output of the previous level. In particular, the generated pages will have to be modified and the classes must be created according to the bean and business delegate design patterns. They then need to be compiled to access and display data from the instance DB.

To clarify the behavior of the environment, Figure 8 shows the generation scheme of the second level of prototyping. According to the information contained in the OWL of the model, accessible through the API Scheme, the "*JSP mutator*" module accepts the HTML pages and modifies them in order that they can use the classes that access the data sourced from the database. The class generator, through the API Scheme, will create all the necessary code for the application to work using the "*Framecode*" library that provides the class-templates on which the produced

Figure 8. Creation of a complete application

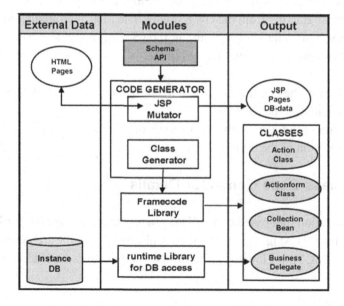

Copyright © 2009, IGI Global, distributing in print or electronic forms without written permission of IGI Global is prohibited.

classes will be based. After the compilation of the aforesaid classes and the copying of possible libraries and other common files (such as the runtime libraries for database access), the prototype is ready to execute the application.

CODE GENERATOR FOR P-IDM PROCESS DESIGN METHODOLOGY

P-IDM Process Code Generator Overview

The code generation tool presented in this paragraph is focused on the design of process-oriented application.

Starting from the OWL representation of the design of the Web information system for the external users, the tool will automatically generate all the code. In the special case, the generated code will be organized following the structure of files and folders requested by the framework Spring Web Flow already presented in the Chapter XI.

The representation of the model through the OWL file that represents the design turns out to be of the highest importance in this part of the work. A module of the code generator, as described above, will be used to read and understand the model of the Web application, while the information that the final user will read is, instead, in the DB.

The output of the code generator is made up of the JSP™ pages that manage the presentation logic (View), Java™ classes that manage business logic and XML files that manage configurations (controller) and the model that manage the interaction with the database starting from the OWL model. The final Web application follows the model view controller paradigm and will be Spring Web Flow compliant.

Particular attention has been oriented in the:

*   Generation of the configuration files in the special way the *filename-flow.xml* file that manages the page flow
*   Generation of the *jsp* file that is the view of the final Web application
*   The generation of the *action classes*

P-IDM Process Code Generator-Details

The code generation tool based on the IDM process methodology (in particular on the design of the P-IDM process of the Web application) uses the architecture of the framework Spring Web Flow to create the final application. In order to make the

Copyright © 2009, IGI Global, distributing in print or electronic forms without written permission of IGI Global is prohibited.

definition of process flow more flexible using configuration files (better explained after) directly generated on the P-IDM process design, the tool does not use the framework Apache Tiles™. Thus, in this chapter, the generation of the pages (that we assume that have a pre-fixed format) is not explained. The main focus is on the flow configuration starting from the process view of P-IDM process and on the generation of all infrastructures needed to make a full working prototype compliant with the Spring Web Flow.

Keeping in mind the architecture of Spring Web Flow described in Chapter XI, in order to produce a full working prototype, it is necessary:

- To receive as input the directory in which the Web application will be generated, the OWL file, the name of the database to use and the username and password to connect to DBMS
- To generate the XML file to configure the Spring Web Flow, the *log4j.properties* file (necessary to Spring Web Flow to test the application), the account file for the user that accesses to the generated application. The login page will be the index file of Web application.
- To copy all the .jar file needed for the Web application to work, and hence all the files needed to Spring Web Flow to execute correctly the action; furthermore, to copy all the images to be shown into the pages. The Spring Web Flow is a modular framework; thus it is important to establish (in base of the chosen Spring Web Flow configuration) the appropriate .jar files to be included in the generated Web application.
- To correctly read the model used to generate the code: the code generation tool uses as input the OWL file obtained as output from the design tool (described in the previous chapter). The information read by the OWL files are used to create the JSP™ pages of Web application, to define the template of each JSP™ pages, to create the xml configuration files compatible with the format used into the framework.
- To access to the database (fixed schema) expressly created to contain the instances to populate the dynamic JSP™ pages.
- To generate the java™ classes that are the action of Spring Web Flow and that allow to manage the flow of the operation of the generated application.
- To build the java classes using ANT.
- To modify, using the JDOM technology, the XML flow configuration file and actions description file (called servlet-config.xml) each time that the JSP™ pages and the Java™ classes (the actions) are generated.

Copyright © 2009, IGI Global, distributing in print or electronic forms without written permission of IGI Global is prohibited.

Briefly, the code generation tool allows generating:

- JSP™ Pages
- Classes
- Static configuration files
- Dynamic configuration files

Generation of the JSP™ Pages

The tool generates two types of JSP™ pages: JSP™ pages useful for the login and registration of the user and the others JSP™ pages used for the view of the Web application. The generation of the login pages is static, and it is made up by the framework Apache Velocity™ (http://velocity.apache.org). They have a pre-defined structure, and they need only data about a database with read and/or write data. The second type of JSP™ pages is generated based on a pre-defined schema and are modified with information read from the model and from the database. All pages use the same layout.

Generation of the Classes

To generate the Java™ classes means to generate the action classes of the Spring Web Flow architecture. Action classes allow to execute the operation and to move in the flow of the business process. The Java™ classes are generated after the model reading and after the generation of the JSP™ pages.

The Generation of the Static Configuration Files

The Webflow-config.xml file and the *services-config-xml* file are static files generated using Velocity. The input useful to generate these files is the name of the folder where the Web application will be generated.

The Generation of the Dynamic Configuration Files

The dynamic configuration files are the XML files that describe the application flow and the file *servlet-config*. These files are made up starting from a basic template, and they will be updated reading from the model. The description of the flow will be updated when a JSP™ and/or a Java™ class will be generated and the *servlet-config* will be updated for each Java™ class.

Copyright © 2009, IGI Global, distributing in print or electronic forms without written permission of IGI Global is prohibited.

Database Connection, the Business Delegate Pattern

In order to connect the Web application with the database, the "business delegate" pattern has been used: it concentrates in only one interface all the functionality to retrieve and update data.

The code generator will connect to the database and retrieves the information about users login and about what to show to the final user.

Action classes will update data that will be presented to the final users.

Class Diagram

In the Figure 9, a block diagram shows the structure of the code generation tool.

In the following, the main classes of each module are described. In the Figure 10, the diagram of all classes is shown.

SpringAppGUI

The module *SpringAppGUI* is the module at the highest level. It provides the graphical application interface, used to set by the user the needed information to generate the Web application.

This information is the OWL file (including its path) used as input, the name and the path in which the generated application will be saved, the username and

Figure 9. Diagram of the structure of the code generation tool

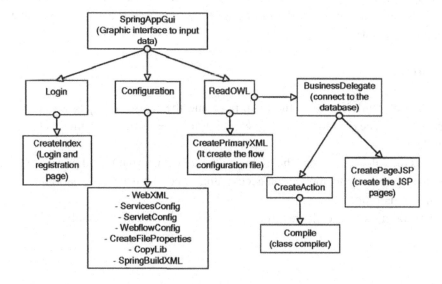

Copyright © 2009, IGI Global, distributing in print or electronic forms without written permission of IGI Global is prohibited.

the password of the DBMS containing the information needed the generated application and the type of the database. Furthermore, it uses the other modules of the code generation tool.

Configuration

The configuration module is the core module, and it will call all the configuration classes of the XML files needed to create the infrastructure of the Web application compatible with the architecture of framework Spring Web Flow. As configuration class, we intend a class having as input the directory of the application that will be generated and that creates a XML file that is more useful to the generation. The following configuration classes are detected:

- WebXML: to create the *web.xml* file
- SpringBuildXML: to create the *spring-build.xml* file
- WebflowConfig: to create the *nameapplication-webflow-config.xml* file
- ServletConfig: to create the *nameapplication -servlet-config.xml* file
- CreateFileProperties: to create the *log4j.properties* file
- CopyLib: to copy the jar files and jsp files needed to the generated Web application
- CreateXMLPrimary: to create the XML file of flow configuration

ReadOWL

The module "*ReadOWL*" is the parser of OWL file that contains the model of the Web application to generate. This module, in fact, has the main goal to read the OWL file and to extract all the information necessary to the classes that have to generate the code.

Login

The "login" module creates the login page and the registration pages to allow to the users to access to the Web application. Each user accesses using his/her own privileges.

This module, in fact, has the main goal to collect username and password from the users to allow the application access, and to collect user information to allow his/her registration.

The login module calls the procedures of the *CreateIndex* module.

Copyright © 2009, IGI Global, distributing in print or electronic forms without written permission of IGI Global is prohibited.

Business Delegate

The "BusinessDelegate" allows the connection with the database.

The BusinessDelegate module calls the *Create JSP class* (to generate the JSP™ pages), the *CreateAction* class (to generate the Java™ files that are the actions of the Spring Web Flow) and the *ModifyXML* (that allow modifying the XML configuration file and the *servlet-config* XML file that describes the action).

The main module is "*SpringAppGUI*" that contains the "main" method; it manages the graphical interface used to insert the information that allows initializing the application: the path of the OWL files, the path (existing or to be created) of the folder in which the generated files must be saved, the path of the DB containing all the information, the username and the password to connect to the DBMS. This module calls the other modules in the following sequence:

- "*Configuration*" that calls the classes to generate the configuration XML files needed to the correct working of the Web application based on the Spring Web Flow, the *index.jsp* files, a log file. Further, it creates the *Spring-build. xml* files needed to compile the classes. These files are:
  - *Web.xml*: the deployment descriptor of the /WEB-INF that describes the used elements in the application because the final application will be a standard J2EE™ Web application. The deployment descriptor is defined in these terms of:
    - ➢ The contextLoader servlet that initializes the Spring framework when the application is loaded in the server engine such as Tomcat.
    - ➢ A servlet dispatcher of Spring called with the name provided during the initialization of the generation tool. This servlet is also configured to manage all the requests that contain in the URL /name/*.
    - ➢ The JSP™ pages of the generated application using the custom tag library of Spring.
  - "*Login*" that has the main goal to generate the JSP™ pages of login and registration; the login page will be the index page of the generated Web application.
- "*ReadOWL*" has the main task of making the parser of the OWL input file that describes the model of Web application.
- "*BusinessDelegate*" that has the main task of interfacing the DB, to call the classes able to create the JSP™ pages, the Java™ classes (that must be compiled), and to modify the file that describes the flow of Spring Web Flow and the *servlet-config* file.

Copyright © 2009, IGI Global, distributing in print or electronic forms without written permission of IGI Global is prohibited.

Figure 10. Class diagram

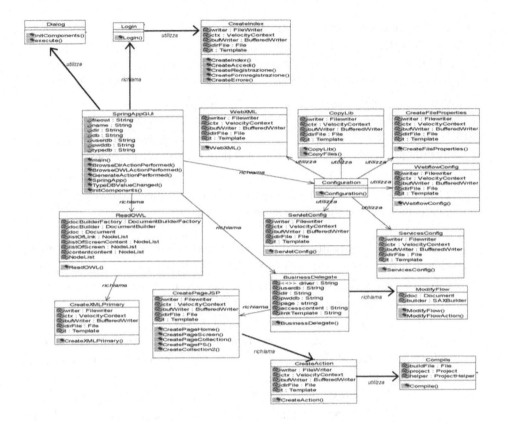

Figure 10 is the final class diagram.
The main tasks of each class are:

- *SpringAppGUI*: It reads all of the information useful to start the code generation that is the OWL file, the directory where the application will be generated, database information (name and type of the database, username and
  password).
- *Login*: It is useful to generate the login and registration pages.
- *Configurator*: It allows generating the XML configuration file. This class
  imports the jar files useful to the final Web application.
- *ReadOWL*: It understands the OWL file and calls the class that generates the
  flow-xml file.
- *BusinessDelegate*:It allows the interaction with the database.
- *CreateAction*: It generates all the Java™ code that allows the execution of the
  operation in the business process.

Copyright © 2009, IGI Global, distributing in print or electronic forms without written permission of IGI Global
is prohibited.

- *Compile*: Using ANT, it compiles the generated Java™ classes.
- *CreatePageJSP*: Using a pre-defined template, it generates the JSP™ pages.
- *Modify:XML*: It modifies the filename-*flow.xml* file and the xml file that describes actions (named *servlet-config*).

The Mapping between P-IDM Process Primitives and the Application Generated

To understand the entire generation process, it is important to understand as the model primitives are mapped on the code generation tool module:

- The access content and their navigational path links are mapped into JSP™ pages that allow the user to explore the collection while the association content and their links generate structures that gives the user access to semantic navigation and, thus they give rise to the link to navigate across the pages.
- The content and the input form are elements of the JSP™ template that contain themselves; moreover, their behavior will be activated through the generated Java™ classes.
- The slots are part of the content and of the input form.
- The screens and the process screens are mapped into JSP™ pages of generated application. The screens are static pages while the process screens make up the process flow pages managed by Spring Web Flow.
- The screen template and their links define the JSP™ page template; in other words, they identify the common elements through the pages.
- The process link and structural link are used to define the process flow and constitute the XML description flow file.

The Flow Configuration

The XML configuration file and the flow configuration are made up in two phases: in the first one the configuration file is made up only by the start and end event; in the second phase, reading the OWL file, the complete flow is created. In the detail, the configuration flow file contains views and action and relative attributes. The views correspond with the JSP™ pages, and they are created by *ModifyFlow* class every time that the *CreateJSP* class generates JSP™ pages (for screen and process screens). The action corresponds to the Java™ class that manages the process flow and are generated by the *ModifyFlow* class every time that the *CreateAction* class creates an action. To generate the process flow compatible with the Spring Web Flow syntax, there is the necessity to find in the representation of the design P-IDM

Copyright © 2009, IGI Global, distributing in print or electronic forms without written permission of IGI Global is prohibited.

process the "start-state" and "end-state;" thus the *CreateXmlPrimary* can create the first part of flow.

The generated file with only start and end event will be completed with the link and all the "*link*" classes of the OWL file. For each link, the source and target screen will be defined using the property defined into the *link owl* class; thus, the xml configuration flow file will be created step by step.

In detail, the structural links, the process links and the association links are used to create the Web application flow.

In the generation of the screens, not only the screens are read but also the child nodes that contain information about the screens nature such as access content or association content.

The business delegate method is invoked after all the screens are read. At the end, the "*ProcessScreen*" class of OWL file is used to generate the JSP™ pages of a process screen, reading for each node the child in order to see if the child is an input form (and thus a form will be created) or a content (and thus a simple HTML file will be created).

The process screen names and the slot names are the input for the *CreatePagePS* of *CreatePageJSP* module.

The Generated Web Application

The Web application is generated in the directory specified using the graphical interface in the generation phase. Of course, if the path is not in a server Web container, it is necessary to copy the entire contents in the appropriate path (such as the *webapps* directory of the Tomcat Web server).

The first page to be visualized will be the login one; after logged, it is possible to access the starting page that contains the link to configuration xml file of Spring Web Flow. The link target is the first Web pages of the generated Web application; now it is possible to navigate the application. The transitions between the pages are intercepted by the Spring Web Flow that checks if the link (transition in Spring Web Flow) is present in the configuration XML file. If the link is present, the framework after it accepts the request, redirects the user to the specific page or action or to the output page of the action operation. The JSP™ pages are the view layer and are formed of a fixed part independently by the contents and of data dependent part.

CONCLUSION

In this chapter, two prototyping tools that use the code generation technique are presented. The tools use different technologies. These tools maximize the benefits

Copyright © 2009, IGI Global, distributing in print or electronic forms without written permission of IGI Global is prohibited.

for the designer not only as case tool to model the Web application but also to evaluate the design and to have a complete working prototype close to the final application.

In particular, the generated application that has as input the ontological representation of the P-IDM design extended with layout information, uses The Apache Struts™ framework (in union with Apache Tiles™); while, the application generated using the P-IDM process design uses the Spring Web Flow technologies. Spring Web Flow allows separating the process logic from application logic. The focus of the second tool (that starts from the definition of the process flow in P-IDM process design) is on the mapping of the model on Spring Web Flow configuration files.

During the explanation, we have considered the three design methodologies:

• The design methodology for the external users of the information system focused on the user experience without the business process
• The design methodology for the external users taking care the user experience design and the business processes design
• The design methodology for internal user focused mainly on the internal user of the information system

In this chapter, the main focus is on the code generation tools for the external users of the information system. During the explanation, the design of the generation tools for the internal users is omitted. Actually, the research activities concern mainly the development of a specific code generation tool for Web application oriented to the internal users; the work is not complete yet, thus, it is not presented in this book. This new generation tool uses the portlet technology that assures to the entire system a great flexibility and modularity. The input of this new generation tool will be only the new BPMN™ design (OMG, 2006) adjusted to the new tool features. The developed editor (presented in Chapter 12) which is fully compliant with the methodology, is good also for the refinement of the design of the Workflow-BPMN.

Considering that it is important to trace the process flow, we have to highlight that the users cannot expand a portlet related to a process task if the previous tasks are not completed. This application logic must be developed in the final application and must be the generation tool that has to implement all the code to manage the constraints. Furthermore, the design team is using also the Microsoft® .NET technology (in details the Web parts).

Copyright © 2009, IGI Global, distributing in print or electronic forms without written permission of IGI Global is prohibited.

REFERENCES

Bolchini, D., & Paolini, P.(2006). Interactive dialogue model: A design technique for multichannel applications. *IEEE Transaction on multimedia, 8*(3), 529-541.

Engelberg, D., & Seffah A. (2002). A framework for rapid mid-fidelity prototyping of Web sites. *Proceeding of the IFIP 17ʰ World Computer Congress-TC13 Stream on Usability: Gaining a Competitive Edge,* (pp. 203-215).

Isensee, S., & Rudd, J. (1996). *The art of rapid prototyping.* International Thomson Computer Press.

Jung, R., & Winter, R. (1998). Case for Web sites. *Proceedings of the 1998 ACM Symposium on Applied Computing,* (pp. 726-731). Atlanta, GA.

OMG. (2006). *Business process modeling notation specification.*

Rumbaugh, J., Jacobson, I., & Booch, G. (2004). *Unified modeling language reference manual.* Addison-Wesley

W3C. (2004). *OWL Web ontology language reference.*

Copyright © 2009, IGI Global, distributing in print or electronic forms without written permission of IGI Global is prohibited.

Chapter XIV
Case Studies

INTRODUCTION

This chapter presents the detailed output of the two code generators showed in the previous chapter. For the first code generator software, the main focus is on the design of layout that, modeled using the specific editor integrated into the case tool showed in Chapter XIII, can create a complete application. In particular, applying to the generated application a specific cascade style sheet, the generated application is really closer to the original one.

In the use of the second generation engine, the main focus in on the flow definition. Thus, the page has a fixed structure in which the several part of the P-IDM process model takes place. In regards to the first code generation tool, we present two cases studies: the first case study is about an application developed for a local bank while the second is about the site of the department of engineering of the University of Lecce. In the second case study, the main focus is about the gap to develop the final application starting from the prototype considering the graphical aspects too.

The presentation is split in three parts: the first one that introduces application through the requirement elicitation, the second one introduces the IDM model

Copyright © 2009, IGI Global, distributing in print or electronic forms without written permission of IGI Global is prohibited.

(Bolchini & Paolini, 2006) and the last one explains the code generation output using such page as example.

The other generated application is the same used as the case study in the presentation of the IDM-process methodology. This application is focused on the analysis of the process flow. The final output shows that the application flow is perfectly adjusted to the design of the application.

USE OF IDM CODE GENERATOR: INTRODUCTION TO THE CASE STUDY

This paragraph briefly introduces the example that will serve as a guideline to explain the notation and the process. The description will be very informal, that is, realistic. By this we mean that a domain expert/end user/customer do not think in terms of goal-oriented requirements engineering. Rather, they state their requirements in their own way, that is, using their own vocabulary (the domain vocabulary) and their own conventions. Part of the job of the requirements engineer is to elicit the actual, often hidden requirements from the end users' minds (Dardenne, van Lamsweerde, & Fickas, 1993; UWA Consortium, 2001).

The chosen application is in the context of online activities of a bank and in detail about the definition, sale and management of cash/debit cards a specific part to the online services accessible from the Web site of the bank. The application focuses on the sale of cash/debit cards in accordance with current Italian norms.

The application needs to be considered from at least three viewpoints: the end user whose goal is to purchase and manage his/her card, the person responsible for the client within the bank and the employee charged with making sure new cards are available online.

The end user uses the application to choose the best suitable card for their needs, to follow all the phases of the purchase in accordance with current norms, and to manage his/her cards.

For the employees responsible for the clients, the application must allow monitoring of the client situation, tracing the purchase procedure, fulfiling the client requested and suggesting to clients the best possible option based on their profile.

From the point of view of the employee responsible for managing the online cards catalogue, the application must enable producing statistics about the cards available and managing the card catalogue. For reasons of simplicity, the employee responsible has not been taken into account in the case study.

The application must be used in diverse conditions, via various devices in various places, allowing the user access to the service in the best way possible; the ubiquity feature is fundamental for the application; thus, the application must be modeled

Copyright © 2009, IGI Global, distributing in print or electronic forms without written permission of IGI Global is prohibited.

for several mobile devices such as WAP, PDA, and SmartPhone in several contexts. It is clear that not all of the features are used on all devices.

Users

The application will be accessed by various user categories based on the profiles previously described. A clear definition of user types is of fundamental importance for correct design with a user-centered approach.

The characteristics of each category and their most important aspects and features of the application are:

- Generic user: he/she does not have a specific account in the system. He/she has access only to generic information. He/she may access the catalogue of available card, and the deals on offer from bank.
- Registered user (bank customer): he/she has one or more accounts at the bank and needs to use the account to access the system. He/she can carry out the following operations: (i) request the card purchase, (ii) modify the card parameters (e.g., monthly maximum), (iii) change the card, in the event of loss, deterioration or theft, and (iv) block a card.
- Salesman/woman: he/she is like the clerk in a virtual branch and is responsible of the clients. Each client has a specific salesman/woman. When a client requests to purchase a cash-card, the salesman/woman authorizes the sale, after the check about the client (such as the client's debt situation). He/she suggests alternative solutions where these may be more suitable for the client concerned. He/she activates the card when the client accepts and signs the sale contract, following the standard procedure.
- Product manager: he/she manages cash-card catalogue analyzing the preferences and requirements of the clients. Using a CRM (customer relationship management) software, he/she can decide on the addition of new products.

Functional Analysis

The analysis identifies the four categories of users: generic user, registered user, salesman/woman and product manager. The application must provide different functions depending on the accessed user and the used device. The following diagrams show the functions available to the various users in the application as a whole.

The registered user that has an account to access the bank system can access the catalogue of available cards and select one for purchase. The request/purchase process are composed of different tasks such as evaluation by the salesman/woman

Copyright © 2009, IGI Global, distributing in print or electronic forms without written permission of IGI Global is prohibited.

Figure 1. Functional use case diagram for bank customer and generic user

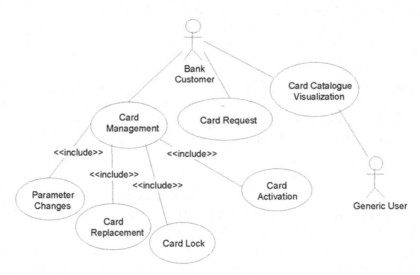

of the request for purchase, acceptance or rejection of the request, suggestion of alternatives, signing of the contract, issuing of the card, and so forth.

The user can access a number of functions for the purchased cards: suspension of the card, substitution, modification of the specific parameters (such as the daily or monthly maximum).

The generic users and registered user can access the cash catalogue to see the various alternatives and their characteristics, but the generic users may not request purchase.

Figure 2 shows the functions of the salesman/woman. This user receives the requests for card purchase. After the decision-making process in which salesman/woman examines the client profile and suggests an alternative card (in the event in which being a solution that better satisfies the client needs), the salesman/woman decides to grant the request for purchase (or otherwise).

If the request is accepted, the salesman/woman draws up the contract (printed in three copies and based on the client's current account) and contacts with the client. The bank issues the cash-card (with a PIN), which the client can activate for use when a signed copy of the contract reaches the bank. The process of modifying the parameters of a card, at the request of a client, follows a similar decision-making process.

By way of example, Figure 3 shows the functions available to the product manager. This type of user analyzes the preferences and needs of the clients and decides to add new products or modify existing ones.

Copyright © 2009, IGI Global, distributing in print or electronic forms without written permission of IGI Global is prohibited.

Figure 2. Use-case from the salesman/woman's point of view

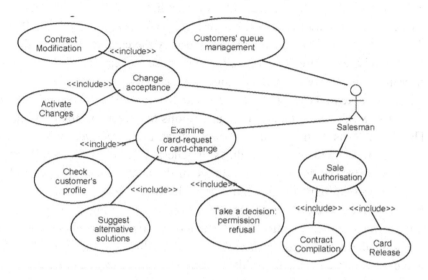

Figure 3. Functional use-case from the product manager's point of view

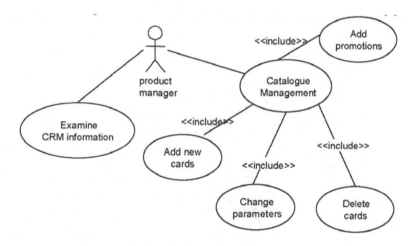

High Level Goals, Goal Refinement Process and Requirements

In the following figures, stakeholder's goals, detailed and subdivided into sub-goals, are shown. In addition, the different requirement to be taken into account in the design of the application are shown for each sub-goal.

Figure 4 shows the sub-goals and requirements of the bank customer without card.

Copyright © 2009, IGI Global, distributing in print or electronic forms without written permission of IGI Global is prohibited.

There are two possibilities taken into account: the user wants to purchase a card or, the user does not yet have a clear idea of what he/she needs. This figure shows the two different situations using the high-level goals *"what to buy"* and *"buy or not buy."* In *"what to buy"* the user reviews briefly the characteristics of the card which to purchase, or directly carry out the purchase request. In *"buy or not buy,"* the user may wish to see the card catalogue or receive suggestions.

These two potential user situations are modeled through *"assess bank's offers"* and *"access bank's suggestions."* The suggestions require a specific personalized goal based on the user's profile *"access customized card catalogue,"* whereas if the user decides to view the bank's products in general, then he/she may wish to see only current offers or the general catalogue of the bank. These two possibilities give rise to the requirements shown in Figure 4.

A user with cards (*bank customer with card*), shown in Figure 5, uses the application to make requests about the card management (*manage his/her own cards"*) or to seek an alternative card (*Wwhat else to buy*). In this case, the user may simply wish to modify some parameter of his/her card (*how to upgrade*), or he/she wishes to purchase a new card (*assess bank's offers*).

Figure 4. Goals, sub-goals and requirements for "bank customer without card"

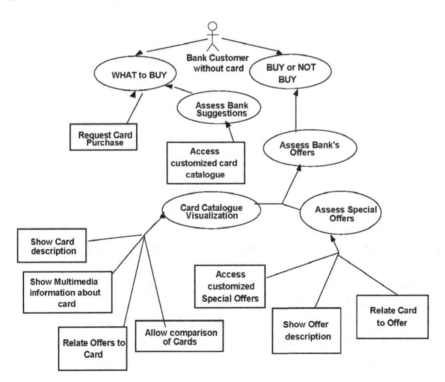

Copyright © 2009, IGI Global, distributing in print or electronic forms without written permission of IGI Global is prohibited.

Figure 5. Goals, sub-goals and requirements of the "bank customer with card"

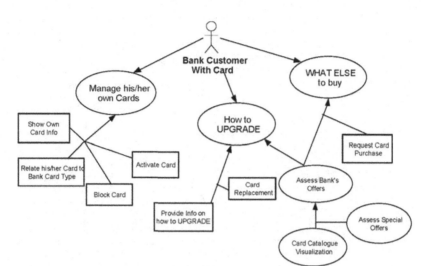

The requirements which derive from this latter goal are the same as in the previous diagram, whereas the goal *how to upgrade* requires the presence of further information (*provide info on how to upgrade*) and ad hoc operations (*card replacement*).

The *salesman/woman* is the intermediary between the bank and its customers. He/she uses information of a statistical nature about the financial situation (*show customer financial situation* and *show statistical information on customer choices*) and accesses the client requests. These two main goals of the salesman/woman give rise to all the requirements present in Figure 6.

The IDM Design for the Generic User

To illustrate the process of prototyping, we describe some meaningful fragments of the model "debit card" related to the generic user.

The generic user can navigate the card catalogue and has access to the special offers; therefore, in Figure 7, the C-IDM diagram of the application for the "Generic User" is shown.

In detail, there are two topics "debit card," and "special offer" and the relative semantic relevant relations "related to" and "associated with." The first one describes the debit cards that can benefit from the specific offer, while the second describes the special offer with which it is possible to purchase the debit card.

Copyright © 2009, IGI Global, distributing in print or electronic forms without written permission of IGI Global is prohibited.

Figure 6. "Salesman's" goals, sub-goals and requirements

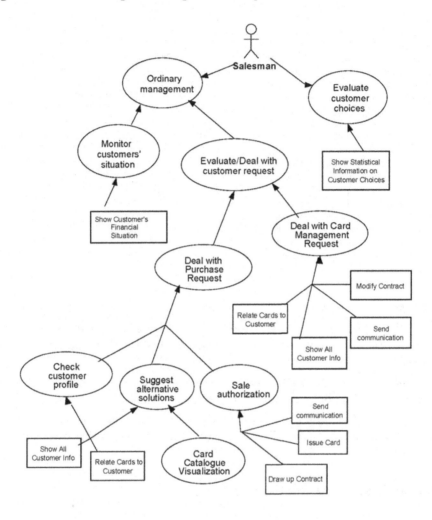

Topic Debit Card

According to the IDM methodology, it is necessary to detail further the analysis using the L-IDM diagram that is shown in the Figure 8.

The topic "debit card" is detailed through the following content dialogue acts:

- Description: card description with text and photos
- Payment charge: charges linked to payments made with the card
- Withdrawal charge: charges linked to ATM withdrawals
- Parameters: monthly and daily maximums for payments and withdrawals.

Copyright © 2009, IGI Global, distributing in print or electronic forms without written permission of IGI Global is prohibited.

Figure 7. A general overview of the Web application design

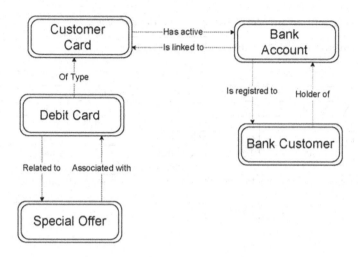

Figure 8. L-IDM of the design related to the generic user

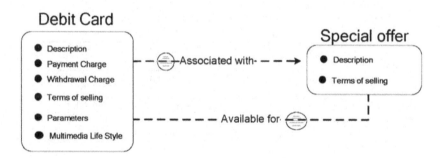

Furthermore, it shows whether a service (e.g., Cirrus/Maestro, etc.) is available for that type of card

- Terms of selling: annual charges linked to the card
- Multimedia life style: descriptions of the lifestyle profile of the typical customer holding this type of card (including photos and video)

The details of the dialogue acts of the topic debit card are shown in Tables from 1 through 6.

The details of the dialogue acts of the topic "special offer" are shown in Tables 7 and 8.

Copyright © 2009, IGI Global, distributing in print or electronic forms without written permission of IGI Global is prohibited.

Table 1. Slot of the dialogue act "Description"

Dialogue act content: Slot of the *Description* dialogue act		
Slot name	**Slot type**	**Description**
Name	Text	Card Name
Small Description	Text	Card small description
Full Description	Text	Card full description
Small Card Photo	Image	Graphic preview of card
Full Card Photo	Image	Card photo
Full Description for PDA	Text	Card full description for the smaller display of PDA device.
Small Description for PDA	Image	Card small description for the display of PDA device.
Card Photo for PDA	Image	

Table 2. Slot of the dialogue act Payment Charge

Dialogue act content: Slot of the *Payment Charge* dialogue act		
Slot name	**Slot type**	**Description**
PBancomat charge on Italy POS	Currency	Charge for payment on Italian debit card (Pagobancomat) Circuit
PBancomat charge on Italy Maestro POS	Currency	Charge for payment on Italian Maestro Circuit
PBancomat charge on foreign Maestro POS	Currency	Charge for payment on foreign debit card (Pagobancomat) Circuit
Fastpay charge	Currency	Charge for payment by Fastpay

Table 3. Slot of the dialogue act Withdrawal Charge

Dialogue act content: Slot of the *Withdrawal Charge* dialogue act		
Slot name	**Slot type**	**Description**
Cash Dispenser charge on Bank	Currency	Charge for Withdrawal from Banca121 ATM
Cash Dispenser charge on MPS	Currency	Charge for Withdrawal from MPS Group ATM
Cash Dispenser charge on other	Currency	Charge for Withdrawal from Other Banks' ATM
Cash Dispenser charge on Italy Cirrus	Currency	Charge for Withdrawal from Italian Cirrus Circuit ATM
Cash Dispenser charge on foreign Cirrus	Currency	Charge for Withdrawal from foreign Cirrus Circuit ATM

Copyright © 2009, IGI Global, distributing in print or electronic forms without written permission of IGI Global is prohibited.

Table 4. Slot of the dialogue act Terms of selling

Dialogue act content: Slot of the *Terms of selling* dialogue act		
Slot name	**Slot type**	**Description**
Yearly Bank Charge	Currency	Yearly Bank Charge for card.
Note on yearly charge	Text	Information about Yearly Bank Charge
Starting Date of card's Validity	Date	Card is valid from this date.
Expiry Date	Date	Expiry date of card

Table 5. Slot of the dialogue act Parameters

Dialogue act content: Slot of the *Parameters* dialogue act		
Slot name	**Slot type**	**Description**
max monthly withdrawal	Currency	Maximum monthly withdrawal
max daily withdrawal	Currency	Maximum daily withdrawal
max monthly Bank withdrawal	Currency	Additional maximum monthly withdrawal from Banca121 ATM
max daily Bank withdrawal	Currency	Additional maximum daily withdrawal from Banca121 ATM
Cirrus withdrawal Availability	{available /not available}	Availability of Cirrus withdrawal
max monthly withdrawal on Cirrus	Currency	Maximum monthly withdrawal on Cirrus Circuit
max daily withdrawal on Cirrus	Currency	Maximum daily withdrawal on Cirrus Circuit
PBancomat Payment Availability	{available /not available}	Availability of PagoBancomat (debit card) Payment
max monthly Payment on Italy PBancomat POS	Currency	Maximum monthly payment on Italian Pagobancomat POS
max daily Payment on Italy PBancomat POS	Currency	Maximum daily payment on Italian Pagobancomat (debit card) POS
Maestro POS Payment Availability	{available /not available}	Availability of payment on Maestro Circuit POS
max monthly Payment on Maestro POS	Currency	Maximum monthly payment on Maestro Circuit POS
max daily Payment on Maestro POS	Currency	Maximum daily payment on Maestro Circuit POS
FastPay Payment Availability	{available /not available}	Availability of FastPay Payment

Copyright © 2009, IGI Global, distributing in print or electronic forms without written permission of IGI Global is prohibited.

Table 6. Slot of the dialogue act Multimedia Life Style

Dialogue act content: Slot of the *Multimedia Life Style* dialogue act		
Slot name	**Slot type**	**Description**
Life style Description	Text	Description of the life-style of the typical owner of this debit card type
Video	Video	Video about life-style of card's owner
Video Description	Text	Description of video (see above)
Photo	Image	Photos about life-style of card's owner
Photo Description	Text	Description of photos (see above)
Customer Review	Text	Customer Review of debit card
Newspaper Review	Text	Newspaper Review of debit card

Table 7. Slot of the dialogue act Terms of Selling

Dialogue act content: Slot of the *Terms of Selling* dialogue act		
Slot name	**Slot type**	**Description**
Charge on Offer	Currency	Charge related to special offer
Note on charge	Text	Information about charge
Offer Starting date	Date	Starting date of the offer
Offer expiry date	Date	Expiry date of the offer
Availability	{available/not available}	....

Table 8. Slot of the dialogue act Description

Dialogue act content: Slot of the *Description* dialogue act		
Slot name	**Slot type**	**Description**
Name	Text	Name of special offer
Description	Text	Small description of special offer
Full Photo	Image	Photo related to special offer
Small Photo	Image	Used for a graphic preview of the special offer
PDA Photo	Image	Photo suitable for PDA display.

- Terms of Selling: economical condition linked to the offer
- Description: the special offer details

According to the IDM methodology, it is necessary to better define the model through the definition of the introductory acts and of the transition acts of the several topics. In detail, the case study application needs to define only two transition

Copyright © 2009, IGI Global, distributing in print or electronic forms without written permission of IGI Global is prohibited.

acts that allow access to the special offers starting from the debit card and to the debit cards starting from the special offer. The two transition acts are "associated with" and "available for." The description of the two transition acts are shown in tables 9 and 10.

The model of the pages is detailed with the definition of the screens for each dialogue acts defined before. It is clear that considering the paradigm of IDM model, the dialogue between the users and the application, several models of the pages could be produced according to the kind of users and the specific device. In Figure 9, the "home page " for the "generic user" of the case study is shown.

Generation of Prototype

The first step to develop the prototype of the case study is to design the model using a graphical editor from which it is possible to obtain a machine readable version of the model. In fact, the code generation tool is the software that creates the prototype and needs the application design in OWL format (W3C, 2004) in order to elaborate it. This model version must be complete with everything needed to create the prototype. From this point of view, the modeled application using IDM methodology must be enriched with all information needed to produce a working prototype. This information is not defined in the design phase because it is not important for the designer. This information is typically related to the graphical aspects

Table 9. Slot of the transition act associated with

Dialogue act content: Slot of the *associated with* transition act		
Slot name	**Slot type**	**Description**
Name	Text	Name of special offer
Description	Text	Small description of special offer
Full Photo	Image	Photo related to special offer

Table 10. Slot of the transition act available for

Dialogue act content: Slot of the *available for* transition act		
Slot name	**Slot type**	**Description**
Name	Text	Name of special offer
Description	Text	Small description of special offer

Copyright © 2009, IGI Global, distributing in print or electronic forms without written permission of IGI Global is prohibited.

Figure 9. Layout model of home page

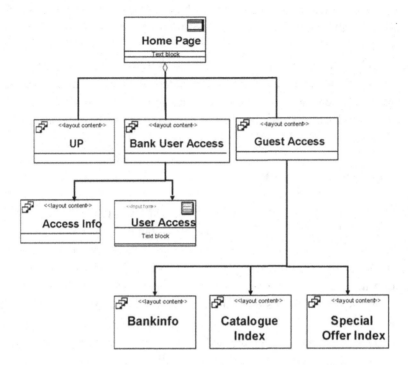

of the application such as the position of the screen in the pages, and so forth. This information is grouped in a specific model called layout model. The layout model is, hence, the collector of the data that the designer does not take in care during the design phase, but they are essential for the development both prototypes and of the final application. In other words, the layout model could be understood as the glue between the methodology and the development architecture, and, thus, it is impossible to standardize it because it is too connected with the technological aspect of the final product. Hence, in the following part of this book, it is not explained in detail, and it is used only in this paragraph because it is fundamental to understand the development of the prototype and the function of the prototyping tool.

The description of the model in machine readable format is made with the editor described before. In Figure 10, a screenshot of the editor is shown.

In order to insert the information of the layout model, the editor specific forms are introduced. In these forms, it is possible to specify the information about the position of the screen in the pages and also as the pages could be configured related to the specific device and user. Furthermore, considering that the main focus of the design is to maximize the dialogue, the two parameters, user and device, are unified because it is nonsense to describe the pages without taking care of the users and

Copyright © 2009, IGI Global, distributing in print or electronic forms without written permission of IGI Global is prohibited.

Figure 10. Home Page model for the Generic User

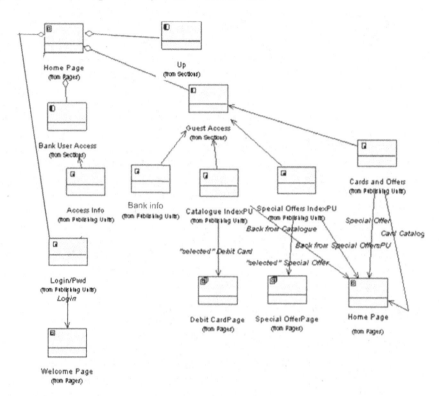

vice versa. In detail, it is necessary to define the position of the screen template into the pages and then in the case in which the screen is an aggregate of more content, it is necessary to define the position of each content into the specific screen. In Figure 11, it is possible to see the form of the layout model of the home page for the user-device "generic user-Web;" while in Figure 12, the layout model of the screen "guest access" in which there are the different contents is presented. The hierarchical structure of the layout model is directly derived from the IDM methodology and from the elements that must be completed with the layout model itself.

In the same way, for each screen it is necessary to specify the content position.

At the end of each page, it is necessary for each kind of device to define the layout template (that displays the screen to the users) and for each link (derived from the view of the navigational structures) to define the slots from which the navigation will be activated.

After the definition of the layout model, it is possible to export the model in OWL format; thus, each part of the home page will be translated in a specific OWL fragment (Figure 13).

Copyright © 2009, IGI Global, distributing in print or electronic forms without written permission of IGI Global is prohibited.

Figure 11. Layout model of the "home page"

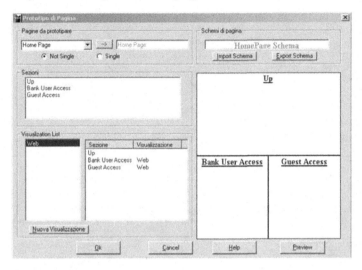

Figure 12. Layout model of the "guest access" screen

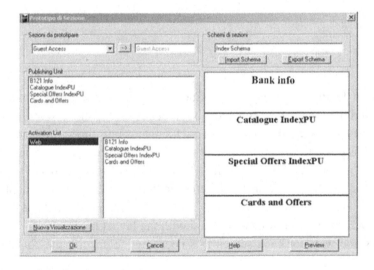

Starting from this design, the complete application prototype is developed; in the following part of the chapter, the main steps in the creation of the prototype of "home page" will be explained. After the design of the application using IDM methodology, the prototype is developed using the framework (explained before). In detail, through a standard HTML editor, the designer creates the graphical template in which the tiles take place. The application data stored in a repository are inserted using a specific tool called "*IstanceDbManager*." The IDM model

Copyright © 2009, IGI Global, distributing in print or electronic forms without written permission of IGI Global is prohibited.

Figure 13. The model of home page in OWL format: the OWL keywords are not present in this image because we speak about the model starting from the meta-model where primitives of the methodology has been defined

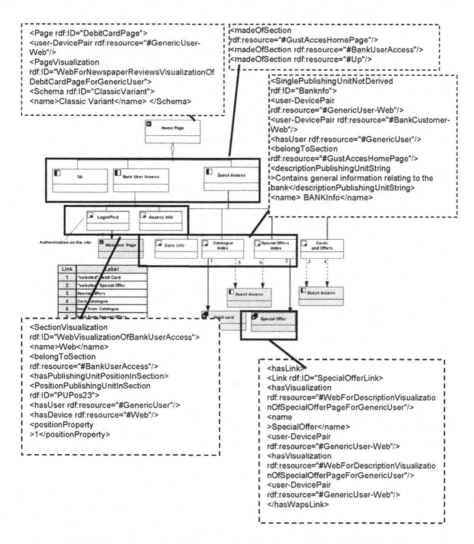

(integrated with layout model) designed and exported in OWL format, is used by the other application modules through the Schema API. The model-dependent environment, using this information, will create all the infrastructures needed to the complete fruition of the scaffold prototype. The HTML output of the home page is shown in the Figure 14.

Over the HTML output, the module model-dependent environment creates the configuration file *tiles-defs.xml*. The file is produced using the IDM model of Web application. Seeing only part of the file for the homepages we have:

Copyright © 2009, IGI Global, distributing in print or electronic forms without written permission of IGI Global is prohibited.

Figure 14. Home page structure

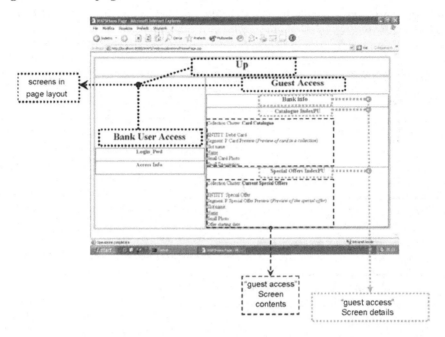

```
<definition name="webvisualizationofbankuseraccess"
path="layout_WebvisualizationofBankUserAccess.jsp">
    <put name="publishing_unit0"
            value="Login_Pwd.jsp" />
    <put name="publishing_unit1"
            value="AccessInfo.jsp" />
</definition>
<definition name="webvisualizationofguestaccess"
        path="layout_WebvisualizationofGuestAccess.jsp">
    <put name="publishing_unit0"
            value="BankInfo.jsp" />
    <put name="publishing_unit2"
            value="SpecialOffersIndexPU.jsp" />
</definition>
<definition name="webvisualizationofhomepage"
            path="layout_WebvisualizationofHomePage.jsp">
    <put name="section0"
            value="Up" type="string" />
    <put name="section1"
        value="webvisualizationofbankuseraccess" type="definition" />
    <put name="section2"
        value="webvisualizationofguestaccess" type="definition" />
</definition>
```

Copyright © 2009, IGI Global, distributing in print or electronic forms without written permission of IGI Global is prohibited.

For each JSP™ path specified in the *tiles-defs.xml* file, the corresponding piece of HTML code is generated. Considering only the generated home page and its layout the output is:

```
(layout _ WebvisualizationofHomePage.jsp)
<%@page contentType="text/html"%>
<%@ taglib uri="/WEB-INF/struts-bean.tld"prefix="bean"%>
<%@ taglib uri="/WEB-INF/struts-html.tld" prefix="html" %>
<%@ taglib uri="/WEB-INF/struts-logic.tld" prefix="logic" %>
<%@ taglib uri="/WEB-INF/struts-tiles.tld" prefix="tiles" %>
<html>
<head><title>
      Home Page
</title></head>
<body>
<table border="2" style="table" width="100%"
bordercolor="#0066FF">
    <tr><td colspan="2" align="center">
          <tiles:insert attribute="section0"/>
    </td></tr>
      <tr><td colspan="2" align="center"> Bank User Access
          <tiles:insert attribute="section1"/>
    </td></tr>
      <tr><td colspan="2" align="center"> Guest Access
          <tiles:insert attribute="section2"/>
    </td></tr>
</table></body>
</html>
```

The page used as an example is based on the visualization schema, stored in the repository of the page template used by the prototyping system. In the visualization schema, the layout elements (in this case the screens) take place. In the code, the "placeholder" is in bold style; at the run-time (using the information of the *tiles-defs. xml*) tiles replace the placeholder with the specific JSP™ pages. In detail, *section0* is the section *Up* of the screen, while the placeholder *section1* will be replaced with the section *BankUserAccess*. The *webvisualizationofbankuseraccess* in the *tiles-defs.xml* file, is a definition in order to include into itself the contents; furthermore, *webvisualizationofguestaccess* is declared as a definition.

To check the behavior of the *struts-config.xml* file, generated by the model-dependent environment, it is necessary to analyze the *SpecialOffersIndexPU.jsp* page that contains the homonymous screen (derived by the introductory act that is the collection of the special offers). In others words, selecting an item in the pages, a new page is opened with the specific special offers.

The part of the specific page is:

Copyright © 2009, IGI Global, distributing in print or electronic forms without written permission of IGI Global is prohibited.

```
<body>
<h3 align="center">Special Offers IndexPU</h3>
<p>Collection Cluster: <b>Current Special Offers</b></p>
<p>ENTITY: Special Offer<br>
   Segment: P Special Offer Preview (Preview of the special
offer)<br> Slot name:<br>
   <html:link action="/SpecialOffersIndexPU__selected_SpecialOf-
fer_Action"> Name<br></html:link>
      Small Photo<br>
      Offer starting date<br>
</p>
   </body>
```

The "html:link action" tag allowsto activating the action to navigate. For this action in the file *struts-config.xml* a specific mapping exists. This mapping defines the link between the logic name of the action used into the page and the class action that implements it.

```
<action-mappings>
    <action path="/SpecialOffersIndexPU__selected_Special-
Offer_Action" type="action. SpecialOffersIndexPU__selected_
SpecialOffer_Action" scope="request" input="Webvisualizatio
nofHomePage.jsp" />
</action-mappings>
```

In this way, the link between the PATH (the logic name used in the page) and the class (attribute TYPE) is defined; in this case, to make the explanation more clear, the logic name and the class action have the same name; however, in general they could be different. The action, created using the information of the IDM model by the model-dependent environment is:

```
/* @author Model-Dependent Environment */
public class SpecialOffersIndexPU__selected_SpecialOffer_Action
extends org.apache.struts.action.Action {
    public ActionForward execute(ActionMapping actionMapping,
ActionForm actionForm, HttpServletRequest httpServletRequest,
HttpServletResponse httpServletResponse)
    throws Exception {                      return actionMapping.findfor-
ward ("DescriptionVisualizationWEBofSpecialSpecialOffersIndexPU");}}
```

As defined in the goal of the design of this module, the generated class allows only making the navigation according to the IDM design of the application; in fact, the "EXECUTE" method makes only the FINDFORWARD method that open a new page. Moreover, in this case, the name of the page is not the physical one but a logic name. The association of the logic page and the physical pages is defined in

Copyright © 2009, IGI Global, distributing in print or electronic forms without written permission of IGI Global is prohibited.

the *struts-config.xml* in a specific section different from one in which the action are defined:

```
<global-forwards>
   <forward
   name= "WebForDescriptionvisualizationofSpecialOfferPageSpecial-
OffersIndexPU"
   path="/WebForDescriptionvisualizationofSpecialOfferPage.jsp"
redirect="false" />
</global-forwards>
```

In this way, we have generated the scaffold and checked its behavior. In the following of this chapter, we analyze the behavior of the data-dependent environment. Using the intermediate pages generated in the scaffold, the data-dependent environment will view in the page the data taken from the data repository called instance DB. In the test phase, the instance DB contains random generated data. The random generation is based on the IDM model for the data multiplicity. In Figure 15, the prototype of homepage is shown.

The layout aspects are close to the scaffold (because a CSS is not applied), but the contents are not model structures (as in the scaffold), but they are mock-up data taken by the database. Not taking into account the changes to the *struts-config.xml* and *tiles-def.xml* files, we analyze the generated classes used to insert the information into the pages: the business delegate and the beans that represent the introductory act SpecialOffer.

The collbean that contains the slots of the introductory act as property and its constructors:

```
Package generated.bean;
import java.beans.*;
import javax.servlet.http.*;
import org.apache.struts.action.*;
import java.util.*;

public class SpecialOfferIndex extends ActionForm {
    /** Holds value for property ID */
    private Integer ID;
    /** Holds value for property SmallPhoto */
    private String Small_photo;
    /** Holds value for property OfferStartingDate */
    private String Name;
    /** Holds value for property Name */
    private String Name;
...
```

Copyright © 2009, IGI Global, distributing in print or electronic forms without written permission of IGI Global is prohibited.

Figure 15. Home page of the prototype

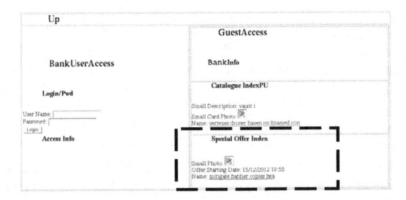

Considering the business delegate classes, the code is:

```
private static final String[] SpecialOfferCollSlots = {"ID",
        "SmallPhoto", "OfferStartingDate", "Name"};

public void loadSpecialOfferIndex(HttpServletRequest
        httpServletRequest) throws Exception {

        SpecialOfferIndex SpecialOfferIndex;
        ServletContext context;
        ResultSet rs;
        Connection conn;
         app.runtime.StandardResultSetProvider prv;

        context =
              httpServletRequest.getSession().getServletContext();
        prv =
             app.runtime.StandardResultSetProvider.singleton();
        conn = prv.getConnection();
        SpecialOfferIndex = new SpecialOfferIndex();
        rs = prv.getCollection(conn, "SpecialOfferIndex",
        SpecialOfferCollComps, SpecialOfferCollSlots);

        while (rs.next()) {
            SpecialOfferIndex.addSpecialOffer
                  (populateSpecialOfferIndexCollection(rs));
        }
             rs.close();
        conn.close();
        context.removeAttribute("SpecialOfferIndex");
        context.setAttribute("SpecialOfferIndex",
                              SpecialOfferIndex);   }
```

Copyright © 2009, IGI Global, distributing in print or electronic forms without written permission of IGI Global is prohibited.

The collbean will be used in the page; in detail, the tile fragment is used in the specific page fragment. The piece of code is:

```
<%@ taglib prefix="html" uri="/WEB-INF/struts-html.tld" %>
<%@ taglib prefix="bean" uri="/WEB-INF/struts-bean.tld" %>
<%@ taglib prefix="logic" uri="/WEB-INF/struts-logic.tld" %>
<%@ taglib prefix="tiles" uri="/WEB-INF/struts-tiles.tld" %>
<%@ taglib prefix="htmlex" uri="/WEB-INF/DebitCard-htmlex.tld" %>
package generated.bean;
import java.beans.*;
import javax.servlet.http.*;
import org.apache.struts.action.*;
import java.util.*;

public class SpecialOfferIndex extends ActionForm {
    /** Holds value for property ID */
    private Integer ID;
    /** Holds value for property SmallPhoto */
    private String Small_foto;
    /** Holds value for property OfferStartingDate */
    private String Name;
    /** Holds value for property Name */
    private String Name;
...

<logic:present name="SpecialOfferIndex">
    <logic:notEmpty name="SpecialOfferIndex" property="ID">
        <bean:define id="ID_SpecialOfferIndex" name="SpecialOfferIn
dex"
           property="ID" toScope="page" type="generated.bean.Spe-
cialOfferIndex" />
    </logic:notEmpty>

    <logic:notEmpty name="SpecialOfferIndex" property="Small_pho-
to">
        <bean:define id="Small_photo_SpecialOfferIndex"
         name="SpecialOfferIndex" property="Small_photo"
toScope="page"
           type="generated.bean.SpecialOfferIndex" />
    </logic:notEmpty>

    <logic:notEmpty name="SpecialOfferIndex" property="Name">
        <bean:define id="Name_SpecialOfferIndex" name="SpecialOffer
Index"
           property="Name" toScope="page" type="generated.bean.Spe-
cialOfferIndex" />
    </logic:notEmpty>

    <logic:notEmpty name="SpecialOfferIndex" property="OfferStarti
ngDate ">
        <bean:define id="Name_SpecialOfferIndex" name="SpecialOffer
```

Copyright © 2009, IGI Global, distributing in print or electronic forms without written permission of IGI Global is prohibited.

```
Index"
        property="OfferStartingDate " toScope="page"
        type="generated.bean.SpecialOfferIndex" />
    </logic:notEmpty>
 </logic:present>

<H3>Special Offer Index</H3><BR/>
Small Photo:
<img  src=
<bean:write name="SpecialOfferIndex" property="Small_photo_Spe-
cialOfferIndex" />
    alt="logo" border="0" height="71" width="760"> <BR/>

Offer Starting Date:
<bean:write name="SpecialOfferIndex" property="OfferStartingDate"
/><BR/>
Name:
<bean:write name="SpecialOfferIndex" property="Name" /><BR/>
```

All of the code shown is generated in an automatic way and allows having a complete application prototype. At the end of the prototyping process, a prototype will be available that, even if based on the IDM model, is completely independent from it during the run-time phase because the generated structure will not be linked to the model. This is a great advantage for the developers for the following two reasons:

- The generated prototype has a great independence; in other words, it is possible to deploy the prototype without the code generation engine; in fact, it is sufficient that on the server there is a J2EE™ servlet container to use the prototype.
- The prototype consists of classes and JSP™ pages: all elements that a developer can use, extend and complete in order to have a final product without to know the IDM model. For example, as we will see in the next test application, it could be possible to use cascade style sheets to improve the layout aspect without changing the prototyping process.

Figure 16 shows the home page after that the developer has applied the images and inserted the correct CSS.

Debit Card for Mobile Device PDA

Now, we consider the case in which the designer has to produce the application for a mobile device such as PDA. The code that manages the application related

Copyright © 2009, IGI Global, distributing in print or electronic forms without written permission of IGI Global is prohibited.

to the framework Apache Struts™ (http://www.apache.org) is the same, while the framework tiles manage the layout aspects of the mobile device: tiles manage the request of the page considering the calling device. If a PDA page is requested, tiles uses the "*tiles-defs_html_pda.xml*" instead of the "*tiles-defs_html.xml*" in order to have the correct page definition. In this case, the complete definition is:

```
<definition name="alias.CatalogueIndexPU.selectedDebitCard"
 extends="page.DebitCardPage. PDAForDescriptionVisualizationOfDeb-
itCardPageForGenericUser"/>
```

The resulting visualization is completely different by the case of the Web browser as it is possible to see in Figure 17.

In this case, the visualization is quite different from the one for the Web channel. Not only the position of the dialogue acts but also the dialogue act itself is changing because they are specific for the PDA device.

Figure 16. The prototype of the homepage with CSS

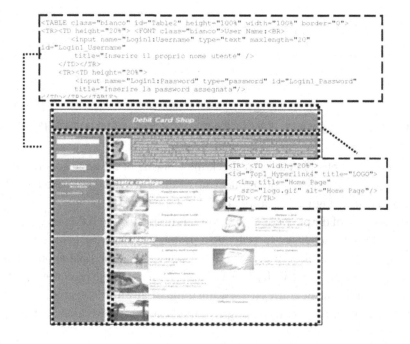

Copyright © 2009, IGI Global, distributing in print or electronic forms without written permission of IGI Global is prohibited.

Figure 17. Home page for generic user on PDA

CASE STUDY ABOUT THE "FACULTY OF ENGINEERING"

The second test application used to check the working of the code generation tool is the Web site of the faculty of engineering of the University of Lecce (now University of Salento). Figure 18 shows the C-IDM model.

The main goal of the previous case study was to check if the IDM model contains all of the information needed to generate a prototype; while the main goal of this case study is to check the gap between the prototype and the final application. In other words, we want empirically to verify the goodness of the prototype. The test application is online at the address (www.ing.unile.it), and it aims to provide services and information on the faculty of engineering. There are several stakeholders of

Copyright © 2009, IGI Global, distributing in print or electronic forms without written permission of IGI Global is prohibited.

Figure 18. C-IDM design for the Web application

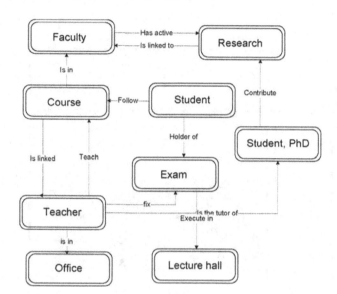

this Web application: faculty staff (professors and researcher, administrative staff), students (final year students, post doctoral students, in-course students and prospect students), the external companies (for the information about activating stages) and all of the people that are interested in accessing the engineering faculty.

The design of the application, developed using IDM methodology integrated with the layout model, has been designed using the specific editor; it is exported in OWL format in order to be used by the prototype engine through the Schema API. Furthermore, in this case, like in the previous case study, the main focus in only on some pages in particular the home page (Figure 19) and on the professor presentation page.

Figure 20 shows a piece of the entire Web application model. The home page is composed of three screens: UP (faculty logo and data), left (the main menu with the links derived by the relevant relationships), and faculty content (in the centre of the page where all the information of faculty take place). Each screen contains inside several dialogue acts.

In order to use the model as a starting point for the prototype process, the designer added the layout model; in Figure 21, it is possible to see the inserting of the information of the layout model such as the page schema and the dialogue acts into the screen schema. These schemas will be used in the prototyping phase to create the HTML page structure in which Apache Tiles™ (http://www.apache.org) put the application screen shown in Figure 22.

Copyright © 2009, IGI Global, distributing in print or electronic forms without written permission of IGI Global is prohibited.

Figure 19. The Web site of the faculty of engineering: Homepage

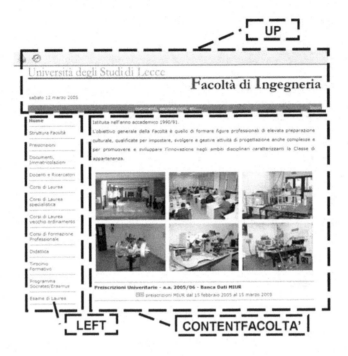

Figure 20. IDM model of the Web site of the faculty of engineering

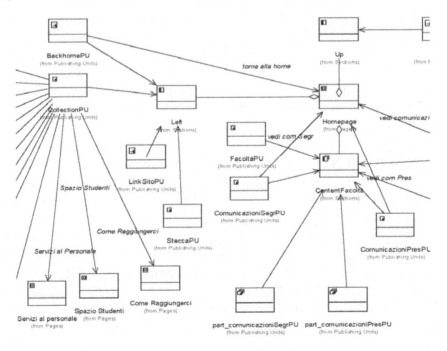

Copyright © 2009, IGI Global, distributing in print or electronic forms without written permission of IGI Global is prohibited.

Figure 21. Adding items to layout Model

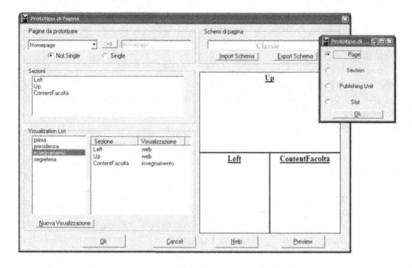

Figure 22. Layout Model of the home page

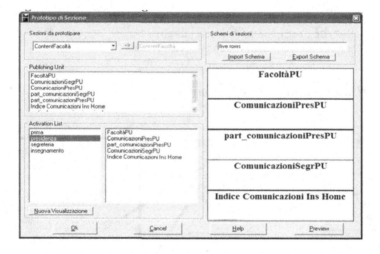

Through the model in OWL format, obtained by the export of the model, it is possible to create the scaffold of the application: the *struts-config.xml* file, the *tiles-def.xml* file and the HTML pages are generated using the information of the model. In Figure 23, the generated scaffold of the application is shown. For each JSP™ page, a specific entry in *tiles-def.xml* exists.

In addition to the HTML structures and to configuration files, the code generation engine for each links creates the corresponding action of which in the *struts-config.xml* exists the reference:

Copyright © 2009, IGI Global, distributing in print or electronic forms without written permission of IGI Global is prohibited.

```
<?xml version="1.0" encoding="UTF-8"?>
<!DOCTYPE struts-config PUBLIC "-//Apache Software Foundation//DTD
Struts Configuration 1.1//EN" "http://jakarta.apache.org/struts/
dtds/struts-config_1_1.dtd">

<struts-config>
  <form-beans>
    <form-bean name="itemChooserForm"
        type="it.unile.straps.generated.bean.ItemChooserForm"/>
  </form-beans>
  <global-exceptions/>
  <global-forwards>
    <forward name="home" path="/App_home.jsp"/>
  </global-forwards>

 <action-mappings>
    <!-- Action mapping per i link. Nota formato:
                    <NomePublishingUnit>_<NomeLink> -->
<action path="/BackhomePU_TornaAllaHome"
   type="generated.action.ChangeItemAction"
   name="itemChooserForm" scope="request">
       <forward name="details" path="alias.BackhomePU.tornaAlla-
Home"/>
</action>

<action path="/CollectionPU_VediStruttura"
   type=" generated.action.ChangeItemAction"
```

Figure 23. Home page with the definitions of tiles

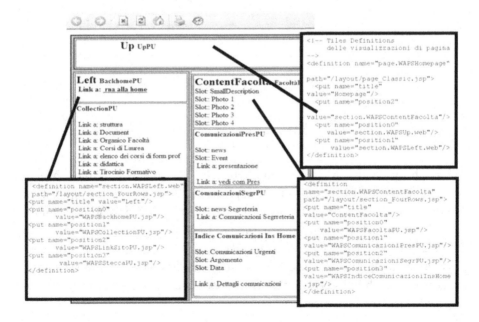

Copyright © 2009, IGI Global, distributing in print or electronic forms without written permission of IGI Global is prohibited.

```
    name="itemChooserForm" scope="request">
        <forward name="details" path="alias.CollectionPU.vediS-
truttura"/>
</action>

<action path="/CollectionPU_VediDocumenti"
    type="generated.action.ChangeItemAction"
    name="itemChooserForm" scope="request">
        <forward name="details" path="alias.CollectionPU.vediDocu-
menti"/>
</action>

<action path="/CollectionPU_OrganicoFacolta"
    type="generated.action.ChangeItemAction"
    name="itemChooserForm" scope="request">
        <forward name="details" path="alias.CollectionPU.organico-
Facolta"/>
</action>

<action path="/CollectionPU_VediCorsiDiLaurea"
    type="generated.action.ChangeItemAction"
    name="itemChooserForm" scope="request">
        <forward name="details" path="alias.CollectionPU.vediCor-
siDiLaurea"/>
</action>

    ...
```

Each intermediate action, of which the specific code is not described because it was presented in the previous case study, allows activating the link between the different page visualizations in order to make the scaffold work.

After the intermediate phase, in which the output is the application scaffold, the data-dependent environment using the generated structures creates the new code needed to allow the prototyping fruition (using the data stored in the layout database). The complete home page prototype (the main output of the prototyping engine) is shown in Figure 24 where the same notation used in the presentation of the scaffold in order to highlight the page schemas and the screen are used.

In order to better explain the prototype behavior for the screen *"ContentFacolta,"* the generated code of JSP™ pages is placed in the call-out; inside it, there are the generated calls to the bean object.

The bean *FacoltaForm* is used to insert into the page the data contained in the database of the prototype. In the following, a piece of code of the bean is shown. In the code, the slots of the page are the private members (the getX and setX methods are omitted):

Copyright © 2009, IGI Global, distributing in print or electronic forms without written permission of IGI Global is prohibited.

```
package it.unile.straps.generated.bean;

import java.beans.*;
import javax.servlet.http.*;
import org.apache.struts.action.*;
import java.util.*;
public class FacoltaForm extends ActionForm {

  /** Holds value for property ID. */
    private Integer ID;
  /** Holds value for property infoGeneraliFacolta_BreveDe-
scrizione. */
    private String infoGeneraliFacolta_BreveDescrizione;
  /** Holds value for property infoGeneraliFacolta_FotoCollection.
*/
    private Collection infoGeneraliFacolta_FotoCollection;
  /** Holds value for property infoGeneraliFacolta_FotoPiccola. */
    private String infoGeneraliFacolta_FotoPiccola;
  /** Holds value for property infoGeneraliFacolta_NomeEdificio. */
    private String infoGeneraliFacolta_NomeEdificio;
  /** Holds value for property infoGeneraliFacolta_Via. */
    private String infoGeneraliFacolta_Via;
  /** Holds value for property infoGeneraliFacolta_CAP. */
    private Object infoGeneraliFacolta_CAP;
  /** Holds value for property infoGeneraliFacolta_Citta. */
    private String infoGeneraliFacolta_Citta;

   ... ... ...
```

Figure 24. Prototype of the home page of faculty Web application

Copyright © 2009, IGI Global, distributing in print or electronic forms without written permission of IGI Global is prohibited.

The properties of the bean are set through business delegate (generated by the prototyping engine). In the following, a piece of code of the business delegate for the *FacoltaForm* bean is shown.

```
public void loadFacoltaForm(HttpServletRequest httpServletRequest)
throws Exception {
        FacoltaForm facoltaForm;
        ServletContext context;
        it.unile.app.runtime.StandardResultSetProvider prv;
        Connection conn;
        ResultSet rs;

        context = httpServletRequest.getSession().getServletCon-
text();
        prv = it.unile.app.runtime.StandardResultSetProvider.
singleton();
        conn = prv.getConnection();
        rs = prv.getInstancesOfEntity(conn, "Facoltà");
        if (rs.next()) {
            facoltaForm = populateFacoltaForm(rs);
        }
        else {
            facoltaForm = null;
        }
        conn.close();
        rs.close();
        if (facoltaForm != null) {
        }
        context.removeAttribute("facoltaForm");
        context.setAttribute("facoltaForm", facoltaForm);
    }
```

The entire generated infrastructure (completely integrated with the Apache Struts and Tiles™ frameworks) (http://www.apache.org) allows the fruition of the test application that has the goal of testing the quality of the generated product. All of the generated code can be modified in order to have the final product without modifying the IDM model. It is possible to apply to the prototype the layout in order to make it closer to the original application. By adding the images and using the specific style sheet in Figure 25, the final prototype is presented; the final screenshot is really similar to the original application.

As it is possible to see, comparing the two screen shots, Figure 19 (original home page) and Figure 25, the output is in practice the same. The unique difference is in the data displayed: in the prototype the data are taken from the instance DB populated using a random algorithm (the title of the communications for the academic head staff is "stranger event" mock-up data).

Copyright © 2009, IGI Global, distributing in print or electronic forms without written permission of IGI Global is prohibited.

Figure 25. The home page prototype added with the style sheet

The generated prototype is complete; in Figure 26, the presentation page of the professor is shown (also this page has mock-up data).

USE OF P-IDM PROCESS CODE GENERATOR

To present the output of the code generator for the P-IDM process, we refer to the design of the case study developed in Chapter VII. In particular, the case is focused on the support of an operator of a travel agency that has to plan the trip to the final user considering his/her requirements.

The P-IDM process design, obtained using the methodological guidelines, is shown in the Figure 27.

In the following, we describe the view of the template (Figure 29) and the view of the process (Figure 28) that are useful to understand the case study.

The process view is fundamental to understand the whole process and, thus, to have a good mapping with its BPMN™ design (OMG, 2006).

From the process view, all of the needed information to generate the configuration file (in general filename-*flow.xml*) are taken. In the specific case, the configuration files are called *fornitore-flow.xml*.

Focusing on the process flow generation and on the pages that allow its execution, we take into account only the template view of the topic "supplier" (this topic is the

Copyright © 2009, IGI Global, distributing in print or electronic forms without written permission of IGI Global is prohibited.

Figure 26. The prototype of the professor presentation page

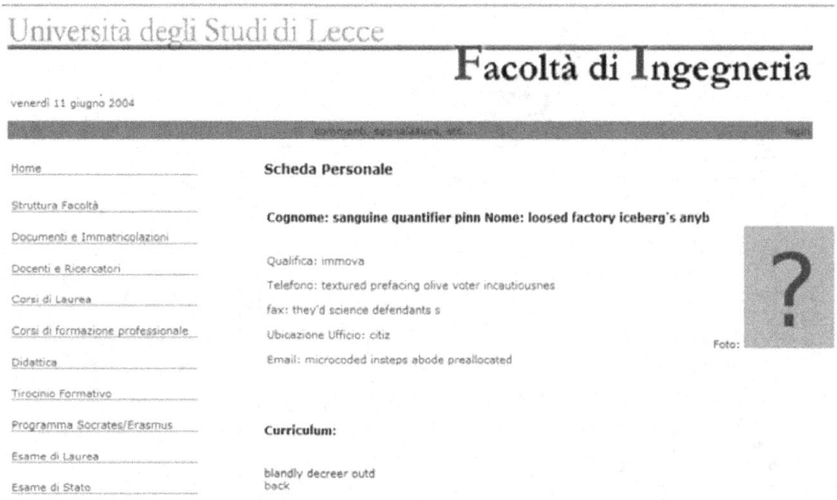

center of the process flow). The highlight is on the presence of the layout content that allows the semantic navigation through the supplier information. There are, also, a set of screens to access to the various steps of the process. These screens are shown to the final users according to the process state defined using the "state" property of the same screen and referred into the configuration file of the flow generated by the code generation tool. The layout of the generated application is fixed because we are focusing on the workflow aspects. The generated pages have a simple layout in which the contents take place in a prefixed order. In Figure 30, the layout template is shown for each contents area.

It is clear that the generated application operates according to the process flow defined during the design phase. It is possible for the user to stop and to resume a process according to the process design exported in OWL format. In the application, the process links (in the left part of the page) and the semantic links (on the right) are present. Thus, the user can both navigate freely between the information and led by the process for the operation.

The Process Flow

In the code generation tool, each process screen becomes a JSP™ page associated with action (developed in Java™). The action contains all of the information needed to link the pages. In the generated application, the first process page is the screen *supplier_data_determines_supplier_availability* associated with the input form that

Copyright © 2009, IGI Global, distributing in print or electronic forms without written permission of IGI Global is prohibited.

Figure 27. A P-IDM process design for the case study

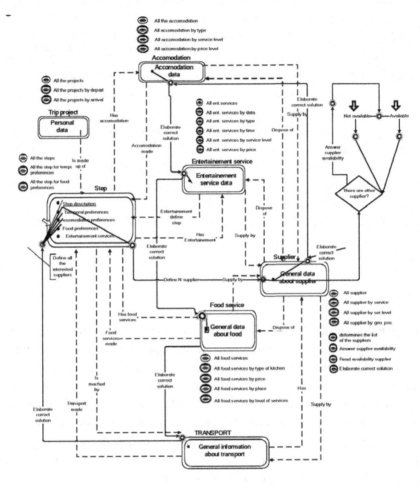

Figure 28. Process view of the case study

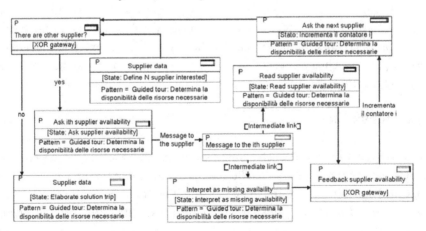

Copyright © 2009, IGI Global, distributing in print or electronic forms without written permission of IGI Global is prohibited.

Figure 29. Template view of the case study

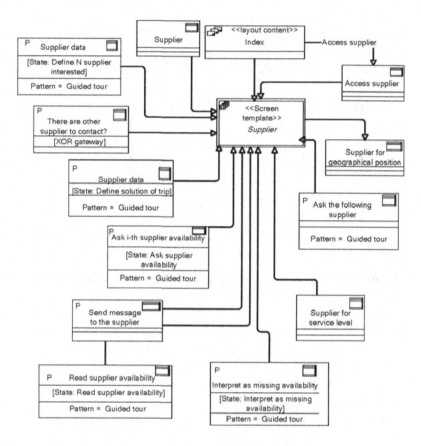

allows the user to look for the suppliers interested to the specific service. The actions associated to the input form are managed by the action *determines_supplier_avail-ability*. If the output of the action is valid (success), the navigation goes on to the next step; while if it is a failure, then the user remains on the same page.

The next pages will be (according to the process flow), *there are supplier to contact*. This page is characterized by a XOR gateway. Thus, the user choice defines the next page: *ask availability of the ith supplier* in case of success, and *elaborate solution trip* in case of failure.

Figure 31 shows that the generated pages are perfectly compliant with the process flow defined in the P-IDM process design of Figure 9 in Chapter VII. To make the explanation more clear, for each screenshot we report the P-IDM process model. The generated page template is always the same, just the contents change.

In case in the user suspends the navigation in the process step, the detailed information on a specific supplier will be shown in the following screenshot (Figure 32).

Copyright © 2009, IGI Global, distributing in print or electronic forms without written permission of IGI Global is prohibited.

Figure 30. An example of layout with a description of each area

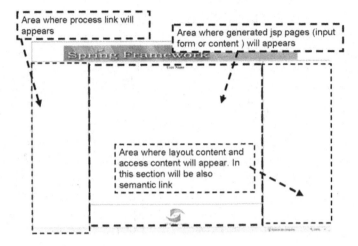

Figure 31. An example of navigation through the process flow designed in P-IDM process model

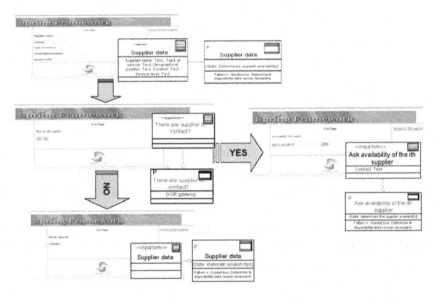

In the screenshot, the specific contents are visualized instead of the input form. The contents contain the same data of the input form, but they are not editable: the data are stored in the database (with fixed schema) and are displayed in the page using a query generated by the prototype engine.

Copyright © 2009, IGI Global, distributing in print or electronic forms without written permission of IGI Global is prohibited.

Figure 32. Process stop in the "determine supplier availability" task

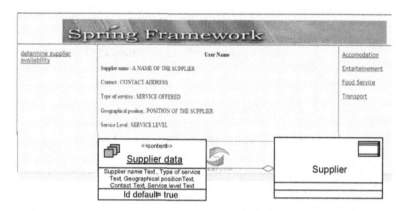

On the left, there is a link that allows to restart later the suspended process. On the right, there are the links that allow the user the semantic navigation between the information of the supplier.

The *supplier-flow.xml* flow starts with a start state generated considering the first task of the BPMN™ design. In the described flow, the tags "*view-state*" represent the JSP™ pages and the tags "*action-state*" represent the Java™ classes able to execute the operation. The two kinds of tags have the child (transition-node) that allows passing from one kind to the other. In Figure 33, the mapping between the *supplier-flow.xml file* and the P-IDM process design is shown.

The following piece of code is about the action of the *determines supplier availability* screen:

```
<form name commandName="determines_supplier_availability "
method="post" enctype="application/x-www-form-urlencoded">
                                <tr>
                <td>Type of services</td>
                <td>
                 <INPUT type="text" name="Type_of_services"/>
                </td>
        </tr>
            <tr>
                <td>Geographical_position</td>
                <td>
                 <INPUT type="text" name=" Geographical_posi-
tion "/>
                </td>
        </tr>
            <tr>
                <td>Service_Level</td>
                <td>
                 <INPUT type="text" name="Service_Level"/>
```

Copyright © 2009, IGI Global, distributing in print or electronic forms without written permission of IGI Global is prohibited.

```
                                </td>
                </tr>
                    <tr>
                        <td>Supplier_name</td>
                        <td>
                         <INPUT type="text" name="Supplier_name"/>
                        </td>
                </tr>
                    <tr>
                        <td>Contact</td>
                        <td>
                         <INPUT type="text" name="Contact"/>
                        </td>
                </tr>
                        <tr>
                            <td colspan="2"
class="buttonBar">
                            <input type="hidden" name="_flowExecu-
tionKey" value="${flowExecutionKey}">
                            <input type="submit" class="button"
name="_eventId_submit" value="GO">
                        </td>
                </tr>
        </form>
```

The code generation tool, accessing to the model has to generate an input form to collect the user data (as it is possible to see in the previous lines of code). The reference to the process flow is an input type = "hidden." The following piece of

Figure 33. The mapping between the configuration file "supplier-flow.xml" and the P-IDM process design

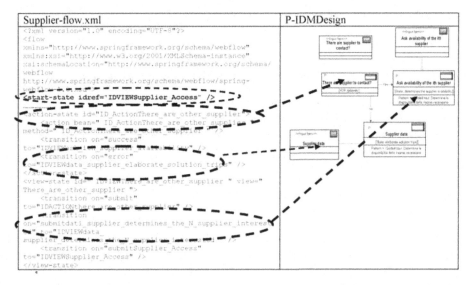

Copyright © 2009, IGI Global, distributing in print or electronic forms without written permission of IGI Global is prohibited.

code is about the JSP™ page generated to visualize (after the executing of the query on prototype database) the supplier information.

```
<%
    Connection con=null;
        try
        {
            Class.forName("org.gjt.mm.mysql.Driver");
            con = DriverManager.getConnection("jdbc:mysql://local-
host:3306/idm","root","admin");
            Statement statement = con.createStatement();
            ResultSet rs = statement.executeQuery("SELECT topic
FROM utilizza WHERE user='"+session.getAttribute("name")+"'");
            while(rs.next()){
            %>

            <p align="center"><a href="supplier.htm?_flowExecution
Key=${flowExecutionKey}&_eventId=submit<%= rs.getString("topic")
%>&id=<%= rs.getString("topic") %> %>"><%= rs.getString("topic")
%></a> </p>

        <%            }
```

CONCLUSION

In this chapter, the outputs of the two generation code tools are presented. In the first part, the focus is on the use of two frameworks: Apache Tiles™ (that allow, starting from the P-IDM model added with the layout information, to place in the pages the several design elements described using the layout model), and Apache Struts™ (that implements the MVC design pattern). The generated application is perfectly compatible with the two frameworks.

The second part of the chapter focuses on the prototyping engine that uses as input model the P-IDM process. In this case, the explanation does not consider the layout (it uses a fixed design in which the different elements of the model take place). The main focus is on the process flow generated starting from the BPMN™ design. The generated flow is compatible with the framework Spring Web Flow that can be used to deploy the prototype.

REFERENCES

Bolchini, D., & Paolini, P. (2006). Interactive dialogue model: A design techinique for multichannel applications. *IEEE Transaction on multimedia, 8*(3), 529-541.

Copyright © 2009, IGI Global, distributing in print or electronic forms without written permission of IGI Global is prohibited.

Dardenne, A., van Lamsweerde, A., & Fickas, S. (1993). Goal-directed requirements acquisition. *Science of Computer Programming, 20,* 3-50. Amsterdam: Elsevier North-Holland Inc.

OMG. (2006). *Business process modeling notation specification.*

UWA Consortium. (2001). *General definition of the UWA framework.* (Tech. rep. EC IST) UWA project (IST-2000-25131).

W3C. (2004). *OWL Web ontology language reference.*

Copyright © 2009, IGI Global, distributing in print or electronic forms without written permission of IGI Global is prohibited.

Chapter XV
Conclusions

In this chapter, we briefly summarize the results achieved in this book, and we will provide some indications on possible future developments.

In the book's coverage, we mainly focus on the design and on the development of complex Web information systems that are information systems that aim to manage, in an explicit way, the design of the processes inside the Web application as support for them.

By the way, it has been necessary to join the know-how coming from two worlds that, up until the present moment, have evolved in parallel: the design of the business processes and the design of the Web applications as support for the information systems.

Of course, to do this, it has been necessary to face different problems: first of all, it has been necessary to create a methodological background in order to analyze:

* Methodologies of design of business processes
* Methodologies of design of Web applications
* Extension to the business processes of the methodologies of design of Web applications

Copyright © 2009, IGI Global, distributing in print or electronic forms without written permission of IGI Global is prohibited.

This analysis, reported in section I of this book, has been essential for the continuation of the job itself because it has allowed identifying the open issues that still exist in the scientific panorama relative to these problems; then, we proposed guidelines to solve such open issues defining a new methodology of design.

However, this has not been the only result reached through this analysis: it has been interesting to discover, in fact, what the different typologies of users were involved in the complex Web information systems are, and it has been possible to distinguish among two macro categories of users:

- The users inside of the companies that do not need other information besides that tightly relevant in the carrying out of their daily assignments connected to their own job. They primarily use the information system through the intranet;
- The external users that require a series of information both for the carrying out of their own tasks inside of the process and to be attracted by the Web application in which they are working in order to avoid abandoning it in a few minutes. Of course, this second category of users uses the information system primarily through Internet.

However, this subdivision among the two macro categories of users is not categorical: it is possible that for particular processes, the external user does not need other information besides that related to the process; as it is possible that the inside user needs other information as support useful to performing his/her daily jobs. Furthermore, it is possible that a big company needs both the intranet system and the Web information system partially sharing the database and/or part of the same business process. This is possible using both methodologies here proposed. The important message that is wanted to transmit with this book is that it is necessary to realize the design and the following implementation of the information system using two different methodological approaches according to the typology of the user to which the information system is turned. A first approach, that for external users, has to merge together the know-how coming from the design of the business processes with that coming from the design of the Web applications (in particular the design of the user experience); in the second approach, since the alone design of the business processes is enough, it is just necessary to refine the draw of the process to a level of detail useful for the following implementation.

Another fundamental problem that is found in this book consists of the strong existing cultural difference among the two typologies of analysts that have called to collaborate in designing the information system. On one hand, in fact, there are the business experts that have the assignment to analyze the processes abstracting themselves completely from the implementation details of the information system

Copyright © 2009, IGI Global, distributing in print or electronic forms without written permission of IGI Global is prohibited.

that will be developed; on the other hand, there are the IT experts that, also participating in the analysis, try to direct the design toward the implementation more than toward the abstraction.

To address these problems, during the book's coverage it has first of all been fundamental to identify a notation for the representation of the business processes easily understandable for both the involved typologies of expert and at the same time rich of all the necessary details for both the business experts and the IT experts. The identified notation is BPMN™ (OMG, 2006) proposed by OMG™ and by now de facto standard in the design of business processes.

From the methodological point of view, the methodology of design of Web applications IDM (Bolchini & Paolini, 2006) already affirmed in the international scientific area has been chosen; IDM, thanks to its different methodological levels, allows, in the initial phase to analyze the information content and then to join it to that necessary for the design of the business processes, and it allows subsequently drawing the pages that will appear to the user.

In order to provide a structured approach, described in this book is an architecture of reference that introduces a fundamental characteristic that differentiates it from the traditional architectures of the information systems: we have, in fact, a level of process that well distinguishes itself from the levels "presentation," "data" and "logic" already present in the traditional architectures.

This level provides the indisputable advantage to separate the logic of process from the application logic allowing the business experts to also operate directly on the design of the process in phase of redefinition of the process (always possible during the life cycle of an information system); this capability allows, for small changes to the process, an almost immediate adjustment of the relative information system. The process level, in conclusion, avoids that, in phase of implementation, the logic of process is bound to the application logic making it very difficult and expensive to maintain the information system itself. Such flexibility is particularly interesting, above all, today in a world in which the information systems are constantly hard to adapt themselves to the changeable demands of the companies (both public and private): this need of change might originate both from the inside of the company (you could think about an organizational rearrangement) and from the outside (i.e., a change of the market's conditions in a highly competitive environment).

Conscious of the fact that the alone methodology is not very effective if not combined to a set of tools that constantly drive the designer in its job, we also provided further to a methodological imprint also a technological impress to drive the designer up to the implementation of the information system.

The goal has been, in fact, to realize a set of tools as support to the design combined to a tool of rapid generation of code that allows the designer to immediately

Copyright © 2009, IGI Global, distributing in print or electronic forms without written permission of IGI Global is prohibited.

verify the design choices done over whether to provide a good base to the developers for the following development and deployment of the information system.

The first problem faced in this area has been to identify a language of interchange that allowed instructing the environment that is wanted to create with the realized design choices.

Covering this topic, after seeing the large number of primitives existing in the proposed methodologies and seeing the elevated degree of interaction existing among the different primitives, we used the ontologies that, thanks to their undisputed semantic and syntactic expressiveness, better than any other technique, they allow fully expressing the whole intrinsic complexity of the methodologies.

Therefore, a knowledge base able to represent both the design of the processes and that of the Web applications and to integrate together the two design models has been created. In particular, a meta-model of the proposed methodologies has been realized (founding itself on the approach proposed by MOF™) on which to find the models coming from the particular designs.

The possibility to import, in a unique knowledge base, ontologies coming from different sources, has allowed besides, building separately the meta-models related to IDM methodology and to BPMN™. The meta-models have been, subsequently, merged together without denying the possibility to use each of them separately. The possibility to use in a separated way the various meta-models is noticed particularly useful in the application of the methodology proposed for the inside user of the system (in which the alone design BPMN™ opportunely refined is enough for the realization of the information system). In the development of the tools, we have been selected open source platforms; in particular, the methodological editors have been realized as plug-in of the Eclipse™ framework, and they are very configurable and extensible while, for the part of generation of code, the Spring Web Flow framework (ww.springframework.org) and the Apache Struts and Tiles™ (http://www.apache. org) frameworks broadly detailed in the relative chapters have been used.

The research work is even more oriented to the DSM philosophy focusing the attention of professional people about the modeling of a domain from which automatically to obtain the final application; this way will be the pole star that will drive our efforts: allowing all focus to solve the specific problem forgetting the complexity of notations, meta-models and developing issues.

Finally, according to the topics discussed above, we will approach the development process in order to provide the professionals with a guide to optimize the time and cost efforts, although the managers will be completely free to adopt the management style considered more suitable for that project.

The development of a complex Web information system is divided into two main aspect: the design of the information system and the development of reusable tools for code generation according to the selected open source framework.

Copyright © 2009, IGI Global, distributing in print or electronic forms without written permission of IGI Global is prohibited.

This second activity, which is not related to the first one by any time constrain, is often well defined: it "translates" the model primitives into the code needed to build an application using a selected framework. The requirements are stable and certain. Therefore, to effectively manage this activity is possible even to use the waterfall model. However, we do not suggest any development process model letting the project manager use the development process model more suitable to the team.

The first activity, instead, is much complex; the design activity involves different stakeholders with different skills. The project management is a very hard task considering that the requirements may change quickly and that the several experts use work approaches quite differently.

As discussed in the preface, considering the flexibility of our approach, we consider the development process similar to the agile unified process; however, a new trend is emerging: the software rhythms (Lui & Chan, 2008).

It is not really a new development software model, but rather it is necessary to harmonize the development phase whatever iterative model used.

It is, therefore, a style and a guide of management to be used in complex projects. For this reason, we think that a suggestion about the better use of iteration in a harmonic way will be helpful for the practitioners while they have to manage a project of a complex Web information system.

FUTURE WORK

The book, in conclusion, represents the point of arrival of a research work on which the group has been working by now for 10 years. However, because of the importance of this approach, we are working on the following future developments:

- To subsequently refine the proposed methodologies: this may be realized making an extensive session of test on other cases of study opportunely selected.
- To refine the realized editor adding both a tool of validation of the design and a tool of simulation of the business processes in order to evaluate the benefits of the re-engineering. Furthermore, the editor must be adapted to the new publishing IDM model.
- To refine the tool of generation of code also considering the real layout of the pages and the connection to a real database creating an interface that it dynamically allows the Web application produced to interface itself with a database compatible with the design. In conclusion, the tool of code generation, according to the actual tendency found in the international scientific

Copyright © 2009, IGI Global, distributing in print or electronic forms without written permission of IGI Global is prohibited.

panorama, has to come to a level of maturity to make useless, if not to improve the generator itself, the figure of the developer.

Furthermore, we are working on two other directions:

- To make more general the BPMN™ editor allowing the export of the diagram in XPDL format; the goal is to allow using the BPMN™ editor without forcing the business analysts to use the whole suite but allowing them to use another tools XPDL complaint.
- To use the new evolution of the framework Apache Struts²™ that has interesting features such as AJAX support and an easy integration with Spring Web Flow allowing us to have a unique suite to generate code according to IDM and P-IDM process methodology.

The work here presented and the future works described, are oriented to simplify as most as possible the design and the development of the complex Web information systems. The approach here proposed, thanks to the set of tools that allows translating the design in a machine readable format and to obtain the overall code, allows reducing the effort of the implementation phase allowing the designer to concentrate itself in the design phase surely most important and delicate.

REFERENCES

Bolchini, D., & Paolini, P. (2006). Interactive dialogue model: A design techinique for multichannel applications. *IEEE Transaction on multimedia, 8*(3), 529-541.

Lui, K.M., & Chan, K.C.C. (2008). *Software development rhythms: Harmonizing agile practices for synergy.* John Wiley & Sons, Inc.

OMG. (2006). *Business process modeling notation specification.*

Copyright © 2009, IGI Global, distributing in print or electronic forms without written permission of IGI Global is prohibited.

About the Authors

Roberto Paiano graduated with a degree in electronic engineering from the University of Bologna. He worked at IBM for 10 years. He was team leader at IBM RNSL (now TIVOLI Laboratory) and project manager at the CORINTO Consortium (National Research Consortium about Object-Oriented Technology). He is a member of the IEEE. Currently, he is assistant professor at the University of Salento (Italy). He has authored papers about information systems, Web modeling and design, and metrics for the Web development. His current research interests are: the methodology of design of Web information systems, the automatic code generation using open-source frameworks and information systems based on the MAS.

Anna Lisa Guido graduated with a degree in computer science engineering from the University of Lecce in 2004 and earned her PhD in computer science from Salento University (Italy). Her research area is in Web information systems, and she is oriented to develop a framework light for small- to medium-size companies that allow to management of business processes. The framework will be made both by a methodology and by tools that help the designer in the design, development and management of process-oriented Web information systems. Methodology will link the know-how of Web application design and the know-how of process design. She is the author of papers about methodology of design of Web information systems.

Andrea Pandurino is an information and communication engineer with a PhD, a contract professor at the department of engineering innovation at the University of Salento in the field of computer graphics, and a coordinator teacher in the field of information systems in the bachelor degree program in computer science engineering. Since January 2007, he has been a researcher and engineer at ISPESL (Italian Superior Institute for Health and Safety on the Workplace). His research is

Copyright © 2009, IGI Global. Copying or distributing in print or electronic forms without written permission of IGI Global is prohibited.

based on market surveillance for the machines subject to the Machinery Directive 98/37/EC absorbed in Italy with DPR n. 459/96.

Paolo Paolini graduated with a degree in physics from the University of Milan and earned his master's degree and PhD in computer science from the University of California at Los Angeles (UCLA). He is currently full professor at Politecnico di Milano (Italy), and is also lecturing at the University of Lugano (Switzerland).He has authored papers in fields like database design, database languages, information systems, office automation, document generation, hypertext modeling, Web modeling and design, multimedia authoring, e-learning, e-health, and multimedia applications for cultural heritage. He has founded active ICT laboratories in Milan, Como, Lecce and Lugano. He has taken part in more than 40 research projects, being scientific director for more than 12. His current research interests are: collaborative e-learning, 3-D collaborative environment, accessibility, audio-interactive applications, ICT for cultural heritage, e-learning, and mobile interactive applications.

Copyright © 2009, IGI Global. Copying or distributing in print or electronic forms without written permission of IGI Global is prohibited.

Index

Copyright © 2009, IGI Global. Copying or distributing in print or electronic forms without written permission of IGI Global is prohibited.

Copyright © 2009, IGI Global. Copying or distributing in print or electronic forms without written permission
of IGI Global is prohibited.

N

O

P

R

S

T

Copyright © 2009, IGI Global. Copying or distributing in print or electronic forms without written permission of IGI Global is prohibited.

Copyright © 2009, IGI Global. Copying or distributing in print or electronic forms without written permission
of IGI Global is prohibited.